Search for the Paradise Land

*An Introduction to the Archaeology of Bahrain and
the Arabian Gulf, from the earliest times to the
death of Alexander the Great*

MICHAEL RICE

LONGMAN
LONDON AND NEW YORK

'A scribe who knows not Sumerian –
what kind of a scribe is he?'

'The traveller from distant places
is a perennial liar.'

Sumerian proverbs

Longman Group Ltd,
Longman House, Burnt Mill, Harlow, Essex CM20 2JE

Associated companies, branches and representatives
throughout the world.

© *Michael Rice 1984*

First published 1985

British Library Cataloguing in Publication Data

Rice, Michael, *1928–*
    Search for the paradise land: an introduction
    to the archaeology of Bahrain and the Arabian
    Gulf, from the earliest times to the death of
    Alexander the Great.
    1. Archaeology – Persian Gulf Region
    2. Persian Gulf Region – Antiquities
    I. Title
    935   DS326

ISBN 0-582-75664-2

Produced by the South Leigh Press Ltd, Lavender Cottage,
Chilcroft Road, Kingsley Green, Haslemere, Surrey.
Printed in Great Britain by
St Edmundsbury Press, Bury St Edmunds, Suffolk

Contents

Introduction

This book is the consequence of some twenty years of involvement in the present-day affairs of Bahrain and the other Arabian peninsula and Gulf states with whose past it is concerned. My involvement has swung, on the one hand, between a concern with the contemporary politics of the region and, in particular, with some of the issues which have arisen from the dependence of so much of the western world on the region's oil reserves and, on the other, with the uncovering of its extraordinary antiquity. It is perhaps difficult to imagine two such extreme perspectives, but straddling them has given me an immense degree of pleasure and only occasional discomfort. I have learned much about the people of the region, who have become my friends and I believe I have gained some understanding of the role which eastern Arabia and the Gulf played in the development of many of the beliefs which are common to those of us who draw our cultural inheritance from the lands which lie to the west of the Zagros mountains.

The archaeology of the Arabian peninsula is very largely a new phenomenon. I have been singularly fortunate in having been involved with it, almost from its beginnings. In some cases, indeed, I have actually been present at the reawakening, as it were, of a long forgotten past. But my interest in the archaeology of the ancient world long preceded my first visit to the Gulf, back in the early 1960s. When I came to Bahrain, I quickly became aware of the remarkable work of the Danish Expeditions, promoted by the Forhistorisk Museum at Moesgard, an idyllic place near Aarhuis in Jutland. The Danes had already been working in and around Bahrain for some years when I arrived. In common with the excavators, I was alarmed at the risks to which a lack of understanding of the importance of Bahrain's antiquities exposed the sites and at the increasing quantity of artefacts which was being excavated from them. I urged my friends in the Government of Bahrain (even then a particularly enlightened one) to cause a museum to be built, both to house the products of the excavations and to set them, and the archaeology of Bahrain itself, into some sort of coherent context; one that I myself, for example, might understand.

To my surprise the Government asked my colleagues and myself, who had some modest experience of design and communications, to prepare the museum. This we did working closely with Geoffrey Bibby, of the Danish Expedition; his book, *Looking for Dilmun* which tells of the work of the expedition in Bahrain and others of the States will, I believe, come to be one of the classics of archaeology. The museum was housed initially in the Government's own headquarters building, later to be moved to what had been the RAF Officers' Mess at Muharraq, Bahrain's sister island. The museum was well received. We were able to work with a free hand and to introduce ideas then only beginning to be employed in contemporary museum design.

For fifteen years now my colleagues and I have been deeply immersed in Arabia's past and in communicating it to the present day, as a result of this well-omened Bahraini precedent. Over the intervening years we have designed and installed museums in Qatar, Oman and Saudi Arabia.[1] We have also been concerned with the making of films on the region's past and in two other particularly satisfying activities. These have been the launching and editorial preparation of two important academic journals concerned with Arabia's archaeology,[2] and helping in the creation, staffing or development of Departments of Antiquities for several of the States. In the case of two of them, Bahrain and Saudi Arabia, the direction of the Department is now entirely the responsibility of people from the States themselves; the journals too, increasingly, are locally edited and this is entirely as it should be.

In the course of planning the various museums for which my colleagues and I are responsible, we tend to become much concerned with the research which must underlie any well conceived museum exhibition. In some cases we carry out the research ourselves, or at least direct it; in others we work closely with the ever increasing number of specialist scholars in the peninsula States, in Britain, Europe and the United States, who are now engaged on studies relating to the past of Arabia and the Gulf.

One of the compensations (and they are many) of working in museums in Arabia and the Gulf is that the people who use them are prepared to read far longer explanatory texts than would many Western audiences. To people who are as involved with communications as my colleagues and I, this is highly satisfactory. It is also the reason for a great deal of the basic material of this book being readily accessible.

Its preparation, particularly in its final stages, has been much helped by the fact that I have also been concerned, for some three years past, with the planning, organization and publication of a major archaeologial and historical conference which was held in Bahrain in December 1983. The Proceedings of the Conference will provide the basis for a great deal of new research in the years to come: the findings of several of the distinguished scholars who took part will be a revelation to many. I have been in the privileged position of having access to their papers before publication and I have used this privilege quite unreservedly.

I am conscious that, despite my own considerable commitment to the region and its archaeology, it is very largely the findings of other men that I am presenting here. It used to be said that there were two sorts of archaeologists, *diggers* and *classifiers*. I suppose I might scrape into the latter category, but I would rather plead for a third to be accepted, that of the *presenters*, and I will contentedly take a humble place amongst them. In archaeology the presenters are those who delight in communicating the lives of those who lived long ago to those who live today.

I acknowledge most gratefully a debt to those scholars whose work forms the substance of this book. Such facts as there are, are theirs; much of the interpretation is mine and I have attempted to make it clear where this is the case. The errors and omissions are wholly my own.

Perhaps I should end this introduction on a note of apology. I hope that my friends in the States of the Arabian peninsula other than Bahrain will understand the prominence which I have given to that island principality. There is good academic reason for it; also I confess to a special affection for a small state which has been exceptionally kind to me and where I have always felt peculiarly at home. My affection for Bahrain does not, however, mean that I do not as much enjoy the other states nor regard their past as highly. But you have to make a start somewhere, even in taking a look at a past as distant as that with which this book, however inadequately, tries to deal.

MICHAEL RICE
LONDON – BAHRAIN – CRETE

I
The Arabian Quest

Four thousand years ago a man walked barefoot across the newly plastered floor of a curious building on a small island, close to the placid waters of an enclosed and distant sea.[1] What manner of man he was we have no way of knowing, except, a little absurdly, that his feet were remarkably large; we know, too, that he was not alone, for he was one of several to walk over the plaster laid down on the floor, and that one of his companions was a dog. Whether he was a labourer engaged on the construction of the building (though surely a singularly careless one), or a stranger who did not know of the work which was in progress so close to the whispering sea and, perhaps at night and in the darkness, stumbled across the still damp surface, are speculations now beyond recall.

In this remote episode it is the location, and not the walker by the shore, which is important; the building was a sacred place, part of a complex of monumental buildings raised to the glory of gods who, at the time when the careless or deliberate feet crossed the plaster floor, had already been worshipped there for upwards of five hundred years in handsome stone-built temples and, in less substantial structures, perhaps for longer still. Almost from the beginning of recorded history a temple had stood upon this site, skirted by palm trees and lapped by the nearby, shallow seas. Here men had sought both to honour and to propitiate the forces of nature and the unknown which they eternalized as gods. It is possible only to guess at the name of the principal divinity who was commemorated in this ancient place; but everything that now is known about it leads to the conviction that he was a great god, the lord and protector of a people for long totally forgotten, without whose lives the world would not be quite like it is today.

The temples on this distant island stand at a special point in time and space: from the earliest of them to the latest they span a time which represents arguably the most intense social, technological and cultural change which mankind has undergone until the present day. The island and its temples lie close to the origins of the modern world; the search for their own origins was a preoccupation of the people most closely identified with the mysteries enshrined in the temples.[2] That search itself forms much of the substance of this study.

The island itself will represent the region of which it is the geographical centre as well as being the focus of much legend and perhaps of cults. Its oecumene, if that is not too pretentious a word for so modest a land, stretched far to the north, deep into Iraq, and southwards out into the Ocean far beyond the horizons of the Arabian peninsula, of which it is a geographical dependancy.

The island lies in the shallow waters of the Arabian Gulf: today it is called Bahrain. In ancient times it was variously named: Dilmun, Tilmun, Tylos, Awad, Samak, Awal,[3] but whatever its name it was the epicentre of a region which was to exercise a profound influence on the history of the western world. That region was bounded by the marsh lands of southern Iraq to the north and, to the south, by the mountains of Oman; between these points lie the scatter of little shaikhdoms which make up the states of the Arabian (sometimes called the Persian) Gulf.

Only in the very recent past has the rest of the world been reminded even of the existence of this small part of it and then not for reasons of its high antiquity nor for any contribution which it may have made to an understanding of some of the most deep-seated preoccupations of mankind. For its people, entire millennia passed in neglect and forgetfulness. Fifty years ago or less the Arabian shores of the Gulf supported some of the least endowed of the world's populations, living in tiny settlements on the edge of the harsh and inhospitable desert.[4] With infinite toil and in the face of a merciless climate its people wrested a bare subsistence from the sea and the lean herds which the land could barely nourish. In twenty years the kaleidoscope of human fortune has shattered and reformed totally; today the people of the Gulf enjoy per capita incomes amongst the highest in the world and a level of prosperity and social welfare which makes them the object of the often malicious envy of those who have been less favoured by the caprice of fate.

It was, of course, oil which effected this phenomenal transformation from abject poverty to wealth limited only by the extent of the black lakes on which much of Western Asia floats. With the accession of such great riches came the interplay of politics and the complex games of greater nations which quickly saw the control of the Gulf lands as a prize worth any amount of conflict and chicanery.

Half a century of external influence has marked the region's most recent history, an influence not always entirely maleficent. But, curiously, in all that time and with the hordes of Western officials, engineers, buccaneers, businessmen and their attendant flocks of journalists, academics and all manner of miscellaneous commentators who followed in their train, few people ever gave thought to what had preceded the Gulf's sudden plunge into the twentieth century.

To their credit, however, some few did. Archaeological excavation of a sort had been carried out, with varying degrees of intensity, efficiency and perception, for over a century, notably in Bahrain itself.[5] The work of more recent years and the improved techniques of excavation and analysis now available to the archaeologist's hand are beginning, if still only dimly, to suggest the profoundly important role which this region played in the early centuries of the development of urban cultures and in their diffusion (a word which must be heavily qualified nowadays) over formidable distances.

As with so many other disciplines, in the past twenty years archaeology has witnessed an extensive recasting of many of its most fervently defended concepts and the precepts of an earlier time. Archaeology is concerned with the extraction and evaluation of those material evidences of the past which can either be recovered or reconstructed. More scientific methodology, a greater awareness among many of the nations, the successors of the ancient cultures, of the significance of their heritage, and the sophisticated processing and publication of the results of an ever increasing number of excavations throughout the world, have contributed to the transformation of what modern man believes he knows about his predecessors and hence about his own origins. At the same time there has been, amongst all types and conditions of humanity, an immeasurably increased awareness of and concern for the origins of these societies which have been constructed, in the course of an uncertain progress from a brute nature to the prospect, diminishing though it must seem to be in our own time, of enlightenment. Ironically, two of the less elevating accessories of our contemporary culture, television and tourism, have done much to make the public at large aware of antiquity.

The Near East, despite increasing competition from other areas, is still the most profitable region for the study of man's past. But the inevitable shortcomings of the reliance by archaeology on the evidence which is actually available is nowhere more tellingly demonstrated than in considering the case of Arabia's position in scholarship. Even today, few works of general archaeological or historical reference contain any mention of the Gulf in their indices or indeed of Arabia in pre-Islamic times at all, except perhaps for the trade in aromatics, usually mentioned incidentally, with perhaps a passing reference to the southern Arabian Kingdoms which grew out of its prosperity. But beyond these, virtually nothing. It may be a trifle invidious, but to demonstrate this extraordinary lack of scholarly reference, two otherwise magisterial publications may be cited. The *Cambridge Ancient History* (3rd edition), the most authoritative conspectus in the English language of the state of knowledge of the ancient world, has one reference to the Arabian peninsula in 1058 pages. The *History of Mankind: Cultural and Scientific Development: Prehistory and the beginnings of Civilization*, published by the United Nations Educational, Scientific and Cultural Organisation (UNESCO) has one reference in 873 pages.

A little more than thirty years ago Henri Frankfort, one of the most percipient and sensitive of the archaeologists of this century, could write in the preface to *The Birth of Civilisation in the Ancient Near East*:[6] 'I have confined myself to Egypt and Mesopotamia, the cultural centres of the Ancient Near East; for in the peripheral regions civilisation arose late and was always, to some extent, derivative.'

In this case Frankfort was notably wrong. He was, however, hardly likely to think otherwise for, in his day, the evidence was scarcely available though some scholars did perceive, however dimly, that Arabia and its littorals represented a blank page in man's history which demanded to be filled.

It might be imagined that it would be difficult to overlook the Arabian peninsula, the 'Island of the Arabs', that great land mass which divides Africa from Asia and which in land surface area is approximately the size of Western Europe. Yet, historians and archaeologists had largely succeeded in doing this, from late Roman times to the very recent past. Such neglect is careless, to say the least, the more so because by no stretch of even the most perverse imagination could Arabia ever really have been said to be *terra incognita*. For over 1400 years now it has been the focus of one of the most pervasive and powerful of the world's faiths, whose adherents are enjoined to travel to the Arabian holy places at least once in their lifetimes. This fact alone has meant an accumulation of a gigantic traffic of humanity and of experience over the centuries; that traffic's existence at least has been well known to Europeans since Crusader times, if not before.[7]

Nor has Arabia experienced any lack of spirited if variously motivated foreigners who have sought to penetrate the peninsula's wastelands of sand and wind-scoured rock. From them have descended the potent and enduring myths of the dauntless, fierce but noble-hearted tent dwellers, customarily but inaccurately called the 'Bedouin'. The desert was furrowed with the tracks of all manners and conditions of purposeful explorers, seeking who knows what enchantment or release in the harsh purity of Arabia's empty spaces.

But, for whatever reason, few of Arabia's explorers were even of a modest archaeological bent. Admittedly the pickings were sparse when compared with Egypt, the Levant or Mesopotamia; politics, too, largely ignored Arabia in the nineteenth century, the high point of Near Eastern exploration and western exploitation, leaving the peninsula generally, with the exception of its western littoral and the south which controlled the route to India, to slumber under the apparently dead weight of the Ottoman Empire. Egypt had been opened to the west and to the pursuits of scholars, first by Napoleon's expedition ('Four thousand years look down on you, Soldiers') and then by Mohammad Ali's Europeanizing policies. Mesopotamia attracted an early interest and her sites were being dug, however inexpertly, early in the nineteenth century. But, as was most markedly the case in the Levant and the Syrio-Palestinian desert, one of the primary motivations for archaeological activity in the land of the Two Rivers was to prove the historicity of the Bible.

The Biblical orientation of much European archaeology survived well into the twentieth century; the Bible was still considered a primary, if somewhat selective, source of an understanding of the ways of the ancient world, before the Redemption. All over the lands of the ancient Near East there continued to plod, sometimes in extreme discomfort but always in confident certainty, an army of learned men. They were often clergymen (and hence might be thought to have a prescriptive interest in the results of their own labours), who espoused passionately the claims of this or that small piece of desert or river bank as the site of such and such a recorded intervention of the Divine in the affairs of man. That the topography often did not fit, at least according to the Bible's directions, did not deter them at all.

Sadly, the winds of time have, as often as not, blown away the theories that they laboured so hard to construct. But Arabia shared rarely in these Biblical excursions, mostly, perhaps, because, other than in certain instances, Arabian sites do not feature largely in the Biblical record, and even taking into account the often over-excited terms which seem to have determined the character of much Biblical archaeology there were few scholars who would readily venture into such unpromising territory. Then, of course, there was the uncomfortable fact that Arabia was firmly held, as it were, by the competition, which, despite all the efforts of the missionary societies of the day, had shown a marked and peremptory disinclination to accept the precepts of Christian proselytizers and firmly resisted any attempt by infidels to involve themselves with the exclusive land of Arabia. From this land, in its inhabitants' view, had sprung the last and greatest of the Prophets and the ultimate Revelation of God's purpose to man. Ideological constraints, too, militated against the unearthing of the material evidences of 'the Age of Ignorance', which to the devout Muslim was represented by the whole course of human history prior to AD 622. Deep revulsion was also expressed at the actions of those who disturbed the tombs of the dead, even if they were not, in strict terms, the burials of believers.

Then, of course, there was the simple but compelling fact of Arabia's extreme physical discomfort. Whilst this did not actually discourage all interested scholars it may be that the pleasures of excavation in the Nile Valley or by the shores of the sun-blessed Aegean were discernibly greater than those attending similar work in Arabia. Also, there were the discommoding facts of the sheer immensity of the desert and the lack of enthusiasm towards foreigners looking for gold (for the search for gold is a fact well known to every desert-dweller about every archaeologist) which was demonstrated, sometimes fatally for the would-be searchers, by its people.

Arabian archaeology is in fact essentially a twentieth-century phenomenon; indeed, with one or two exceptions, it is to all intents and purposes a post-war development. It is one of the less immediately predictable by-products of the exploitation of the Arabian peninsula's staggering reserves of fossil hydrocarbons, the oil for which the industrial world so desperately thirsts.

The West's remitting pursuit of the one resource which is all that most of the oil-bearing lands possess, has been, generally speaking, fairly shameful. The West has almost exhausted itself in devising machines and whole economies which depend upon this sole resource of a people whose consequent prosperity is not only dependent upon those very machines and economies, but is also often bitterly resented. The political power deriving from the ownership of so much of the world's energy resources has given the states of the Arabian peninsula a disconcerting influence on the lives of a substantial portion of the people who live on this planet. It is perhaps as well to try and understand something of their history. In doing so, we will find that we are discovering much about our own.

Thus far we have spoken of Arabia and the Arabian peninsula. Now we must become a little more specific, narrowing the focus down to one particular part of the peninsula with which this study will be concerned. This region is that which contains, in contemporary geo-political terms, Kuwait, the Eastern Province of the Kingdom of Saudi Arabia, the State of Qatar, the archipelago of islands which comprise the State of Bahrain, the seven shaikhdoms of the United Arab Emirates and the Sultanate of Oman. Collectively this region is described as 'eastern Arabia'; it is also the western littoral of that inland sea, the gulf which divides Arabia from Iran and which, by reason of the controversy which attends whichever territorial adjective (Arabian or Persian) is employed to identify it, is most generally described simply as 'the Gulf'. This term results in the infinite confusion of those living in the Americas, to whom it only means the Gulf of Mexico.

This story therefore is concerned with the antiquity of eastern Arabia and, most particularly, of Bahrain, which lies in the very centre of the Gulf. As such it is partial and limited, necessarily disregarding by far the largest part of the Arabian peninsula and concentrating only on one quadrant of it. There are three main reasons why this should be so.

The first is that compared with the rest of Arabia the eastern quadrant has generally been far better researched, to the extent at least that it is possible to lay out, with reasonable assurance, an historical sequence for it based on the evidence brought to light by the combination of chance and archaeology. For the past fifty years or thereabouts, access for non-Muslims to eastern Arabia has also been much easier than to any other part of the peninsula. Because they are the oil-bearing parts of Arabia, the States which are contained within the region have all of them maintained a substantial and increasing degree of contact with the outside world, sustaining significant populations of foreigners, including Europeans and Americans. Secondly, the opportunities for a fulfilled social and cultural life have in the past been limited in these parts, often notably so. In consequence the foreigners living in eastern Arabia have frequently turned to archaeology by way of diversion. The third factor provides the essence of this book: in eastern Arabia and the Gulf lies much of the earliest mythical and iconographic material which informs many of the most profoundly-rooted beliefs of the modern world.

The foreign, if originally largely amateur, preoccupation with archaeology led in time to an awareness by professional archaeologists that the region did contain important and hitherto largely overlooked material. Gradually professional teams began to work there, in several of the states freely and with official support and involvement.

To anyone with a taste for such things there is a pleasing symmetry in the return of eastern Arabia to the consciousness of the world.

By geomorphological chance, a very substantial part of the world's reserves of fossil hydrocarbons, in oil-bearing strata laid down hundreds of millions of years ago, lies under these peninsula states. The earliest commercial exploitation of oil from the Arabian Gulf took place in 1932 when the first commercial quantities were exported from Bahrain:[8] in the light of what will be seen to be the almost mystical role which Bahrain has exercised in the region as a land of the beginning of things, this chance seems peculiarly appropriate. Since 1932 the region has become the most sought after commercial and financial market on the globe. It would nonetheless be an exaggeration to describe the Gulf States today as the very centre of the world's trade: it would not have been so great an exaggeration four thousand years ago.

Throughout most of the third millennium BC and into the early centuries of the second, the Gulf was part (arguably the most important part) of the principal highway for the movement of international trade. The route ran from western Anatolia, down the twin rivers of Mesopotamia, the Tigris and the Euphrates, through the Gulf to India (or more strictly, in contemporary political terms, to Pakistan) and up the Indus Valley riverine system to huge forbiddingly monumental cities such as Harappa and Moenjo-Daro. This route may also have touched or have been connected with other routes to even more distant regions; westwards the traders may have penetrated even to the Nile Valley.

Thus the Gulf played a major role in that extraordinary period, from c. 3300 BC to c. 2200 BC, when a great surge of energy seems to have possessed the populations of the Nile and the Tigris-Euphrates valleys, in consequence of which many of what have subsequently come to be regarded as the distinguishing marks of civilization and culture were first laid down.

The organization of urban societies, the management and direction of large bodies of citizens, the conduct of the inundation and hence of the introduction of agriculture, hierarchies, kingship, monumental architecture, writing (branching soon into administrative and literary usages), formalized rituals both religious and civil, the codification of laws, the specialization of crafts, the growth of defensive systems and military levies; indeed all the paraphernalia of developed societies which largely remained unchanged until our own day, either erupted into the world in this brief period of human history, or else, during it, were refined out of recognition from their early forms. From this time everything was totally changed in the societies which experienced these phenomena and in those which have descended from them, including our own. From these valley peoples, through a process of exceptional practical and intellectual energy, emerged the magnificent cultures of Pharaonic Egypt and of Sumer, the one arguably the most human, engaging and, paradoxically, the most majestic of ancient societies, the other the most inventive and dynamic.[9]

The discoveries of the postwar period have not diminished the splendour of the achievements of the two remarkable peoples who brought these cultures to birth; but equally they have revealed that, with regard to certain important aspects of what had seemed to be peculiarly their achievements, they were not, in fact, the first. Thus to the Sumerians is credited the origin of the curious human practice of building and living in cities; certainly man had to wait for the emergence of the Sumerian city-states in the early third millennium for the particular form of city, in hierarchy, organization and structure, that modern man would recognize as something like his own. But thousands of years before even the earliest of Sumerian cities was raised up at Eridu, on a small island in the extreme south of the Mesopotamian marshlands, a ten-acre fortified settlement had been built at Jericho (c. 9000 BC)[10] far away to the west in Palestine. Great watch towers guarded Jericho's walls against the incursion of the wild desert tribes who sought control of the wells which the people of Jericho had tapped and organized for their economy in the tenth millennium before the Christian era. Perhaps more remarkable still, four thousand years before the first tentative temples began to be raised beside the god-infested Nile, painted shrines with the evidence of elaborate rites and worship were set up within the towns (for it is difficult to use another word to describe them) that flourished on the Anatolian plains at Catal Hüyük and Haçilar, on sites more than three times larger than Jericho.[11]

Even in this remote and obscure period of man's development, at least seven thousand years ago, sophisticated art, so much the most surprising of man's achievements, flourished. The carvings and paintings of these lonely Anatolian townsmen have a strangely chilling quality. Their principal divinity seems to have been a great goddess, massive and fecund, who, with her boy-consort, is portrayed supported by leopards and bulls: somehow, terror never seems to be very far distant from her and the creatures that attend her.[12] After a few centuries of richly productive life the Anatolian settlements disappear: a long night descends until a second dawn heralded the first appearance of those civilizations which were to set the pattern for all the ages which followed them. With the invention of writing, at its earliest in the middle of the fourth millennium, history begins and with it the record of urban man.

There was a time in man's experience when everything was new under the sun. To many people, educated conventionally, the ancient world meant an inaccurate and often somewhat stickily sentimentalized picture of life in a Greece and a Rome that never were. Such a view was fostered by nineteenth-century educationalists, often to satisfy their own emotional needs and frequently to warrant the moral and political ethics of the Europe of their day: Winckelmann, as it were, hand in hand with Dr Arnold (an association not wholly unthinkable, surely?). Otherwise, and with only a passing nod to the Egyptians (who were considered odd and rather disturbing), the problems of the remoter reaches of human history could be readily resolved by the simple reliance on biblical revelation.

Myth, religious belief and fairy stories acknowledge no frontiers. Throughout human history most peoples have felt compelled irresistibly to seek for a time when the world was young and free, when men and animals lived at one together. In this quest, so often identified with an imagined land of innocence and abundance, man unknowingly proclaimed his protest against the debased, troubled and guilt-laden condition of his own humanity. Out of the need to explain his own existence came his hope that he was not entirely alone and that providence had some care of him. Thus man created, both as a means of consolation and because he was a highly creative animal, some of mankind's most splendid legends: in seeking for Eden, the primaeval garden of tranquillity and fulfilment, man revealed something of what, wistfully, he would have liked his world to be.

As it is described in the book of Genesis, the episode in the Garden of Eden is a depressing event which condemned man to perpetual misfortune and woman to perpetual ignominy. It was a story which gave nineteenth-century Biblical scholars profound and particular satisfaction. Less excited intellects might have thought the whole episode, at least as it was recorded in the Old Testament, best forgotten. Nonetheless, mile upon dusty mile of the Near East was plodded over by divines of extreme worthiness and limited historical horizons. As a result of this prospecting, Gardens of Eden proliferated as each scholar advanced the claims of the small piece of desert or river bank whose cause he earnestly and vociferously espoused, leaving behind him, as often as not, twin trails of acrimony and disillusion.

With the revelation of the geological age of the world, even the most besotted protagonists of the Biblical Eden began to lose confidence in their ability ever to discover precisely where man's sinful history had begun. But, little as they knew it, help of a kind was on the way, galloping down the centuries. When it came, however, their plight was like that of the maiden who, rescued from ravening beasts, finds that her most cherished bastion has fallen before the onslaught of her rescuer.

The discovery which demolished much Biblical scholarship of the day, and which accelerated its demotion from antiquarian pre-eminence to the relatively minor place it now occupies, was the unearthing of the earliest civilizations of the Mesopotamian plain lying between and around two great rivers, the Tigris and the Euphrates. This region has always ranked high among the contenders for the putative site of Eden, but its real history was hazy beyond the comparatively recent times dealt with by the historical books of the Jewish peoples. But in the second half of the nineteenth century Mesopotamian history was found to reach immeasurably beyond the time even of the Assyrians and Babylonians, the former of whom were regarded as so significant a people that their name was once given to the entire study of the region. At length, scholars who were not burdened with the necessity of proving the historicity of the Bible, revealed in the land of the two rivers a totally unsuspected culture, humane, highly sophisticated, sensitively literate, with hints of an architectural and artistic splendour which rivalled and perhaps even contributed to the majesty of Old Kingdom Egypt.

In the legends and myths of the mysterious inhabitants of this land the archetypal Eden was at last discovered, not indeed merely as a geographical location to be neatly sited upon a map, but also as 'the land where the Sun rises', a place to be yearned for, the original home of gods and men. In short, there were now revealed the origins of the myth which had been echoed, probably more than two thousand years after it had first been written down, by the authors of the Book of Genesis, who must stand, in this as in so many other cases, as amongst the most successful and respected of plagiarists. Their plagiarism however, was probably quite innocent.

As more was revealed about the people whose poetic insight created the myth of the terrestrial paradise, more was also revealed about many of the most deep-seated beliefs and hopes of their successors. These beliefs, descending through the camp-fire stories of the nomadic tribes who lived belligerently on the periphery of the vastly superior cultures, passed in turn to the Hebrews, the Greeks and the Romans and so to the world of our time.

The early inhabitants of southern Mesopotamia called their land Sumer, or more precisely, they spoke of it as 'Shumer'. They also called themselves, to our ears simply and engagingly, 'the black-headed folk'. Theirs is the earliest great civilization yet to be revealed in any detail: their legacy to us is almost incalculable and yet they remain relatively unknown when compared, for example, with their near and splendid contemporaries, the Egyptians. This may be because the vast and marvellous inheritance of ancient Egypt has come down to us in stone and metal whilst the Sumerians left a gift of words, ideas and legends which has only been revealed as theirs four thousand years after they ceased to exist as a nation. Their most stupendous innovation, which is Sumer's special and unique glory, was the creation of writing: at least no earlier system of writing than theirs is known. Had the Sumerians done nothing else, mankind would eternally have been in their debt for what is perhaps the most benign of all great inventions. But they did much, much more.[13]

The discovery that the myth of Eden had its origins in the records of the Sumerians began another quest, this time for the site of *their* earthly paradise, the name of which is transliterated today as *Dilmun*. Sumerologists were on rather firmer ground than their Biblical predecessors, for it rapidly became obvious that to the Sumerians, and to their Akkadian, Babylonian, Kassite and Assyrian successors, Dilmun was both a mythical land and a geographical location.

The Hebrews (perhaps surprisingly) had never made their Garden of Paradise a market place, yet the Sumerian legends of man's primaeval existence in the blissful 'land of the living' (one of the most frequent of Dilmun's epithets) were matched by matter of fact records of the shipments of dates and onions, stone, metal, timber and pearls from Dilmun. For those who find such quests down the byways of scholarship agreeable, Dilmun was a land well worth the search, more human in scale than Eden, happier by far in its legacy to men. The discountenanced band of scholars who had so earnestly sought for the Biblical Eden were given some small vindication by their Sumerological successors: at least a Paradise land existed after all, even if its gateway was more likely to be guarded by a customs official than by an angel with a flaming sword.

In fact, any distinction between the mythical and the mercantile Dilmun is artificial and unwarranted by any of the Sumerian sources. Goddesses and sea captains are as indiscriminately mingled in the literary remains as they were in Liddell and Scott's first Greek exercises of twenty-five years and more ago. Dilmun's products include, variously, onions shipped to the metropolis of Ur and an entire cycle of vegetation brought to birth in the place of the assembly of gods. It is the home of Ziusudra, the Sumerian prototype of Noah, and of petty kings bowing respectfully before the might of their Mesopotamian over-lords.

For the past century or so there has been occasional but serious academic argument on the issue of where Dilmun may be sited.[14] Allowing even for the asperity with which such disputes seem always to be conducted, the argument over Dilmun cannot be said to have raged, for Dilmunology is a modest science.

From the later years of the nineteenth century onwards, academic opinion has decided that the metropolis of Dilmun, the terrestrial paradise and the flourishing entrepot, was for much of its history located in Bahrain, the island state in the Arabian Gulf, whose name in Arabic means 'the place of the two seas'. But from time to time the term embraced much more extensive territories than the archipelago of islands with which the name is associated today.

One of the most frequently employed epithets of the Gulf itself was 'sea of the rising sun'. This term was often employed by the Sumerians and their successors and it demonstrates the danger of taking the ancients seriously in the matter of geographical descriptions. No one could believe the Sumerians to be so obtuse or so unobservant as to imagine that the sun rose to the due south of their land, which could be the only conclusion if 'sea of the rising sun' is taken literally.

The question will be asked later in this study whether the Sumerians came to Mesopotamia from the south: if, as is also possible, they came along a route skirting the westerly shores of the Gulf, it is conceivable that the Gulf was given this description by its earliest navigators, moored perhaps on the Arabian foreshore and looking out towards the easterly sky. From the Arabian mainland, the sun may well appear to rise across the sea, out of Bahrain itself whose central prominence, the Jebal Dukhan, would be struck by its first rays: it is an improbable concept but one that is not so far-fetched as to be quite impossible. The axis of the Gulf runs south to east: as a ship sails southward down its waters the axis shifts more to west to east. Thus, in the latitude of Bahrain, sailing southwards towards the Straits of Hormuz, the sun would rise apparently out of the sea's eastern horizon. Similarly, from the latitude of Ur, one of the most significant Sumerian cities, at certain times of the year the sun would appear to rise to the south and east, in other words over the Arabian Gulf.[15]

According to the traditions of Sumer the date palm was brought to their land from the Gulf region. The Sumerians, understandably in the light of the barrenness of their own land, respected and sought after trees. They also, almost certainly, destroyed many forests and plantations in the course of providing fuel for one of their staple industries, copper smelting. But the palm tree was supreme in their regard and was honoured in ritual and in legend.

In a hymn to Ninsinna, the goddess proclaims the antiquity of her city, Isin, as greater even than that of Dilmun and says: 'My house, before Dilmun existed, was fashioned from palm tree'.[17] The goddess here acknowledges the extremely important part which the date palm played in Sumerian belief and legend. Growing straight and tall it was unequivocally the 'tree of life' to the Sumerians and as such is often portrayed in their art. By tradition the palm was brought from Dilmun, on whose own seals (a form of art which probably originated in Bahrain) it is a frequent motif: it was extensively cultivated in well planted groves all over Sumer. People had early discovered the high calorific value of the date, and they practised artificial pollination in promoting its growth in their otherwise treeless land.

The palm trees of Dilmun were indeed so renowned that they entered the common language of the Sumerians, as the very criterion of excellence. Thus a King is said to be cherished 'like a date palm of Dilmun'.[18] When glorifying the sacred city of Nippur, the domain of the master of the gods Enlil himself (and a sort of Sumerian Vatican in the precedence which it seemed to take over the other god–ruled metropolitan centres) a hymnodist observes 'My Nippur, before Dilmun existed the palm tree grew there'.[19] This is of course itself a celebration of Dilmun's own vaunted antiquity.

There is an evocative praise of trees from one of the Tammuz liturgies, which mentions Dilmun: Tammuz was Dummuzi, the Sumerian god of vegetation.

> In my right hand is a cedar, on my left is a cypress,
> My pregnant mother is a consecrated cedar
> A cedar of Hasur
> A dark tree of Tilmun.[20]

It is suggested that Hasur represents the source of the two great rivers of Sumer, the Tigris and the Euphrates and Tilmun (or Dilmun) is the place of their outpouring. This again is a reference to the idea that the underground springs of Bahrain (which will be further described below) and of the Hasa province were connected with the rivers and not, as we know to be the truth, part of the Arabian water table.

The repeated references in Sumerian and Babylonian texts to Dil-mun as an entrepot, as an island dominion of the Mesopotamian kings in later times and, accepting that the eastern coast of what is now called Saudi Arabia was included from time to time in the geographical description, as the known source of the best dates in the ancient world, all confirm the view that Dilmun was situated in the Gulf, and Bahrain is the only wholly convincing site for its centre that can be found. If the Sumerians were, as has been suggested, an immigrant people in south-ern Mesopotamia, and if they came originally from the south, the only island landfall they could have made in what would have seemed a treacherous sea would have been Bahrain.

The little island would thus have evoked grateful memories from the wandering people that it sheltered. The strange lowering rock in its centre, the Jebel Dukhan, 'the Mountain of Smoke' and the altogether surprising fresh-water springs which bubble up in the seas around the island, could well have added a touch of mystery and wonder to its sheltering shores. Clearly it was a land redolent of the gods.

Islands have always fascinated men and there is much evidence that all over the ancient world they enjoyed a special reputation and sanctity as shrines of the gods. Several Mediterranean islands shared this attribution of holiness, many of them being provinces of the Great Mother goddess of remote antiquity. The Gulf is not well supplied with islands and the more likely, therefore, that any new people settling on its shores would single out the only significant one as a sanctuary. But now the wealth of evidence which has emerged in recent years as a result of the archaeological work carried out in Bahrain should be enough to satisfy the most sceptical observer. Any doubts that might still have lingered about its identification as Dilmun may now reasonably be dispelled, for research over the past twenty years has revealed the full and remarkable extent of Bahrain's early history and its exceptional antiquity.[21]

Since the nineteen-fifties it has been convincingly demonstrated that, from the closing centuries of the third millennium BC, Bahrain was an important religious centre, important enough to be the site of great temple complexes, markedly but not exclusively Sumerian in in-fluence. Typically Mesopotamian cult and everyday objects have been found there and more undoubtedly wait to be uncovered. At least one great city flourished there; two of the principal sites known so far, the Qala'at al-Bahrain and Barbar, are important by any standards and, in the context of Mesopotamian archaeology to which they must be related, they are particularly significant.

In another respect Bahrain has a wholly unique claim to its inclusion in the annals of man's ancient history in the Near East: it is often described as the largest necropolis of the ancient world. In its desert regions the surface of the landscape is so pitted with burial mounds that it looks like the popular image of a long dead planet. One hundred and seventy thousand and maybe more tombs are there, in which an ancient people, mysterious and unknown, were buried.

Dilmun is the location for the Sumerians' explanation of the origins of agriculture and irrigation: it is even thought of as the place from which originated the god who brought the secrets of science, writing and all the arts to Sumer.[22] It is the place of assembly of the Sumerian high gods who were much given to collective decision-making.

Whilst Dilmun's place in the historical records of Sumer and of its successor cultures, the Akkadian and the Babylonian, is important, the fact that it is found at the centre of the oldest surviving corpus of legends recorded in written form is surely particularly appealing today. Dilmun has an important place in the original Sumerian story of the Flood on which the Old Testament version is unquestionably based. The Flood legend is an episode in the world's first (and one of its greatest) epic histories which introduces the most enduring and powerful figure of ancient legend, the heroic Gilgamesh.[23] His love for man takes him on the quest for the secret of the renewal of youth which he believes is to be found only in the blessed land of Dilmun, at the confluence of the waters where Ziusudra lives, on whom, alone of all mortals, the gods had conferred the gift of eternal life.

'On another level entirely, the control of Dilmun's trade was a matter of concern and pride to the sovereigns of Mesopotamia. From its busy harbours, shipments were made of stone, metals, foodstuffs and other merchandise vital to Sumer's economy. By control of its harbours, the trade routes were kept open to southern Arabia and even possibly to Egypt and, later and above all, eastwards to the extensive and perplexing civilization of the Indus Valley.

The Gulf, a narrow, almost rectangular body of water which, until its outpouring through the Straits of Hormuz into the Arabian Sea, is virtually an inland sea, does more than simply divide the Arabian peninsula from Iran. At its head, its northern extremity, in the marsh lands where sky, lakes and sea all seem to merge into one, it is fed by the two great rivers of Mesopotamia, the Tigris and the Euphrates on whose banks and extended canal irrigation systems so much of the early history of urban man was enacted. Geographically it is central to south western Asia, linking the western edge of that great continent with the eastern lands of the Iranian plateau and the Indian sub-continent. In ancient times the Gulf was called by a variety of names. As well as 'the Sea of the Rising Sun', it may also have been called 'the Waters of Death': if it is the Gulf on which Gilgamesh sailed in search of Ziusudra this term would appear to have had some currency, perhaps only of a literary sort. In Akkadian, towards the end of the third millennium, it was called 'Tantum Shaplitum'. It was also called 'the place of crossing', a mysterious name, or perhaps 'the place of rule', but 'the Bitter Sea' may perhaps be a comment on the extreme salinity of the comparatively shallow waters of much of the Gulf, particularly in the summer months, whilst 'the Lower Sea' was a term frequently employed from the late third millennium on, to differentiate the Gulf from 'the Upper Sea', the Mediterranean. These are both terms which reveal their Mesopotamian origins as well as the gradual swing away from the Gulf to the Mediterranean as the world's principal artery of trade.

To Herodotus[24] and Alexander[25] the Gulf was the Erythraean Sea: 'Erythraean' means 'Red' and confusingly, at this period and later, the stretch of water between Egypt and Arabia, now known as the Red Sea, was then called the Arabian Gulf; thus Ptolemy knew it.[26] To the Gulf waters were added the Red Sea *and* the Arabian Sea, all embraced within the term 'Erythraean' at certain times.

By whatever name it might be known the Gulf was, by early in the third millennium, the focus of considerable activity and development. Along the Arabian shore and particularly on the islands which nestle close to the coast, settlements were established which grew into sizeable and prosperous cities. The principal sites of such settlements, so far to be identified, have been found on Failakah Island, a dependency of Kuwait; on Tarut, a small island close to the Saudi Arabian mainland; inland, around Abqaiq; Bahrain Island, at various times the political centre of the region; small settlements in Abu Dhabi and perhaps at Ras al-Khaima in the United Arab Emirates; and what appear to be several little townships in the Sultanate of Oman, where quantities of copper, the staple trade of the early Mesopotamian cities, were mined.

The phenomenal growth of urban civilization in southern Mesopotamia, the most striking historical consequence of the late fourth millennium, was paradoxical in that the land in which the little cities of Sumer grew and flourished was almost wholly barren of the raw materials – wood, stone or metal-bearing ores – on which the cities depended for their rapidly developing manufacturing industries. These were already specialized and well organized, leading to the production of surplus, far beyond the needs of the citizens to absorb. The invention of the sailing boat expanded the horizons of the river-based cities substantially, making it possible for them to mount expeditions over considerable distances both in search of the raw materials Mesopotamia lacked and to seek out markets for the disposal of the manufactured surplus which the cities' prosperous economies were turning out.

After the more tentative experience gained by the simpler, smaller river craft which no doubt occasionally ventured out on to the relatively open water of the lagoons with which Southern Mesopotamia was liberally supplied, bolder experiments in marine design might be expected. The sail was developed and as a consequence of boats being capable of moving before the wind, journeys of vastly increased range might be contemplated whilst substantially larger tonnages than could be driven by rowers could be built and sent out on wide-ranging voyages. The sailing boats on which much of this far ranging travel depended were nonetheless small: the displacement of one typical boat in the early second millennium (and it probably is representative of the earlier periods as well) is estimated at nineteen tons.[27] Their range was limited by the amount of fresh-water they could carry: their masters were cautious seamen, preferring sensibly to lug down the coast, stopping as frequently as they might to take on water and fresh supplies for the next leg of the journey. Only the Arabian coast could give them the shelter and facilities they required: the Persian littoral was less favoured with natural harbours and inlets whilst its barren, rocky shore discouraged landfalls.

Thus the little communities strung out along the eastern Arabian coast, once established, came to serve a variety of functions. First, they were convenient refuelling points, at least before the long haul from Oman to the mouth of the Indus Valley system far to the east; second, they provided access to the raw materials that Mesopotamia needed; whilst, third, they provided depots and outlets for manufactured goods that could be traded with the people of the hinterland.

In addition to their role as entrepôts, of places of trans-shipment either of raw materials or manufactured products, at least some of the coastal cities were themselves production centres. Thus, at one period, Bahrain sustained a copper-smelting industry, converting (in all probability) the ore which was mined in Oman and smelting it into ingot; it was also smelted in Oman itself. Agriculture, notably the cultivation of dates and onions, was an important element in the economy of eastern Arabia at least from the fourth millennium on, as was fishing, perhaps the most characteristic and the most typical way of life established in the region from the time of the very earliest settlements.[28]

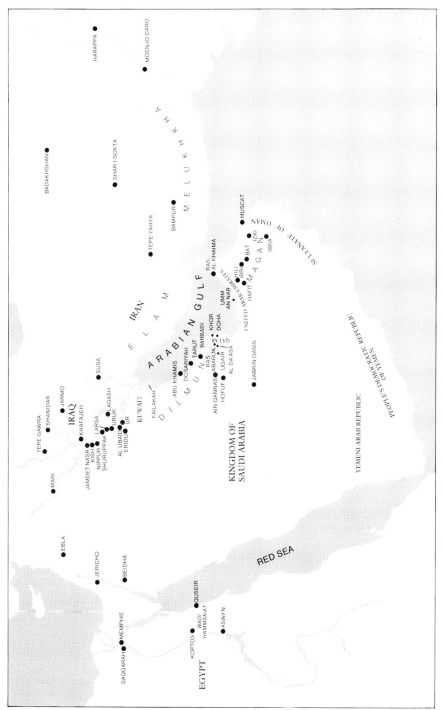

Western Asia, Mesopotamia and Elam showing the principal archaeological sites.

19

Thus in the late fifth to early fourth millennium tiny stone tools from eastern Arabian sites, miniature awls and borers, testify to the probable existence of industrialized pearl fishing, the region's most important industry until well into recent times.[29] Oyster middens of great antiquity on Bahraini[30] and other sites suggest that the oyster beds were fished for pearls and not simply for an elegant addition to the diet of the region's inhabitants. That fishing occupied a place in their ideological and philosophical make-up is demonstrated by the exceptional antiquity of fish-cults in the region and by the identification of at least one of the High Gods of Sumer, Enki, who has considerable connections with Bahrain and the Gulf, with fish and fishing.[31]

But like all other achievements of men, the paramountcy of the Gulf as a commercial waterway was destined to last only for a certain time. By the early centuries of the second millennium the axis of world politics and trade was already swinging away to the north and west, to the Levant and hence to the eastern Mediterranean and to the newly emerging lands of the Aegean. It is even possible that there was some form of population movement from the Gulf headlands up into the Levantine coast, perhaps brought about by one of the marked, often short-term changes of climate to which the region seems always to have been subject, or by the inability of the coastal settlements to sustain the level of population developed during the late third millennium. Such a radical change may perhaps have come about as a consequence, in turn, of the invasions in the east and north which seem to have created havoc, in a time of general disunity and political confusion throughout near-eastern lands, in the early centuries of the second millennium BC.

The Gulf and eastern Arabia sank into relative obscurity after the nineteenth/eighteenth centuries BC with only an occasional incident or contemporary record to illuminate the times' apparent general gloom. Mesopotamian rulers still claimed sovereignty over the Gulf as much by convention and the recollection of the splendours of past conquerors as by any real need to control what had become a total and literal backwater. For over a thousand years this situation persisted; then, from around the eighth century BC, there is evidence of a return of prosperity to eastern Arabia and the Gulf islands.

This renaissance of the region, marked by the development of cities whose luxury and riches were proverbial, arose directly from the fortunes associated with the spice trade, the extraordinary commerce in aromatics such as frankincense and myrrh which grow in abundance in southern Arabia and whose traffic gave rise to societies whose only purpose was to service the caravans, or to take tolls from them.[32] It was this trade, supported in particular by the large-scale domestication of the camel – which made long-ranging land routes possible, comparable in extent even with the earlier sea routes – which drew Arabia again to the attention of the major world powers of the day.

The spice trade was, in its own day, as important a factor in the economy of first-millennium Arabia as fossil hydrocarbons and the oil industry which has grown up to exploit them are to Arabia in the present day. Gerrha was founded around 690 BC: her inhabitants were said by Agatharchides to be the richest people in the world.

The last emperor of Babylon, Nabonidos (589–556 BC), established his capital at Tayma in northern Arabia and burials of neo-Babylonian date have been excavated on Bahrain. No doubt the Babylonians were there for purposes of trade as inscriptions of the period make clear.[33]

This return of Arabia to the consciousness of the larger world later coincided with the first waves of serious scientific curiosity, associated with the intellectual dynamism of the emerging Greek world. From the time of Herodotus onwards, accounts of the Gulf and eastern Arabia appear in the histories, geographies and other scientific treatises which the Greeks and their Roman successors delighted in producing.

At the beginning of his first book Herodotus considers the nature of the Greeks and 'The Asiatics' (the Persians, in other words) and the origins of their conflict. The Persians, he observes, put the responsibility for the quarrel on the Phoenicians who, the Persian learned men say, 'came to our seas from the sea which is called Red and having settled in the country which they still occupy at once began to make long voyages'.[34] In Book Seven, when he analyses the composition of Xerxes' forces, he relates how 'the Phoenicians, with the Syrians of Palestine, contributed 300 tribesmen . . . these people have a tradition that in ancient times they lived on the Persian Gulf but migrated to the Syrian coast, where they are found today'.[35]

The people of Tyre, that once splendid and ancient city, insisted on their Gulf origins. At one time Bahrain Island was called Tylos: it would be entirely consistent with philological precedent for the 'l' to become an 'r'. However, Tylos appears late in the record, certainly long after the establishment of Tyre. Even the Old Testament, not always to be relied on for its historical accuracy, preserves a memory of Tyre in association with 'Eden, the Garden of God'. Thus in Ezekiel the prophet says: 'O Tyre, you have said "I am perfect in beauty". Your borders are in the heart of the sea. . . . You were in Eden, the garden of God: every precious stone was your covering.'[36]

It may be observed that, in this translation at least, Tyre's borders are said to be 'in the heart of the sea' – a description not wholly appropriate for a coastal city, which would certainly not be said to be 'in the heart of the sea', but perfectly proper for an island.

The general mistrust in which nineteenth-century scholars (and those who have thought like them) held poor Herodotus has meant that many of his observations which deserve consideration have often been cursorily discussed. This was certainly the case with the several occasions on which he reported traditions current in his time, of the origins of the Phoenicians being found in the Gulf.

However, Herodotus was not the only ancient author to examine and chronicle the Phoenicians' belief that they came originally from the coasts of the Gulf and, in particular, from the islands. Alexander's contemporary Androsthenes was one whose now lost work was extensively cited by other classical authors, of whom Strabo was the most influential. He records the tradition that the inhabitants of the Gulf islands in his time (the first century AD) believed that the Phoenician cities of Tyre and Arados were seeded by colonists from the Gulf islands which, in his time, bore the nearly identical names of Tylos and Arad (Bahrain and Muharraq as they are known today).

Recently the evidence for a Gulf colonization of the Phoenician coast and the possible authenticity of the traditions here referred to have been reviewed most elegantly by the American scholar G. W. Bowersock.[37] He accepts the Phoenician tradition, as reported by Herodotus, as a genuine expression of that peoples' belief about their origins; he also suggests that in late antiquity this belief about the origins of the Phoenicians was widespread.

He draws attention to a consideration which has been largely overlooked by other commentators. Strabo recalls a reference in the Odyssey in which Homer refers to 'the Sidonians', in association with peoples who came from the shores of what is today called the Red Sea. Strabo suggests that these Sidonians are, in fact, not the inhabitants of the city of Sidon, but rather those who dwell in the Arabian Gulf, from whom the original Sidonians were descended. He draws the parallel between the Sidonians and the inhabitants of Tyre and Arad, as colonists in the same sense, from the Gulf islands.

Bowersock demonstrates convincingly that in late antiquity, in the Graeco-Roman world at least, there was a widely held tradition, concerning the origins of the Phoenician coastal cities, of colonization from the Gulf islands. Herodotus even puts a date on when he thinks the original migration took place, 2300 years before his day. Herodotus was writing in approximately 450 BC, so the migration would have taken place, roughly, in 2750 BC. This is firmly in the middle of the period when there is in fact little evidence of occupation at all in Bahrain, though there seems to have been a good deal going on in the eastern province of Saudi Arabia. However, it is specifically with the islands of the Gulf that the tradition deals and there is no reason to assume that it means anything other than what it says.

One aspect of historical writing often does reveal Herodotus at something less than his best: this is whenever he is dealing with chronology, a subject on which the ancients tended to be as shaky as in their understanding of direction or distance. If Herodotus' date is reduced by a thousand years (admittedly a fairly brutal reduction), the proposed date for the transfer of population from the Gulf to Phoenicia is then sited at the end of the first quarter of the second millennium, just when the high Dilmunite culture of the preceeding five hundred years or so seems to decline sharply. This is the point at which the Indus Valley cities no longer represent the lucrative and ready markets of the east and the Kassite mountain dwellers came down on the cities of Babylonia and the Gulf.

Later in this review of the Gulf in antiquity some consideration will be given to the place in its history of the island of Failakah, in the Bay of Kuwait. Failakah seems to have been associated particularly with religious festivals and cults which featured bulls. If Failakah was involved in this putative migration, which may well have been a relatively gradual process extending over several generations rather than any sort of mass exodus, the bull cults of southern Anatolia and of Syria (of which there is much evidence in their seals, and which are comparable with those of the Gulf cities, particularly Failakah) and, a few centuries later, of Crete, may have their origins in the Gulf islands. It is quite possible that one of the Gulf's short-term climate changes may have been the original occasion for a significant segment of the population finding it necessary to reduce the numbers of their parent settlement and to seek a new place in which to establish themselves. Since Dilmunite merchants had been travelling deep into Northern Syria and Southern Anatolia for centuries they would have been well familiar with the Phoenician coast and with the rich lands which lay behind it.[38] Their predilection for coastal islands, too, would have been well met by the siting of what were to become Tyre and Arados.

The Gulf and its islands continued to figure spasmodically in the reports of the writers of late antiquity. After that period this corner of south-west Asia seems then to have entered one of its periods of relative decline, certainly of obscurity. The reasons for the apparent decline may again have been climatic or the consequences of war. The Muslim historians did not concern themselves with the times before Islam very much, though the Quran itself, as will be seen below, introduces an enigmatic and mysterious element into the region's history or, more exactly, into its mythology. Otherwise long centuries passed during which any importance which once the region may have had was all but forgotten by the world.

After the splendid centuries of the Arab empires, when the thirst for trade drove Arab argosies across the world, from the Gulf to China, the depredations of the Mongols, the rise of the Ottoman Empire, internal dissension and foreign invasion induced a strange lassitude in the lands of the Middle and Near East. Though occasional travellers penetrated into Arabia and returned to tell curious tales of a remote people whose ways were markedly different from those of the Western world, which was growing more and more confident of its role in the management of nations, the peninsula was allowed to slumber undisturbed. As the centuries rolled by, the dead weight of the Ottoman bureaucracy bore down upon eastern Arabia, penetrating in its final years even to Qatar, just across the Gulf from Bahrain.

The Gulf itself began to stir once again in the European consciousness during the eighteenth century. One of the most hardy and dedicated of travellers, a young Dane, Carsten Niebhur, travelled its length and included reports of it in his really quite remarkable book, published in 1774 (in the French edition)[39] which attracted some mild attention among scholars and savants; he did not, however, visit Bahrain, a rather surprising omission. The growing power of Britain in India was the factor which in time induced the principal change in much of European attitudes, and it led in time to an awakening of scholarly interest in the region's past. In the later years of the eighteenth century, Britain, concerned with the need to protect her sea lanes to India which were vital to the prosperity of her developing industrial cities, successfully eliminated French competition in southern Arabia and the lower reaches of the Gulf. The French presence had, for the while, seemed to pose a significant threat to what Britain had increasingly come to see as her essential paramountcy in the area. The French had established a foothold in Muscat; in 1798 the British effected their expulsion and themselves entered into a treaty with the Sultan of Oman.[40] Then another problem reared its head which was deemed to require British action: the nefarious activities of the celebrated pirates of the east Arabian coast.

'Pirates' is of course a term which the European interest in the area has applied to the freebooters who sailed the southern Gulf seas and who were a considerable nuisance to the free passage of the merchant ships sailing to and from the Indian Empire ports. Arab writers of the present day prefer to see them as independent-minded fighters for freedom, kicking against the presence of the colonial power which, with remarkable prescience, they are considered to have recognized as such a good deal earlier than most other peoples.

The truth is more probably that, pirates or freedom fighters or whatever, they were really a sort of sea-borne Badu who, like their land-based brothers, saw any strangers not directly under their protection as fair game. The rich cargoes which sailed to and from India, British and otherwise, also had the attraction of being carried by the ships of the infidel, making their seizure an act of piety as much as of profit.

A series of judicious treaties with the shaikhs of the Gulf coast eventually cut off the freebooters' land support. Gradually their activities ceased, their going marked by the occasional startlingly dramatic incident as in the case of the Qatari-based buccaneer, Rahma bin Jaber. Trapped at last in Khor after a lifetime of merciless harrying of the coastal ports and the shipping that served them, Rahma, with his ten year-old son clasped to his breast, ignited a load of gunpowder in his hold and blew himself, his son and his ship to immortality in the year 1826, off the coast near Dammam in Saudi Arabia.

With the British maintaining a watchful eye on the seas around the Gulf and with British diplomatic activity directed largely towards the shaikhs who were the ancestors of the rulers of the modern States, matters remained relatively peaceful throughout the nineteenth century, punctuated only by the occasional flurry when a dynastic or clan dispute between the shaikhs and their followers might assume proportions which could not be ignored. Such occasions requiring British intervention were rare; Britain had, by virtue of the treaties which she had engineered with the shaikhs, made herself responsible for their relations with such foreign powers as might presume an interest in the area. Thus effectively she prevented any power other than herself taking a real interest in what was going on in a corner of the world which was, in any case, in the eyes of most foreign observers, remote and insignificant.

In the latter part of the nineteenth century relations with the Gulf were administered not by the Foreign Office in London, but by the Viceroy's staff in India. In the winter of 1878 Captain E. L. Durand, who held the post of Assistant Political Resident at Bushire, obtained permission to visit Bahrain and to carry out trial excavations of the tumulus mounds on the island. A report of their existence had excited Durand's antiquarian interest and he journeyed to Bahrain on what was to become the first archaeological expedition to visit the island.

On returning to London Durand presented his findings to a meeting of the Royal Asian Society[41] (he had already submitted a somewhat fuller, chattier and charmingly illustrated report to his superiors in Calcutta).[42] It was as a consequence of his report that Sir Henry Rawlinson, perhaps the most influential English scholar of the time in the study of the history and languages of ancient western Asia, made a brief but profoundly significant appearance in the story of the development of archaeology in the Gulf.

Rawlinson was a phenomenon even for his day when English soldier-scholars flung themselves, with persistence and a blithe disregard of danger, into the most hazardous enterprises, as much in the hope of achieving a fuller understanding of those ancient Empires of which they saw themselves the contemporary heirs, as in the firm suppression of those people who actually inhabited the lands over which they confidently ranged. As a young man Rawlinson had had a major hand in the decipherment of cuneiform and was one of the handful of scholars who recognized Sumerian for what it was, a language with no connection with the semitic languages which succeeded it in Mesopotamia. This little group of scholars was responsible for recalling Sumerian to the world after some four thousand years of silence, perhaps the most moving and romantic episode in the otherwise rather austere disciplines of paleoepigraphy and philology. A linguist of exceptional ability and diligence, he maintained his enthusiasm for decipherment throughout his life. Though he was an old man at the time of Durand's lecture in 1881 (for he was then over seventy, a Major-General, that most Victorian of military ranks, and a baronet), Rawlinson's commentary on Durand's text reads, even today, with freshness and enthusiasm, transmitting something of the excitement which he experienced in language.[43]

The most important outcome of Durand's visit to Bahrain was the discovery of an inscribed stone, the most significant inscription, indeed, yet to be recovered from the island. Rawlinson went to its root when Durand presented it, and showed that it was a votive offering of one who described himself as 'the servant of the God Inzak'. Citing a host of references, Rawlinson identified Inzak as the God of Dilmun: more references testified to Dilmun's island character and, drawing on sources which must have been wholly obscure to the considerable majority of his audience, Rawlinson firmly aligned Dilmun, the legendary Sumerian Paradise land, with the Bahrain islands. His commentary is full of star lore, in which perhaps few scholars would follow him today, and is extensively cross-referenced in Hebrew, Arabian and early Persian sources. It was, by any standards, a brilliant performance, a scholarly *tour de force*; Rawlinson was possibly the first man to speak Dilmun's name aloud in many hundred years.

So convincing is Rawlinson's commentary that it is the more surprising that Durand's expedition, modest in extent but substantial in its conclusions, did not excite greater and more sustained scholarly interest. It is the more surprising still when it is recalled that at approximately the same time George Smith had discovered the Sumerian original of the Biblical Deluge myth.[44] Despite contemporary scholarship's preoccupation with the search for the Garden of Eden, no one at the time seemed disposed to follow up Durand's trail and Bahrain-Dilmun was very largely forgotten.

Other travellers in eastern Arabia of course recorded sites and monuments of concern to archaeology: Palgrave, that strange Jewish Jesuit (he persisted at one point in calling himself, improbably, 'Brother Cohen', that priestly name having originally been his father's) described standing stone monuments in eastern Arabia in the account of his journey which was published in 1865,[45] but his veracity has sometimes been questioned. More recent research in the northern and western parts of the peninsula is however well on the way to vindicating him, if a little vicariously in geographical terms, for monuments not unlike those which he described have been located far away across Arabia, near Sinai.

In the 'nineties a British couple, Theodore and Mabel Virginia Anna Bent, visited several parts of Arabia including Bahrain.[46] Again they described various of the islands' monuments, including the so-called 'Royal Tombs' of A'ali, first in a lecture delivered by Bent at the Royal Geographical Society's headquarters in London, and, after his death, by Mrs Bent in *Southern Arabia*.[47] Their interest was really more ethnological than archaeological; however, their account of Bahrain at the end of the century is of considerable value.

M. Jouannin, a Belgian, excavated in Bahrain in 1903;[48] Colonel Prideaux, then British Resident in the Gulf, excavated some sixty-seven of the burial mounds in 1906 on behalf of the Archaeological Service of India. His report[49] is remarkable for the tone of deep exasperation in which much of it is written. He complains bitterly and frequently about the cost of excavation and of the excessive demands of his workers. However, it was the first serious attempt at a scientific survey of the mounds, well illustrated and with an admirable plan which was frequently reproduced by others afterwards, often without acknowledgment to Prideaux.

The father of Egyptology, Sir Flinders Petrie, made a brief intervention in the Gulf's archaeological development in 1925. In that year he despatched to Bahrain a young archaeologist, Ernest Mackay, who was later to make a distinguished contribution to the archaeology of India. Mackay spent some weeks in Bahrain and in 1929 produced *Bahrain and Hamamieh*[50] (the latter an Egyptian site) in the great series appearing under Petrie's editorship and published under the auspices of the British School of Archaeology in Egypt.

Petrie was one of those who believed that, at least in part, the impetus for the extraordinary flowering of Egyptian civilization in the late pre-Dynastic period came from contact between the people of the Nile Valley and voyagers from south-western Asia, who entered Egypt through the Wadi Hammamat, the great route which cuts through the eastern deserts of Egypt. He also thought that the people who entered the Valley originated in Elam, in south-western Persia.[51] There is, indeed, plenty of evidence of the introduction of Mesopotamian (and perhaps Elamite) elements into Egyptian culture at this time but the actual route that these influences took is still uncertain. Petrie evidently believed that the islanders of the Gulf, with their capacity for long voyages (which he must have sensed intuitively for there was little evidence available during his lifetime), were the means of effecting the connection which resulted in some powerful and significant elements being introduced into the consciousness and artistic repertory of the Nile people, where they were rapidly and firmly Egyptianized.[52]

Mackay's report, sadly, is largely notable for its inaccuracies. On practically every point that he explored he leapt to a quite insupportable conclusion: thus, traces of ivory inlays which he found in Bahraini tumuli he described as Phoenician and he believed Bahrain to be a mortuary island to which the dead were brought from the mainland for burial. However, it is easy to find fault with work done so long ago, with the accumulated knowledge of a lifetime to redress the inadequacies of the slender sources which Mackay would have had at his disposal. In fact his report is useful for the excellent drawings which he provided of pottery and artefacts from the tombs; he was also the first competent authority, other than Prideaux, to attempt to survey and draw the burial mounds which he examined.

In the years immediately preceding the second World War, oil company staffs were beginning to be settled in various parts of eastern Arabia. In the course of their surveying and cartographical duties (and, as was earlier observed, in their spare time, in the absence of much else to do) they had begun to explore the coast and its hinterland and to report on the discoveries of ancient remains which they made there. Gradually, scholarly circles, particularly those in the United States, began to be aware of the prospects of a 'new' region of the ancient Near East, one which had very largely been left in an archaeologically virginal state. In passing, it may be remarked that whilst it is fashionable to attribute many failings to the oil companies and their personnel and whilst such strictures are often no doubt justified, the contribution made by the companies to the uncovering of Arabia's past has been overwhelmingly beneficial. Without them and their enthusiasm it is doubtful whether Arabia would, even now, have been recognized archaeologically for what it is.

A young American scholar attracted to Arabia at this time was P. B. Cornwall, who visited the Hasa province of eastern Saudi Arabia in 1940.[53] He described various of the ancient sites and recorded some of the first evidences of hominid occupation there. Later he visited Bahrain and there he excavated a strange circular 'council chamber' which has subsequently been lost. He published several articles of considerable importance in Bahraini studies: these will be noted in their place. Sadly he did not sustain his interest in the archaeology of the Gulf; had he done so his contribution would no doubt have been a still more distinguished one. His unpublished thesis *Dilmun: a history of Bahrain before Cyrus*[54] is a remarkable compilation of reference and observation. Its value has been surprisingly little diminished by the passage of time.

The Second World War was obviously not the time for any sort of serious archaeological work to be carried out in so remote a theatre. The importance of the Gulf, however, came increasingly to be recognized as the Powers realized their dependence upon sources of supply of petroleum for industry and the machines of war. Bahrain, to everyone's surprise, was bombed by the Italians, presumably by mistake, but it could not be said that the war greatly affected life in the region as a whole. However, its future importance was being laid down in those days and its people, were, unbeknown to themselves, shortly to experience an astonishing abundance as the focus of world energy needs swung towards the Arabian deserts.

In 1953, some seventy years of occasional and fragmentary research came to an end with the true beginning of serious archaeology in the Gulf. In this year the first Danish Expedition arrived in Bahrain[55] and began work. Over the next seventeen years they were to transform the state of knowledge of the Gulf's antiquity and to recall to the world a civilization which had been forgotten for millennia.

The story of the Danish Expedition has been agreeably told by Geoffrey Bibby in his popular book *Looking for Dilmun*.[56] Bibby – and the Expedition's original leader, P. V. Glob – deserve to be remembered not only as great originators and the men largely to be credited with recalling to the world a forgotten and important part of its heritage but also as amongst the century's most fortunate archaeologists: luck is a quality, in archaeology at least, as important as the technical competence and ability which they also possessed in substantial measure. Between them and their colleagues they discovered a new chapter in the world's history and showed that four thousand years and more ago a civilization flourished in the Gulf which bore comparison with its great contemporaries in Mesopotamia, Egypt, Iran and the Indus Valley.

Due to the vagaries of academic publication, whilst their names should be ranked with the most distinguished in the history of archaeology, they are in fact known only to a comparatively narrow field of specialized interest. The loss is as much theirs as it is archaeology's.

The way in which the Danes first received permission to work in Bahrain demonstrates the importance of having fortunate stars, to guide the destinies of archaeologists. The British adviser to the Ruler of Bahrain, Sir Charles Belgrave, a man of some modest scholarly interests but with little experience of archaeologists, received two similar applications for permission to excavate in the same week: one was from the Danish Expedition, the other from the considerably more influential and very much richer University of Pennsylvania. Feeling himself unable to make an informed judgement as to the professional merits of either bidder, Belgrave decided that the most equitable means of reaching a decision would be on the toss of a coin. The coin was tossed and Denmark was free to resume an association with the Gulf which had begun with Niebhur's expedition some two hundred years before. Of such random circumstances is archaeological history made; it is difficult not to wonder what the much more richly endowed Pennsylvanians might have made of it.[57]

The contribution of the Danes – and now of a new generation of archaeologists drawn from many nations, including the Arabs and, increasingly, the peninsula States themselves – to recalling Dilmun to the world is deeply significant. As a result of their work the little island and large parts of the Arabian mainland of which, at various times, it was the capital, stand revealed as a profoundly significant cultural and mercantile state, particularly in the springtime of man's historic experience, the third and second millennia before our era. Just how profound and significant the island's influence was is only now becoming clear; by any standards it must be judged remarkable. This study will attempt to show, in outline at least, how rich is Bahrain's archaeology and how, though largely unknown, its influence lies embedded in the cultural repertoire of all peoples who draw, for better or worse, their inspiration from the great monotheistic religions which drew so much of their original inspiration from the desert dwellers of Arabia and its peripheral lands. To comprehend that significance fully, however, it is necessary to see Bahrain, Dilmun and the Gulf lands as part of the world which they directly influenced and which in turn influenced them. This involves a journey which ranges from Anatolia in the north, Egypt in the west, Mesopotamia and the heartland of the Sumerians in Iraq, Persia, Central Asia and, far to the south and east, the cities of the Indus Valley. To the people of all these lands the little group of islands in the Gulf and its dependencies along the Arabian coast occupied a special and enduring place. Of these lands, in turn, none was more lasting in its importance than Sumer, the land of the black-headed people, who had chosen to establish themselves in one of the most inhospitable regions of the known world, the southern part of the land between the two rivers, whose climate was both vicious and erratic. The environment of the Gulf was to exercise a profound influence on its people and, on the development of the societies around its shores; climate has ever exercised a profound influence on the history of men, and it is to the climate of the Gulf over the period during which settlement has been possible that this study must now turn.

II
The Last Oryx

It is a pleasing thought that the unicorn, that fabulous and magical beast, may still be alive and well and living in eastern Arabia.

Like the phoenix, the unicorn is a creature of the desert as much as it is of fantasy, the product of who knows what tales ancient travellers brought back with them from the further limits of the known world. Yet the probability is that the unicorn is in fact the oryx, a creature which combines massiveness with elegance and power with seeming tranquillity. The unicorn is an inhabitant of that misty land which divides legend from reality; at one moment he is visible and he is gone the next. He is notable for his susceptibility to virgins; indeed, so susceptible is he that he will surrender himself to human captors if a virgin is available in whose lap he may lay his head.

There is no evidence that the oryx, if he is indeed the unicorn's prototype, shares this unusual propensity. But there is no doubt that overhunting of the poor beast has contributed to his imminent extinction, though his pursuers have seldom been notably virginal. It is now estimated that there are probably no more than a few dozen head of oryx left in the wild in Arabia. It is greatly to the credit of governments in the peninsula that efforts to save the species have now been rewarded with success.

In their preserves the oryx maintain a watchful, dignified existence. To go among them is somewhat disconcerting: they turn on new-comers a long look of cool appraisal and then, thoughtfully, lower their massive heads on which grow two long, thin, black, razor-sharp horns. The young of the breed are pretty and delicate creatures; but power, not prettiness or delicacy, is the characteristic of the adults, particularly of the bulls. Their long, slender horns, which look as though they could be deadly, are the cause of the oryx's identification with the unicorn: seen in profile their two horns become one and the equation is exact.

But another factor, other than the depredations of man, has contributed to bringing this rare and beautiful antelope to the very edge of extinction. This is the fact that in all probability the oryx is a relic of an earlier climatic period, in popular terms, a sort of living fossil. It belongs to the fauna of the Pliopleistocene, a division of geological time which ended around two million years before the present. Then the climate of eastern Arabia was somewhat more generous than it is today; it could support, in what was probably a savannah-type environment, herds of animals larger and more dependent on supplies of food and water than are those creatures which survive in the desert today, when the climate is, truly, hyper-arid.[1] The oryx is said never to drink water in the wild; this, however, sounds more like a traveller's tale than an observation of strict scientific fact, though the animal is known to have a phenomenal ability to detect small quantities of atmospheric mois-ture. It also feeds at night when, in desert conditions, plants contain more moisture than they do during the day.

However, the oryx does serve to illustrate one of the characteristics of the climate of eastern Arabia and the fauna which the region sustains: the climate of the Gulf region is liable to quite marked changes which, considered over divisions of geological time, have often been very substantial. It has long been recognized that climate and the geophysical factors which attend his habitation have profoundly influenced the life and development of man. But just how profound such influences are and how fine the tolerances may be which can divide abundance from devastation are only now being apprehended by scholars; they have always been very clearly apprehended, let it be said, by people such as the desert dwellers, living at the whim of nature for millennia.

The margin, taking temperature for example, or the effects of prolonged rainfall or of drought, is fine indeed; a few degrees' change overall, either way, could bring in its train another ice-age or spread the deserts across lands which are now rich and fertile. Man clings precipi-tously to the edges of the inhabitable world; but he is the most malign influence in effecting ecological change and has been so throughout the millennia.

The climate of the last ten thousand years or so, during which the whole of the history of urban man is compressed, has been especially benevolent. Because our planet has been enjoying a phase of excep-tionally favourable climate, cities have been built, empires arisen, art has flourished and man has stepped on to the moon. A degree or two away from the global mean and the development of mankind would have been irreversibly blighted. It would still be.

The extreme nature of the climate in eastern Arabia on the one hand demonstrates the effects which can so easily occur in consequence of climate shifts and, on the other, the extraordinary ability of man to adapt even to the most improbable climatic circumstances. Geomorphologically, Arabia is still a relatively volatile part of the earth's land surface. It is still moving, drifting inexorably in a north-easterly direction, thus separating itself still further from its original union with Africa and pushing steadily against Iran. The Red Sea was flooded in early Pliocene times (c. twelve million years ago) when the final rupture with Africa was effected and the land bridge which had joined east Africa with south west Arabia was broken.[2]

The extent to which the Gulf is still in motion can be demonstrated at both its extremities and in the centre. Thus the Kuwaiti part of the delta at the head of the Gulf has been shown to have subsided by over 100 feet over the past five thousand[3] years, whilst at its south-east limit the Musandam peninsula in Oman has subsided by approximately 180 feet during the past ten thousand years. On the other hand the Bahrain Ridge, in the centre of the Gulf, is thought still to be rising.[4]

The Gulf is a product of the Tertiary period; it was formed as a consequence of tectonic movement, of the great plates of the earth's land surface grinding further away from each other. It is a roughly rectangular depression, approximately one thousand kilometres in length from its head, where the Tigris and Euphrates debouch, to the Straits of Hormuz, guarded on the western littoral by the towering walls of Ras Musandam. The sea bed slopes quite sharply; the Arabian coastline is fairly shallow whilst the deep water is all on its Iranian side. Its maximum depth is approximately 165 metres.[5]

Although the physical profile of the Gulf was laid down long ago (though relatively not so long ago in terms of the geological age of the Earth) it is really only in comparatively recent times that it has assumed the character and appearance with which we are familiar today. The environment of eastern Arabia has been affected by marked fluctuations of the conditions which permit more or less permanent settlement. Some of these fluctuations have continued well into the historic lifetime of man.

The question of the extent of climate change, and its effect upon a region as climatically extreme as eastern Arabia and the Gulf now are, is difficult of analysis or solution. Whatever may have been the true effect of changes in seawater stands, of the different levels in the water table and the apparent variations in the rate of precipitation, one influence on the environment is definitely to be identified – man. If ever the present generation, with its laudable concern for the protection of the environment of our beleaguered planet, needs to call evidence from the past, that of eastern Arabia will stand as a sufficiently awful warning for even the direst prophet of the impending destruction of our species.

One factor alone may be cited to demonstrate the extreme fragility of the conditions under which we live and the hazards which, all unthinking, we inflict on ourselves and our descendants. Much of the wealth of eastern Arabia in antiquity was drawn from the discovery of the uses to which copper could be put; indeed, a neat equation of copper, spice and oil can stand for the last five thousand years of Arabian history and its sum, the acquisitiveness of the world outside the peninsula. But copper, before it can be manipulated by the smiths, must be smelted: smelting demands high temperatures and heat requires fuel. It is thus far speculation, but it is surely not unwarranted to suppose that in Oman, on the terraces perhaps of the Jebel Akhdar (the Green Mountain), in north-west Arabia and Sinai, where extensive fourth- and third-millennium copper mining sites abound, and even on Bahrain itself, millions of trees were sacrificed to the needs of the copper industry. The stripping of the hillsides in Oman, for instance, would immediately reduce precipitation: the value of trees as wind-breaks would be lost and the earth would be swiftly eroded.

How much therefore the needs of the ancient copper industry may be the cause of much of today's deserts is a moot question. Certainly it seems not unreasonable to think that some of the most extreme aspects of the deserts today may be quite recent in origin, the consequence of man's own inability to maintain his environment properly.

The degree of tolerance in these matters is very slight and the extent of change, either of climate or of the environment, in, for example, the level of precipitation in a particular region due to the loss of an ancient stand of trees, need only be marginal to bring about a catastrophic alteration in the balance of nature. Tinkering with the environment is one of the more dismal inheritances of the ancient world.

Of course man is not unaided in his depredations on the world around him. In this malignant process he possessed a most industrious assistant who undoubtedly played a notable part in denuding landscapes; this was the goat whose domestication was distinctly an equivocal benefit, in this respect at least.

There is some disagreement about the extent to which Arabia was affected by the great glaciations which so dominated the last million years or so in the northern hemisphere. However, glacier wasting in the north raised sea levels throughout the world between 20,000 and 10,000 years ago. To whatever degree Arabia shared in these larger climatic changes, the volatility of her own was such that climate patterns were subject often to quite short-term changes: for example making part of the coast for a period capable of supporting a larger population than before, in consequence of a short 'wet phase'. There is evidence of several 'wet phases' in eastern Arabia; of the most recent, the first ended about ten thousand years ago, whilst another began one thousand years ago and lasted for three or four hundred years.[6] This coincides, for example, with the growth and decline of the little fishing settlements at Murwab and Huwailah in Qatar.[7]

The discovery of Dryopithecine remains in north-eastern Arabia[8] demonstrates the extent to which the climate 15–12 million years ago differed from that of its present profoundly desert, hyper-arid character. Dryopithecines are arboreal creatures, tree-haunting and flourishing in a broad savannah-type environment; they may or may not be on the line of ancestors which ultimately produced man. In their hey-day Arabia probably would have looked much like East Africa now, with plenty of cover for larger game. There is evidence that from Pliocene times (from *c*.3.5 million to *c*.1.2 million years ago) Arabia underwent a protracted 'wet phase' when in all probability it enjoyed a warm, moist climate. Its vegetation then would have been lush and tropical. During this long wet phase it is possible that hominids, like those that flourished in East Africa at the same time, were present in Arabia. After this time arid conditions supervened, reaching a level similar to that prevailing now around seventeen thousand years ago. Since then the climate has varied erratically and recent evidence has distinguished a sort of climatic antiphon, with an arid phase being followed by a moist one, in at least eight periods over the past seventeen millennia.

The faunal record in ancient Arabia is still very far from being complete. However the presence of large beasts, such as mastodon in Abu Dhabi (at Jebel Baraka),[9] and in the eastern region of Saudi Arabia,[9a] testify to a marked degree of environmental change over the millennia. To judge from the rock carvings which are found in other parts of Arabia (the eastern region does not seem to have encouraged the development of that characteristic and ubiquitous art form as other parts of the peninsula did), lion, baboon, ostrich and water buffalo, all creatures of the savannah, were common.[10] It is from this sort of ecological environment that the oryx probably descends and, by chance, survives.

It is in the region of the Rub al-Khali, the dreaded Empty Quarter of south-eastern Arabia, so often the focus of all manner of traveller's tales, that the change in eastern Arabia's capacity to support life is shown at its most dramatic.[11] Both at the edge of this tremendous sand-sea, whose arid dunes and sandy wastes stretch from horizon to horizon, and deep into areas which are virtually impervious, are to be found many small neolithic hunting and fishing encampments, perhaps more permanent settlements. The presence of the neolithic Arabians, who lived here 6000–5000 years ago, is marked by the scatter of the fine and elegant tools they made, some of the prettiest artefacts to have survived from stone-age Arabia, or, indeed, from anywhere. Here have been found the skeletal remains of hippopotami, which once lived in the swampy margins of what was a series of lakes and inland waters, reaching deep into the desert.

Generally speaking, however, in the period during which man has inhabited the region, the fauna, some members of which would have contributed to his diet, has probably not changed greatly. The desert hare, the fennec fox, the gazelle, the ibex and the diminishing oryx have all been present, then as now. The onegar, a form of wild ass, was probably once indigenous and has now disappeared; the camel is domesticated now, but that is a relatively recent development. In the third millennium and for much of the second it was probably known but as a relatively rare and certainly wild beast. It did, however, make some contribution to the inhabitants' diet.[12] Some enterprising fisher folk varied this diet significantly by the addition of large aquatic mammals like the dugong or sea-cow hunted by the early settlers at Umm an-Nar in Abu Dhabi.[13]

The richness of Arabia's fauna in the relatively recent past is demonstrated by evidence from the region to the south and west of the peninsula. In the south-west Rub al-Khali, the evidence of the presence of large bodies of standing water well within the life-time of man is also supported in a rich and varied faunal register. This includes the Asiatic wild ass (a relative of the onegar), *Bos Primogenius*, the great archaic bovine which once also roamed the forest lands of Europe, the *hippopotamus antiquus*, the water buffalo and the ostrich.[14] Since the hippopotamus inhabited the east it is possible that at least some of the others were once present there. The probability is that increasing desiccation and the decline of the water table drove the animals further and further south, until ultimately they encountered in man a scourge at least as dangerous (probably more so) as even the most inhospitable climate.

When the Rub al-Khali was lacustrine the coast of eastern Arabia would have had the appearance of a string of little islands with deep inlets reaching into the desert, rather like the creek around which Dubai has developed. This would have affected parts of Qatar and the northern coast of the Omani peninsula where the United Arab Emirates is now located; it also affected Bahrain, for the small al-Ubaid pottery-bearing site at Al-Markh was a little island at the time of the occasional fishing expeditions which were pitched there. It is now part of the principal island of the Bahrain archipelago. In Oman, evidence from Umm as-Samman shows that an arm of the sea once reached there. Today it is many miles distant from the coast, stretching indeed up to and beyond the border with Saudi Arabia.

The level of the Gulf itself appears to have risen and fallen fairly sharply over the past one hundred thousand years.[15] There is considerable evidence that between one hundred and twenty thousand and ten thousand years ago the sea receded, leaving the sandy floor of the Gulf exposed. It would then have been a broad plain, watered probably by an extension of the Shatt al-Arab which may have reached the shelf margin of the Gulf of Oman, representing a fall of some 330 feet below the present level.[16] If ever there were Neanderthalers in the area (a doubtful assumption), it is quite possible that such evidence as they may have left behind them was on the sandy plains which now form the floor of the Gulf. The greatest regression of the Gulf waters happened between seventy thousand and seventeen thousand years ago: then the sea withdrew beyond the Straits of Hormuz.

Whilst there is evidence of marked changes in the sea levels in the Gulf, such changes are far less dramatic in the Gulf's sister, the Red Sea, to the west of the Arabian peninsula. This would appear to be contradictory and the dilemma which it induces has not yet been resolved. No doubt further research will do so.

The sea began to return _c._ seventeen thousand years ago. An acceleration in the process took place _c._ eleven thousand years ago, perhaps by as much as ¾ to 1¼ inches per annum. Bahrain Island became separated from the mainland between six and seven thousand years ago;[17] previously it had simply been a dome-shaped prominence inland.

The sea reached its maximum transgression (that is, its highest level) between seven thousand and four thousand years before the present. Then it was perhaps some two metres higher than it is today.[18] Along the low coastline which characterizes so much of the Arabian littoral of the Gulf even so relatively small a rise in sea level would result in the flooding of large areas.

One of the phenomena which are particularly evident throughout all the Gulf sea-board states are the _sabkha_, the surface salt-pans which

'Bos primogenius', the large bovine herded in antiquity (*Museum of Archaeology and Ethnography, Riyadh*).

are found around the coast and inland where the sea has once transgressed. Essentially, the *sabkha* are formed by the action of the sun on water held in shallow pools on the surface of the desert. The water evaporates as a consequence of the sun's heat and a salt-encrusted layer is formed, the salt being drawn up, as it were, to the surface by the effects of evaporation.

Many of the Gulf *sabkha* are relatively recent in origin. Those in the Abu Dhabi coastal area have been dated by the Carbon-14 process to approximately four thousand years before the present.[19] However, whilst inland *sabkha* tend to be lacustrine in origin, some of them are relics of the transgressions of the sea; thus some of the *sabkha* inland in Saudi Arabia represent a sea level approximately 450 feet higher than at present and in Oman the *sabkha* of Umm as-Samman is thought to have been one such relic.

The importance of the water table, that is, the artesian or other potable waters that lie below the surface of the land, is obviously supreme. In Arabia the water table slopes eastwards, rising as it does so. The aquifers are fed by the winter rains and melting snows of the Syrian and Jordanian mountains; much of the water in the aquifers is fossil water, put down in some cases twenty thousand years and more ago. The fact that the water table rises as it slopes towards the east accounts for the remarkable phenomenon of the fresh-water (or at least brackish) springs which bubble up from the sea-floor around Bahrain and which must have contributed considerably to the island's ancient reputation for sanctity and special selection by the gods. It may also account for the name by which the region has been known, at least since Islamic times: Bahrain, the 'Two Seas'. In this case, of course, the two seas would be the salt water sea and the fresh water sea below the surface. It is probable that the great Arabian Wadi systems, of Sahba, Batin and Dawasir, were active, in the sense that they carried off rain water into the Gulf, during the Pleistocene.

It is one thing to excavate the evidence of man's past from the sites where he has lived and to analyze them, extrapolating from them such assumptions as we may be able to make about the way he lived and the motivations which moved him. It is quite another to investigate the history of the earth which bore him. The evidence of climate in eastern Arabia is complex and often obscure but the very lack of research in the region, compared with other parts of the Near East may prompt scholars to consider recovering such evidence as they can about the factors of climate and the physical environment before development, which is now sweeping across the region furiously, obliterates it forever.

III
Dilmun and the Land of Sumer

To set Bahrain and the lands of eastern Arabia into a coherent historical and cultural perspective it is helpful to look first at the structures and *mores* of the societies which are immediately contiguous to them, and which exercised so notable an influence on the region throughout the course of its history. Of these contiguous lands by far the most important and influential was Mesopotamia, the land of the Two Rivers. It must be borne in mind of course that Iran, Inner Arabia, the Indus Valley and Oman were all, to varying degrees, to exert an influence on the character of ancient Bahrain and the Gulf, but none of these seems to have approached Mesopotamia in the depth of its impact and its enduring quality.

Mesopotamia is today principally contained within the borders of the Republic of Iraq and divides naturally into two regions, north and south. In the early centuries of their mutual and related history, the south was incomparably the more important of the two, though a northern Mesopotamian influence can frequently be discerned, even in the earliest times, until ultimately, in the second millennium BC, it becomes the dominant, imposing its character on the whole of the land between the two rivers.

The essential quality of Mesopotamian culture was its extraordinary capacity for invention, the product of the genius of the land's first and most notable inhabitants, the Sumerians. Whilst the progress achieved in the scientific cultivation of crops and the management of herds owed much of its origins to northern Mesopotamian farmers, it is as city dwellers that the Mesopotamian people are most significant, and the emergence and growth of this phenomenon is to be observed particularly in the south. It was because of the Sumerians' dependence on the city as the basic structural element in their society that their influence spread far beyond their own borders, affecting the patterns of life in lands and times far distant from their own.

It can be misleading to attempt to isolate a specific time in man's historical development and, as it were, apply a stop-action to the world at that moment, thereafter setting it in historical time as a critical point in determining the course of subsequent events. There were, however, a few occasions when conjunctions of powerful forces have come together and wrenched the world out of its course to set it in a new direction. Something like this would appear to have happened during the later centuries of the fourth millennium.

It is clearly significant that in Egypt and Iraq, and later in India and China, the first great urban civilizations grew up in the river valleys. The siting of settlements on the banks of fast-running and capricious rivers and the consequent invention of irrigation permitted the development of sophisticated agricultural techniques and led to the conditions in which a highly developed political organization became necessary, to ensure that the manpower of the community was marshalled in good order, and that the canals and the lands which depended upon them were efficiently maintained and protected in the interests of the community at large. The emergence of the warrior caste and ultimately of kingship itself resulted in all probability from the discovery of the technique of the management of rivers and canals. Thus it may be said that technology played a critical part in the establishment of early societies and the hierarchies and social structures which grew up within their boundaries.

Just as it is usually unrealistic to try and arrest a point in historical time and represent it as marking a fundamental turning point, so it is dangerous to isolate one particular circumstance and see it as the starting point for another, quite dissimilar, set of experiences. However, the notion cannot be wholly discarded that the development of an ability to husband water resources and hence to make a greater acreage available to the community would to a large extent depend upon the willingness of members of the community to behave with responsibility and restraint. Inevitably, since human nature has not changed over the past five thousand years, individuals would try to obtain more than their fair share or to deprive others of theirs. Other, less organized, peoples would cast the eye of envy on the more prosperous community and, in consequence, the leader of the otherwise occasional war-band might well find himself more or less permanently recruited to the community's service. As the community grew and as the more skilful, charismatic or more powerful leader would begin to assert a form of hegemony over more widely dispersed groups, so kingship would be, in the Sumerian expression, 'handed down'.[1]

The principle of government under an autocratic ruler was early on found to be essential to control the resources that the societies had at their disposal and so to produce what was required for the needs of an increasing population. This in turn led to the emergence of a class structure and the fostering of specializations and individual skills by members of the societies, the early artist-craftsmen whose work expanded the horizons of their contemporaries and made it possible for the corporate life of the state, in the person and way of life of the ruler or in the service of the gods, to find expression. Through the invention of writing and of monumental inscriptions it also now became possible for one generation to communicate with others over long periods of time and to eliminate the total dependence on oral tradition which characterized all earlier attempts at formulating the corporate beliefs and intellectual inheritance of the community.

Building in stone and brick led to permanence not only in architecture but in beliefs and social structures; however the use of long-lasting materials in architecture was not, it is now known, an original invention of Near-Eastern societies. Recent carbon datings from Western European megalithic structures suggest that they are earlier in construction than all monumental buildings in the Near East, thus far known. But, equally significant, so far as we know the societies in northern France, Britain and Malta, which produced these remarkable monuments, did not develop structurally as did their Near Eastern peers. But it was the discovery of writing which made still greater controls in the society possible and led to entirely new dimensions of experience.

From the ability to retain ideas in a permanent form came man's discovery of still further potentials, hitherto only dimly realized, within himself. The ability to make permanent records which were capable of comprehension by any with the necessary skills (which, unlike other forms of craftsmanship, required only a normal intelligence and application for the acquisition of proficiency) was arguably the most important single advance ever made by man. It is one with a special relevance to the future of the societies in the region with which we are concerned. Equally, by the better organization of his resources man discovered the means to produce more than he needed of both the necessities and the luxuries of his world. Gradually he found the leisure in which to produce more and better things and in which to enjoy them. From this last discovery, the creation of surplus, the confines of his world expanded dramatically, for now trade and the peaceful intercourse of different peoples became familiar aspects of his everyday life.

In Mesopotamia special conditions prevailed, for man had settled there relatively late in his dispersion over the surface of the inhabited world, although lower palaeolithic sites have been found in the north, as have the remains of Neanderthals.[2] The Neanderthal was once the prototype of the half-human, half-ape, a creature of nightmare whose brutish existence was liable to abrupt termination by his equally brutish neighbour. But in recent years discoveries at Shanidar, in northern Iraq, and the analysis of other remains have begun to present a different picture of a creature who cared for and protected the old and infirm in his group and who, at their death, went out on to the hillside to gather flowers to bury with them. The discovery, too, that the cranial capacity of Neanderthals is on average somewhat larger than modern man's has also begun to qualify the unflattering picture which Neanderthal's modern descendants (if such we are, in part at least) were pleased to draw of him. Instead of the loping brute of earlier belief, Neanderthal is rapidly acquiring an air of pensive and gentle melancholy – a generalization which, though more kindly, may be as specious as the earlier one.

In Mesopotamia, the contrast between north and south is most marked in the earliest periods. In the north, around the tenth millennium BC, the beginnings of agriculture and the controlled breeding of herd animals appear for the first time anywhere in the world; except, perhaps, for the strange and ambiguous evidence from Nubia where incipient agriculture has been detected between the sixteenth and thirteenth millennia.[3] But the southern part of the land offered little inducement for settlers, since it was virtually bereft of minerals, stone or trees. Only when man had learned to control his environment, in particular to manage the rivers and lagoons which formed so much of the southern landscape, and so himself to create the conditions in which his needs could be satisfied, did a settled existence become possible in the southern part of the Land of the Two Rivers.

Over millennia small groups of migrants had drifted into Mesopotamia from the south and the west, where the deserts of Arabia lay, from the mountain lands of Iran in the east, and from Syria and Anatolia in the north. In the north the little settlements flourished and, incidentally, very early on began to produce pottery of an extraordinary fineness and elegance. It is remarkable that some of the earliest pottery in the world is also some of the most beautiful: that which is identified with the cultures known as Hassouna and Halaf is of quite exceptional and superlative quality.[4]

By the end of the fifth millennium another culture of comparatively high development had spread both to the north and south. It is from the south, from a small *tel* not far from Ur, that its archaeological site name of al-Ubaid derives.[5] Little is known of the social structures of the Ubaid people, other than through the traces which were left in succeeding cultures and their most distinctive pottery which is found over an immensely wide-spread area, fanning out from Mesopotamia to the Levant, Iran and, most significantly in this present context, to east Arabian sites. As for evidences of religious cults, in the oldest pre-Sumerian settlement, Jarmo in northern Iraq, a goddess figurine has been discovered but no representations of gods comparable antiquity are known. In the Ubaid region in the south the priesthoods must have been exceptionally powerful. The size of many Ubaid temples is formidable.

The Ubaid pottery levels are followed on southern Mesopotamian sites by the more sombre Uruk pottery and then by that which is typed by its find-site, Jamdet Nasr. In terms of absolute chronology Uruk spans the middle centuries of the fourth millennium and Jamdet Nasr continues until the beginning of the third. It is thus equivalent in Egyptian chronology to Naqada II or the Gerzean period, immediately prior to the first dynasty of Kings. In Sumer (to use the term which by the beginning of the third millennium is appropriate) these early pottery sequences are followed by the Early Dynastic period, which, divided archaeologically into three phases, continues until the appearance of Sargon the Great in the twenty-fourth century BC.[6]

By the beginning of the fourth millennium southern Mesopotamian society has become recognizably Sumerian, in language, custom and in the development of that most Sumerian of institutions, the city. The Ubaid people disappear and are subsumed into the predominantly Sumerian mass. However, the transition from Ubaid to Sumerian is virtually unmarked and whilst it was once thought that the Sumerians were a 'new people' who arrived at some unspecified point in the first half of the fourth millennium, this view is today much less firmly held. Rather, scholars believe that Ubaid society evolved into the Sumerian, perhaps with the leavening of some alien elements but with no evidence of a major population change having taken place. The evidence of a long pottery sequence from Ubaid to early Sumerian forms is one of the more convincing arguments in favour of a cultural continuity in the south over the thousand years or so which anticipate the first certain appearance of the Sumerians as a distinct and identifiable group around 3500 BC.[7] The evidence of language is less clear however; whilst the first pictographic tablets to be found in Sumer are thought to be written in Sumerian, many of the place names which were adopted as the names of the cities and shrines of Sumer are not themselves Sumerian words.

They appear to be the names of some pre-Sumerian strain which once was thought to be the remnants of the language of the Ubaid people – 'proto-Euphratean' as it was sometimes called. It is by no means certain, however, that such a separate language ever existed and the issue is yet another of the perplexing elements still unresolved in the history of this distant epoch.[8]

The problem of the origins of the Sumerians themselves is one of the most tantalizing of the unresolved mysteries of the ancient world. At one time or another, practically every possible origin (and a variety of quite impossible ones) has been suggested for them, but still the question must, for the present, end in uncertainty. Their language, usually one of the surest means of pinpointing an ethnic group's origins, bears absolutely no relationship to any other language, living or dead. Sumerian is agglutinative, that is to say its clauses are built up by adding syllabic elements to the original root. In this it is similar to Finnish, Turkish, Hungarian and Basque, but it is connected with none of these nor with any other known tongue.

Sumerian was a rich and flexible language and it soon became one of the most powerful media for the expression of the Sumerians' exceptional creative genius. Sumerian literature, with its amazing repertory of epic poems, of the sagas of heroes, 'wisdom' literature, hymns and songs, love poetry, proverbs and laws is immensely rich;[9] it boasts the oldest surviving corpus of literary texts in the history of the world and, in many ways, one of the most noble, full of humanity and with a deep concern for the human condition. No account of Sumerian ways can ignore the literature of the Sumerian people and in the present context extensive use will be made of extracts from that part of the literature which bears upon the Holy Land of Dilmun, a particular theme of these early epic writers.

Perhaps the most important single contribution which the Sumerians made to the progress of mankind was the invention of sophisticated writing systems. It is difficult, maybe even impossible, to think of any invention which has contributed more to the fulfilment of man's destiny, nor one which has added more to his enjoyment of the world in which he found himself placed by the whim of the gods.

It is not certain that the Sumerians were the first to invent the *concept* of writing. In Upper Palaeolithic times, it has been suggested, some form of calendrical notations may have been employed to keep track of the seasons and the passage of the days.[10] A group of tablets excavated at Tartaria, in Rumania, bears some resemblance to early Sumerian forms and may, indeed, be ancestral to them, hinting at yet another point of origin for the Sumerian people themselves, or, as likely, a direction from which some powerful influence travelled.[11]

Recent research has opened up another remarkable and exciting vista to the origins of writing.[12] For many years past workers on sites in the Near East have been turning up quantities of small baked clay objects in a variety of seemingly arbitrary shapes, spheres, half-spheres, cones, tetrahedrons and the like. These have been variously described – as toys or ritual objects – or dismissed outright as inexplicable.

These tokens are found on sites dating back as far as the ninth millennium BC. This is astonishingly early, coinciding virtually with the first appearance of agriculture in the Near East, one of the most momentous of all social changes which man has experienced since Neolithic times.

These various shapes seem to have been used over the many thousands of years which separate their first appearance from that of the first tablets from Sumer to carry what may properly be called 'writing'. What makes the discovery so momentous, however, is the recognition that they are the earliest device for recording the numbers and species of animals possessed by a temple, for example, and that the scribes of several thousand years after their introduction used the same symbols, incised on stone or clay, as were represented by the clay tokens.

Frequently the tokens were contained in hollow clay bullae, roughly the size of tennis balls. On the outside of the bulla the number and type of tokens which it enclosed would be incised, to prevent fraud or the passing of incorrect information. The only example so far known to have come from an east Arabian site is stated to have been 'an isolated surface find near Dhahran in Saudi Arabia'. Sadly, it was removed from Saudi Arabia and is now in the United States.[12a]

However, neither of the precedents, the 'tokens' or the Tartaria tablets, which may have gone before the Sumerians' introduction of writing in any way diminishes the splendour of the Sumerian achievement; they were the first to devise a technique of making permanent records which was also flexible enough to be capable of expressing concepts and ideas and of recording for ever the very speech of the people.

The earliest known examples of Sumerian writing come from Kish[13] and Uruk,[14] two of the most ancient antediluvian cities in Sumer; those from Kish are marginally the earlier but both sets of tablets are dated to the Uruk period. On these small, cushion-like stone tablets, excavated from levels *c.* 3500 BC, were found pictographs, representations of the object about which it was required to record

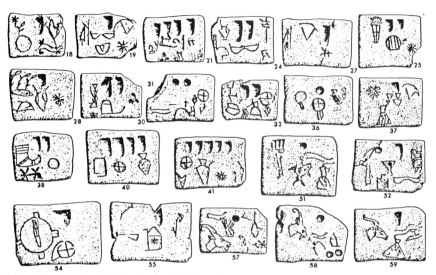

Tablets like these from Uruk, the city of Gilgamesh, are amongst the earliest examples of writing known. (*Müller Karper*).

quantities. From this point the technique developed rapidly, with the pictographs becoming more extensive as the records became more complex. It was soon realized that the simple representation of an object by drawing a picture of it was both cumbersome and limited. Then the great leap forward was taken in synthesizing the pictographs with abstractions which would represent the object on one level but also the sound of the word or syllable concerned on another. By this means it was possible to develop a form of writing which could itself record observations without being wholly dependent on the representation of objects alone. This form of writing is known as cuneiform, for the characters are wedge-shaped, the product of Sumerian 'pens': sharpened reeds whose angled writing points most easily produced the combination of lines and wedges which made up the Sumerian script. Ultimately there were some 2000 standard signs of which 600–700 were in general and relatively frequent use. To learn them and to inscribe them competently must have demanded a formidable standard of education for the boys who attended the schools specially set up for the purpose of training scribes. The scribal profession was one which was greatly to be envied, a situation which also prevailed in Egypt. The sophistication of the Sumerian intellectual establishment even in the fourth millennium BC was quite extraordinary. This is demonstrated by the fact that, like many early-formed languages, Sumerian originally had an extremely complex and cumbersome vocabulary. Thus it was particularly rich in nouns with many words for objects which would more conveniently be classified by adjectives. At some point in the latter part of the fourth millennium, the language was reformed and instead of there being, say, twenty-six words for various types of sheep, the number was drastically reduced and qualifying adjectives (or their equivalent) employed.

The script itself went through some six stages of adaptation[15] before it was finally stabilized into what might be called its classical form around 1800 BC. When the semitic-speaking hordes from the Arabian and western deserts began to move into the Sumerians lands, since they were of course illiterate, they adopted cuneiform as their own form of writing though it is illsuited to a semitic language. As a consequence, however, of the tribes' adoption of it, its use spread to other semitic language-speaking states around the Near East, so that by the middle of the second millennium BC, two thousand years after the Sumerians had invented it, cuneiform was widespread in use throughout the Near East, though Sumerian itself had become purely a liturgical language by then. Typically, since they believed that nothing of theirs could ever be improved upon, only the Egyptians did not employ cuneiform characters (except under diplomatic duress) preferring their own system of hieroglyphic and hieratic scripts, the first of which is surely the most elegant script yet invented by man.

It has been suggested that the Egyptians must have borrowed the idea of writing from the Sumerians as the chances of both peoples independently making the same so revolutionary an invention at roughly the same time (the earliest examples of Egyptian writing appear shortly after the Sumerian) is thought to be stretching the theory of independent development too far. However, the Egyptian system bears little or no relationship to Sumerian forms, and it seems strange that this should be so if the Egyptians did borrow the idea originally. In the later centuries of the second millennium, when all the kingdoms in the Levant and Mesopotamia were using cuneiform, even the scribes of the Egyptian foreign office, who maintained an extensive correspondence on the Pharaoh's behalf with his contemporaries, were obliged to conduct this part of their correspondence in cuneiform. With the Egyptian conviction that their ways were so unreservedly superior to all others, this necessity of writing in another people's orthography must have been a trying experience.

The texts which have survived from Sumer, and which are to be reckoned in tens of thousands at least, are preserved on clay tablets, the most convenient and accessible substance which the scribe could procure on which to write. Following the same cushion-shape of the earliest stone tablets, the clay tablets were first smoothed, the characters swiftly incised on them with the wedge-shaped reeds and then baked, in which form they are virtually indestructible. Often they were sealed in envelopes and then (like the earlier tokens from which, in a sense, they may descend) neatly filed away in archive rooms which have become familiar and important elements in the excavation of many a Near-Eastern palace or city site.

The consequences of the Sumerian preoccupation with writing – and they were an almost compulsively literate people – was to be of profound importance to the people of Bahrain and the Gulf settlements. The Sumerians did not invent writing primarily to record their folk epics or the proverbs which show them to have been a worldly-wise people with a nicely ironic cast of mind. Their purpose was, some might think, a less elevated one; they were concerned to maintain accurate records of their trading activities. These activities were to become perhaps their greatest single preoccupation and trade accounted in no small part for the diffusion of Sumerian and Mesopotamian influences over a wide area of the known world. In this aspect of their life Bahrain and the Gulf islands and settlements played a particularly significant part.

The Sumerians were the first people to organize trade, to a large extent making it the very basis of their societies. Southern Mesopotamia is an odd part of the world; it is now, as it was in the days of the Sumerians themselves, a land of harsh, wind-swept desert, of fast-running rivers that lay down rich silt and mud fields which are capable of exceptionally high yields when managed carefully, of lagoons stretching from horizon to horizon, teeming with fish and game, but virtually without any other natural resources whatsoever. There is hardly any stone in Sumer and the few trees, such as there are, with the exception of the ubiquitous palm tree, are of little value to the craftsman or builder.

Because of the nature of their land the Sumerians, in the latter part of the fourth millennium, were faced with a singular dilemma: a burning creative enterprise which was prevented from finding expression in the conversion of the products of nature into the artefacts of man. To obtain the raw materials their craftsmen needed, therefore, the city and temple administrators were forced to search for sources of supply far distant from their own ungenerous land. From early times we read of trading expeditions reaching out to far distant lands, of treaties between Sumerian states and foreign powers for the supply of Sumer's needs and the mounting of military expeditions to keep open the caravan routes or to subdue brigands and the other barbarians whose activities might prejudice the free flow of trade to and from the ports of Sumer's cities.

In the course of developing a trade which ultimately stretched from Anatolia to the Indus Valley, from the Levant and the islands of the Mediterranean to central Asia and north and south through Bahrain and the east Arabian towns, the Sumerians devised a complex series of techniques to facilitate the exchange of goods on an international scale and to finance the activities of their professional merchants.[16] In the course of doing so they invented the bank, the concept of capital and equity holding, mortgaging and the advancing of working or risk capital against securities, indeed much on the paraphernalia of international finance which still oils the wheels of commerce to this day. Later this study will examine the surviving correspondence of an Old Babylonian merchant who, in immediately post-Sumerian times, operated a trading enterprise of doubtful probity between the city of Ur and the city of Dilmun, located on the north shore of Bahrain's principal island.[17].

Sumerian trade operated in two ways: first by establishing sources of supply of the raw materials which were needed and, second, by creating export markets for the surplus goods the cities made, as a result of their enterprise and the skilful management of people and resources. The actual processes of manufacture were industrialized and highly organized. Factories were operated, turning out a particular product range, with a well organized and generally well cared-for labour force. Sumer's manufactures included textiles, furniture, jewellery, copper and bronze objects, and fine inlays; in addition she exported her surplus agricultural products. Her imports were first and foremost copper, and all sorts of timber and stone for her lapidaries, sculptors and architects. Timber came from Indian forests and from Oman; stone from Persia, perhaps from Oman and, in the case of the precious lapis lazuli much favoured by the gods, from distant Badakhshan. Gold was mined in Elam, in south-western Persia and in Syria.

The staple of Sumerian trade was copper; its conversion by man is very ancient and there is evidence of it being smelted in Anatolia in the seventh millennium.[18] Indeed some scholars have suggested that the Anatolian sources were lost to the Sumerians in the fourth millennium BC;[19] in consequence, they were forced to look for other sources of supply, which they found, it is suggested, to the south: Oman may have been one of her principal sources discovered in this search. But the idea of Sumer's discovery of the Gulf being the consequence of her search for copper is improbable. No doubt the need to prospect the Gulf lands for this vital element in her economy added greatly to Sumer's knowledge of the region but there is really nothing to suggest that Anatolian copper was so significant in the early history of the people. However, it is certain Bahrain played an important role as an entrepôt in the movement of copper from its sources, notably in Oman, to Mesopotamia. There is evidence of a considerable quantity of copper being handled in Bahrain, through the quays of the successive cities at the Qala'at al-Bahrain site.[20]

Trade was conducted, as will be seen from the correspondence which survives, by barter in part but also by the much more sophisticated technique of giving equivalent values in a standard of currency, in the Sumerians' and Babylonians' case in silver. They did not, however, find it necessary to take the conclusive step of introducing a coinage.

Whilst the idea does not receive the same degree of support today, it has in the past been often suggested that the immigrants into southern Mesopotamia, who were to become the Sumerians, came to the land from the south, travelling up the Gulf or along the Arabian coast.[21] The presence of the Ubaid in southern Mesopotamia has already been observed, and their pottery has been found, in very recent years, on many east Arabian and Gulf sites. However, there is as yet no evidence that the Ubaid progressed, as it were, from south to north; indeed the pottery seems to suggest that the earliest examples are to be found in the north, whilst the analyses of Ubaid sherds which have been carried out on the Gulf examples connect them with potteries at Ur.[22] But the fact remains that the Sumerians believed that the arts of civilization had been brought to them from the Gulf by the fish-man Oannes, who may be a manifestation of Enki, the benign creator god of whom much more will be heard before this present work is done.[23] One cycle of legend makes Dilmun, which featured paradoxically in the Sumerian consciousness both as a commercial trading centre and as an idealized Paradise land, the place of creation, from which concept undoubtedly the Biblical story of the Garden of Eden is derived.[24] It would be unwise to dismiss absolutely the possibility that the people who became the Sumerians, or perhaps other immigrants who influenced them considerably, did come up the Gulf from some as yet unknown southern point of origin.

The centre of the land of Dilmun, which exercised so powerful an appeal to the Sumerians, was the principal Bahrain island. However, its borders were never immutably fixed; at certain periods it was known to include the eastern Arabian coastline up to present day Kuwait and to include Failakah island on which important third-millennium remains have been found. Dilmun was 'the place where the sun rises', 'the land of the living', in Sumerian *Kirlu Ti-La*.[25]

There has been considerable speculation whether the Gulf in Sumerian times reached significantly further north than it does today. The view was widely held, until fairly recently, that it did, this opinion being strengthened by the historical record of such cities as Eridu and Ur which boasted of a sea trade and which now lie up to 150 miles from the Gulf. At one time it was thought that the shorelines of the Gulf had not much changed since relatively early times, certainly since the lifetime of man. However, some doubt is now being cast on this view.[26] It may be that the region of southern Iraq, now inhabited by the Marsh Arabs, a people who could well be the last survivors of the Sumerian (even pre-Sumerian) way of life, was then, even more than it is today, an area of lagoons, reaching far into the Sumerian hinterland. Thus some of the principal Sumerian ports in the south would have been situated on the shores of a lagoon and linked by a chain of them each opening into another, down to the Gulf.

Eridu, the most southerly of all the Sumerian cities, was also the most ancient. It was one of the great pre-diluvian cities, for the Sumerians reckoned historic time from the legendary ages before the Flood. Archaeology has borne out this tradition of Eridu's antiquity and suggests that it is fact: so far, no city has been found that is of earlier date. A long series of temples was excavated at Eridu; the four oldest,

An early Temple at Eridu, *c.*3300 BC. The base on which the temple stands is formed by the ruins of earlier structures and retained by a substantial wall. (*Museum of Archaeology and Ethnography, Riyadh*).

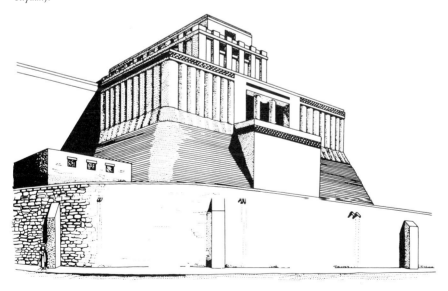

reaching ultimately down to the virgin sand, are the earliest identifiable as Ubaid buildings.[27]

In the context of Bahrain and the Gulf, this fact of the antiquity of Eridu is extremely important, for Eridu was sacred to Enki, the god of the Sweet Waters. Throughout Sumerian history Eridu was the cult centre of the one Sumerian divinity who was well disposed towards humanity.

According to the evidence of legend, Dilmun and Enki were closely identified in Sumerian belief; the worship of the god, it has been argued, might have originated in the Paradise Land.[28] Enki is sometimes conflated with Oannes, the amphibious monster who swam up the Gulf, accompanied by a train of outlandish marine creatures. Oannes' epiphany has been cited as evidence that the Sumerians came from the south, it being suggested that Oannes was a sort of abstraction of the people themselves and also, more pertinent to this story, that on their northward journey they had settled for a time on Bahrain island. This, it was supposed, accounted for the tenderness with which they looked back to Dilmun and for the sanctity with which they invested the island, making it in truth the island of blessedness and innocence. It has been suggested too that the palm tree, that profoundly important element in Mesopotamian agrarian economy, was not native to southern Iraq – as indeed it is not – but was brought to Sumer by the migrating black-headed people, travelling northwards up the Gulf.[29]

The exceptional antiquity of Eridu has further been called in support of the contention that it was the first true Sumerian settlement, the landfall as it were of the immigrants, who commemorated their sea-borne journey by consecrating their first mainland city to the water-god Enki. In this context, too, it has been noted that in the second half of the fourth millennium, Uruk, the city which was to give birth to the greatest of Sumerian heroic kings, Gilgamesh, shows a marked and sudden increase of population.[30] It has been suggested that this increase might have been the consequence of a migration of people from the Gulf region. If such a migration took place (for which, at present, there is no archaeological evidence), it would account for the infusion of myths and legends which are centred on Bahrain – Dilmun, revered as the original home of gods and men.

It has been noted already that most authorities see an uninterrupted sequence of occupation in southern Mesopotamia from early Ubaid times through to the first appearance of writing, and hence to the first appearance of the Sumerians when it was possible to put a name to them, in the latter part of the fourth millennium.[31] The most compelling evidence for this view comes from the Eridu temple itself: the earliest humble shrine which underlays the great, late-third-millennium ziggurat (which was consecrated to Enki and thus honoured the god of fish and the deep waters), displays a startling continuity from the days of Mesopotamia's earliest occupation, around 5000 BC, down to the lifetime of the ziggurat some three thousand years later. The evidence of pottery too, is quite clear. From the products of the Ubaid people, through the types associated with the Uruk and Jamdet Nasr periods, the succession of each type from its predecessor is evident. Pottery is a certain marker in these matters and its evidence is unequivocal. Thus, if the Ubaid or the Sumerians, or any part of them, came from the south then they must have moved along the Arabian shore; but such Ubaid pottery evidence as there is at present, which does not come from sites further south than Bahrain and Qatar, indicates connections with the later Ubaid and, in all probability, with established communities in Mesopotamia.

Two of the most significant artefacts from the very beginnings of the Sumerian period both come from Eridu; they are amongst the only surviving examples of Ubaid statuary. The first is a clay figure of a man, naked, holding a mace and wearing a high *polos* headdress, a type of conical cap which later became one of the distinguishing marks of many Near Eastern divinities, and which is not unlike the white crown of Upper Egypt. Companion female figures, somewhat older and shown suckling a child, have also been discovered; both male and female share the same strange and rather frightening reptilian heads. On the shoulders of the male figure dots of clay may, it is suggested, represent tattoo markings.[32]

The other, deeply significant, survival from fourth millennium Eridu, in the late Ubaid period, is the oldest model of a sailing boat yet found anywhere in the world.[33] With little modification, this type of vessel continued to sail the waters of the Gulf and, where they were navigable, the rivers of Mesopotamia, far into historic times. The Eridu boat would have been seaworthy and further supports the belief that the Gulf could easily have been explored by men in prehistoric times. It was on the Gulf's tricky waters, or on the waters of southern Mesopotamia's marsh-bound lagoons, that man first developed the art of harnessing the winds to his service and using their power to drive the early sailing craft of which the Eridu boat is the prototype. How far these early voyages reached is yet a matter of speculation but the presence of shells, which can only have originated in India, in a very early grave at Tepe Gawra far to the north in Mesopotamia, could be taken as

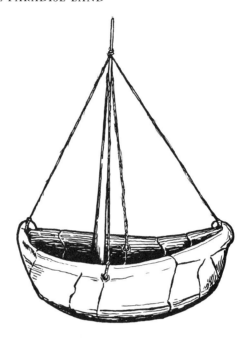

Sailing boats like this one from Eridu were probably the first to travel on the waters of the Gulf, early in the fourth millennium BC (after *Illustrated London News*).

evidence, even this early, of a route to India through the Gulf. A land route cannot be completely ruled out, however, though the experience of historic times makes it less likely. Shells from the Gulf have also been found in Egyptian graves of the Naqada I period, equivalent to the Uruk period in Sumerian chronology. Similarly, lapis lazuli have been found in predynastic Egyptian contexts and can only have reached the Valley from the east. Whilst again a land route cannot entirely be dismissed, the probability of these materials having reached Egypt by sea is generally thought to be more likely.

The most notable characteristics of Sumerian society grew out of the land and the conditions necessary to organize it in such a way that it would support a rapidly growing population with increasingly sophisticated needs. There is some evidence that the earliest Sumerian political unit was an assembly of free men who, under the leadership of the elders, together openly debated issues affecting the community.[34] Some commentators have, perhaps a little optimistically, seen in this

institution the earliest recorded example of democratic, even of par-
liamentary, government.[35] In the event, however, this phenomenon is
much more likely to demonstrate the lingering vestiges of the old tribal
assemblies of neolithic times, possibly an inheritance from the Ubaid
communities, and one which clearly proved to be unworkable in the
earliest phases of the true Sumerian period. However, the Sumerians
remained throughout their history a fiercely independent and indi-
vidualistic people. It would certainly not have been out of keeping with
their nature if the citizens had demanded a share in their own government. The most inspired of Sumerian rulers, Gilgamesh, is, albeit in a
purely literary context, shown consulting the elders of the state – and
then going against their advice.[36]

There is evidence that the earliest centre of administration and
authority in the fledgling Sumerian cities was the temple: this is logical
enough, for the city is merely the central point of the earthly domain of
the god to whom the city was consecrated. In the early centuries the
city, and the state which depended on it, was, literally, a theocracy,
god-directed and god-ruled. All land was owned corporately on the
god's behalf and managed by his vicars, the stewards of his estate who
in early times no doubt formed a powerful confraternity of priests
under the rule of the *En*, the high priest. The title was sometimes also
used in a purely political context, divorced from any cultic role.

To these practical priesthoods the world may owe much. In the
early centuries, trade, that essential aspect of Sumerian society, was in
the hands of the temple authorities; merchants bought and sold on the
temple's behalf and all the goods involved were the temple's property.
The practice of writing was invented, so far as we may judge, principally to effect a system of accounting for the temple's treasure; the
earliest pictographic texts are inventories of goods and animals in all
likelihood belonging to the temple.

One of the puzzles incidentally, and a most intriguing one, about the
process of disseminating an invention like writing is how, in so
fragmented a political society as the Sumerian cities undoubtedly were
in the historic period, they managed to develop a writing system which
rapidly became accepted throughout the land, paying no apparent
regard to the distinctions which one city state might vaunt over another
or the pretensions which the adherents of one divinity might advance
against the other gods. It seems that the sort of freemasonry which the
priesthoods represented must have been powerful enough and sufficiently organized throughout the country to make the decisions of
some central college outweigh local differences or preferences. It is

perhaps the first historic example of a bureaucracy at work, maintaining its own larger interests at the expense of any short term policies which might otherwise have supervened.

But, though their states were governed either corporately or auto-cratically, the Sumerians nonetheless retained throughout their exist-ence a respect for the individual and for the rule of law applied equally to all citizens, to a degree remarkable in antiquity. In most ancient societies it is generally the state, perhaps personified by the king, which is all-powerful and all-pervasive, private interests being liable to be sacrificed to a frequently arbitrary judgement of what was represented as the general or national interest. The Sumerians were the first people to attempt to define the role of the individual in society and to establish a formal, written code governing behaviour and defining responsibilities between the citizens themselves and between the citizen and the state. In doing so, they invented law and rightly prided themselves on the fact.[37]

The Sumerians thought of themselves as one people, and as quite distinct from their neighbours, but they early on fragmented into a constantly changing mosaic of little states, competing noisily with each other, though their frontiers sometimes barely stretched outside the city walls. One after another claimed the paramountcy over the others, to be overtaken quickly by a marginally more powerful or politically more agile neighbour. Only rarely was the land harnessed under one leadership for longer than a lifetime and in general terms Sumerian political history is made up of the records of the mass of little cities constantly squabbling amongst themselves like puppies in a basket.

Sumer was thus never a unitary state for longer than a few decades at a time, the individual cities often maintaining much of their auton-omous character meanwhile. When the distribution of cities, built perhaps on earlier Ubaid settlements, was established in the pattern which was to persist throughout the historic Sumerian period, Sumer could be said to stretch from just below modern Baghdad in the north to the sealands of the Gulf in the south, bordered by the Arabian desert in the west and the foothills of the Iranian plateau in the east; it was only some 10,000 square miles in extent, a tiny portion of the world's surface when measured against the influence its people exerted. Amongst the earliest cities, in addition to Eridu, were Ur, which provides much of the best known archaeological material of the region,[38] Uruk, the city of which Gilgamesh was king, and Nippur which was always the most sacred of Sumerian cities, consecrated to Enlil; Kish, Badtibira and Lagash were other cities of immense antiquity. By Early Dynastic times, in the first centuries of the third millennium there were some twenty city-states which made up the polity of Sumer.[39]

Each of them followed a similar if not identical political pattern: there would be a king or governor, a *lugal* or *ensi*, a temple to the principal god of the city and other lesser fanes consecrated to his or her coadjutors. Built around and beyond the sacred enclosure of the temple which formed the heart of any Sumerian city (and which was indeed the city's reason for existence, for the city was the personal property and domain of the divinity to which it was consecrated and the temple his or her dwelling place) were the citizens' houses of baked mud brick. The city's roads criss-crossed with blank walled alleys from which opened gates into the houses. These might be little more than one or two-roomed huts, or in the case of the more prosperous craftsmen, merchants or administrators, spacious buildings on two floors, with pleasant courtyards and loggias elegantly decorated,[40] but like all well-designed Near Eastern dwellings to this day, looking inwards to the household and the family which it enveloped. None of the cities covered very large acreages; the most famous, Ur, covered about half a square mile. Uruk, the city of Gilgamesh, was much bigger however, ranging over almost two square miles.

As Sumerian society developed and expanded, shops, factories, schools and barracks for the enlisted men became conventional land-marks in any Sumerian town. As, almost beyond anything else, the Sumerians believed in trade, the rivers' quayside market-places, where far-ranging ships would disgorge the merchandise of many lands, became more and more important in the life of the cities and central to the experience of its people.

A busy, properous, creative and largely cheerful people, the Sumerians had, by the beginning of the third millennium, established themselves securely upon their land. In essence, the cities which they built, the clothes that were worn in their market places, and the buzz of many tongues would have made their society seem little different from that of any Middle-Eastern country up to the beginning of the twentieth century AD.

The racial origins of the people of Sumer, it has already been observed, are unknown. They have not helped the matter by tending, throughout their history, to portray themselves as rather tubby, short-necked, round-headed people. In fact, the evidence of their skeletons indicates that their grasp of morphology was slight, but nonetheless many early commentators were led to believe that they were racially entirely distinct from the desert peoples to the west of them, who were Semitic-speaking and who constantly pressed upon the established urban communities which the Sumerians developed. But linguistic distinctions do not reveal themselves in skeletal remains: a Sumerian skeleton is indistinguishable from one of a Semitic-speaking desert dweller.

The successors of the Sumerians – the Akkadians, Babylonians, Kassites and Assyrians – were Semites and the language and culture of the land became progressively semiticized over the centuries to the extent that Sumerian was totally lost as a living language. However, from evidence so far available, it is impossible to argue anything conclusive about the Sumerian race. Certainly all the peoples of southern Mesopotamia intermarried freely and Semitic names in early Sumerian times are almost as frequent as Sumerian names surviving into the early Babylonian period. Within the present limits of knowledge, the terms 'Sumerian' and 'Semitic' are to be understood simply as cultural and linguistic divisions rather than as indications of distinct racial groupings.

The recorded history of urban man opens with the Sumerians having established themselves on their land and with the transformation of what were perhaps tribal or clan settlements, small villages which felt the need for some sort of 'central place' either for exchange or for ritual observance and so gradually led to the beginnings of city life. The earliest settlements of the Near East, which had developed erratically in Iraq itself, in Egypt, Palestine, Syria and Turkey, rapidly grew in Sumer into what modern man would consider properly organized cities. By the end of the fourth millennium a sizeable proportion of the Sumerian population spent its life within a city's boundaries. Unhappily, what may have been one of the primary considerations in drawing man to urban life, security, proved illusory in Mesopotamia, for the nomadic desert and mountain tribes, which hedged the cities about, quickly decided that they were prizes worth devouring and their riches worth seizing. Further, in moving to the city man had put himself at one remove from nature and the stress of city life began to weigh heavily upon him.

It was an entirely new experience for mankind, this living together permanently in highly organized, usually tightly walled, settlements. Economic pressures and the need for firm political controls in a powerfully developing economy were added to the hope of limiting the depressing cycle of onslaught and invasion which marred the enjoyment of life (or even its continuation) in post-neolithic societies, newly awakening to the prospects which that life had to offer. The evidence available and the interpretations, particularly those which are in-

fluenced by modern psychological analysis, suggest that the transformation from neolithic village communities to urban settlements and
the development of political structures and technology brought in train
a series of acute and radical changes and attendant tensions. The most
profound of these were experienced, first, in the emergence of art as a
formal discipline, which both in its origins and in its later practice was
concerned with the unseen world as much as the real one; and, second,
in the change from magic to religion, and consequently the organization of belief and the responsibility of man to the gods in terms which
the modern world could comprehend. Art and religion were as inextricably intertwined in Sumer as indeed they have always been practically everywhere else.

There is little trace in early Sumerian art of the propitiatory role
which religion customarily fulfilled in hunter-gatherer societies. It is
much more concerned with the declared worship of the gods, the
decoration of their temples and with binding them to care for the world
of men. The cults which the people developed were, in the manner of
religious observance ever afterwards, a method of catharsis, of the
release of tensions and the assuaging of fear and apprehension. The
uncertainty of their environment, the constant menace of the desert
tribes and, eventually, the rivalries of the little cities themselves, all
created a degree of uncertainty amongst those early city-dwellers which
some may see manifested in the works of art which they produced.
Monstrous shapes, reflecting man's deepest fears, began to emerge into
tangible, artefactual form and so lost some of their terror.

Although the judgement is necessarily a highly subjective one,
much early Sumerian art often seems to be pathological in origin and
demonstrates a neurotic, tense, introverted quality which can still be
deeply disturbing. As man tried to accustom himself to living in the
mass, these monster forms seem to betray the Sumerian's anxiety and
uncertainty about coping successfully with the tensions which this
communal life provoked. However, it is essentially this quality which
makes the art of early Sumer so especially interesting: it is the first
produced by a predominantly and consciously urban society.

Although Sumerian art softened over the centuries and reduced
many of the bleak and fearful qualities it early manifested, it never
wholly lost this characteristic undercurrent of disquiet. It must also be
admitted that, with important exceptions, the early art of Sumer is
often notable, when compared for example with that of contemporary
Egypt, for its technical incompetence. The Sumerians may be partly
worsted in the comparison by the strict discipline displayed by Egyp-

tian artists from the earliest times; but in any event they were better with words and ideas than with plastic materials, the result perhaps of living in a land bare of wood and stone. This peculiar blend of the neurotic and the incompetent did not, however, reduce the marvellous quality of Sumerian sealcutting, in which perhaps the black-headed people achieved their highest and happiest artistic skills.

Sumerian unhandiness, in any case, is rather endearing. Exceptions must be made to this denigration of Sumerian attempts at art in the case of such works of very high technical achievement as the splendid head of a woman from Uruk (the finest sculpture from any culture of its date, the thirty-third century before our era)[41] and a sinister creature of nightmare in polished limestone, the lioness-headed woman of unknown provenance, now in the Brooklyn Museum.[42] Here the neurotic quality of Sumerian art is well demonstrated: in this beautifully moulded figure the creature seems to be struggling to break out of its monstrous, part-animal, part-human shape.

The Sumerians were not entirely alone in developing that corner of south-western Asia which they occupied. To the west development was erratic, but to the east and south, in what is today south-western Iran, another talented people was establishing its place in the world.

One of the imponderables of the archaeology of the Gulf in early times, in the late prehistoric period for instance, is the extent to which its culture and way of life were influenced by this people, one of the more mysterious of the Sumerians' neighbours, the Elamites. Elam broadly occupied the Iranian province known historically as Khuzistan, centred on the great and enduring city of Susa which, in turn, has led to the region sometimes being referred to as Susiana. By whatever name it is called, Elam was a powerful western-Asiatic state, in many ways the peer of Sumer itself; it was also an important Gulf power, with a long reach of the eastern coastline under its control.[43]

The origins of Elam are as obscure as Sumer's. Their frontiers marched together in the region of the southern Zagros foothills. In historic times they were frequently in conflict with each other. Elam seems to have been a more integrated state than Sumer usually was, except on the infrequent occasions when a dynast in one of the little states emerged with sufficient power or charisma to impose his hegemony over the whole land. Cities in Elam, it has been suggested, were the consequence of the need for staging and exchange posts to be established to serve the search for raw materials and resources.

Elam shared with Sumer the early use of sophisticated writing systems. The system the Elamites employed is an adaptation of Sumerian cuneiform; the paramountcy in its use is still unquestionably Sumer's. Unfortunately nothing is known of ancient Elamite; at present it remains indecipherable and consequently far less is known about the early Elamite kingdom than would otherwise be the case.

The Elamites early on adopted the practice of seal making, a skill they shared with their Sumerian contemporaries. Elamite seals are exceptionally rich in design themes and in the skill which the seal cutters demonstrate in achieving their often very complex effects. Even more than their Sumerian colleagues, Elamite seal cutters were remarkably able at bringing about positively monumental effects in a tiny compass.[44]

Many Elamite themes and designs were incorporated into Gulf seal forms, and Elamite influence was at least as considerable as Sumerian. But no one equalled the Elamites in making *pictorial* seals which show monumental buildings or scenes of ritual or of palace life.

Many Gulf and east Arabian sites, of the third and second millennia in particular, yield quantities of a soft, easily carved stone which is frequently identified as soapstone or steatite but which is more accurately called chlorite. This is a dense, rather plastic-looking stone which varies in colour from brilliant green, through blue to grey and black. Its ease of handling meant that it was ideal for the manufacture of everyday containers, ones that, as it were, required mass-production as a consequence of the ubiquity of their use.[45] It has been demonstrated that much of the raw material required for this trade came from southern Persia and was traded through cities like those at Shahr-i-Sokta and

Designs like these from Elamite seals show the richness and variety of the seal-cutters' work in the late fourth/early third millennium. They show affinities both with contemporary Mesopotamian and Egyptian designs and with the Gulf or Dilmun seals. (*Amiet, P. 1961*).

Tepe Yahya; there were also steatite mines in western Arabia.[46] The variety of forms and designs used by the chlorite craftsmen is very extensive but certain themes repeat themselves with remarkable persistence. The vessels used range from tiny household jars, many with side-lugs allowing them to be suspended, to huge ritual vessels with designs of complex and often extravagant pictorial detail.

To what extent, if at all, there was contact directly between Elam in the east and Bahrain and the western Gulf littoral is, in the present state of knowledge, unclear. With the amount of traffic which the Gulf must have borne, certainly in the second half of the third millennium and in the beginning of the second, it is difficult not to conclude that there must have been some regular and familiar contact. There are evidences of influences percolating into the Gulf from even further east and north (from the Caucasus and Transoxiana for example) and in all probability running through Elam. There was a temple at Susa, Elam's principal city, consecrated to Enshag the tutelary divinity of Dilmun.[47] There may perhaps have been a colony of Dilmunites resident there.

It has often been proposed that many of the western-Asiatic influences which become apparent in Egypt in late pre-dynastic times came in fact from Elam. The pear-shaped maces, whose changing form seem to some commentators to mark the invasion of a new people in the Nile Valley, may be Elamite in origin; some of the elaborate ceremonial carving on votive palette and knives may also come ultimately from the same inspiration.[48]

The extent of Elam's influence on the history of the societies of late fourth- and early third-millennium western Asia is still awaiting study and quantification. When this is done the degree to which that influence extended westwards to Egypt, if at all, will be better known as will its contribution to Dilmun. It may be recalled that it was suggested by no less a figure than Sir Flinders Petrie that the islanders of the Gulf may have been the carriers of Elamite and Mesopotamian influences to Egypt in the late Gerzean (Naqada II) period.[49] It seems very much more likely to the scholars of today that such influences were transmitted peacefully, more probably by merchants than by warriors.

The achievements of the people of Sumer were extraordinary: it is one of the injustices of history that they are still generally deprived of the credit for them. Their exceptional antiquity, reaching back to the very invention of history, has of course not helped them. The fact that, in a sense, they invented the means of history itself, by inventing writing, merely piles irony on unwarranted neglect.

IV
Kings of the Four Corners of the World

The one Sumerian sovereign of whom most people will have heard is Gilgamesh.[1] By his appearance in the story of Dilmun in an episode in the Epic which describes his quest for the flower of restored youth, he highlights the essentially mystical nature which the land enjoyed in the minds of the people of Sumer who lived during and after Gilgamesh's time. More than this, in the person of Gilgamesh of Uruk, Sumerian legend and historical reality come into conjunction. To the people of the land he remained one of the greatest of heroes throughout their existence and indeed beyond it, for he was still a potent symbol to their Babylonian and Assyrian successors. His appeal, apart from the universal characteristics of his legend, seems to have rested upon the real achievements of his reign and the memory which the people retained of its glories. The exploits of later kings may also have contributed to it by being absorbed into the older legend.

The kings of Uruk are some of the better documented of the earliest rulers of the Sumerian states.[2] The historical existence of Gilgamesh has been proven by the discovery of the records of temple building in his name at Uruk and by the confrontation between himself and an historical king of Kish, Agga; he reigned c. 2700 BC.[3] Gilgamesh was preceded on the Uruk throne by his father, Lugalbanda, by Dummuzi-Tammuz (subsequently a god) and by Enmerkar, who seems to have been the first of the hero figures to catch the imagination of subsequent generations. It is, incidentally, likely that the Sumerians were the first people to have developed the concept of an heroic age, the time of these early kings, in much the way made familiar by the legends of the Mycenean age in Greece, the Northern sagas and the Vedas of India, many hundreds of years later.

Uruk has provided some of the earliest surviving Sumerian documents referring to Dilmun and dating from well back into the fourth millennium. One of the earliest such references comes from a tablet,

Gilgamesh, the archetypal hero and protagonist of the *Epic of Gilgamesh*, the first heroic epic known. (*Bahrain National Museum*).

c. 3000 BC,[4] and appears to refer to a tax official. It is not certain that at this time Dilmun implied Bahrain; it is more likely that it meant eastern Arabia.

In the surviving texts relating to the reign of Gilgamesh, the record of a number of the characteristics associated with Sumerian kingship may be found. Kingship was an essentially practical function in Sumer and seems, in its early days at least, not to have been overladen with any specifically mystical significance. Kings emerged comparatively late in the early period of Sumerian history. The king ruled but he did so by consent and frequently had to persuade his men of the rightness of the course of action which he proposed. He probably descended from the war-band leader, appointed by the city or state in times of emergency. The levies of warriors which he led were always ready themselves to urge a policy on their sovereign and, clearly, he was obliged to take their representations into account, though not necessarily to accept them. The Sumerians were an independently-minded people and were not usually prepared to abdicate absolute power to their kings, other than in times of extreme crisis.

The succession to the kingship seems generally to have been by the hereditary principle but most of the dynasties were shortlived, rarely lasting for much more than a century or so. The kingship could be assumed by humble citizens who, doubtless by the process of assassination or other political device, might be seen to manifest the favour of the city divinity, in whose hands the gift of kingship rested. A gardener is listed amongst the kings, as is a women tavern-keeper.

The Egyptians neatly solved the problem of the evident contradictions of monarchic rule as a political system by an absolute identification of king and god. It is difficult to argue with the administrative decisions of an immanent and divine ruler: treason and blasphemy become identical. Indeed, happy is the society which may see its god in the flesh every time he chooses to show himself, discharging his divine role in public. Much of the permanence and apparent changelessness of Egypt came from the sense of security which the king's divinity brought to the Two Lands: there, all was patently for the best in the best of all possible human situations. The Sumerians, who do not seem to possess the same quality of innocence of view which often typifies the Egyptians at much the same time, did not have the comfort of knowing that God was living in a handsomely furnished white-walled building, only, as it were, a short distance down the road. Such was the happy case of the people of Memphis and of others of the early capitals of Egypt.

To the Sumerians, the concept of kingship was more significant than the person of the king. In the Sumerian phrase, 'kingship was handed down' from heaven, mirroring the system by which the divine world was organized: 'As above, so below'. The king was originally conceived as little more than the overseer of the labour force required to farm the god's land. The gods recognized that their workers needed overseers and, therefore, kingship was delegated from heaven to earth: the king became, in the first place, the steward of a divine master. But in Sumer kingship also had its darker side.

Of all the cities of Sumer the most celebrated is Ur, first by reason of its Biblical celebrity and then because of the extraordinary discoveries of Sir Leonard Woolley.[5] Until the 1920s the mention of the city of Ur was inevitably followed by the Biblical epithet 'of the Chaldees' and it was pigeon-holed as the putative birthplace of Abraham, the Friend of God. This ancestor of the Hebrews and the Arabs, if indeed he existed at all, would have been a desert shaikh whose immediate forebears had migrated to the city probably at the beginning of the second millennium, amongst the waves of semitic incursions which characterized all phases of Sumerian history. Ur, however, had been great long before Abraham, and the discovery of the tombs of the Sumerian kings in the city by Sir Leonard Woolley in 1922 revealed its greatness in a startling, indeed, in a chilling manner.[6]

In the twelfth tablet of the series from which the most complete version of the Epic of Gilgamesh is drawn, there appears to be the description, in part, of the burial rites of a Sumerian king.[7] From this it seems that, sometimes at least, servants, courtiers and members of the royal family may have gone into the Underworld with the king, sacrificed to his royal eternity. Whilst this tablet does not really constitute a part of the Epic proper, it is particularly interesting in the light of Woolley's quite exceptional discoveries.

After working in the ruins of Mesopotamian cities for many years, during which he greatly advanced the knowledge of Sumer's contribution to the world that succeeded it, Woolley discovered a number of complete burials of the Early Dynastic period at Ur, now dated to the middle of the third millennium BC and probably, within a century or so, nearly contemporary with the reign of Gilgamesh, and just after the great pyramids were built at Gizeh in Egypt. One grave was contained in a deeply sunk pit and was very richly furnished with gold, silver, bronze, ivory and copper artefacts of a singular beauty and high craftmanship. Goblets, cups, jewellery, regalia and the rich trappings of a powerful and luxurious court were released from their four and a half thousand years of entombment. What was even more remarkable was the discovery of the court itself, or at least some seventy-four members of it, who had been sacrificed and laid in orderly rows to wait upon the eternity of their sovereigns.

The practice of such ritual sacrifice, by which individuals were put to death to accompany their chieftains into the darkness, is of great antiquity. It is a practice which is to be found in all historical periods over most areas of the world. It is still not unknown in Africa where, for example, thirty-two members of the court of Asantehene, the somewhat more than mortal paramount chief of the splendid Ashanti people of Ghana and the guardian of its collective soul, were clubbed to death in the tribal capital, Kumasi, some forty years ago on the death of the last but one holder of the office. Naturally, to the modern world which reckons the numbers of its sacrifices in millions, there is something particularly frightful in finding evidence of the deliberate slaying of seventy-odd courtiers, whose deaths were occasioned solely by religious belief and not by the demands of politics.

The rationale of the practice is, of course, not difficult to see; usually the king so served also exercised a priestly function as the mediator between his people and their gods, and in this capacity he would be required to carry out complex and extended rituals to achieve the prosperity of the folk. Rainmaking ceremonies, rites connected with the fecundity of herds, the fertility of the crops or the averting of natural disasters needed many participants and acolytes to the principal celebrant. Obviously any such ceremonies would be vastly more effective if they were performed in the presence of the gods whom they sought to influence; therefore, the king's closest assistants would be required to attend upon him and to assist him when he carried out the sacrifices in the afterlife.

The contents of the great tombs at Ur inevitably came to be compared with Tutankhamun's which was discovered earlier in the same decade. But the elegant daggers, the slender cups of gold, the great electrum helmet of Prince Meskalamdug, are so superlative in their simplicity and restraint of design, brilliantly compounded with the costliest materials, that they make the glitter of most of the sad little boy-pharaoh's weirdly-designed death-gifts seem more meretricious even than they really are. The contents of the Ur tombs are simply extraordinary, the most sumptuous ever made by any people. They are quite untypical of the general run of Sumerian work, even of the finest. Nothing that has survived from Sumer encourages the expectation of works of such quality. Only the art of the seals, some of which have the quality of jewels, has something of the same brilliance of form and design. But the objects in the tomb are really unparalleled and are witnesses to what must have been a culture of the most remarkable material splendour. It is difficult, however, to suppress the suspicion that the contents of the Ur tombs were not the sole unaided work of Sumerian craftsmen, though whence they may have come is quite beyond speculation.

The Ur burials are sharply mirrored by others in China, south of Peking, dating from the Shang dynasty, several centuries later. There is one important difference between the two, apart from the differences which ought to be expected to exist between two cultures so disparate in time and place. The attendants in the Shang tombs have all been violently killed and the grave is in effect an execution site, a Bronze Age shambles. The tomb in Ur is at first sight even more chilling, and yet reflection may suggest otherwise; the members of the court who went to their deaths evidently did so willingly, without force being used upon them and without regret at leaving the world. There is evidence that they laid themselves down in the pit and that each one took a drug, witnessed by the many small cups found in the tomb, which would ease their passing. When they were dead or unconscious, their bodies were neatly laid out to remove any evidence of the convulsions of death which they might experience; then the earth was brought down upon them, as they thought, forever. One woman, it appears, was nearly late for her own funeral and lay down hastily amongst her companions.

Altogether Woolley found sixteen 'Royal Tombs'. In one of the tombs seventy-four courtiers were buried; in another, known as Pur-Abi's (for a long time she was mistakenly called Shub-ad), there were seventeen. In the so-called 'King's Tomb' (there is actually no evidence that the principal occupant was a king) there were fifty-nine bodies; Meskalamdug, he of the magnificent helmet, had forty companions. It would appear that the practice ran out after the examples in Ur. It is no more clear why it should have ceased than why the practice began in the first place or who introduced it. It must always be remembered that archaeology can only base its assumptions on the evidence before it. We do not know whether these ritual holocausts were practised in earlier times because there is no evidence yet found to indicate it. However, the references in the Gilgamesh Epic may suggest that they were part of Sumerian custom at an earlier date.

It has been suggested that the persons who occupy the principal places in the Ur tombs may have been surrogates for the living princes, sacrificed at the end of the celebration of the *hieros gamos*, the sacred marriage of god and goddess enacted in Sumer on the upper platform of the ziggurat, the sacred mountain, to ensure the fertility and prosperity of the land.[8] As yet there is no positive evidence to support this suggestion, but it does seem certain that the practice of the killing of a mock-king was known at certain other periods of Mesopotamian history.

The ready acceptance of death by those who went with the main figures in the drama was warranted by the certainty of immortality as they waited upon their king in the eternal exercise of his office. It was a comforting doctrine to a people to whome the afterlife was a matter of deep uncertainty and it suggests a modification, at least for the period during which the practice was current, of the traditional Sumerian disbelief in any satisfactory afterlife at all. Generally speaking, the Sumerians, like their semitic successors, believed that whatever fate awaited man after death, it offered little attraction. The souls of the dead were conceived as huddled together in dusty wind-swept corridors of some unamiable underworld where they were battered by the scaly wings of predatory birds. It may be that the custom, which seems to have been practised only for a short time, was originally foreign to Sumer and may therefore have been introduced by an alien dynasty. With all the rationalization in the world, however, it is still disturbing to think about the large and handsomely accoutred procession of men and women with the pack animals who would die with them, their harness and trappings jangling, winding its way down through Ur to the place of ceremonial death, one bright Sumerian morning.

The kings of these early Sumerian states are shadowy figures and little is really known of them. Compared with their Egyptian contemporaries of the Archaic period and the early Old Kingdom, they are obscure indeed. Occasionally the record of a campaign, of a benefaction to a temple or the conclusion of a successful merchanting venture survives.

The material and intellectual heritage of Sumer is so immense, however, whether in practical invention or in the creation of the world's first great literature, that we may presume that life in the little cities was, at this time, especially vibrant, resembling perhaps that of the Italian cities of the Renaissance, with which, in political character as well, the Sumerian cities may to some degree be compared.

However, conflicts between the little city-states and the resulting tensions continued unabated and eventually became insupportable; first one, then another enjoyed a brief spell of the paramountcy of Sumer, and dynasty followed insecure dynasty in the palaces of the land. The black-headed folk had always been a disputatious people. As the temple and city lands of one state became insufficient to support its people, or as the possessions of one divinity seemed disproportionately greater than another whose adherents coveted the riches of their neighbour, or as a palace servant seized the *lugal-ship* from a failing master, so the pressures began to mount which eventually would lead to the collapse of the Sumerian state.

Now another problem, though already a familiar one to all the cities, obtruded itself still more urgently into the consciousness of the people: the threat, ever present but now increasing, posed by the barbarous tribes who surrounded them. These were nomads of the desert or wild hill-men with no understanding of the fragile culture which the little cities had so patiently built up over the centuries, but with an unthinking envy of their material wealth. From all directions these restless and destructive hordes menaced Sumer, but the cities were unable to produce a common policy even to protect themselves.

In the twenty-fourth century BC, the beginning of the end came for Sumer, and it was heralded by the emergence into history of one of the most remarkable men of the ancient world. But for the poverty of the surviving information about him, he would deserve to rank with the greatest political leaders of any era. Whilst he preserved for a time the fabric of the Sumerian way of life, he also introduced elements into the society which eventually made its destruction certain. For a century or so he created an empire which was wholly Sumerian in its manners and customs, although he himself was a civilized member of one of the barbarous desert hordes which pressed upon Sumer. He was a Semite, of those people who were to make so profound a contribution to the end of the Sumerian period.

In the palace of Kish, the king Ur-Zababa had in his service as his cup-bearer (an office of importance in the state and evidently not possessing the equivocal overtones associated with the same appointment, as frequently horizontal as vertical, in later, Greek monarchies) a young man who was to be known to history as Sharrukin, or Sargon. He was to prove a man of exceptional military ability, an outstanding administrator and a political innovator of genius.

A fascinating legend about the birth and early life of Sargon has survived and it bears a remarkable resemblance to the legendary origins of another, later, and historically even more shadowy, Semitic leader, Moses. In the text it is Sargon himself who is speaking:

Sargon the Mighty King, King of Agade, am I.
My mother was a changeling, my father I knew not.
The brothers of my father loved the hills.
My city is Azupiranu, which is situated on the banks of the
    Euphrates.
My changeling mother conceived me, in secret she bore me.
She set me in a basket of rushes, with bitumen she sealed my lid.
She cast me into the river which rose not over me.
The river bore me up and carried me to Akki, the drawer of water.
Akki, the drawer of water, lifted me out as he dipped his ewer.
Akki, the drawer of water, took me as his son and reared me.
Akki, the drawer of water, appointed me as his gardener.
While I was a gardener, Ishtar granted me her love.
And for four and forty years I exercised kingship.
The black-headed people, I ruled, I governed.
Mighty mountains with chip-axes of bronze I conquered.
The upper ranges I scaled.
The lower ranges I traversed.
The sea lands three times I circled.

Dilmun my hand captured.
. . .

Whatever king may come after me
Let him rule, let him govern the black-headed people.
Let him conquer mighty mountains with chip-axes of bronze.
Let him scale the upper ranges.
Let him traverse the lower ranges.
Let him circle the sea lands three times
Dilmun let his hand capture
. . . from my city, Agade.[9]

There is more than bombast in these last lines; narrow-eyed menace seems to hiss down the more than forty centuries which separate Sargon from our own day. By this time (approximately 2370 BC) Dilmun was evidently so significant to anyone seeking the kingship of the land that its capture was a matter for pride, even for the man who was to be the mightiest conqueror of his time. But the inscription above was written at the end of his long and tempestuous reign and much was to be accomplished before he could boast that his hand had captured Dilmun.

Sargon's master, Ur-Zababa was attacked and evidently killed by the ambitious ruler of Umma, Lugalzaggesi, who had marched on Kish after razing to the ground the holy places of Lagash. Lugalzaggesi claimed the kingship of all Sumer, the first occasion on which a formal claim in terms of the 'Kingship of the Land' was made to the paramountcy; having evidently taken power in his own city, Sargon set out to avenge Ur-Zababa, and to destroy the usurper. He gathered an army together and attacked Uruk, where Lugalzaggesi had established himself; despite a powerful confederation brought in to defend the city, Sargon was victorious and Uruk fell. Lugalzaggesi apparently escaped when Sargon attacked, for the next we hear is of a pitched battle between the king's host and Sargon. Again, the Semite was totally victorious: he destroyed Lugalzaggesi's army and this time captured him. Nothing more is heard of Lugalzaggesi except that he was led before Sargon by the neck, haltered like a dog, and it may be assumed that his end came swiftly.

Sargon now assumed the highest power and swept through Sumer, eliminating any pockets of resistance that were still loyal to Lugalzaggesi. Eventually he subduded not only the cities of Sumer but many of the lands which bordered it; he was forced to this course in order to check for a time the further incursion of the tribes from one of which he had himself come, and the others like them which menaced what had now become his extensive empire. After the subjugation of the Sumerian states, Sargon 'washed his weapons' in the waters of the Gulf, by this act perhaps demonstrating his claim to sovereignty over them and the lands which bordered them. It was now that he could set out on the conquest of Dilmun.

In the ruins of one of the principal sites of this period on Bahrain island, the Qala'at al-Bahrain, there is evidence of the abrupt destruction of the earliest city, here identified as City I.[10] It is believed that the city's apparently insufficient defences were overthrown during Sargon's conquests and that it was his troops which carried the evidences of his power even to the sacred land of Dilmun. The next occupation level shows extensive ramparts having been built around the new complex of buildings (City II) presumably to ensure that Sargon's governor or vassal prince was not so easily conquered as his predecessor in Dilmun's rule.[11]

Sargon's accession to the kingship of Sumer marks a fundamental change in the political organization of southern Mesopotamia. Hitherto each little state has been the be-all and end-all of its inhabitants' lives. Sargon was evidently an altogether more sophisticated politician than his predecessors in the Sumerian kingship, with the Semitic sense of race and kinship which he strongly evinced; he swept away, for the period of his empire, the little loyalties of each city and imposed instead the absolute sovereignty of the king. He moved closer to the concept of kingship which was characteristic of Egypt (although at this time without the direct identity between god and king which the Two Lands so successfully developed) making the office a manifestation of his own personal power, rather than the more metaphysical concept of a responsibility delegated from the gods. The Sumerians conceived kingship as transcending the human vicars who might temporarily exercise its power on behalf of their divine principals; Sargon made kingship a political reality and in doing so inaugurated the long line of oriental autocracies which ended with the deposition of the last Ottoman Sultan.

The empire which Sargon created, the first political entity in world history to warrant being so called, now entered upon a phase of unexampled splendour and power. As if to mark the fact that a new period in Near-Eastern history had been inaugurated, Sargon decided to build a new capital, away from the traditional cities of Sumer. The place he chose came to be known as Agade (the Akkad of the Bible) and whilst its exact site is now unknown it was located somewhere in the vicinity of Kish, near the neck of the two rivers, strategically one of the most important positions in all Mesopotamia, as the cities built there by successive rulers after Sargon testify. It would be pleasant to think that this choice of site for his new city might demonstrate a streak of sentiment in Sargon, that he should decide to build his own magnificent city within the sight of the lesser one from which, as a relatively minor official, he had started out on his great chain of conquests: more likely it was evidence of his powerful command of the site's strategic potential. In any event, its selection represents the first evidence in Sumer's history of the movement towards the north which was to influence both the political and economic directions of the Middle East from the later centuries of the third millennium onwards, and which was to result in the axis of world communications being shifted away from the Gulf to the Mediterranean.

Soon Agade was the most powerful and gorgeous city of the time and into its harbours sailed ships bearing tribute and merchandise from the four corners of the world, of which Sargon claimed the sovereignty amongst his titles. An inscription survives in which Sargon speaks proudly of the ships of Dilmun riding fearlessly at anchor in the harbour of Agade, some measure evidently of the power that now he exercised and of the peace which he had brought to the Near Eastern world:

> Sargon, King of Kish, was victorious in thirty-four campaigns and dismantled all the cities as far as the shore of the sea. At the wharf of Agade he made moor ships from Meluhha, ships from Magan and ships from Dilmun . . . Enlil did not let anyone oppose Sargon the King. 5400 soldiers ate daily in his palace.[12]

This extract is from an inscription on a statue, probably from the period following Sargon's reign.

Though he came from the desert Sargon evidently understood the importance of trade to the Sumerian nation and to the prosperity of the cities. The emperor was always sharp-eyed in the protection of his merchants' trade routes and was quick to punish any marauders or those jealous princes who might menace the free movement of trade across the wide sweep of lands that came under his *imperium*.

Sargon was, by all reports, a devout follower of the gods of Sumer and, like other *arriviste* conquerors before him, he saw as his destiny the honourable preservation of the wonders of the world he had inherited and of the worship of its gods. The arts flourished during his reign and by an extraordinary chance one of the masterpieces of early art surviving from the Sargonid period is thought to be a portrait of the conqueror himself or of his grandson and successor, Naram-Sin.[13]

Sargon the Great (or perhaps his grandson, Naram–Sin), who conquered Dilmun in the twenty-fourth century BC. (*The Bagdad Museum*).

The head, which was found at Nineveh to the north of Sumer, is an early example, and one that is difficult to parallel, of the art of the bronzesmith; a powerful and dramatic work which achieves much of its impact by the firmly defined and compelling features of the Emperor himself (if it is he) which it delineates. Although the once-inlaid eyes have been gouged out, the expression of the King's face is one of tranquillity. These do not seem to be the features of a stern and ruthless warrior, but rather of a compassionate and reflective man who yet exemplified the exalted and puissant majesty of ancient kingship. The contrast in physical type between Sargon and his Sumerian predecessors is strikingly demonstrated by the finely drawn, slender-boned Semitic face of Sargon when compared with the frankly rather pudgy features of the native Sumerians who, by some curious convention, always seemed to portray themselves, to modern eyes, singularly unflatteringly. The 'Sargon head' is an astonishing piece in the very highest rank of naturalistic portraiture, comparable with the finest work of the Old Kingdom in Egypt, and it is by a happy chance that it should have come down to the present age.

Sargon's empire preserved much of the best of Sumer but at the price of its becoming virtually entirely Semitic in language, administration and influence, thus paving the way for the later Babylonian and Assyrian empires, which were its eventual successors. These, too, were Semitic states, though they preserved, like Sargon, much of the essential qualities of Sumerian culture, manners and beliefs.

Sargon, who, it has been remarked, had the unmistakable physical appearance of a desert shaikh, evidently possessed other characteristics in common with that distinguished but kin-conscious profession (if to be a shaikh can be thus described) in that he appointed his own relations and members of the Semitic tribes to many of the most powerful positions in the state. There was, no doubt, an element of policy as well as nepotism in this, for Sargon probably recognized that in the long term it would be hopeless to try and hold back the growing involvement of the tribes in the affairs of Sumer; he may have persuaded himself that a policy of involving the desert peoples in the management of the state would prepare more of them for the responsibilities of empire and subdue their destructive and unthinking envy of Sumerian culture. On the other hand, he may simply have liked to have his relations around him.

It may be that this policy worked, for when the reckoning with the tribes came it was not the Semites who overwhelmed his empire but the Guti, a tribe of equal barbarity and even greater ferocity, who surged down on Sargon's state, probably from the Zagros mountains in the east. The Guti were a people 'which brooks no control'. They came from the region that was later to nourish the Kassites, another of the successor nations to Sumer's greatness and, later still, in the first millennium BC, the centre of the remarkable metal-working and horse-loving people of Luristan. Anarchy and desolation followed the Guti invasion, which had apparently been brought down on the land to revenge some dreadful but unspecified sacrilege perpetrated by Sargon's grandson, Naram-Sin. It was Enlil himself, the master of the high gods, who called the Guti, 'the mountain dragon', down upon Agade. The once glorious city was utterly destroyed and over its ruins a terrifying curse was wrathfully spoken by the gods.[14] The people who once slaughtered animals for sacrifice are willed to 'murder their wives instead of slaying sheep'; the hope is expressed that they may slaughter their children and, in the case of the poor, specifically to drown them. 'Agade,' the curse proclaims, 'may your palace built with a joyful hand be turned into a depressing ruin.' It concludes on a baleful note: 'Who says "I will lie down in Agade" will not find a good sleeping place'.

The curse seems to have worked, for to this day the site of the golden city so proudly built by Sargon the Great King, the King of the World, is undiscovered, buried beneath the debris of the Mesopotamian plain and the anger of the gods.

With the exception of Ur, the Sumerian city-state which is perhaps most generally remembered today is Lagash, in the south-eastern part of the land. Its modern celebrity derives from the many statues, scattered over the world's museums, of one of its rulers, known to us as Gudea, who reigned at the end of the third millennium.[15]

Lagash, however, emerged into prominence several centuries before Gudea, at the time when Sumer was still powerful. It would seem that the city was not one of those which bore a special mystical significance to the peoples of the time, as many cities did, for a record of its sovereigns does not appear in the surviving king-lists. One of the early rulers of Lagash was Ur-Nanshe who governed the city in the middle of the twenty-sixth century before our era. His inscriptions, of which many survive, are particularly interesting in the present context in that they record the bringing of tribute from far distant countries to him, borne to Lagash 'by the ships of Dilmun'. Ur-Nanshe's inscription is now some four and a half thousand years old. It is apparent that 'the ships of Dilmun' had, in his time, become a symbol of a wide-ranging maritime power, rather like the 'hearts of oak' in the popular English ballad.

Gudea, the *ensi* of Lagash, *c.* 2200 BC. He traded extensively with Dilmun. (*Louvre*).

Later, when Sargon's empire was destroyed by the barbarous Guti, Lagash became for a time the most important Mesopotamian city-state, for the conquerors seem to have favoured its rulers, an early example perhaps of the fruits of collaboration with the occupying forces. The dynasty which came to power, by accommodating itself with the wild men who were now in command of Sumer's destiny, is largely memorable because of Gudea, its second king. If the dynasty is to be judged by Gudea's many surviving portraits, it was a worthy, solid family, rather bourgeois in appearance, with a firm approach to the business of managing the splendid heritage which the capricious gods of Sumer and the intervention of the Guti had handed to them.

Gudea would not have felt out of place at the Tudor courts, even if he was, to his credit, substantially less shifty-eyed than so many of the members of those dubious assemblies. Certainly, as for the Tudor kings, trade was a principal concern for Gudea; quite properly so, since much of Sumer's splendour depended upon the importation of the raw materials and merchandise that was needed to embellish the court and the temples of the gods.

In the manner of his kind, Gudea seems to have been a man of somewhat complacent piety who has left generous records of his many benefactions in the service of the gods. Whilst it is perhaps difficult to warm to Gudea, it is impossible to resist completely the placid self-assurance of a ruler who records, in the detail usually reserved either for the breakfast table or the analyst's couch, a dream which, when he had had it explained, he recognized as the sound of the divine word.

A long poem survives, inscribed on a large prismatic cylinder in the British Museum, from which the story may be extracted.[17] Gudea goes to sleep in his palace at Lagash, comfortable in the knowledge that things could hardly be better in the city. He dreams: and there appears to him a tremendous figure, a crowned man with wings of a lion-headed bird, the lower part of his body a flood-wave. He is supported majestically by lions crouched heraldically on either side of him. This god commands Gudea to build his temple; Gudea, who, if judged only by this dream, cannot have been overbright, seems not to understand him. The sun appears and then a glorified woman holding a clay tablet on which the stars are drawn. Then another figure, once more of heroic dimensions, manifests himself and draws a plan of a house and places bricks on a brick mould together with a carrying basket. At the same time, a donkey 'of special breed' is pawing the ground impatiently.

One might have imagined that an averagely intelligent five year-old Sumerian child could have explained the dream to Gudea, whose incomprehension must have tested the always uncertain tempers of the Sumerian divinities almost beyond endurance. Gudea had the dream professionally interpreted, and it was then revealed as an instruction from the tutelary god of the city to rebuild his temple. Each part of the dream is explained to Gudea by a priestess with oracular powers; each part conforms to a Sumerian concept of the different roles played by the various gods.

It is hard to resist the thought that the gods of Sumer, although they were customarily a difficult group to have many dealings with, were not entirely lacking in humour. To the bemused Gudea it is finally explained that the donkey in the dream is himself, impatient to begin building; the qualification that the donkey was 'of special breed' is particularly engaging.

Gudea builds the temple to the satisfaction of the gods, for they proclaim an abundance of blessings on Sumer. To celebrate the divine pleasure, Gudea throws an enormous party for everyone concerned, including of course, the divinities. Lagash, purified and morally up-lifted, rejoices.

Gudea lists proudly the merchandise which flows into his city, recording that much of it was trans-shipped from Dilmun where it was brought from many lands. The ships bring to him gold from Egypt and Anatolia, silver from the Amanus, copper from the Zagros, ironite from Egypt, carnelian from Ethiopia, and from Dilmun itself, timber.

In the reign of his successors, there are reports that copper utensils, lapis lazuli, tables inlaid with ivory and other ivory objects, combs, breastplates and boxes, ornaments for furniture and semi-precious stones were commonly to be found in Dilmun's market places. Then there are reports of other imports from Dilmun, no less essential than gold and ivory to the life of a rich and prosperous city: the island's onions and dates which were famous throughout the ancient Near East, and what the Sumerian texts refer to as 'fish-eyes'.[18] It is generally agreed that this term can only signify pearls. Pearling was, until recently, an important industry in Bahrain and the Gulf, although it is now sharply in decline. Oyster middens, mounds of discarded oyster shells, have been found on the island which date back beyond historic times.[19]

Gudea's dynasty was eventually overthrown by a brilliant usurper of the throne of Ur, whose previous ruler had broken the power of the Guti. Without the invaders' support, the Lagashite dynasty fell to the newcomer, Ur-Nammu, who ushers in the last of the great periods of Sumerian history, the third and final dynasty of Ur.

Ur-Nammu was one of the outstanding rulers of Sumer, a capable administrator and military leader, a builder and, perhaps more important than any of these, the promoter of a legal code which regulated man's conduct to his fellows and the state, and anticipated the more famous code of Hammurabi by several hundred years.[20] In law, as in so many other departments of life which today are taken for granted, the Sumerians seem to have been the innovators. But despite its brilliance, his reign was a short one: Ur-Nammu seems to have possessed the kingship for only nine years; he was then killed in one of the battles that Sumerian leaders had constantly to face. The portrait which survives of him shows him as delicate of feature, sensitive in appearance.

One of the most splendid sequences in Sumer's history began with the accession to the kingship of Sumer and Akkad of Ur-Nammu's son, Shulgi, in the year 2095 BC. His reign was to be long and glorious; when he died in 2048 BC he had created an empire as extensive as Sargon's and, in many ways, more integrated and coherent. It was a time of great ziggurat building, the remains of some of them, built in Shulgi's time, standing to this day.

Shulgi, like his father, was a notable law giver, always one of the most creditable activities of Sumerian sovereigns, and a distinguished soldier who extended far afield the influence of his empire and of his capital city. His family seems to have been of a strong religious bent, manifested both by their extensive programme of temple building and by a thoroughly un-Sumerian practice of proclaiming themselves to be divine. A state cult, involving offerings to the statues of the king and the naming of one of the months of the calendar in his honour, was introduced and is reminiscent of Roman practices under the Principate. Shulgi is commemorated in one of the principal texts to survive from this time: it describes the sacred marriage (the *hieros gamos*) and contains passages reminiscent of the Song of Solomon, that ecstatic invocation of the splendours of the beloved. In it Shulgi is addressed in terms of the most passionate longing by the priestess, with whom he was to enact one of the most important of Sumerian religious festivals, ensuring the fertility of the year.

An inscription of Shulgi's reign records the king having sent a royal messenger to Dilmun, Ur-Dumuzi, to bring home two invalid officials, a perhaps not altogether usual example of royal concern at so early a time.[21] At his death, the venerable Shulgi was succeeded first by one son and then by another, Shu-sin (2038–30). In common with the other members of his family, Shu-sin was divine but he had rather more problems to test both his divinity and his statesmanship than his predecessors had. The nomads of the Syrian desert on the western borders of the empire were once more stirring and for the rest of the dynasty's rule, and indeed for more than a thousand years afterwards, constant incursions of fierce semitic tribesmen (amongst whom may have been Abraham and his followers) continued to harry the foundations of the Sumerian state and those of its successors. Dilmun once more appears in the archives of this time, when one of Shu-sin's officials, Arad-Nanna, lists amongst his titles 'Prefect (*gir-nita*) of Dilmun';[22] the first of the elements in his name seems to prefigure one of Dilmun-Bahrain's own later names. It was around this time that the richest period of Dilmun's trading empire flourished with Ur as its headquarters.

A peculiarity of the house of Ur-Nammu was its burial customs which are unlike those of other Sumerian dynasts. Large, richly furnished tomb chambers built deep in the ground contained the bodies of the kings of this time which recall the royal burials of early dynastic Egypt and of the Royal Tombs at Ur, though without the human sacrifices which attended those interments. It seems likely that the

Third Dynasty burials were associated with the rites of Dumuzi, the Sumerian god of vegetation and rebirth who, as a dying god ruling over the underworld, has many parallels with the Egyptian Osiris, with whom the Pharaoh was identified in death.

Like most of the dynasties founded on the rule of the agglomeration of city states with its constant round of intrigue, power politics and decline, that created by Ur-Nammu was not destined to last for very long. With its fall, and apart from one or two uneasy and temporary survivals, the end of Sumer must be recorded, after a period of nearly two thousand years during which time its peoples had given more of importance to the world than ever did any other nation of antiquity, other than Egypt. But by now the land of Sumer was exhausted.

For too long the society had sought to withstand the friction of the different cities, the unpredictability of the two rivers between which they had first tried to build a nation, and the constant onslaught of barbaric and envious tribes on every frontier. Unlike Egypt, for which some of its most splendid times were just dawning and which would take another fifteen hundred years to exhaust its strength, Sumer had too volatile and fragile a structure to withstand the pressures which were mounting within and around it. The world, however, was fortunate that a ruler of the northern city of Babylon, a Semitic prince named Hammurabi with something of Sargon about him, succeeded eventually to Sumer's empire. At his accession, around 1750 BC, the history of Sumer ends and that of Babylon begins. It is the peculiar glory of Babylon that she conserved much of Sumer's legacy to the world, which still draws a handsome dividend from it to this day.

The Sumerians now pass from history, their very existence eventually to be forgotten. But this gentle people, energetic, often bewildered, perpetually creative, inventive seemingly beyond even the customary boundaries of genius, often fearful but never wholly despairing, may seem closer to us than most ancient peoples, precisely because they display so intense a quality of humanity. The monuments which they left behind were not only, or even principally, of stone or precious metals, but were words, images, concepts and ideas which have deeply influenced the life of every civilized man who ever lived in the lands which draw their intellectual origins from western Asia. The magnitude of the achievements of Sumer, like those of its contemporary Egypt, down to the end of the third millennium, can only be measured when it is realized that when their high and elegant cultures were flourishing, the rest of the world was virtually empty of anything even remotely approaching civilization.

Although Sumer's days were over and her name survived only as an archaic formula in the titularies of some of the more antiquarian-minded sovereigns of the later Mesopotamian states, her influence was never wholly lost, for the successor states retained much of her heritage. But before examining the outline of Mesopotamia's post-Sumerian history it may be pertinent to take a view of the world as it was at the end of the Sumerian period when, as we reckon historical time, the second millennium before the present era was beginning.

The processes of change once again began to accelerate as they had done so remarkably at the end of the fourth millennium. Even Egypt, seemingly imperturbable if not eternal, experienced the shock of a brutal disruption of her tranquil way of life. The first and greatest period of her dynastic history ended with a collapse into chaos and anarchy after the nearly interminable reign of Pepi II who doddered on into the ninety-fourth year of his kingship having been proclaimed Lord of the Two Lands when he was six years old. The rule of god-kings works admirably when they are in possession of their faculties; a senile divinity is both politically and philosophically an appalling concept. The long years of Pepi's reign, when the great grandsons of the men who watched his coronation were old before its end, must have made some of his more conscientious courtiers long for the days when the god had been sent back to rule other gods, before the decline of his powers could prejudice his rule of men.

After a long and harrowing period in which famine, anarchy and a total disregard for all the most respected Egyptian values stalked the banks of the Nile, order was painfully restored by the austere and dedicated Pharaohs of the early Middle Kingdom. Peace returned to the Valley; Egypt regained her soul and the successive Montuhotpes, Amenemhets and Senwosrets added new splendour to the majesty of the Two Lands. Then new pressures began to bear upon Egypt and a weak, increasingly decentralized monarchy in the shadowy Thirteenth Dynasty let power and resources ebb away and, an unheard-of calamity, Egypt was invaded by a semitic people related to those who had already assumed the sovereignty in Mesopotamia. The 'Hyksos' princes (who used to be called, charmingly but as it happens quite inaccurately, 'the shepherd kings') seem never to have been entirely happy ruling this mysterious and, to foreigners, bewildering land. They tried anxiously to adopt Egyptian ways and to gain the acceptance of the people, but settling self-consciously in the Delta, where they could feel that their ancestral Syrian and Arabian deserts were not so very far away, they never wholly penetrated Egyptian life. Probably undeservedly, they were cursed with an unparalleled vituperation and hatred when finally they were expelled by a family of Theban nobles whose chief was exasperated by the presence of aliens upon the throne of the sacred land. Rising against the usurping kings, he restored the rule of the gods and the prosperity of his house. The long late summer of Egyptian greatness now began with the creation of her magnificent, luxurious and paradoxical empire – for, deep in her heart, Egypt still distrusted all that lay beyond her frontiers – which exalted the throne of the Pharaohs of the New Kingdom high above all other thrones in the world.

In other lands, the wheel of change was revolving irresistibly. In the west, Crete was inaugurating her rule of the Mediterranean and a distinctive if, later, somewhat neurotic culture, many elements of which were probably Asiatic in origin. Far to the north, the early cities of Troy were built to guard the route which linked the Aegean with the Black Sea, on whose shores wild savages with discouraging habits roamed in search of human prey. Across the mass of European lands, as far as the islands in the North Sea which, shrouded in mist and fog, were known if at all only by legend and the discounted reports of occasional travellers, new people were moving, seeking new pastures or the protection of new gods. In Greece, a new race came down from the north with different gods and broad, handsome faces, whose gold-masked chiefs were buried on the wind-swept and menacing hills at Mycenae. The great ports of the Syrian coast sent argosies to Egypt and Crete and wherever a profit might be made.

In Mesopotamia, too, profound changes were in train. The final disappearance of the old Sumerian states and the dominance of the Semitic rulers meant a shift away from the south and the creation of northern kingdoms, first in Babylon and then Assyria, which looked to the Mediterranean lands, those of the Upper Sea, as their natural outlet for conquest and trade. In time the southern cities of Sumer, once the most important in the world, declined to the level of simple village settlements and so most of them have remained to this day. Occasionally a ruler with a taste for history or in the hope of pleasing the almost forgotten gods, would build a temple or repair a ziggurat. But most of the cities disappeared, buried beneath the mounds of dust and sand which, wind-blown, piled over them and hid them until the modern world, happily more careful of its ancestry than were its own ancestors, painstakingly uncovered them.

In the middle of the second millennium a series of spectacular cataclysms overwhelmed much of the ancient world. In the Mediterranean the eruption, as it is now believed, of Santorini brought down the cities of Crete, admitting both the harsh Achaeans to the island's splendid palaces and in all probability, the myth of Atlantis into the modern world. Somewhat earlier, in what is today the state of Pakistan, the mighty civilization of the Indus Valley, including the powerful cities of Harappa and Moenjo-Daro, collapsed, by whatever cause. The impact of these events was brutal and absolute. In what had once been Sumer the poet lamented piteously: 'Who was King? Who was *not* King?'

As the political and economic axis of the world began to shift to the north, so the Gulf too declined in importance. Bereft of its main market by the destruction of the Indus Valley cities and with the establishment of caravan routes more reliable and better policed than in the early days, the Lower Sea became, literally, a backwater.

Dilmun-Bahrain had witnessed many changes of political control in Mesopotamia and always her religious and commercial appeal, then as now an irresistible combination, ensured her prosperity. Now, however, it was different, for her commercial significance seems to have been destroyed by the collapse of the great Indus Valley cities which were the outlet for much of Sumer's merchandise. From this time onwards, Dilmun ceases to be important; only occasionally does a mention of the island appear in the ancient sources and then it sinks into an obscurity from which Bahrain has only tentatively emerged in this century. Certainly, never again would it occupy the special place that it did for the Sumerians and their immediate successors. Already the world had begun to change and the decline of Dilmun's commercial significance even produced a decline in her legendary status as the island of the gods. Soon the Sumerians themselves were forgotten and only occasionally was Dilmun noticed, for now it was merely a distant province of whatever power ruled Mesopotamia.

In the fourteenth century BC, during the reign of Burnaburriyas, a contemporary of that odd-looking religious innovator Akhenaton of Egypt, two letters were sent by the incumbent governor of Dilmun to his superior in Babylonia, then ruled by the Kassites, of which the island was a province.[23] This correspondence is especially interesting for it throws a light on a number of characteristics which had come to be identified with Dilmun historically and which confirm its association at this time with the principal Bahrain island. Very recently (1970) extensive evidence has been discovered, in the Al-Hajjar graves, of the period during which the island was under Kassite domination; it suggests that circumstances in the islands were much more ebullient than had appeared to be the case.

It is apparent from the text of the first letter (Ni 615) that the writer is awaiting a 'Sutean Woman' to cross the water and visit him. From this may be deduced that the writer is living on the mainland of Arabia, which, at this and at other times, was included in the term Dilmun, which thus becomes the name of a substantial region, far exceeding the confines of the island itself. However, it is reasonably certain, from the evidence of City III at the Qala'at al-Bahrain, where the remains of the Kassite occupation have produced quantities of their rather unattractive pottery as well as some as yet unpublished cuneiform tablets, that Bahrain was the capital of what might be thought of as the Dilmun province in Kassite times. The writer knows that the Sutean woman has reached Dilmun proper, in other words, Bahrain, but has not yet crossed the straits to the mainland. The Sutean woman is a mysterious figure but it is known that in many of the north-east Arabian tribal groups of this and later times women were powerful, often as priestesses, even as queens.

> To Ililiya speak! This is what Ili-ippasra thy brother said: Unto thee be well-being! May Inzag and Meskilak, the gods of Tilmun, guard thy life!
> Iltam who will arrive, I have met. Also the Sutean woman has crossed the sea and she will arrive. Of the coming of this Sutean woman I am not so sure. Now I have directed her to Babil. Before the month of Epuly draws to a close she will reach there. Around me the Ahlamu have carried away the dates, thus with me there is nothing I can do. But a single town must not be allowed to be pillaged.
> In the town which I am living in when from Sin-nun I heard and the temple I heard about is the old house of Nin [. . .] the house was old and had collapsed. Now he has done nothing at all he let it go. And from that day on they keep on seeing dreams and the destruction of the palace has been indicated for the fifth time.

The writer complains that the Ahlamu have carried off the dates, evidently stored ready for shipment back to Mesopotamia. The dates of Dilmun were always specially favoured in ancient times and probably the best of them came from the oasis of Qatif and Hofuf in Saudi Arabia, another indication of the likely extent of Dilmun's territories in this period. In the ruins of Qala'at al-Bahrain (City III) extensive store rooms have been found which suggest that they were used for the warehousing of dates before they were shipped and also for the pressing of date juice, which, when fermented, produced an agreeable and very intoxicating drink.

In both letters the texts are preceded by a benediction in which Inzak (the Sumerian Enshag), the guardian god of Dilmun, is invoked with a goddess, Meskilak, 'the lady of pure decrees'. She was a divinity most appropriate for Dilmun, for one of its epithets was the 'land of pure decrees'.

The first letter contains a reference to the antiquity of certain temples in Dilmun and to their deplorable state of disrepair. Where the text mentions 'the house of Nin . . .' it is tempting to restore the missing word to read 'Ninkhursag' or 'Ninsikilla', both of them the island's patrons. Prophecies about the destruction of the 'palace' are also reported in conjunction with the unruly behaviour of the thieving Ahlamu and indicate the generally anarchic situation which prevailed in the Gulf at this time as a result of the depredations of the Badu tribes.

The second letter is less informative than the first, but still complains of the difficulties which the Kassite administration was experiencing at the hands of the Ahlamu.

> To Ililiya speak! This is what Ili-ippasra, thy brother said: Unto thee be well-being! May Inzag and Meskilak, the deities of Tilmun, guard thy life! The Ahlamu certainly talk to me only of violence and plunder: of conciliation they do not talk with me. The lord put it upon me to ask them, but they did not comply.

These two letters are important for their references to two peoples, the Suteans and the Ahlamu, whose descendants are in all probability the Arab tribes of the Gulf and Saudi Arabia today.[24]

Both groups were nomadic Badu who constantly harassed the settled communities on the shores of the Gulf and in the nearby oases, like those from which Dilmun's dates came. The Suteans were originally drawn from the area between Mari and Qatna, well to the north of Mesopotamia in Syria, a region in which the semitic and Sumerian strains in Mesopotamian culture possibly were first integrated. Contact between the cities and the shaikhs of the Badu tribes had for long been established but frequently the tribes got out of hand and had to be put down severely. At the end of the fifteenth century BC the king of Babylon gave instructions for the extermination of the Suteans, but they survived, no doubt by withdrawing into the desert which was always a hopeless obstacle to town-bred soldiers.

The Ahlamu were a long established tribal group, formed originally perhaps by the occasional confederation of nomads who constantly disturbed the peace of states from Syria to the Gulf. They were, in all probability, ancestral to the Aramaeans who secured a powerful place for themselves in the later history of the region and who, by the eighth century BC, formed an important linguistic family, to the extent that Aramaic became eventually the common language of much of the Near East. The Arabs themselves, another linguistic family closely related to the groups already mentioned, are first recorded in the Assyrian annals of the ninth century BC. The semitic elements which, throughout Sumer's history, alternately menaced and, by adopting so many of its institutions, sustained the land, came out of the Syrio-Arabian deserts, like the nomads who still, though in diminishing numbers, live in the desert to this day.

The correspondence addressed to Ililiya in Babylon at this time is one of the few evidences of a concern with the affairs of the south to survive from the troubled centuries which followed the collapse of Hammurabi's dynasty in Mesopotamia. From this time onwards, Dilmun's history becomes increasingly obscure. The world had expanded enormously since the days of the Sumerians and there were more rewarding markets and richer civilizations to conquer than small islands and barren tracts of desert on the coast along the Gulf.

Occasionally Dilmun is mentioned in the dismal recital of conquest and repression which characterizes the history of the kings of later Babylonia and Assyria, the latter being arguably the most repellent of all the princes of the ancient Near East. Thus Tukulti-Ninurta I, one of the greatest warrior kings of Assyria who reigned from 1242 to 1206 BC, conquered Babylon, dragged its king in chains to his capital at Assur and went on to absorb the whole of the land that had been Sumer. Dilmun became subject to him and he proclaimed himself 'King of Sippur and Babylon, King of Dilmun and the country Melukhkha, King of the Upper and Lower seas, King of all mountain regions and the deserts'.[25] Tukulti-Ninurta's barbaric reign ended appropriately when he was assassinated by his own son.

In the annals of Sargon II, the king of Assyria who reigned from 721 to 705 BC, nearly two thousand years after his namesake, the great Emperor of Agade, there is mention of one of the few kings of Dilmun whose name is known: 'Uperi, who lives like a fish in the midst of the sea of the rising sun'.[26] This reference to the 'sea of the rising sun' echoes the similar terms which were used of the Gulf and Dilmun in some of the earliest references in the epic works of the Sumerians.

Islands were often said to be, reasonably enough, 'in the midst of the sea'; it was an expression commonly used by Assyrian monarchs of island nations which they conquered in the Mediterranean or in the Gulf. Uperi may seem to be dismissed rather contemptuously by his suzerain, though 'like a fish' could, just possibly, recall a fish cult which was associated with Dilmun and its earliest divinity, Enki. Dilmun, in Sargon II's time, as in the days of Burnaburiyas, probably covered much of the eastern Arabian coast, possibly including Kuwait. One of the names of Bahrain in pre-Islamic times was Samak which, curiously, means 'fish' in Arabic.

In 694 BC Sennacherib was king of Assyria and famous – at least in Byron's recension – for his attack upon Jerusalem. He also conquered Elam in the south-west of Persia; like many of his forebears, he attacked and overthrew Babylon and it is reported that the debris from the sacking of the city floated down the Gulf to the shores of Dilmun.[27] This improbable circumstance so intimidated the island's inhabitants that they quickly swore allegiance to the Great King.

The king of Dilmun of the day, whose name is unknown, evidently considered it politic to demonstrate his adherence to Sennacherib's interest more positively than by the mere expression of loyalty. He sent a team of labourers to assist in the razing of Babylon after the city had fallen to the Assyrian. They brought with them the tools which are described as typical of their country, 'bronze spades and bronze pikes'. Metal working, even at this late date, was evidently still one of the most readily recognized characteristics of Dilmun, as it had been in Sumerian times when it was the centre of the copper trade.

From late Assyrian times comes a most curious text, which was published originally in a study of Chaldaean astrology. This purports to be an astrological prediction which forecasts a disaster for an unnamed king of Dilmun.[28] The prediction links the fate of various kings to eclipses of the moon in different months. The relevant parts of the prediction read:

> Contemplate its eclipse, a decision will be given for the King of Dilmun. Someone will kill the King of Dilmun during an uprising, a stranger will ascend the throne.
>
> If the eclipse takes place on the 15th day someone will kill the King of Dilmun during an uprising, a stranger will ascend the throne.
>
> If the eclipse takes place on the 16th day then the King will be killed during his procession, a fool will ascend the throne.

No date is known for the origin of this mysterious piece of astrological forecasting. One commentator[29] has suggested that some of the other

I. The great temple site at Barbar, uncovered during the excavations undertaken by the Department of Antiquities and Museums in 1983. The sacred well is on the left, with the processional way leading up to the terrace.

II. Rescue archaeology at Medinat Hamed, a new town in central Bahrain, has revealed several early intact tombs from the latter half of the third millennium.

III. *Following page*. These steps lead up to the terraces of the second temple at Barbar. They commence at what was ground level when the temple was built, around four thousand years ago.

events with which it seems to deal relate to the troubled and dangerous times when the Guti, the wild tribes from the mountains dividing Sumer from Persia, swarmed down on Sumer and wrought such devastation.

The brutal and relentless Assyrians tore up the established order in the Near East and imposed their harsh absolutism upon all the lands that came under their influence. The inscriptions of the Assyrian kings are catalogues of terror and oppression. In the early years of the seventh century, Sennacherib's son Esarhaddon lists Dilmun high amongst his conquests and supplies us with the name of another Dilmunite king:

> Upon Qanaia, King of Tilmun, I imposed tribute, due to me as his lord.[30]

Later still, Assurbanipal (668–631 BC) proclaims his power by assuming some of the most ancient royal titles which recall the titulary of Sargon the Great, from nearly two thousand years earlier. Now Dilmun appears as one of the boundaries of his empire and is used by him to demonstrate the extent of the world that he ruled:

> Assurbanipal, the Great King, the legitimate King, the King of the world, King of Assyria, King of all the four rims of the earth, King of Kings, prince without rival, who rules from the Upper Sea to the Lower Sea, had made bow to his feet all the other rulers and who has laid the yoke of his overlordship upon them from Tyre which is an island in the Upper Sea as far as Tilmun which is an island in the Lower Sea – and they pulled the straps of his yoke.[31]

Still another of the shadowy kings of Dilmun is mentioned in the annals of Assurbanipal. The Assyrian king's general, Bel-ibai, launched a campaign against southern Mesopotamia to consolidate the northerner's rule over it. He conquered Bit-iakin, possibly the region of Kuwait in the north-eastern corner of the Gulf, and Elam in the south-western part of Persia. In his correspondence from the field, Bel-ibai mentions 'Hundaru, King of Dilmun'.[32] The king of Assyria seems to have thought it expedient to deal with the Dilmunite ruler by diplomacy rather than by force of arms and in a letter he offers to confirm Hundaru's rule in exchange for an acceptance of Assurbanipal's suzerainty and for support in his war against Babylon. This the lesser king evidently thought was a prudent course and a Dilmunite ambassador, I'idm, is reported as being accredited to the Assyrian court. At this same period, the arrival of what is either tribute booty, or an exchange of gifts between two rulers – the point is not clear and probably depends on whether it is Assurbanipal's or Hundaru's point of view that is considered – is recorded as arriving at the Assyrian capital from Dilmun. Whatever it was, it was a rich consignment of merchandise; it included twenty-six talents of bronze, goods manufactured from that metal and from copper, and sticks of precious woods, testifying convincingly to the wealth that Dilmun evidently still enjoyed. The excavations at the Qala'at al-Bahrain of this Neo-Babylonian period (c. 700 BC) reveal an extensive town with handsome public buildings.[33]

The ancient world reached its climax and its end in the colossal figure of Alexander the Macedonian. Perhaps the only man so far born of woman (in his case the appalling Olympias) who was entitled to suspect that he was a god, Alexander bridges the ancient and modern worlds, the West and the East. In many parts of western Asia he is still a living presence; there is much in the intellectual heritage of the West that can be traced back to Alexander's unleashing of the flood of knowledge, ideas and technology which the Near Eastern states possessed and which, pouring over the intellectually-barren lands of Europe, made them flourish.

In the last year of his life, shattered by the death of Hephaestion, his companion from boyhood, Alexander's never wholly stable personality toppled over into what was, in all probability, acute disturbance. With the memory of the appalling march through Gedrosia (Makran) on the south-eastern side of the Gulf still vivid in his mind and in the minds of his unfortunate coadjutors, commanders and men, he turned his eyes towards Arabia.

He was, it is alleged, angered at the refusal of the Arabians to allow him the homage which, as the world conqueror whose dominions were vaster than those of any emperor who preceded him, he felt entitled to demand. Already the stark and matter-of-fact sense of total independence of spirit, so characteristic of the desert dwellers, made the prospect of acknowledging even Alexander's sovereignty unthinkable to the people of the peninsula. Alexander had hopes, similarly unfulfilled, that he might be recognized as divine by the Arabians who, he was given to understand, only worshipped two gods who were identified by the Greeks with Uranus and Dionysos. It was not, Alexander considered, unreasonable that he should be regarded as worthy of divine honour since his achievements surpassed even those of Dionysos; Uranus was, of course, far too old a divinity to be considered as an Alexander.

All of this we learn from Arrian, a Bithynian civil servant in the service of the Roman Empire, who flourished in the second century AD and who wrote the most monumental surviving history of Alexander's lifetime. Though he lived several hundred years after his subject's own career it is evident that he was able to draw on sources contemporary with Alexander himself. Amongst these were the logs of several of Alexander's sea captains including his most celebrated admiral, Nearchos the Cretan. Arrian lived in the days of Hadrian, perhaps the most agreeable and certainly the most civilized of Roman emperors, himself a worthy successor to Alexander, whom he held in deep admiration.

Arrian gives a detailed description of their voyage, particularly Nearchos'; it is appropriate now to turn to his words in the late Aubrey de Selincourt's translation:[34]

> Alexander had ideas of settling the seaboard of the Persian Gulf and the off-shore islands; for he fancied it might become as prosperous a country as Phoenicia. The naval preparations were directed against the Arabs of the coast, ostensibly because they were the only people in that part of the country who had sent no delegation to wait upon him, or shown their respect by any other normal act of courtesy; actually, however, the reason for the preparations was, in my opinion, Alexander's insatiable thirst for extending his possessions.
>
> Report has it that Alexander had heard that the Arabs worshipped only two gods, Uranus and Dionysus, the former because he is seen to contain within himself not only the stars but the sun too, the greatest and clearest source of blessing to mankind in all their affairs, and the latter, Dionysus, because of the fame of his journey to India. Alexander accordingly felt it would not be beyond his merits to be regarded by the Arabs as a third god, in view of the fact that his achievements surpassed those of Dionysus; or at least he would deserve this honour if he conquered the Arabs and allowed them, as he had allowed the Indians, to retain their ancient institutions. Moreover, the wealth of their country was an additional incitement – the cassia in the oases, the trees which bore frankincense and myrrh, the shrubs which yielded cinnamon, the meadows where nard grew wild: of all this report had told him. Arabia was a large country, its coast (it was said) no less in extent than the coast of India; many islands lay off it, and there were harbours everywhere fit for his fleet to ride in and to provide sites for new settlements likely to grow to great wealth and prosperity.
>
> He was further informed of the existence of two islands off the mouth of the Euphrates. One of them lay fairly close, at a distance of, perhaps, fifteen miles from that point on the shore where the river joins the sea. This, the smaller of the two, was densely

wooded, and contained a temple of Artemis the regular service of which was performed by the islanders themselves. Deer and wild goats found pasture there, and as they were held sacred to the goddess it was unlawful to hunt them except for the purpose of sacrifice. For this reason only was the ban upon taking them removed. Aristobulus tells us that Alexander decreed that this island should be called Icarus after the Aegean island of that name.

The second of the two islands, called Tylus, lay off the mouth of the Euphrates at about the distance a running ship can cover in a day and a night. It was of some size, most of it neither wild nor wooded, but fit to produce all sorts of cultivated crops in their proper seasons.

Some of this information Alexander got from Archias, who was sent out in a galley to reconnoitre the coast for the proposed expedition against the Arabs. Archias reached Tylus, but did not venture beyond; Androsthenes, who went in command of another galley, got further, sailing round a part of the Arabian peninsula, and Hiero, the shipmaster from Soli, made greater progress than either. Alexander put him in charge of a third galley and gave him instructions to circumnavigate the whole peninsula as far as the Egyptian town of Heröopolis on the Red Sea. But even he found his courage fail him, though he had sailed round the greater part of the Arabian coast; he turned back, and stated in his report to Alexander that the peninsula was of immense size, nearly as big as India, and that a great headland ran far out into the ocean. This headland had, indeed, been sighted at no great distance by Nearchus' men on their voyage from India, before they altered course for the Persian Gulf.

This passage is of considerable interest for the light which it throws on the Gulf in antiquity. It may be worth pausing for a moment to consider it in greater detail.

Arrian draws on Aristobulus for some parts of his account and Aristobulus was a contemporary of Alexander. However, most of his analysis of Nearchos' voyage depends upon the admiral's own authority; it appears in the form of 'The Indica' which Arrian based on Nearchos' journals.

The first point to observe is perhaps that Alexander has ideas of settling the seaboard of the Gulf and the off-shore islands; he fancied it might become as prosperous a country as Phoenicia. If nothing else Alexander demonstrates here a remarkable foresight for after his death colonies of Greeks established themselves along the Arabian shore and inland in Arabia.[35] The colonies flourished greatly for they lay athwart the spice routes from the south which, even in Alexander's time, were already bringing great riches to the peninsula, a point which Arrian himself records.

It is in his geographical observations however that the greatest interest in Arrian's narrative lies. He describes 'two islands off the mouth of the Euphrates'; one of them densely wooded and rich in game, was sacred to a goddess whom the Greeks identified with their own Artemis. Alexander decreed that the island should be called Ikaros, a curious choice despite the explanation which the text provides. Ikaros in the Gulf puzzled commentators greatly until the discovery, in the 1950s, of an inscription set up by Alexander on the island of Failakah on the Bay of Kuwait which, with the later discovery of a substantial temple also of the Hellenistic period, unmistakably Greek in architecture and attributes, made it clear that Failakah is Ikaros.[36]

The second island is called Tylos; this is Bahrain, and it features in most of the records left by ancient historians and geographers. Indeed it has a quite unique recorded history for the first literary reference to it was more remote from Arrian's day than his time is from our own.

The seriousness of Alexander's intentions towards the exploration, if not the conquest of Arabia is manifested by the fact that other senior officers of his staff, beside Nearchos, carried out voyages of exploration in the Gulf. These were Archias, Androsthenes and Hiero, the last having evidently sailed beyond the Gulf and begun the formidable task of sailing round the Arabian coast, through the Red Sea to Egypt. He did not complete it.

According to Nearchos, Alexander sought intelligence about the people of the peninsula's coast, their habitations and in particular the distribution of safe anchorages, sources of fresh water and of game or other victuals. It has been speculated that one of the most extraordinary acts of Alexander's life was connected with his interest in Arabia and the unexplored regions to the south and west of his dominions.[37] In his later years, seized compellingly with the idea of his divinity, Alexander saw himself fulfilling a destiny which had never before fallen to the lot of any man, divine or merely mortal. He became subject to one of the strangest and most persistent preoccupations of his lifetime. This seems, in essence, to have consisted of a deliberate attempt to sweep away, or at least to symbolize the sweeping away, of the barriers which had divided east and west of his dominions, the Greeks and those others who inhabited European lands from their brothers in the Persian lands which had been brought under his hegemony. The remarkable and spectacular marriage of 10,000 at Susa when Greeks and Persians were mingled in what seems to have been a consciously sacramental, if somewhat Hollywood-styled, occasion, was the must curious manifestation of this idea. As he moved towards his death Alexander became more and more exalted; a sort of transcendental quality seized him, manifested in his conviction (one which indeed it is difficult perhaps entirely to disregard) that his destiny was different in kind from those of all other men. The control of the Gulf and of its western littoral (he already held the eastern shore by his subjugation of the Persian Empire) would have enabled him to bring all of his wide dominions into coherent and mutual contact, to unite the two great divisions of the world under his divine sovereignty. Then, no doubt, he would have turned towards the west and to a destiny which is, alas, beyond speculation.

His death in Babylon, which he entered in defiance of the Chaldaean soothsayers (who were amongst the most skilled in what must have been a generally difficult and often risky profession) ended any prospects of the universal brotherhood of man being introduced in this early dawn. If the King had lived out a more generous life-span, the bleak two thousand years which ultimately succeeded his time might have been suffused by a kinder light, had the precepts of the Academy prevailed rather than those of the synagogue and the several Romes.

Unawed by the claims of Alexander's divinity, the people of Arabia and the Gulf, accustomed perhaps to less equivocal godheads, ignored his tremendous presence and were thus never brought into his short-lived empire. But for a region which for three thousand years before Alexander's day had had the reputation of being the meeting place of an entire and formidable pantheon, a slight, obsessive Macedonian, divine or not, did not perhaps mean very much. The gods of Sumer assembled in Dilmun were certainly more elemental than Alexander and, as gods, more practised in inspiring awe amongst their followers. However, even they did not achieve his extraordinary posterity.

Whatever may have been Alexander's role as a divinity, we are on firmer ground with the inscription which he caused to be set up on Failakah island in the Bay of Kuwait, preserving it as a sanctuary. The finding of the great inscribed stone is described by Bibby and it is now to be seen in the Failakah Museum.[38]

In this inscription, Failakah island is called Ikaros, though whether this commemorates the son of Daedalos who fell to his death by flying too close to the sun is not known. However, Ikaros is mentioned in Arrian's life of Alexander, as we have seen, and is described as an idyllic place like its sister island Tylos, a literal paradise, a park reserved for game, though hunting, except for sacrifice, was forbidden.

One of the many remarkable discoveries which have resulted from the past years of excavation in the Gulf and eastern Arabia has been the hitherto entirely unexpected penetration of the region by Greek influences. Alexander's interest in Arabia was, of course, well known and his determination to conquer it among his last recorded acts of policy. What had not been expected was the extent to which settlements quite unmistakably Greek had been established in Arabia in the years following his death.

The involvement of the Greeks in the region marks one of the high points of its history. All over the area, in Bahrain and in eastern Arabia as well as on Failakah, even far down into the Arabian desert, Greek influence indicates a degree of prosperity and importance for the region which it had hardly enjoyed since Old Babylonian times. The evidence of the grave fields in Bahrain is notable in this regard: no accurate count has been made, but, whilst a substantial percentage of the tens of thousands date from the late third and early second millennia, a large number can be traced to Hellenistic times. It is, indeed, curious how the inhabitants of Bahrain and the nearby mainland in the third and second centuries BC reverted to the practice of mound burial employed by their predecessors. Not all the bearers of Greek traditions, however, favoured (or perhaps could afford) interment in a family or individual grave mound. A Greek burial ground, in which the graves are simple shafts, though set beneath one large mound, was found by chance in Bahrain's capital during a construction project.[39] No doubt the inhabitants of the graves were modest people, seamen perhaps, who lived in or were connected with the fourth city level at the Qala'at al-Bahrain, which is associated with the times immediately succeeding Alexander's lifetime. Two skeletons were found intermingled in the same grave.

In Failakah, Greek influences were of great significance. Whether this was because of Alexander's interest in the island or whether the Greek involvement was of longer standing is unknown, but a substantial Greek settlement has been identified. One of its buildings was evidently a factory for the manufacture of pottery figures;[40] since most of these seem to be cultic, it may be presumed that they served the sacred nature of the island, perhaps indicating the presence of pilgrims who would make use of the products of the factory.

The Greek presence is also to be detected deep into the Arabian desert. At Fau, about 370 miles south of Riyadh, a caravanserai with considerable evidence of Greek influences is being excavated by the University of Riyadh.[41] A whole chain of settlements was strung out across the desert, linking the spice-producing regions in the south with the Gulf coast in the east. From the cities on the eastern seaboard, including Bahrain, Arabian spices were exported to the Greeks of Persia and as far away as those who settled, in the wake of Alexander, in India.

But the most significant remains on Failakah, other than the Alexander inscription, are those of a small Greek temple, excavated by the Danes, perhaps sacred to the goddess Artemis, the guardian divinity of the island.[42] It is a handsome construction, though modest in scale; it is, in fact, a very pretty miniature Greek fane. The quality of its architecture, however, shows nothing provincial about it; indeed, it would seem likely that its construction was supervised by a Greek-trained architect perhaps using craftsmen imported for the project. The temple was built after Alexander's lifetime and perhaps its quality is a consequence of the importance which his decree gave to this distant outpost of the Greek world.

According to another inscription, dedicated by one Soteles, a citizen of Athens, Artemis in Failakah bore the surname Suteira and is hailed as 'Sarconices'.[43] The Greek presence on Failakah was not only religious however. Presumably to defend the little temple, the factory and the township from marauders, a fort was built. The inscription left by Soteles joins 'the soldiers' with him in its dedication; it is difficult not to feel some concern for Greek soldiers so far from their homeland in so very remote and distant a place as Failakah must have seemed, far from the customary entertainments and civilities of Greek life.

V

The Gods of Sumer and the Myths of Dilmun

Like most of mankind before or after them the Sumerians were puzzled by the world and felt deeply the need to explain it to themselves. Through the medium of their language they created splendid images and stories to link the worlds of gods and men, with the facility with which the Egyptians carved in stone to the same purpose. They wondered at the world and took, on balance, a rather humble view of their place in it. Their gods, an unappealing and generally disagreeable race, were, with few exceptions, largely ill-disposed or at best indifferent to man.

The Sumerians saw all life as vain and man as the powerless creature of a capricious and often malevolent destiny; they are a people with whom it is easy to find much in common. It may be that their dispiriting view of the world was in part the result of their geographical location; in part it may have been the inheritance of the generally pessimistic religious view of the Semitic-speaking component in their society. Their land lay between two powerful and unpredictable rivers, which, despite all the controls they might exercise, in one year could bring abundance and in the next ruin. In considering this sense of impending catastrophe – the apparently basic Sumerian belief that something dreadful was always about to happen – it must be remembered that the Biblical story of the Flood is the record of a Sumerian cataclysm, dimly recalled by the descendants of one of the nomadic tribes who wandered the deserts beyond the cities' limits. The social and political structure of their society was weighted against permanence and tranquillity and, as in Greece two thousand years later, constantly led to war and the destruction of one little state by another.

Nor did they find any consolation in creating comforting fantasies about an after-life, which on the one hand might redress the pain and suffering of the earthly existence, or, on the other, would be an idealized extension of life on earth. To the frankly rather smug Egyptians, for example, no more perfect life could be imagined than a perpetual sunlit existence in the Nile valley. But the Sumerians, anticipating alike Freud and the doctrine of original sin, said 'never has a sinless child been born to its mother'[1] and in some of their moods (though fortunately not their most characteristic) they bore a frightening load of quiet despondency around with them, which manifested itself most strongly when they considered their likely fate after death. Forlornly, they described a state in which the souls of the dead crouched, hungry and thirsty, beaten by the scaly wings of dreadful birds in the dusty, windswept corridors of an appalling underworld[2] which has many features, if so they may be termed, of the Christian or Muslim Hell and the pre-Christian Hades; indeed the dispiriting idea of the place of eternal punishment and suffering may well descend from this dismal Mesopotamian concept.

The gods of Sumer were responsible for many, if not all, of the problems which beset mankind. The Sumerians invented a splendid and colourful theogony but it was one in which the gods are rarely seen to advantage for, in the Sumerian view, there was little good that might be said for them.

The dispassionate view which many of the ancients took of divinity is in sharp contrast to the more respectful attitudes of later ages. Everyone is familiar with the discreditable antics of the Greek pantheon whose members, obsessed by alternating waves of greed, lust and ill-temper, mirrored only too exactly the character of humanity itself. The Hebrews, influenced by the harshness of desert life and apparently responding to the darker aspects of Sumerian beliefs (though *their* ancestors may have been responsible for the blacker sides of Sumerian convictions), created the jealous and temperamental Yahweh, who only emerged as the sole god, hidden on his Jerusalem mountain-top, after his adherents had disposed of those other deities whom once the Hebrews worshipped and of whom they long sustained nostalgic memories. Only the Egyptians, typically insulated alike by their desert boundaries and the immensely high opinion they held of themselves, blessed the gods unreservedly, feeling compassion towards those less happy races of mankind who had the misfortune not to be born Egyptian. If there was one thing of which, for example, a Memphite landowner, living in the early centuries of the third millennium, could be certain, looking out contentedly over his estate as evening came on, it was that God was an Egyptian; there was no comparable comfort to sustain the Sumerians.

In the Sumerian canon of belief the greater and the lesser gods, the latter often the servants of the former, were brought into existence first; and the world (by which was really meant the land of Sumer and the Gulf, the sea whose waters washed its southernmost shore) was made ready for them. Every major divinity received a plot of land which was to be his or hers, and the elements and all visible and hidden things were each apportioned to the charge of one of them. All the great gods, collectively known as the Annunaki, were given households of lesser gods who, in addition to serving their divine masters, also served the useful purpose of interceding between mankind and the gods, when men had been created. They were, it has been suggested, the spiritual ancestors of the Christian 'guardian angels', and every Sumerian family head had his personal divinity to whom he would address his prayers, begging him to take a petition to the High Gods, for they were too awful for man directly to approach.

When, in the beginning, the world was made and parcelled out to the various gods and goddesses, all was admirably conceived, but the divinities felt that their world lacked something: it needed docile and obedient creatures who might cultivate the earth and harvest it, and maintain order amongst the other animals. Indeed the first recorded strike took place when the lesser Sumerian divinities, the Igigi-gods, downed tools and, glowering at the Annunaki, the High Gods, intimidated them into accepting their just demands for leisure and their belief that largely agricultural pursuits were unsuitable occupations even for minor deities.[3] The ruling divinities were thus forced to take action and to improve the conditions of their junior colleagues. Clearly the work had to be done by someone, and so man was created for the purpose of carrying out such menial and ungodly tasks. Having made man, the gods also decided it would be both pleasant and useful for a system of worship to be introduced, thus showing that from the earliest times they suffered from that curious and recurring sense of insecurity to which divinities seem much to be subject, an insecurity which needed to be assuaged by their constantly being told, by legions of believers, how sublime they were. For these humble purposes, therefore, was mankind created, to be the creatures of each god and the workers on his estate. This was the time of primaeval innocence, when, dutifully,

> The whole universe, the people in unison,
> to Enlil with one tongue, gave praise.[4]

The Sumerians' concept of the trappings and attributes of divinity still, in some respects at least, haunt contemporary man. When the gods manifest themselves they are fully realized in what might be described as the classical divine mould. They are superhuman, invisible, unbound by time and space, rulers of the elements and hungry for worship. They are represented in human form but are gigantic, with distinctive clothing and, in the case of the male gods, with rather alarming hats, apparently a sort of horned turban with which they are invariably portrayed.

Male divinities predominated in Sumer; the Mother, by many names known but in her most potent form called Ninhursag, is a great one, but never supreme. Unlike Egypt, where in the case of ancient gods like Ptah, Horus and even Osiris, it is possible to speculate about dimly observed human originals, mighty heroes who left the memory

A Sumerian divinity, wearing the horned turban with which gods are often depicted, including the representations of them on Dilmun seals. (*The Trustees of the British Museum*).

of their rule so vivid in the people's consciousness that they raised them to the most honoured rank they could conceive, Sumer's gods are far more elemental and harshly absolute. They never achieved the numinous quality of that most mysterious of Egyptian gods 'Him whose name is hidden', the nobility of the later 'unknown' Amon, or even the philosophically rather tepid beneficence of Akhnaton's Aten.

The Sumerian cosmology held that in the beginning was the primaeval sea, represented as female; her oceanic form possibly again commemorates the Sumerians' own preoccupation with the sea, in this case the waters of the Gulf. From the chaos of the waters, the cosmic mountain was begotten in which form heaven and earth were united in the persons of two great divinities, An, the god of Heaven, and Ki, the goddess of Earth. From their union sprang Enlil, the Lord of Air, who then became the executive leader of the Annunaki, the assembly of the Great Gods, and the recipient of the chorus of praise offered by all the people.

An and Enlil were associated with two other major divinities: Enki, Lord of the Abyss, the water god, one of the most popular in the pantheon, and Ninhursag, the Lady of the Mountain, the Great Goddess. Other important members of the divine family included Utu, God of the Sun (whose Akkadian name 'Shamash' survives in the Arabic word for sun, 'Shams'); Nanna, God of the Moon, later to be known as Sin; and Inanna the Ishtar-Aphrodite goddess of love and lust. Inanna was a highly equivocal goddess. She softened when she became the Semitic Ishtar under the Babylonians, but as will be seen from the Gilgamesh epic later in this story, the Sumerians themselves were very much in two minds about her. Inanna has part of her legendary connections linked with Dilmun and hence to the subject of this study. She says of herself: 'I am Inanna of the place where the sun rises'.[5] She is also reported to have 'washed her head in the fountain of Dilmun',[6] a reference perhaps to the many fresh water springs which may be found in the north of the island, and, more surprisingly, in the sea itself which divides Bahrain from the mainland of Arabia. The subterranean waters of eastern Arabia and the central Gulf were a particularly powerful element in giving the region its reputation for sanctity and the special favour of the gods.

Enlil and Enki were the most important of all the gods to the Sumerians. Enlil was thought of as a sort of divine Chief Executive, stern but usually just. Enki was the most beloved of the gods of Sumer, for he is the friend of man who brought knowledge of the arts and sciences to the black-headed folk, riding up the Gulf accompanied by

Enki, the Lord of the Abyss, God of the Sweet Waters, one of the most powerful members of the Sumerian pantheon and particularly associated with Dilmun and its legends.

rejoicing fishes. In this he seems to share in the myth identified, in much later times, with Oannes. Enki's epiphany is marvellously described.

> When Enki arose the fishes rose and adored him,
> He stood, a marvel unto the Apsu,
> Brought joy to the Enqu,
> To the sea it seemed that Anu was upon him,
> To the Great River is seemed that terror hovered about him,
> While at the same time the South Wind stirred the depths of the
> Euphrates.[6]

Although Dilmun had its own tutelary divinity, Enshag or Inzak, who will be revealed further in the legend of Enki and Ninhursag where he is spoken of as 'Lord of Dilmun', Enki was possibly the land's first and most important god. It has been suggested, indeed, that the veneration of Enki, Lord of the Abyss, and patron of the fishes, may have originated in Dilmun and from there have moved north to the Sumerian lands.[7] If this were so, and if Enki was the original tribal god of the

Sumerians, it could well be the reason for the belief that Enki brought the arts of civilization to Sumer from Dilmun. It would also be another reason for the reverence and affection in which the black-headed people held Dilmun as the Terrestrial Paradise.

Enki was beloved by the Sumerians for the sympathy he displayed towards humanity and the kindly interest he seemed to take in the well-being of the race of men. He was less remote and terrible than most of his colleagues, more inclined to behave predictably and with good-will towards man. He is among the most frequently portrayed of all the great gods in the vibrant and revealing glyptic art of the time. He appears in countless seals in various manifestations, on the water, in his reed house which bears a close resemblance to the houses built by the Marsh Arabs to this day, amiably wrestling with wild beasts, receiving petitions. He is also represented in one of the most important activities of Sumerian Gods, the sacred marriage, the *hieros gamos* which was celebrated down to Ninevite times, with the King enacting the god's role, partnered by one of the sacred temple women masquerading as the goddess. In many of his appearances, two streams of crystal water cascade from Enki's shoulders, in which his creatures the fishes disport themselves joyfully. Water is Enki's special element, in particular the sweet waters hidden beneath the earth whose management was essential to the Sumerians. In their rather confused view Enki rode the waters of the Gulf and, by thus agitating them, filled the Tigris and Euphrates with their overflow, so bringing prosperity and abundance to his people.

Enki is a chthonic divinity, his dwelling place the Abyss, far from the haunts of man. His name means 'Lord of Earth', and by it his original sovereignty over the world is proclaimed. At some time, however, Enki's supremacy was challenged and overthrown by Enlil, the Lord of Air, who then became the head of the Annunaki, under the kingship of the distant An. An was, incidentally, conceived of as some sort of Demiurge who, having created the world, largely withdrew from it to the higher heavens.

The reason why Enki lost his primacy is, in the present state of knowledge, uncertain: it may be that once the Sumerians had settled down to an existence on land and no longer depended so exclusively on the sea (as evidently they did originally, in witness of which are the offerings of fishes which were piled on Enki's altars at Eridu and the nets which were hung about them) they became more conscious of the mysterious powers of wind, storm and rain which whipped to fury the rivers and lagoons on which they had established themselves. The more kindly god of the sweet waters and the fishes was replaced by an elemental and implacable divinity whose officers were the bringers of storm and deluge. But it is likely that Enki is the most ancient male divinity whose name we know. Certainly the little shrine at his city, Eridu, piled high with the offerings of his creatures, the fishes, is the earliest of all temples that can be identified as such for certain. Enki, incidentally, was the god who was responsible for marking out the ground plans of temples.

An early text describes Enki as the father of Enlil, suggesting that, as was repeated again in Babylonian times with Marduk, and with the triple sequence of Uranos, Kronos and Zeus, the son could become greater than the father. Another legend survives which shows Enki, here described as the son of An, to have been the original creator god, displaying a brisk and cheerful attention to all the needs of the earth. A long and complex myth, *Enki and the World Order*,[8] describes his joyful bringing of order and all its blessings to mankind, to animals and to the land and cities of Sumer. Responsibilities are allotted by Enki to all the smaller divinities who have power over specific functions, elements or sections of the economy.

The myth gives the impression of bubbling enthusiasm on Enki's part and it emphasizes his joy in the work which he had wrought.

Enki proclaims his divine titles:

> I am the first son of An . . . I am the Lord of the Land
> I am the father of all lands
> I am the 'Big Brother' of the gods
> I am the record keeper of heaven and earth
> I am the leader of the Annunaki.

Enki turns to the organization of the earth and amongst the first lands to be blessed are Magan and Dilmun:

> The lands of Magan and Dilmun
> Looked up to me, Enki,
> Moved the Dilmun–boat to the ground
> Loaded the Magan–boat sky–high.

In Sumerian times Magan was in all probability located on the coast of Oman and also perhaps on the Makran coast across the Gulf.

Sumer itself next receives Enki's blessing and he proclaims its glories. Ur, the city whose fate has been decreed by Enlil, and Melukh-kha, probably the coastal regions of modern Pakistan, together with the cities of the Indus valley are celebrated by the god; then back to Dilmun:

He cleansed, purified the land Dilmun,
Placed Ninsikil in charge of it.
. . . he eats fish . . . he eats its dates.

Enki's blessing of Dilmun is especially generous and gives it a strong
identification with the sea, emphasizing the land's dependance on the
fruits of the sea as well as on the products of agriculture:

May the sea bring you its abundance,
The city – its dwellings are good dwellings,
Dilmun – its dwellings are good dwellings,
Its barley is very small barley,
Its dates are very large dates.

Dilmun dates, incidentally, were celebrated throughout antiquity.
Even late in the second millennium BC, long after the Sumerians had
disappeared for ever, Dilmun's dates were still greatly sought after by
the rulers of Mesopotamia. They were also responsible for a notably
high rate of caries in the teeth of the early inhabitants of Bahrain.

Amongst those whose power is called up by Enki is Utu, the sun
god, whose home is in Dilmun. One of the Paradise Land's epithets
may be recalled in the following passage in which he identifies Dilmun
in the same terms as the goddess Inanna, quoted earlier:

The hero, the bull who comes forth out of the forest,
Who roars lion-like,
The valiant Utu, the bull who stands secure,
Who proudly displays his power,
The father of the great city, *the place where the sun rises*,
The great herald of holy An,
The judge, the decision maker of the gods,
Who wears a lapis lazuli beard,
Who comes forth from the holy heaven,
Utu, the Son born of Ningal,
Enki placed in charge of the entire universe.

In some of the legends which survive and recount the doings of the
Fish-God, Enki presents a slightly disreputable, even a faintly absurd
figure. But the Sumerians seemed to have loved him, whilst the other
divinities they feared. In one of the most important and complete of the
early legends, Enki comes into full conjunction with Dilmun, for the
story begins in that land, before time was. Dilmun is already Enki's
home.

The myth concerns the rather fraught and complicated relationship of Enki and Ninhursag, one of the manifestations of the great and terrible primaeval goddess who survived into Sumerian times, her supreme authority then being subjected to that of the male gods.[9] Dilmun is splendidly described, a land of joy and peace, whose creation has been an unreserved success. Ninsikil is a tutelary goddess of Dilmun: her name means 'the pure queen'.

> The land Dilmun is a pure place, the land Dilmun is a clean place;
> The land Dilmun is a clean place, the land Dilmun is a bright place;
> He who is all alone laid himself down in Dilmun,
> The place after Enki had laid himself by his wife,
> That place is clean, that place is bright,
> He who is all alone laid himself down in Dilmun,
> The place, after Enki had laid himself by Ninsikil,
> That place is clean, that place is bright,
> In Dilmun the raven uttered no cries,
> The kite uttered not the cry of the kite,
> The lion killed not,
> The wolf snatched not the lamb,
> Unknown was the kid-killing dog,
> Unknown was the grain-devouring boar,
> The bird on high . . . not its young,
> The dove . . . not the head,
> The sick-eyed says not 'I am sick-eyed',
> The sick-headed says not 'I am sick-headed',
> Its old woman says not 'I am an old woman',
> Its old man says not 'I am an old man',
> Its unwashed maid is not . . . in the city,
> He who crosses the river utters no . . .
> The overseer does not . . .
> The singer utters no wail,
> By the side of the city he utters no lament.

Only one thing apparently mars life in this happy land, the lack of sweet water, but the cohabitation of Ninsikil and Enki soon overcomes this problem. Ninsikil, a practical if somewhat opportunistic goddess, prevails upon the relaxed and good-tempered Enki, evidently in a state of post-coital euphoria, to provide the island with the water it needs. He at once calls upon Utu the sun-god, to make the sweet waters flow. Utu does so, and all that is possible for the enjoyment of men is realized in Dilmun. Even the economy is transformed.

Her city drinks the water of abundance,
Dilmun drinks the water of abundance,
Her wells of bitter water, behold they are become wells of good
    water,
Her fields and farms produced good grain,
Her city, behold it is become the house of the banks and quays of
    the land.

An alternative translation[10] of the last line would have Dilmun as the place of assembly of the gods, their meeting place and, so far as the Sumerians were concerned, the place of their origin. A fragment of a cuneiform tablet found at Asshur, the capital of the later bloodstained Assyrian Kingdom, indicates that *e-karra*, 'the House of the Quay', was the name of a temple in Dilmun.[11] It may be recalled in the last line of the extract above and it is entirely in keeping with the Sumerians' commercial preoccupations that the quays of mercantile Dilmun should be so commemorated, even in the context of a hymn of praise to the most lofty of the gods.

Now, however, the story takes another turn, and a strange and slightly sinister element enters it. Clearly no place so well endowed as Dilmun should be without plants and the benefits of cultivation. Enki proceeds to deal with this by inducing a complex and cumbersome series of pregnancies on successive generations of plant goddesses, brought into being for that purpose.

The process starts with the Great Mother herself, Ninhursag, whose nine months of pregnancy is equivalent to nine human days. Their daughter is Ninsar; Enki rapidly lies with her too and in nine days her daughter Ninhur is born. Enki, indefatigable and undeterred by the fact that he is now dealing with his grand-daughter, fathers Uttu, the Plant Goddess, on Ninhur.

Ninhursag, who apparently has been absent during this succession of pregnancies, now returns to the goddess-littered island and takes an ill-fortuned hand in the affair. She offers Uttu some helpful advice on the predictable course of her relations with the still tumescent Enki. What she proposes is, unhappily, lost from the tablet which contains the legend but Uttu, like a dutiful great grand-daughter, takes Ninhursag's advice seriously and, as a result, promptly if unexpectedly, gives birth to eight plants, unaided by Enki.

The god, despite his divine nature, is now apparently exhausted by the efforts which he has so urgently been making in the cause of agriculture, and is lying 'stretched out in the swamp-land'. With him is his attendant, Isimud, and from him he learns the names of each of the eight plants which Uttu has mothered. As Isimud pronounces its name Enki eats the plant concerned. Are there portents here of other myths reaching us from this Sumerian Eden: the Hebrew legend of the Forbidden Fruit and the Greek story of the ingestation by Kronos of his children?[12] It is also remarkable that when Enki is lying alone in the marshes, he masturbates,[13] like Atum the Egyptian creator god, who, in one of the Egyptians' explanations for the process of creation, since he is the unique being, is obliged to resort to this procedure to start off the sequence of divine births which ultimately leads to the making of the earlier generations of the gods.

When Enki has eaten all the plants, Ninhursag returns again, this time in a wild and angry epiphany. In a swirling rage she curses Enki for having eaten the plants: 'Until thou art dead, I shall not look upon thee with the eye of life'. Wrathfully she disappears and Enki is stricken with a mortal sickness which affects eight parts of his body, each plant that he had eaten taking its revenge on a different organ. It is also possible (if confusing) that Enki is impregnated by his own semen in this phase of the story, again recalling an Egyptian parallel, the story of the conflict of Horus and Seth where something not dissimilar occurs.[14]

A peculiar characteristic of the gods of Sumer seems to have been a tendency to fall to pieces in times of stress. The Deluge myth will demonstrate how badly they could behave when things became really difficult for them. The High Gods become discouraged: seeing the powerful Enki himself brought down by Ninhursag, they fall into a deep despondency and sit hopelessly in the dust. The peace and happiness of Dilmun is clouded by their distress and lack of resource.

A new element is introduced at this point into the legend. The Sumerians, seemingly, were fond of animals and were the first people to record stories in which animals play a human role, like those to which Aesop later gave his name, and of the same order as those in the engaging animal cartoons which survive from Egypt and for which, indeed, there are also many Sumerian parallels. In this case it is the fox, not a creature normally noted for his sagacity and resource in Sumerian fable, who takes the initiative in the matter of Enki's sickness.

Finding the miserable gods hopelessly watching their divine comrade sinking into what looks suspiciously like mortality, the fox offers to bring back Ninhursag so that she may heal Enki. As Enlil, the Lord of Air and prince of the gods, can think of nothing better himself, he accepts the fox's offer swiftly.

At this point the text is indecipherable and we do not know by what means the fox persuaded Ninhursag to return. But return she does and she agrees to heal the hapless Enki by means of the facility (a routine matter apparently to Sumerian goddesses) of giving birth to eight deities, each of whom acts as an antidote to one of Enki's ailments. Abu, Nintul, Ninul, Ninsutu, Ninkasi, Nazi, Dazimira, Ninti and Enshag are successively sprung from the goddess's fecund womb and each, having healed the appropriate part of Enki, is either appointed the tutelary of certain lands or married to another. Ninhursag then places Enki by her vulva and speeds his healing. Enki is restored to his full godly powers. The poem ends with a paean of praise to him.

The two last named gods in the sequence brought to birth by Ninhursag to heal Enki, Ninti and Enshag, are of special interest in the present context. Kramer has suggested that Ninti may be the original of the legend of Eve, the 'first mother' of the Genesis creation myth and thus, possibly, a remote link with the two Paradise myths.[15]

Enshag is not one of the great gods of Sumer but he has a vital role to play in the identification of Dilmun and Bahrain. The discovery of the island's principal cuneiform text with its mention of this god has its place in a later section of this study.

It may be appropriate here to refer to the discovery of a text which was found on Cythera, in the distant Aegaean far away from the islands of the Gulf, and which also refers to Enshag.[16] It is written in an archaic cuneiform and appears to refer to the god Enshag and the goddess Lakhamun, the gods of Tilmun, to whom it said 'the king of Tilmun Naram-Sin, son of Ibiq-Adad, king of Tilmun, for his life has made an offering'.

Naram-Sin is evidently not the king of Sumer and Akkad who was the grandson of Sargon the Great. Ibiq-Adad seems to be unknown. What an inscription of this comparative obscurity was doing on an Aegaean island so far from its own supposed island of origin is totally mysterious. Tilmun, incidentally, is the transliteration of the Semitic-language form of Dilmun.

Enki was a fish-god; the charming readiness of the fishes to adore him has already been recorded. One of the more remarkable and certainly one of the most ancient legends associated with the Gulf and the origins of knowledge concerns Enki in a curious manifestation of a creature, part fish, part man called Oannes, a Hellenized form of his Semitic name, Ea. Enki is almost invariably shown in human form in Mesopotamian art. Fishes were sacred to him and so was the ibex, a creature which features frequently on the seals which are so notable a product of the societies flourishing in the Gulf in antiquity; sometimes, indeed, Enki is manifested in the ibex, and his boat, in which he is often portrayed, was called 'Ibex of the Absu'. The story of Oannes is contained in the work of Berossus,[17] who was a contemporary of Alexander the Great; he was Priest of Bel in the great temple of Babylon. He seems not to have been a very remarkable man nor, to judge by the parts of his *Babyloniaca* which have survived in extracts quoted in other men's work, a particularly gifted one. He was given a somewhat more exalted posthumous biography by the hand of legend, however, including fathering the Erythraean Sibyl.

Berossus was a hellenized Babylonian. He was an admirer of things Greek and he sought to reconcile the history of his own people with that of the new masters of the world. He wrote for Antiochos I, one of Alexander's successors and set out to make available, in the Greek language, books of stupendous and quite unbelievable antiquity preserved at Babylon which contained the origins of his people, the transmission of the arts of civilization to them by the bizarre amphibious creatures which manifested themselves in the Gulf, and a list of kings, from before the Flood to Alexander. The books, suggested Berossus, contained 'the histories of heaven [and earth] and sea and the first birth and the Kings and their deeds'.

The weird and mysterious creatures of which he tells suddenly appear and attach themselves to the race of men, proceeding to teach them all knowledge. The leader of the team of didactic monsters is 'a beast named Oannes' which 'appeared from the Erythraean Sea in a place adjacent to Babylonia. Its entire body was that of a fish but a human head had grown beneath the head of the fish and human feet had grown from the fish's tail. It also had a human voice. A picture of it is still preserved today.' 'This beast spent the days with the men but ate no food. It gave to men the knowledge of letters and sciences and crafts of all types. It also taught them how to found cities, establish temples, introduce laws and measure land. It also revealed to them seeds and the gathering of fruits and in general it gave men everything which is connected with the civilized life. From the time of that beast nothing further has been discovered. But when the sun set this beast Oannes plunged back into the sea and spent the nights in the deep, for it was amphibious. Later other beasts also appeared. He [Berossus] says that he will discuss these in the book of the Kings. Oannes wrote about birth and government and gave the following account to men.'

Oannes, himself, then describes the 'time when everything was darkness and water'. Strange monsters appeared; all manner of creatures came forth, to be ruled by a woman called Omorka. Then Bel, the great god, arose, split the woman in two, destroyed the monster forms and created men and beasts able to endure the air.

The second of Berossus's books was *The Book of Kings*. He records in it the names of the kings of Babylon from the beginning of things. The earliest kings ruled for many thousands of years. They were attended or advised by other creatures, like Oannes, who came up from the Gulf; Berossus gives the names of these creatures, which were known collectively as *apkallus*, a term which may mean something like 'sages'. They were all of them mixtures of men and fish.

The 'Kings' are the legendary sovereigns who reigned before the Flood. The last of them is Xisouthros, a figure from Greek myth whose name is a Hellenized form of Ziusudra, the Sumerian hero of the flood myth in the Epic of Gilgamesh.

Berossus describes the Flood. The warning of its impending approach is given to Xisouthros by Kronos, the Greek equivalent of Enki. He includes a curious little story which purports to describe the birth of Gilgamesh, his being saved from an early death by an eagle and his upbringing, like Sargon the Great, by a gardener.

The events which Berossus charts are, he says, based on records reaching back more than 400,000 years. This can safely be discounted, but his description of the fish-men *apkallus*, coming up to Babylonia from the Gulf is, if nothing else, a charming legend which enshrines the belief of the Babylonians and their Sumerian predecessors that their civilization originated from the Lower Sea, the place where the sun rises.

Oannes and his attendants are clearly Enki and his familiars. Even in relatively late times priests of Enki/Ea were depicted wearing fish costumes, with fish headdresses above their own features, thus impersonating quite convincingly the form of the *apkallus* described by Berossus.

As to the *apkallus* themselves, none of the representations (so far as we know) to which Berossus refers, survives. However, there is a group of strange little figures, of uncertain provenance, which appear to come from very early urban levels in south-western Iranian city sites.[18] These are in the form of men, covered with fish scales (though otherwise human in form) and each with a deep scar running down his face. These little figurines are made in segments: they are remarkably powerful and quite unlike anything else from Sumer or from early Elam. Whether they actually represent *apkallus* only Enki knows.

The earliest of all temples discovered in Mesopotamia is at Eridu and was consecrated to Enki. It dates from Ubaid times, a simple sanctuary built on the virgin sand; it is the ancestor of all Sumerian

One of a group of figurines, made in mixed stone segments, said to be found in early coastal sites in south-western Iran; probably late third millennium BC. (*Louvre*, after *Art in the Ancient World*, Faber).

temples. It was overlaid by seventeen successive buildings, each one more elaborate than its predecessor, culminating in a great third-millennium ziggurat, a splendid structure raised to the glory of Enki, more than two thousand years after the little Ubaid shrine had introduced his worship to the land.

In the first sanctuary was an altar piled with offerings six inches deep in fish bones, the relics of sacrifices placed there more than five thousand years ago. The fish were sea-perch, creatures of the brackish lagoon waters. Enki was also much honoured, understandably, by sailors who courted his favour and goodwill in launching themselves upon the uncertain mercy of his kingdom's waters. If it is possible that Enshag-Inzak may be a manifestation of Enki himself, the suggestion that his worship in Bahrain may have preceded his cult in Sumer is wholly tenable. According to Rawlinson, the Babylonians acknowledged having received all their knowledge from 'the mysterious islands of the Persian Gulf' – which, as the Babylonians were the direct cultural successors of the innovating Sumerians, they patently did not. It is another matter, however, with the Sumerians themselves.

The gods of Sumer are to be seen at their best perhaps in the context of their place of assembly, the land of crossing, which was Dilmun. After the disaster of the Flood, they were said to cluster around the sacrifices provided for them by the prototypical survivor, Ziusudra, 'like flies',[19] a somewhat distasteful metaphor. But they also clustered around the sacred land of Dilmun, the original Holy Land, from the legends of which all the others in the Western World actually descend. In these legends they are revealed as a tremendous presence, great if intangible forms which were to exercise a profound influence on the world; so profound as to endure over the five or six thousand years since the people who invented them first began to fill their world with the stories of their intervention in the affairs of men. The modern world, when it takes account of such matters, draws its inspiration of the divine from the great monotheistic faiths which have moulded society over the last two thousand years. Hebrew, Christian and Muslim religious beliefs have all drawn their inspiration from a common, though of course not from an exclusive, source. That source had its beginnings in the people of southern Mesopotamia; to those people Dilmun was a magical land, a faery place, half realized, half a place of myth. This was the Garden of Eden, the place of origins; there was no Fall there, though. In Dilmun all was pure and enduring. It is not surprising perhaps that its very existence was forgotten for so long, but the fact remains that without this little island and the legends which it bore, the world would not be quite the place that it is, nor would people, for at least the past three thousand formative years, have believed quite what they came to believe.

VI

Bahrain: The Paradise Land

When, in the winter of 1878–9, Captain E. L. Durand, an officer in the service of the Government of India (he bore the appointment of Assistant Political Resident, The Persian Gulf and was based in Bushire on the Persian coast), visited Bahrain, relations with the state were under the administrative control of the Viceroy in Calcutta. Britain's interest in the Gulf in those days was simply the protection of her routes to India; she was not particularly interested in Arabia or the Gulf as such, though the curious long-lasting myth of the special relationship which is said to persist between the Arabs and the British presumably dates to this time.

In subsequent times, Bahrain provided a convenient base for the British political presence, such as it was, when it was removed from the Persian mainland. The island was the seat of successive Political Agents and, later, of Political Residents who represented British government interests in the Gulf until 1971: they were the last of the pro-Consuls, surviving majestically into the modern age.

Bahrain was no doubt chosen for this faintly equivocal eminence by reason of its island character and the relative sophistication of its people. The Bahrainis' ancient trading history and their latter-day pre-eminence in the Gulf's pearl trade made them ideal associates for the British, who had, after all, their own strongly developed mercantile interests. The essentially Arab character of the State was however never affected; apart from a few rather oddly expressed treaties and a visitation by Lord Curzon in his most august manner, his dignity only marginally impaired by his allegedly being hoisted ashore in an armchair covered in Persian carpets, the British influence in Bahrain was superficial, not profound. However, all that lay in the future when the Viceroy's Foreign Department despatched Captain Durand to Bahrain.

In the course of a three-week stay Captain Durand, a keen amateur archaeologist by all accounts, and a talented water-colourist, opened several of the tumulus burial mounds which dominate the Aali district, near the village of the same name. He reported to his government enthusiastically on his findings. In one of the tombs he appears to have come up against a wall, inconveniently sited for his further exploration; with disarming succinctness he observes: 'We blew this out'.[1]

However, the practice of dynamiting tombs is not a fair measure of Captain Durand's contribution to the uncovering of the early history of the Bahrain islands, for one discovery which he made in the casual manner of those days was to be of crucial significance in establishing the part that Bahrain had played in the early history of south-west Asia and, indeed, in the developing awareness of the extent of man's history. Embedded in the outer wall of a mosque in the principal settlement on the island he found a black basalt stone which had engraved on it a plaque of cuneiform script, one of the few examples of early epigraphy yet discovered in Bahrain, and incontestably the most important.

Before examining Durand's stone and its importance, it is worth recording the melancholy fact that Durand evidently considered, in the all frequent manner of antiquarians of his day, that having discovered the stone he was entitled to retain it. This he proceeded to do. Since his time the stone, a particularly important document in the history of early Arabia, has never been seen again. It is believed that it found its way back to Britain when Captain Durand returned home. It probably lay hidden in an attic somewhere, in that event sharing the dismal fate of the multitude of curios, inexpertly stuffed animal heads and unhappy fragments of Oriental furniture which the servants of the Victorian Empire habitually brought home, the source of remembrance of imperial glory for themselves, and of inconvenience and embarrassment to their heirs. In fact, it is suspected, though not proven, that it was lost in London during the Second World War. One of Durand's relatives recalled seeing the stone in his London home which was subsequently destroyed in the blitz. Some of Durand's effects were sold at Christie's a number of years ago and enquiry of the firm elicited this information, the stone having passed some of the intervening years in Scotland.[2]

The inscription was found embedded in the wall of a mosque in the Bilad ed Kadim, the ancient capital of Bahrain. Of this the only substantial remains today is the Suq al-Khamis mosque, once ruinous, now disastrously restored. Durand's stone was c. 26 inches in length and its discoverer described it as being like the prow of a boat or an animal's tongue: it has also been said to look like a foot. Towards the narrower end of the stone an upright palm branch was inscribed. Beside the branch a rectangular 'box' contained four lines of inscription in the style of cuneiform script which prevailed during the eighteenth century BC, at the time of the first Babylonian empire, roughly contemporary with Hammurabi, the great law-giver. 'Old Babylonian' cuneiform had by then become the customary script for most Near Eastern countries' official and business correspondence and for the literary productions of the Babylonian and Assyrian heirs of the civilization of Sumer.

Durand's account of his researches in Bahrain is published in two forms: the first and most frequently quoted was contained in the proceedings of the Journal of the Royal Asiatic Society.[3] This version contains Sir Henry Creswicke Rawlinson's comments: he was the Society's Director-General at the time and a most remarkable man.[4]

There is, however, another version of Durand's report. This is the original version,[5] which he submitted to the Foreign Department of the Viceroy's administration in Calcutta where, in view of its evident originality and importance, it was printed.

The Calcutta text differs in a number of particulars from that published in the Society's proceedings. For one thing it is written a good deal less formally and is much more engaging. Durand was, after all, writing for colleagues and presumably felt that he could indulge what sometimes amounts almost to whimsey. Thus he introduced a very agreeable bull-terrier pup whose antics he related; in describing the fauna of Bahrain he recorded the appearance of a species of fish evidently unknown to him which, with little ichthyological precision, he describes as wearing a coat. He went into detail on the economy of the island, regretting the decline of the palm plantations, an observation which will strike the visitor still, a century and more later.

The most significant difference in the two versions is that the Calcutta text is enriched with a series of lively water-colour sketches. Durand was a competent draughtsman, a handy quality in the days before the general availability of the camera. He was the first to draw the burial mounds of Bahrain: he showed the entrance to one piled fearsomely high with rocks, in a positively Gothic formation. He drew the fish which caught his interest but not, alas, the bull-terrier pup.

In the Calcutta text he reproduced his most famous discovery, the inscribed stone from a 'squeeze' which he had made on the spot. A squeeze was a popular method of copying inscriptions in the last century and consisted of applying a papier-mache or similar pulp to the inscription thus making an exact copy. However, the illustration published in the Calcutta text must have puzzled his colleagues for it is reproduced back to front and upside down. This is corrected in the

Society's version and it is this drawing which is always reproduced today. Rawlinson attempted a translation in the Calcutta version: it is not, however, satisfactory and he evidently was able to revise it during the time which lapsed between the publication of the two versions.

Rawlinson was a distinguished public servant as well as being one of the most important figures in the uncovering of the early civilizations of Persia and Mesopotamia. In no little part due to his phenomenal ability in linguistics and a preparedness as a young man to risk life and limb in the decipherment of ancient inscriptions, the secret of the cuneiform script was finally broken.[6] He was, as a comparatively junior figure, one of those scholars who was set the task of decipering what turned out to be Sumerian cuneiform. Rawlinson early on recognized that the language was not a Semitic one and that it was anterior to the already familiar ancient languages of Mesopotamia, like Akkadian, Babylonian and Assyrian. A remarkable combination of scholar and man-of-action he was, perhaps more than any other, responsible for unlocking the rich storehouse of Sumerian literature and releasing it to the world. Rawlinson was also, in the style of the scholars of his day, a great deal more speculative and imaginative than his more austere successors might consider altogether proper, for they are jealous of the scientific reputation of their discipline and resent the charge, often levelled in archaeology's early days, of being mere treasure hunters. A little informed speculation is surely no bad thing, however, provided that it is recognized as such: Durand's stone gives plenty of opportunity for it.

It can be accepted with reasonable certainty that the stone is from Bahrain itself, perhaps the last fragment to survive of a palace of one of the island's merchant princes. Who 'Rimum' was will perhaps never be known, but at least his act of piety in invoking his god has assured him some small immortality. The text reads:

> e-gal ri – mu – um eri din – za – ak LU a – ga – rum
> The Palace of Rimum, the Servant of Inzak, of the tribe of Agarum.

The mention of Rimum's tribe, the Agarum, provides an example of the quite extraordinary continuity which may be found amongst peoples whose way of life remained traditional and predominantly tribal. It has been proposed that 'Agarum' is perpetuated in 'Hagar', as the Hasa province of eastern Arabia and Bahrain itself were collectively called in mediaeval times. A tribe of nomads called the Beni Hagar still occupies land in the Hasa province of what is now Saudi Arabia and may, therefore, be related to Rimum's tribe. The Beni Hagar are an

The inscription found by Captain Durand when he visited Bahrain in 1878–9. It records the name of Rimum, perhaps a ruler of Dilmun *c.* 1800 BC, and identifies the god Inzak (Sumerian Enshag) as the island's tutelary divinity.

interesting phenomenon, incidentally, with a knack of appearing at significant moments of history. They seem to have been one of the Christianized Arab tribes in late pre-Islamic times and, having moved up to the north, to have been present at the fall of Jerusalem when it was captured in the seventh century AD by the Caliph Omar.

'Inzak' was the Akkadian form of the name of the Sumerian god 'Enshag' who featured in the last stage of the chain of births which took place in Dilmun and is described in the legend of Enki and Ninhursag. He was one of the principal divinities of the ancient inhabitants of Bahrain and in the legend referred to is proclaimed 'Lord of Dilmun'; he is said to control reason and wisdom, an area of concern which clearly he inherited from his father. Temples were dedicated to him in Sumerian and Elamite[7] cities and he was worshipped in Babylonian times, under the name Nabu; later he became an influential member of the pantheon. He is, according to Rawlinson, the god represented in the sky by the planet Mercury, the sun's closest attendant and a divinity of considerable power and mystery in the ancient world.[8] The planets, incidentally, were called by the Sumerians 'the big ones that walk about' distinguishing them from the stars, 'the little ones which are scattered about like grain': both are pretty concepts.

Enshag Inzak-Nabu-Mercury was the 'dark' god, a wise and supple deity. His name has been interpreted (again by Rawlinson) as meaning 'the nearest Lord', referring perhaps to his position as Mercury in the solar system. Rawlinson further suggested that the ancient name of Bahrain might mean 'The Blessed Island', an intriguing and pleasing suggestion in the light of its significance to the Sumerians.

Rawlinson referred to the fact that in his *History* Herodotus reported Phoenician legends of their origins in which they too ascribed their beginnings to the islands in the Gulf. If there is any truth in this myth at all, the far-famed ability of the Phoenicians in the arts of commerce and of navigation might reasonably have been attributed to their island origins. For if the Gulf islands did see their beginnings, they made their eventual home in Syria/Lebanon, one of the most important centres of trade of the ancient world.

It would be unwise to postulate any firm conviction on the basis of an Herodotean report alone. But it cannot be said too often that peoples in ancient times did cover extraordinary distances and, seemingly quite cheerfully, undertook great migrations. The founding of the Greek colonies around the Mediterranean and far into Arabia, demonstrated this procedure in comparatively late times: the Phoenicians themselves were renowned for the practice in earlier times still. It now seems not improbable that the report recorded by Herodotus was based on some historical reality.[9]

The theory of 'wave-migration' has demonstrated that groups, a tribe (whatever that may be) or a congeries of more or less related families or clans can cover vast distances over a few generations simply by advancing almost imperceptibly year by year across grazing lands or territory other than that which requires settled cultivation. If, as seems quite probable, there was a decline in climatic conditions in the Gulf area during the early second millennium, its people may have started to move westwards until, in a few decades, they found themselves moving up or down the Levantine coast.

It may be appropriate to turn aside for a moment and consider further, and from the standpoint of a remarkable but little known philological study, the identification of Dilmun with Bahrain and the Island with the idea of the Terrestrial Paradise. It should perhaps be said that the Sumerians did not, so far as we know, suggest that Dilmun was a place to which the spirits of the dead were translated. They had only the haziest and, as has already been demonstrated, generally pessimistic views of an afterlife. Paradise meant for them the place of origins, the site of the original and benevolent creation. The original concept of the Garden of Eden has something of the same idea.

In essence Dilmun is the Holy Land, the first land in the world perhaps to be accorded this sacred character. Dilmun was holy ground and the legends which grew up around it all emphasise its sacred nature.

Of all the earliest studies on Dilmun and Bahrain which deal in particular with this aspect of Dilmun as a Holy Land, none is more remarkable than that published in *Scriptura Sacra et Monumenta Orientis Antiqui* under the august imprimatur of the Pontificii Instituti Biblici of Rome, in 1928.[10] It was the work of a notable scholar, the Jesuit epigrapher, Fr E. Burrows, SJ.

The extract from the Pontifical Journal from which these notes have been prepared is, in its original form, a remarkable document in its own right: inscribed in the author's own hand, line perfectly balancing line, each of the several languages into which Burrows slips with effortless practice, commanding its own font; similarly, italics, bold faces and other typographical devices are indicated by a variation in calligraphy.

Burrows' 1928 article, 'Tilmun, Bahrain, Paradise' is at least the equal, in its profundity of erudition, of Rawlinson's pioneering sweep nearly fifty years before around the cuneiform and other texts. Its compass is narrower since it is concerned purely with the etymology of Tilmun/Dilmun and the textual references, in Sumerian, Akkadian, Phoenician, Hebrew and Arabic originals, which contributed to Burrows' contention that Bahrain was not only Dilmun but was also the origin of the idea of the Terrestrial Paradise; though its compass is confined it is yet profound. No other scholar has attempted so deep a penetration into the mists of Bahrain's antiquity.

His argument is developed in something like the sequence which follows; in his original text he tends to prefer the spelling 'Tilmun', in this following the practice of the time. However, when referring to Sumerian sources, 'Dilmum' is now recognized as being a more exact transliteration of the Sumerian form. Tilmun is, strictly speaking, appropriate for the transliteration of the word in Semitic languages but it seems tedious to use it here, thus Dilmun will appear throughout.

The cuneiform characters used to write the word which is now transliterated 'Dilmun' have the values NI and TUK. The determinative for a country or place KI is added to these two syllables, giving the typical Sumerian agglutinative NI-TUK-KI. It was once thought that the composite sign formed by these elements was pronounced as it is written. However, most Sumerian signs have more than one way of being pronounced: NI-TUK was spoken DILMUN – the element KI was not articulated at all, serving simply to indicate that the group of signs which preceded it delineated a place or country.

Now, to complicate matters still further, Burrows goes on to

IV. This enigmatic site at Diraz was excavated in 1972. It appears to date from the latter part of the third millennium BC and is thus contemporary with the Barbar temple complex.

V. The well at the temple complex at Barbar is part of the second temple and its presence on the site probably identifies the divinity worshipped there as Enki, the Lord of the Abyss.

VI. The oryx was in danger of extinction in eastern Arabia until this herd, and another in Oman, were set up to re-establish the species. The oryx may be the origin of the legend of the unicorn.

VII. Two small elephants, in lapis lazuli and, possibly, anhydrite, which were said to have been bought at Qatif in the nineteen-thirties.

suggest that NI and TUK sometimes had the value DU-GUD in Sumerian. He believes that the Sumerian ideogram might primarily have the value NI-TUK, meaning 'terrible'. In this it approaches very closely the meaning of DU-GUD which Burrows translates at 'majestic'; he indicates too, that it may, similarly, mean 'great one'.

DU-GUD would be a most appropriate name for Holy Dilmun, the original home of the gods, in its meaning 'venerable'. However another shade of meaning perhaps links it even more directly with Dilmun for DU-GUD can also mean 'massive', 'steep' and, particularly, 'dark', a nuance derived, Burrows proposes, from the ideogram's pictographic origins as a rain-cloud. These meanings, 'massive' and 'dark', would be especially appropriate when applied to Dilmun – Bahrain's central topographical feature, the Jebal Dukhan. This name is usually translated 'Mountain of Smoke' and thus perpetuates the idea of darkness, even of mystery; that it is still so called to this day would seem to be another remarkable instance of the immensely long time over which names can survive in the Middle East.

Burrows thinks that the name 'Dilmun' may be Semitic in origin, not Sumerian. He suggests that it is a 'native proto-Arab name', an interesting suggestion indeed, but one which perhaps would not attract a great deal of support today. The speculation about a pre-Sumerian language, proposed in particular by the distinguished American Sumerologist Samuel Noah Kramer, is a consideration which has arisen since Burrows' day.[11] Kramer believed that certain words – the names of the two great rivers of Sumer, many place names, and some of the most common terms in use in Sumerian times – were inherited from an earlier people who occupied the land before the Sumerians entered it. This language has been variously called 'proto-Euphratean' and 'Ubai-dian'; however, though the words concerned do not appear to be either semitic in origin *or* Sumerian, most authorities are satisfied that the Sumerians and the people who made Ubaid pottery are one and there is no evidence of an earlier people occupying southern Iraq before the Sumerians entered it. It is puzzling, nonetheless, this intrusion of what appear to be wholly alien names, particularly those which apply to places and which we know persist over very long periods of currency and time. Whether Dilmun may be one of these pre-Sumerian names is not certain, but certainly the name is of immense antiquity.

There is another interesting comment that can be made about Burrows' study, though its implications are far beyond the competence of this author to judge. He dismisses as 'rather improbable' the suggestion that NI-TUK may be derived from a word for 'pearl', represented in

Old Turkish and Hungarian, two languages which have some structural similarity to Sumerian. Writing in the late 'twenties, Burrows believed that there was no connection between Dilmun-Bahrain and pearls in antiquity; thus he considered this suggestion to be insupportable. But since Burrows' day, of course, the evidence for Dilmun being renowned as a source of pearls has multiplied notably. The Danish excavations identified vast oyster middens on the island, dating back five thousand years and more, showing that the oyster was harvested from early times.[12] Groups of these piles of discarded oyster shells were found between Ras Noma and Ras al-Jaziyia. 'Fish-eyes', mentioned in the cuneiform texts as products of Dilmun, are now generally accepted as being a term (rather a graphic and descriptive one) for pearls; in eastern Arabian sites miniature tools have been found which may have been used in adapting the pearl as an item of jewellery. If Burrows had known of the close link between Dilmun and pearls he might have pursued further this intriguing connection with two other ancient agglutinative languages. However, it cannot be assumed that the pursuit would have been particularly profitable since Sumerian is *sui generis*, without any evident connection to any other known language, one of its most mysterious characteristics.

Whilst considering Burrows' ideas on the etymology of Dilmun it may be worth noting the remarkable fact that one authority considered that NU-TUK-KI meant 'the place of the bringing of oil', the oil, in this case of course, being naphtha. A distinguished German scholar, writing like Burrows in the 1920s, proposed that NI-TUK meant 'oil-ship'.[13] The peculiar element here, of course, is that oil (in the sense that the word is used today) was not discovered until the 1930s, but when it was, the first Arabian source for it was Bahrain. 'The oil-ship' is not at all a bad description of the island that was the first Arabian territory to recover its oil deposits in commercial quantities and make them available to the world at large.

Bahrain's long tradition as a centre of trade continues today. The merchant community is rich and sophisticated; its prosperity is based upon the island's modern facilities and location, and the natural acumen and agreeable nature of the Bahrainis, not always found in combination. The State is ruled by a Shaikh of the dynasty of the al-Khalifa, one of the great families of Arabian princes, who conquered Bahrain in the eighteenth century. The Amir is a prince of humanity, wisdom and perception; the extraordinary progress which his state has experienced in the past decades is due, in no small part, to the character of his rule. Since the discovery of oil, successive rulers have used their compara-

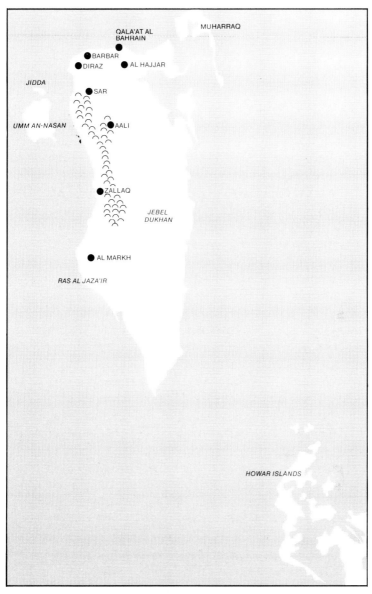

Principal archaeological sites in Bahrain.

tively modest revenues wisely and in the interests of their people to the point where today Bahrain has three generations of its people educated in the western manner, living in a state which may claim one of the first national welfare services of modern times. Hospitals, schools, roads, harbours and all the harassing paraphernalia of a modern social infra-structure have been assimilated into the island's life, with, so far, remarkably little disturbance or difficulty.

Even in the modern world Bahrain has one unique characteristic which makes it quite distinct from its neighbours: it is the only island state in Arabic-speaking lands. The insular quality of Bahrain is, of course, what has marked it throughout history and determined, to a degree greater than any other single factor, its development. The character of the people has similarly been conditioned by the fact of their being islanders. To an extent far greater than most of their contemporaries in the Arabian peninsula, the Bahrainis have a sense of nationality, developed to a high degree, even amongst those who descend from those desert dwellers who migrated to the island in the latter half of the eighteenth century.

Much of Bahrain is desert, sharply contrasting with the northern limits of the island which are richly fertile. Small farms, in extent and often in character like European private gardens, were once a familiar and pleasing characteristic of the landscape. They represented an agreeable custom amongst the more prosperous people, where the family may withdraw in the evening or in the humid summer months.

During the splendid centuries of the Islamic Caliphates, Bahrain was a quiet backwater, though the arts of poetry and architecture flourished there. The island had a kindly part to play from time to time in the often troubled history of the nearby states, for, cut off by the sea from the mainland, it was a place of refuge for fallen dynasts and those unfortunate people who had backed the wrong side in dynastic or religious disputes. Bahrain was then a land too insignificant to excite the ambitions of conquerors, content with its small prosperity drawn from the sea, in the form of the pearls much sought after by the princes who had succeeded to the rule of the Prophet's widely dispersed peoples.

Bahrain is a prosperous and pleasant land, its population of around three hundred and fifty thousand, largely Arab in race, with a mélange of Persians, Indians, Omanis and Europeans. The allegiance of its indigenous population is split, roughly equally, between the two great sects of Islam, the Sunni and the Shi'a. By temperament, the Bahrainis are a courteous and kindly people who go about their daily business with little of the flurry, acrimony or lighthearted frenzy of many of their neighbours in the Middle East. They display the dignity and reserve of their Arab stock on the one hand, mingled with the ability and sensitivity of the Persians and Mesopotamians whose blood runs in their veins. Like the later settlers, the earlier inhabitants of Bahrain must have come from the mainland: in the present state of knowledge, it would appear that this first landfall was made more than seven thousand years ago. Whether it was by chance or by deliberate and resolute policy, these earliest settlers must have crossed the narrow seas which divide the Arabian mainland from the island which is, on a good day, visible from the neighbouring coast. The periodic falls in the level of the Gulf probably facilitated their crossing.

At some time, in the very distant past, man took to the water. No doubt his early excursions on it were involuntary, but no amount of speculation will ever disclose to us how seamanship began. All we can reasonably assume is that the real breakthrough may have come when the making of reed-boats was adopted by the people living on the banks of the Tigris and Euphrates and the lakes and marshes which were connected with them, and by those who lived in similar though more favoured circumstances on the Nile. How this remarkable discovery was made is not known, but the building of reed-boats which depended on the 'wash-through' principle for their buoyancy and which would carry very considerable loads was one of the key discoveries of ancient technology. Reed-boats built to this principle also had the merit of being virtually unsinkable.[14]

Even when the Sumerians had perfected the construction of sea-going vessels of timber, the reed-boat was still the form that they preferred, certainly when it came to depicting water or sea-borne voyagers. It was, invariably, associated with their gods, who were determined travellers. Unlike their Egyptian colleagues, however, who used boats principally for their journeys across the stars, the Sumerian gods were more inclined to use the river system for their visits to one another's cities and in the course of their godly activities.

Islands, such as Bahrain, have always been invested with a mysterious and numinous quality. Early seamen must always have recognized gratefully their presence in the middle of an otherwise hostile element; often they have been consecrated to the great goddesses who, in remote antiquity, ruled the assemblies of gods which were later to be dominated by male divinities. To the Egyptians an island was the place of beginnings: 'the Divine Emerging Island' which first rose out of the chaos of waters which formed the Abyss in which the original creator god lay inert.

All islands, if they are to fulfil their mystical character, tend always to be filled with a sense of presence, of something half glimpsed out of the corner of the eye, of sounds heard in dream, uncertainly recollected on awakening, of groves stirring with unseen and elemental forces, of Apollo or Dionysos. Though Bahrain is essentially a desert island (some four fifths of its land surface are stark and barren desert), it nonetheless possesses this mystical quality in generous measure. There are – or were until very recently – parts of the island, near the shore at Zallaq for instance, where the vegetation grows lushly, densely indeed, like primaeval forest. It is not difficult to believe that this is what the world was like, once upon a time. To the early voyagers a landfall near these groves must have seemed like an evidence of the protection of a powerful god, whose presence might be manifested at any moment.

The shore line of Bahrain, in common with other parts of the Gulf, has advanced over the past six thousand years. Many neolithic sites, originally on the shore, are now inland. Bahrain's main Ubaid site, at Al-Markh south of Zallaq, where sherds of Ubaid pottery have been found, was, during the time it was used as an occasional camping area for small fishing expeditions, a little islet, separated from the main island of which, with the fall in the level of the Gulf, it is now a part.[15]

Bahrain is the only safe harbour between the head of the Gulf, where Sumer's seamen would have left the relative safety of their rivers and marshes, and Oman, the source, it is believed, of the copper which they so eagerly sought. In this voyage of some 620 miles, Bahrain must have been singularly well-omened for them.

Bahrain has probably changed little in physical character, other than in its buildings, road systems and all the appurtenances of modernity, since the time of its first settlers. Then as now only the northern part of the island was fertile. Roughly in the centre of the island is its most striking natural feature, the Jebal Dukhan, the Mountain of Smoke. It could only be described as a mountain in a land which is otherwise almost wholly flat: the Jebal Dukhan may be said to tower only modestly, to a height of 432 feet. In the white heat of midday it does shimmer in haze and thus may have earned its 'smoky' epithet.

On and around the mountain some of the earliest remains of Bahrain's history have been found. Here, and more particularly at sites on the coast, the hunters of the late Stone Age chipped their flints, making tools often beautiful as well as efficient.

These once-coastal sites have yielded one of the most significant of Bahrain's archaeological finds: they are the only sites in the lower Gulf from which sickle-blades have been reported.[16]

This suggests that Bahrain participated in early agricultural experiments and practices with which such sickles are associated, although it may be that they were used simply for the harvesting of wild cereals and do not imply their domestication. These sickles, though they must have been somewhat inefficient, for the teeth were set in highly friable materials including earthenware, were used for gathering corn. This is demonstrated by the glitter on the sickles' teeth caused by the silica in cornstalks. Sickles of this and similar types are known from Egypt, Mesopotamia and early Palestinian settlements.

The journey from Bahrain's modern capital city to the site of the city of Dilmun itself takes less than half an hour, turning off the main highway into what was once a dense plantation of palm trees. The landscape changes perceptibly, scrub appears and, as it is penetrated further, the terrain is broken by masonry and blocks of stone straggling over and in the ground, the remains of successive but relatively recent occupations. Suddenly the horizon widens and towards the sea the rearing mass of a great fortress comes into sight, the impressive ruins of one of the guard-forts built by the Portuguese during their occupation of the island in the sixteenth century. A road runs round the castle's moat and, following it, the visitor suddenly comes upon a deep depression in the ground. Within it, below the fort and close to the sea, lie the remains of the cities on which Dilmun's early prosperity was founded.

Amongst the many archaeological sites of importance on Bahrain there are two outstanding ones which demonstrate undoubted links with Sumer (as indeed they do with other cultures to the south and east); one is this large and complex *tel* known as the Qala'at al-Bahrain, whilst the other lies about four miles further along the coast at Barbar. Many similarities in building technique, architectural detail and evident purpose proclaim their Sumerian connections, but with an important difference. Whereas in Sumer itself stone building was comparatively rare, due, reasonably enough, to the absence of local materials, the Bahrain remains are all stone-built and thus preserve more faithfully than many in Mesopotamia the format of buildings from early times. For this reason alone the Bahrain remains should warrant a reputation as some of the more important survivals from the ancient Near East. When the age of some of the Bahrain structures is considered, they deserve to be credited as amongst the most ancient of buildings indeed, for the earliest of them, particularly those at the temple site of Barbar, must have been erected not long after the first centuries of man's discovery of stone architecture itself.

Both sites demonstrate the importance which Bahrain must have held in the minds of the Sumerians and their successors. An interesting light is thrown by the stone-built Bahrain temples on the origins of that most familiar of Sumerian structures, the ziggurat, the stepped temple platform from which the legend of the Tower of Babel descends. The idea of the ziggurat seems to have originated in the need to keep sacred buildings clear of the flood plain and in the very ancient Sumerian practice of regarding certain areas as irrevocably sacred.

A building erected on a sacred site was thought of as being conse-crated for all time. When the mud brick structures needed major repair or when a larger place of worship was called for, the Sumerians simply filled in the courts and chapels of the original temple, raised a mound over it and erected another building on top of it. This procedure produced a stepped effect after the second of such rebuildings. Then the idea grew until the form itself became holy and, all over Sumer and the later Babylonian and Assyrian empires, stepped and terraced ziggurats were built, on the topmost level of which was built the god's most sacred shrine. The essential, if rather obvious, fact that produced this sequence may well have been the realization that mud brick walls cannot be re-used. The destruction of the original temple was thus rationalized by preserving it forever under the mound raised above it.

In Bahrain this did not happen, except perhaps vestigially at Barbar, because the buildings were of stone which, once it was cut and shaped, required a more intensely developed religious sense than the pragmatic Sumerians possessed, to resist re-using it.

The mound which covers the city remains at Qala'at al-Bahrain is some 400 by 800 yards east to west, rising to a height of fifteen yards. This is a very substantial area and compares favourably in scale with the *tels* of Mesopotamia which cover some of Sumer's greatest cities. By no means all of it has been excavated and it is possible that if the whole area were cleared an entire archaic city would be revealed. From its position near the shore and from the visible stone works which lie out in the shallow water, the second of the cities on the site is probably the city from which the Dilmun merchants conducted their wide-ranging trade at the beginning of the second millennium, thus perpetuating a com-mercial tradition already centuries old.

Five ancient (pre-Islamic) levels have been established at the Qala'at al-Bahrain site by the Danish expeditions working there since 1953:[17]

> i. City I, probably contemporary with immediately pre-Akkaddian times, late Early Dynastic III in Sumerian termi-nology *c.* 2450 BC
>
> ii. City II, perhaps founded in the time of Sargon the Great, King of Sumer and Akkad, *c.* 2370 BC and flourishing parti-cularly at the end of the third and the beginning of the second millennium.
>
> iii. City III, corresponding to the Kassite period in Mesopota-mia, *c.* 1600 BC

iv. City IV, corresponding to the Neo-Babylonian period, *c.* 650BC

v. City V, the Greek period, *c.* 300 BC, continuing into the early centuries of the Christian era, before the Revelation of Islam.

It will be seen readily that the second city is probably the most important of those identified on the site. The list of settlements at the Qala'at also shows that there is little significant occupation to be detected in Bahrain before the closing centuries of the third millennium. One solitary Umm an-Nar sherd was found in the lower levels of the foundations, suggesting connections with a culture originating in Oman, whence Dilmun probably obtained the bulk of her copper.[18]

Traces of copper fragments have been found on the beach close to Qala'at al-Bahrain, lending material support to the record of Dilmun's

The city-site at the Qala'at al-Bahrain; an early aerial view showing the extent of the mound and the rich vegetation which, at the time, surrounded it.

trade in which that metal played so considerable a part.[19] Within the ruins have been found the remains of a metalsmith's forge, including a double bellows. It seems likely that Bahrain's exceptional fertility and the fact that the island was well-wooded contributed to her value as a metal-working centre. Only with abundant timber could the fires have been kindled to smelt the raw copper into ingots.

The distillation of liquor also played a part in the early Dilmun economy and rooms specially designed for the pressing of date juice demonstrate the antiquity of a process which may still be seen in use in parts of Arabia. Pottery was manufactured there and inside the ruins was uncovered the workshop of a maker of the distinctive Bahrain stamp seals, the discovery of which has added a new dimension to Bahrain's archaeology and to the minor arts of the ancient world.

The walls of Qala'at al-Bahrain have survived the long ages since they were built remarkably well. In the area still uncovered today the buildings that remain date, in the most part, from the seventh century BC and, like many others in the island, are built with limestone cut from Bahrain's little neighbouring island, Jidda. Broad stairways and high gates also survive and still show the finely carved semi-circular hinge stones designed to bear the weight of massive doors. But Qala'at al-Bahrain has a history which reaches back two thousand years before this city flourished, at the very end of Dilmun's history.

The first city at Qala'at al-Bahrain was built in the second half of the third millennium and endured until it was destroyed, probably during the twenty-fourth century BC and maybe by the conquering armies of Sargon the Great who, it will be recalled, proudly claimed Dilmun as part of his Empire. When he 'washed his spears in the waters of the Gulf' he may have referred to his conquest and pillaging of the sacred island, whose ruler had presumably displayed some reluctance at being drawn into the Akkadian's empire.

This period has yielded one of the characteristic pottery types, particular to the island. These vessels are large with a highly distinctive chain ridge decoration; a number of early seals and a handsome steatite *pyxis* engraved with geometric designs and whorls, of which other examples have been found at Barbar, were also found in the first city levels. The steatite (or, more strictly, chlorite) vessel is typical of a product found extensively in other eastern Arabian contexts. One of the steatite vessels is intact and of fine workmanship. It had three lugs which suggest that it may have been suspended. This, with its slightly curving sides and outline, gives it the appearance of the alabaster vessels from the Cyclades with which it may be approximately contemporary.

Chlorite, as well as being the most popular and the most practical material for the fashioning of the Dilmun seals, was also favoured by Sumerian craftsmen for making all kinds of vessels.[20] Its use continued for over two thousand years with the same general profile and decoration being turned out throughout that time. One steatite pot from Bahrain has a cross engraved on it as well as the typical dotted circle which frequently runs round the rims of the pots. One of the anomalies of Bahrain's archaeology is that no examples have yet been found[21] of the highly decorated chlorite vessels which are a characteristic of early Sumerian sites and of those in eastern Arabia and Elam in the early centuries of the third millennium. These objects were clearly highly regarded and were traded over extensive distances; their decoration is remarkable and their workmanship often very fine. It is curious that none has been found, so far, in Bahrain and there is no immediately obvious explanation why this should be so.

From the Qala'at al-Bahrain City I comes a fragmentary inscription, impressed on the inner rim of a large clay jar so that it could easily be read by tilting the pot; it gives a measure of capacity. The mount is expressed as:

2 pani 4 sar 7 qa

and has been equated to c. 118.8 pints.[22]

Excavations at Qala'at al-Bahrain; most of what can be seen here are buildings from City IV, c. 650 BC.

After its supposed Sargonid destruction, this city was rebuilt, but this time with a high stone rampart, presumably in the hope that its people would be secure against a second attack. At various places around the perimeter of the mound the city wall of the second foundation can be seen.

This second city probably survived until well after the turn of the third millennium and was the southern location of the Alik Tilmun, the guild of energetic merchants from Ur who were responsible for so much of Bahrain's ancient prosperity. More seals were found on this level as well as Indus Valley weights, which reflect the close commercial relations which existed between Bahrain and the cities of Harappa and Moenjo-Daro. City II is now thought to be contemporary with the first temples of Barbar.[23] There is no doubt that the time during which it flourished was the highest point of Bahrain's ancient prosperity and influence.

Recent estimates of the number of burials represented by the Bahrain moundfields have also produced an estimation of the likely population of City II at the Qala'at al-Bahrain. The latest informed figure is 6700, based on the area occupied within the city walls; setting this figure against the population of the island as a whole, indicated by the number of burials, would suggest a total population of upwards of sixty thousand inhabitants.[24]

The extensive and perplexing necropolis of Bahrain will be described later and the point made that little enough is known of the people who were laid in the mound-tombs; however, there can be little doubt that they were the people who lived and flourished at the various cities at Qala'at al-Bahrain. Ivory ornaments were often placed in the tombs and ivory was worked at the Qala'at al-Bahrain, for a tusk prepared for further working by an ancient craftsman has been found there.[25] In all probability the ivory came from Melukhkha, the Indus Valley region where the elephant was indigenous and much venerated.

The next level at Qala'at al-Bahrain, the third city, appears to be contemporary with the period when the Kassites, a people from the mountains of Iran, ruled Mesopotamia. They were a rather barbarous people whose art was certainly not as distinguished as that of others among the ruling peoples of the land; however, they left their traces in Bahrain: tall, slender, roughly made pots and some of the very few cuneiform tablets yet to be found there, which are, as yet, unpublished. By the Carbon-14 process it has been possible to date the destruction of the city to a median date of 1190 BC ± sixty years. This reading was obtained from date stones found in ruins, a witness to the product (the

The walls of City II, *c.* 2000 BC, surrounded the site. They are substantial constructions, built after the destruction of the first, much smaller City I settlement.

Sum Dilmun in Sumerian) whose excellence identified Dilmun in the minds of the ancients as strongly as its role as the Holy Land. The 'Kassite' city was clearly handsome, with a large, rectangular palace with parallel rooms on either side of it as one of its principal monuments. It is from the later years of the Kassite period that the correspondence survives between Ili-ippasra and Ililiya, who was resident in Dilmun. It may be that Ililiya's letters were sent from this very place, around 1370 BC.

The fourth city was rich in finds, dating from the neo-Babylonian period. From this time, much later than the first great days of Dilmun, came a hoard of silver dated, by means of a fine silver signet ring bearing an Egyptian-style cartouche,[26] from the seventh century BC. This hoard was first thought to demonstrate the several links between Bahrain and the great civilization of the Nile Valley, which existed despite the two seas and the immense Arabian desert which separate them. However, later research suggests that the ring is Egyptianized Phoenician work (one of the few positive Phoenician links with Bahrain actually to be identified) and probably indicates a connection with that other great emporium of the ancient world, Byblos in the Lebanon. It was thought that the hoard had been buried deliberately, probably by a silversmith to whom it belonged, during the time of the invasions and wars in the Near East which the records of the period reveal. However, recent research has proposed that much of the silver may be an early evidence of 'money', the tokens and silver pieces that were used before the introduction of coinage.

It is this city which is open to the sky and the exploration of visitors, and is approximately contemporary with Uperi, a King of Dilmun known from the Assyrian records.[27] One of the most readily identifiable remains is a large, almost square, white limestone pillar base, near the bottom of a flight of broad, shallow steps, Behind the pillar base a woman was found buried in one of the terracotta, bitumen-coated 'bath-tub' coffins, reminiscent of, but in no sense connected with, the Mycenaean *larnax*. Scattered around this area other burials were discovered, including one which yielded some finely-made bronze objects, including a bowl and a wine-dipper. Some of the burials were of children, their small bodies placed in simple pots.[28] Others, however, were such that a new light was cast on the beliefs and cult practices of the people of Dilmun *c.*700 BC and on their continuity over a very long time. The cult also revealed much more ancient connections.

Sunk in the floor of the buildings were several small pits, seven of which contained the coiled skeletons of serpents. Beads were also found in close proximity to the snake burials.

The discovery was made in 1957 and it set up echoes of one of the incidents in the Gilgamesh epic (see Chapter IX), when the serpent steals from the King of Uruk the flower of eternal youth which he had wrested from the sea-bed after many long and perilous adventures.

In Zallaq, a small town in the centre of Bahrain's western coast, so-called 'phallic' stone pillars were discovered in 1956; they have been removed from their original location.[29] Phallic objects, like beauty, tend often to be in the eye of the beholder. Whatever these are, one now

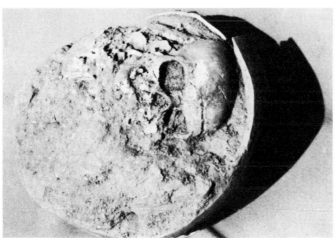

A bronze 'wine-dipper' and other objects excavated at Qala'at al-Bahrain, suggesting a fairly sumptuous way of life. (*Bahrain National Museum*).

Babies, who died prematurely, were often buried in pots. (*Bahrain National Museum*).

137

stands at Barbar, whilst the others are in Denmark waiting to be returned to Bahrain. Though they date from a much earlier period than the snake burials (probably from the third millennium or the early second) and their allegedly phallic character depends upon a fairly subjective judgement, it is tempting to associate Gilgamesh-Serpent-Fertility-Phalloi-Snake Burials all in one neat equation and postulate the existence on the island of a snake cult of great antiquity. To many of the ancients, the serpent embodied the mysterious, hidden powers of the life-giving earth. An architectural fragment from Abu Dhabi, down the Gulf from Bahrain, whose archaeology is closely linked with it, demonstrates this strongly since snake and phallus have become one.[30]

The last level of Qala'at al-Bahrain in the pre-Islamic period, the fifth city, testifies to the extent of Bahrain's trade at the time with the Hellenistic world, for extensive finds of Attic ware pottery have been made there. This was the city which followed Alexander's blazing career but it has also yielded artefacts which suggest that once again the trade to India was open, demonstrated in particular by an attractive pottery figure of a girl of unmistakably Indian type.

Throughout the early history of Bahrain there are evidences, as might well be expected, of connections with cultures on the mainland of Saudi Arabia. The fifth Qala'at al-Bahrain city has for example, produced a number of miniature altars in pottery and a fragment of a steatopygous (i.e. with abnormally fat buttocks and thighs) pottery figure which make it clear that the island shared, to some degree at least, the goddess-cult then prevailing in Saudi Arabia. This was perhaps centred around Thaj, where similar material has been recovered from surface sites in the vicinity of that extensive desert city.

After this period, the Qala'at al-Bahrain site appears to have been abandoned until Islamic times. On the face of it, this long time gap seems improbable and merely points again to the importance of further excavation in the area. But, as with the written records of the island, it is Alexander and his times that close the Qala'at's record in antiquity.

Just outside the gateway of the fifth city was found a pottery jar, buried in the ground, presumably to hide it either from its owner or from potential robbers. Inside the vessel were found some 300 silver coins dating from the reign of one of the Antiochid kings, of the same house as he for whom Berossus wrote his *Babyloniaca*.[31] The coins are magnificent, most of them seemingly uncirculated tetradrachms. The coins bear a portrait of Alexander himself, wearing the horned head-dress in which he is identified as Herakles, that over-muscled hero whose legend seems to have absorbed incidents from the much earlier,

One of the so-called 'phallic' stones, now erected near the temple site at Barbar.

if equally substantially legendary career of the noble Sumerian king Gilgamesh. Alexander assumed the horns after he had been recognized by the priests of Siwa as the son of the ram-headed god Amon and hence true Pharaoh of Egypt. The Alexander hoard makes a splendid *terminus* to the record of the cities which had been established on the island's northern shore and which had flourished there at least two thousand years before the Macedonian's lifetime.

About four miles to the west of the Qala'at al-Bahrain lies the island's other principal site, this time one with still more striking Sumerian connections, the great temple complex of Barbar.[32] Barbar lies on the northern shore of Bahrain facing up the Gulf to Sumer. Remarkably enough, its significance was first suggested by Durand on his pioneering survey of the island in 1878–9, a tribute indeed to his perception.[33] The Barbar mound is just under an acre in extent and at once demonstrates the size of the complex of buildings it conceals. It is

The hoard of silver coins, many of them apparently uncirculated, found in the ruins of City V, which flourished during a time of considerable commercial activity by the successors of Alexander in the area. Many of the coins bear the portrait of the king; they were minted by Antiochos I, the Seleucid king, *c.* 280 BC.

now encircled by palm plantations, the second and third temples are each superimposed upon its predecessor.

The earliest temple was built on a rectangular platform approximately 80 feet long and 50–55 feet wide which may have been enlarged at a later stage. It was surrounded by a stone wall and there were a number of small stone-built rooms on its summit surrounding an open courtyard. The temple appears to have been built on a carefully laid layer of clean sand, above which, in turn, a layer of blue clay had been put down. A further layer of sand was then piled over the mound, presumably to ensure its ritual cleanliness before building actually began. Even in its first phase, the element of water which, as will be seen, was probably the most important factor in the rituals enacted at Barbar, already appears. In the south-western corner of this early complex two staircases led down to a square-built well.

It has been noted already that the Barbar temples have marked Sumerian connotations, though with notable differences which may well be the consequence of local Dilmunite influence. Two essentially Sumerian characteristics in relation to their sacred buildings may, however, be observed here: first, the buildings of the Barbar temples followed the practice of building over temples and shrines which had outlived their purpose or which required renewing, thus demonstrating the belief in the inalienably sacred character of a place once it had been consecrated to the service of the gods. This custom was observed when Temple II came to be built. Temple I was largely dismantled but the central cult complex was allowed to stand and the new altars raised above it, showing this aspect of Sumerian influence at work over a period of five hundred years.

The other Sumerian practice which is represented at Barbar is to be seen in the burying of 'foundation deposits', quantities of pottery and metal objects ceremonially laid in the earth at the time of building,

Excavations below the Qala'at al-Bahrain.

presumably as votive offerings to the chthonic gods. At Barbar the excavators found nearly a hundred conical clay beakers, all ritually broken, in the fill of the temple platform.[34] These beakers were perhaps used in a ritual feast at the time when the temple was first inaugurated. A small cylinder-shaped jar of limestone was also found under the ramp leading up to the temple.

The second temple was an extension and enlargement of the first, but it broadly followed the same design. The central platform was retained though it was raised. It marked the sacred area but it was surrounded by a lower terrace, confined by an oval wall, some 220 feet in length; about 90 feet of the outer wall still remains. To the south of the temple a wide staircase, which is still standing, led up to the oval terrace. The foot of the staircase, incidentally, marks the ground level as it then was, showing how the land has risen over the ensuing forty-five centuries: this area around the temple is still largely unexcavated.

An additional feature, the 'sacrificial area', was added to the complex at this time. It is to be seen to the east of the site: an oval courtyard, lying somewhat below the level of the principal terrace and reached by a gradually descending ramp. In this area was found a thick layer of ash (still indeed to be seen towards the end of the oval, to the right), which contained the burnt bones of sacrificial animals.

The most notable feature of the second temple was, of course, the sacred well, or spring, perhaps the very *absu* (the Abyss of subterranean waters) of Enki. A long staircase, now partly destroyed, led from the terrace to the well, the stone steps actually reaching down into

Pottery beakers were frequently buried in the foundations of Sumerian temples. These were found in the foundations of the first temple at Barbar.

The small, densely packed stone work of the 'sacrificial area' at Barbar.

These alabaster vases were found beneath one of the stairways of the second temple. (*Department of Antiquities, Bahrain*).

The well, still unexcavated, associated with the third temple at Barbar.

the water. The well, like so much of Barbar, is constructed from finely cut stone blocks, from stone brought from Bahrain's nearby island, Jidda; Temple I, on the other hand, was built from a local Bahrain stone.

That the temples, given their Sumerian connections, are built largely of stone is itself of great interest: for the Sumerians built in baked mud bricks, their land being entirely bereft of stone, which in Bahrain was plentiful. Evidently, the island even then possessed skilled craftsmen who could handle the fine-grained limestone, working to the designs and instructions of some unknown architect who, if not a Dilmunite (though he may well have been), knew much about the techniques of building in a material which must largely have been strange to the people who apparently inspired the temple's construction.

The third temple, perhaps built around the end of the third and in use during the early centuries of the second millennium BC, was larger again than its predecessors. In the centre of the site a square platform was enclosed by a massive stone wall of finely cut masonry. Along the wall towards the west and north, are remains of a room whilst the platform itself was paved with limestone slabs. Two circular offering tables of finely cut stone with a low altar between them still stand in the middle of the courtyard. East of the offering tables three stone altars once stood. To the south-west, three stone blocks are standing, each pierced with a round hole. It has been suggested that these were used for tethering the sacrificial animals.

In the north-eastern corner of the courtyard was a square pit containing rich foundation deposits, all of copper.[35] This itself is of some significance since the mercantile Dilmun, the secular counterpart of Dilmun the sacred land, depended on the copper trade for its exceptional prosperity.

The third temple's terrace probably covered an area some 50 square feet and faced to the north. It is not known for certain if the sacred well, and the handsome processional staircase that led to it from the temple platform built for the second temple, were incorporated into the new structure. Standing high above the surrounding buildings, which probably clustered around its walls and the landscape in which the whole complex was set, the temple, gleaming white, would have been impressive indeed.

One curious survival from the third temple may still be seen in the gypsum mortar or 'juss' which was used to bond the stones in the wall foundations on the west side of the upper terrace and on the floor of another building to the north-west of the main temple. The print of a large naked foot is clearly impressed in the mortar.[36] A number of footprints and some handprints have been found in the temple area; there are also the paw-marks of a dog, showing that even in such remote times, where men were, dogs were close-by. The foot was one of the most frequently employed symbols in the iconography of the Dilmun seals which are described later in this survey. However, there is no evidence whether the footprints at Barbar are deliberate or merely the consequence of chance, the footsteps of a workman on the site, perhaps preserved by accident for the past four thousand years.

Many of the objects which have been recovered from the Barbar site are of very fine quality indeed and testify eloquently to the high standard of culture which flourished in Bahrain in the third millennium BC. Barbar produced a very distinctive type of pottery (now known as 'Barbar Ware') which was first identified on the site. It can be recognized easily by its marked horizontal ridging.

The Sumerians respected the tools of the trades which the people practised. Gods were placed in charge of them and poems celebrated their qualities. It is not surprising therefore to find at Barbar, in the second temple deposit, a copper axe and a copper adze, the one concerned with building, the other with agriculture.[37]

Copper 'models' of spearheads and crescent-shaped shafthole axes were found in the 'fill' of the central platform, as well as beads of

At various places on the gypsum plasterwork at the Temple site at Barbar are footprints, probably of the workers who built the third temple. At least one of them must have been notable for the size of his feet (*Forshistorisk Museum Moesgard*).

marble, lapis lazuli and carnelian. Lapis was one of the products frequently identified with Dilmun; it was traded as far as Egypt but its only known source is far to the east at Badakhshan, in Afghanistan. A small strip of gold was also found in the deposit.[38]

Some of the most attractive products of ancient Bahrain recovered from the Barbar site are examples of the 'Dilmun seals' which are so specially identified with Bahrain and the lands around it at this time. Several seals were found at Barbar, including a group from the sacred well itself. It has been suggested[40] that these were thrown into the well in some sort of ritual act, presumably to draw to the attention of the resident divinity, Enki himself no doubt, the needs and aspirations of the seals' owners.

The seals all come from the third temple levels. They are of the fully developed type typical of Bahrain and Failakah at the end of the third millennium and the early years of the second.[41] This was the time of Dilmun's commercial greatness and the seals, in all probability, are the 'trade marks' of merchant companies and families based in Bahrain but trading with Sumer in the north, Oman in the south and, to the east, the great Indus Valley cities such as Moenjo-Daro and Harappa.

A particularly fine pottery sherd also survives which shows a Dilmun seal's impression very clearly.[42] This was found actually in the well at Barbar, and shows a heroic figure grasping two animals by their necks, exercising his will over them.

This design is of great antiquity. It is known from late fourth millennium Sumer, from south-western Iran, where some authorities believed it originated and, far away to the east, from Egypt.[43] There its presence in late pre-dynastic times, at the end of the fourth millennium, has prompted speculation about the extent of influences from the Gulf and Mesopotamia which Egypt experienced at the time immediately before the unification of the two Kingdoms of the Nile Valley under the

This pottery sherd is impressed with a Dilmun seal. The design is of great antiquity; versions of it are found throughout Mesopotamia and as far away as Egypt (*Forshistorisk Museum Moesgard*).

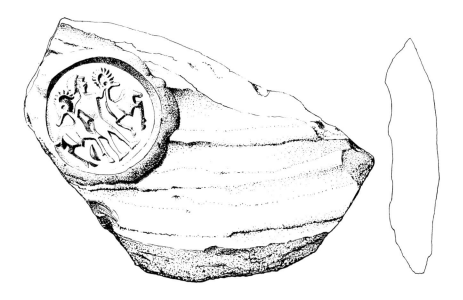

first Pharaohs. Some authorities, including Petrie, have believed that Mesopotamian influences came to Egypt by the intervention of 'the islanders of the Gulf'.[44]

Music was a notable feature of all Sumerian religious ceremonies. Many representations of musical performance have come down to us, including some enchanting scenes featuring animals as the musicians. But in the temple ceremonies at Barbar we must assume that solemn and sonorous melodies would have risen from the courtyards, to charm the gods. The chanting of the priests was no doubt matched by the sound of pipes, harps, flutes and percussion instruments, including drums, rattles and something very like modern castanets.

This concern of the Sumerian life-style with music is hinted at in Barbar. Amongst the deposits of the second temple was a small copper rattle, perhaps from the percussion department of an ancient orchestra, and the most important and handsome find of all, a majestic bull's head, finely cast in copper.[45] Though it is supposition, it is possible that this fine piece ornamented the sounding box of a Sumerian lyre, of the type which was found in the great death-pit at Ur and so miraculously preserved by Sir Leonard Woolley. Stringed instruments bearing richly adorned animal heads were characteristic of Sumerian temple and royal ceremonies and it is certainly possible that the Barbar bull-head served this amiable purpose. A Dilmun seal from Failakah, which during the third millennium was part, in all probability, of Dilmun's 'empire' (together with much of the eastern region of Saudi Arabia) shows a bull-headed lyre of just this sort.[46]

The artefacts recovered from Barbar are among the most interesting and significant to be found in Bahrain and contribute much to an understanding of the religious practices and beliefs of the Dilmunites of four thousand years and more ago. Within the precincts of the first and most ancient temple was a double line of cut stone blocks, eight in all, set by the temple's western side. Cut into the blocks' upper surfaces were two square holes (in one case, three holes) which were originally lined with a copper sheeting, bonded to the stone with bitumen. Through the copper, nails had been driven, their points inwards and in some cases with wood still adhering to them. It seems likely that they were either the supports for wooden columns or for the bases of wooden statues: the third hole in one of the blocks is explained as having secured a staff or wand carried by one of the figures. On the side of one of the blocks two figures of men are roughly carved, one with down-turned arms, the other with his arms raised, the fingers of each hand splayed out.

Though the remains of the second temple are much the best preserved and extensive on the site, the third temple at Barbar was probably the most complex and sophisticated. By the time it was built, the consecrated area, the main sanctuary, was raised high above the surrounding landscape. A double circular stone plinth supported the temple's main altars with, facing them, a stone seat or throne with a libation altar before it. A pit of offerings, stone-lined and thus deliberately built as an integral part of the Barbar temple like its Sumerian parallels, was found beyond this altar and in it were alabaster vases, the copper figures of a naked worshipper, perhaps a priest (which may originally have served as a handle of a mirror) and of a bird. Three of the alabaster vases were virtually in perfect condition, the others in fragments; similar ones have been discovered at Ur and can reasonably be ascribed to the latter part of the third millennium.[47]

An extensive collection of the horizontally-ridged type of pottery, which is now described using 'Barbar' as its find-site, has been recovered; the other most distinctive Bahraini pottery is the 'chain-ridge' ware. Some of this pottery would seem to have been exported to Sumer, for examples have been found in early dynastic tombs in Ur. A

The great third-millennium temple site at Barbar during its re-excavation. At the left is the *absu* or sacred well; a processional way leads from the well to the upper terrace, whilst, to the right, the 'sacrificial area' (oval in shape) is also connected with the terrace by a ramp. (*Department of Antiquities, Bahrain*).

stone vessel decorated with concentric circles is also similar to others found in Ur burials of the same period.[48]

As would be expected in what appears to have been the most important sanctuary on an island whose ancient economy was derived, to a significant degree, from the copper trade, a considerable amount of copper (and later bronze) artefacts has been recovered from Barbar. Among them were numerous arrowheads of a type which once again recalls similar examples from Ur, and a quantity of copper axeheads. Many of the axes recovered from Bahraini sites are purely votive and could never have been functional.

The presence at Barbar of the bull head mentioned above, with its great upcurving horns, provides an echo of that remote time when the Sumerians and their predecessors were beginning to develop the most important characteristic of their splendid and beneficent culture. The bull or ox head, the *bucranium*, is one of the earliest pictographs and was used to symbolize, reasonably enough, an ox. This sign appears on the earliest tablets of what was to develop into formal writing: the early pictographs developed successively through abstractions of the original ox-head shape to the final cuneiform characters.[49]

The *bucranium* was a powerful symbol from times as early as the Anatolian settlements at Haçilar and Catal Hüyük on the Konya plain.

Amongst the copper votive offerings found in the temple at Barbar were this figure of a worshipper, probably the handle of a mirror, and a bird.

Barbar is the type-site for a distinctive style of pottery which is now identified with third-millennium Bahrain. Examples of it have been found in other sites around the Gulf and in Sumer.

There, bull heads were set up as elements in the design of the shrines which were so important a feature of these little 'cities'. Similarly, Egypt honoured the bull head; in one of the First Dynasty royal tombs at Saqqarah a number of bulls' skulls were placed on a low platform at the sides of the tomb of King Udimu.[50] Queen Her-Neith was also buried in a tomb decorated with the skulls of bulls.[51]

In the Gulf the *bucranium* appears frequently as a motif on the seals which are peculiar to the culture of the region. All in all it is a potent and enduring symbol from the earliest times. However, descending through a different line, through the north of the land into Syria, the ox head became the first letter of the Phoenician script which is accepted as the origin of the modern Latin alphabet. Thus the Sumerian ox head symbol became eventually the alpha of the Greeks and is also preserved in the first sign of the Roman script. The *bucranium* was a favoured motif in Mesopotamian design from the very earliest, where it underwent many refinements and adaptations, moving from the naturalistic to a more and more abstract interpretation, a development which was

151

repeated in its progress from pictograph to cuneiform. It is particularly striking in the beautiful, very early pottery from northern Mesopotamian sites: in a stylized form it is also found in the repertory of Ubaid potters and painters.

It is possible only to speculate about the god or gods who were worshipped at Barbar. Although the most important divinity to be worshipped in Dilmun was probably Enki, other Sumerian deities were identified with the island. Thus, Inanna was worshipped in a temple at Ur called E-Dilmun-na, commemorating her links with the island.[51a] Dilmun was a land of the gods, and it is not surprising, therefore, that majestic temples should have been set up there in their honour. The kings of Sumer congratulated themselves on their piety in restoring the temples when they fell into decay. Thus Warad-Sin (second half of the nineteenth century BC), in a long inscription in Ur which refers to E-Dilmun-na, says:

> For Inanna the lady clad in great splendour wielding all the powers, eldest daughter of Sin, his lady: Warad-Sin, the prince who favours Nippur, nourisher of Ur, who takes thought for Girsu with Lagash, who reverences E-barra, King of Larsa, King of Sumer and Akkad, the strong one who seeks out the [divine] oracles and executes their purpose, who builds anew the house of the gods, am I: on whom Enki bestowed a wide understanding to perform the duties of the City. Because of this, for Inanna my lady, with my prayer [I restored] E-Dilmun-na her dwelling of rest and of heart's delight. That the eye might see and its interior might be liked I enlarged its area more than before. Unto days to come for my life I built it: its head I raised and made like a mountain. Over my works may Inanna my lady rejoice. Length of days, years of abundance, a throne securely based, a sceptre to subdue the people as a gift may she grant me.[51b]

E-Dilmun-na seems always to have been of special significance to the Sumerians, again, perhaps because of the nature of Dilmun itself. If it was 'the place of assembly' of the people on their journey to Sumer, this is understandable enough. The cult centre of Sin-Nanna was at Ur, at the edge of the desert out of which poured perpetually floods of wild nomads who variously threatened and were absorbed by the Sumerian cities, eventually enriching them immeasurably but at the expense of their survival. Sin-Nanna was one of the greatest of the gods and many cities other than Ur honoured him with temples and shrines. The successive levels of Sin temples found at Khafajah show that from the earliest times, the moon-god was a divinity to whom worship was elaborately given. It has been observed that the moon is the prototype of the universal god to desert people and that the Semitic tribes followed this practice. Moon temples were built by the pre-Islamic Arabs who, like their ancestors, considered the planet mild and beneficient, an understandable view for a people who had to endure the daily torments of the sun at its height. Thus it is argued, Sin-Nanna would naturally be a god of special significance and affection to the people of the desert as they first settled in the city of Ur, on the desert's fringe.

In the light of the discovery of a temple at Barbar in Bahrain, which is very similar in at least one important respect with the temple built to the glory of Sin in Khafajah, it is interesting that a fragment from a hymn to the moon-god speaks of 'the temple [Sagnamsar] which is the mount of Dilmun'. It seems wholly possible that this refers to a temple complex in Dilmun, perhaps that at Barbar itself. Whilst the hymn is addressed to Sin-Nanna, some commentators have seen the divinity being celebrated as the ubiquitous Enki. This view is strengthened by one interpretation of Sagnamsar as meaning that it is consecrated to the 'benefactor of writing', an appropriate epithet for the god of wisdom.

Two recent studies into the meaning of the name 'Barbar' are of interest in that, whilst both of them point to quite different conclusions, both suggest that the origin of the name may reach back to the time when the temples themselves were flourishing. 'Barbar' is not an Arabic word: its meaning must therefore be sought elsewhere.

One scholar[51c] suggests that 'Barbar' may convey the meaning 'foreigners': this would imply perhaps that the builders of the temples were not indigenous to Bahrain and were identified by the local Dilmunites as such. However, the same authority goes on to note that Samas, the sun-god, a significant divinity in Sumer and, like Enki, generally well disposed to man, was worshipped in the Sumerian city of Larsa in temples called e-babbar, which, he notes, is usually translated as the 'White House'. In Sumerian bab bar also means 'sunrise' and Dilmun was celebrated as 'the land of sunrise'.

The two principal Bahraini sites known to date, the Qala'at al-Bahrain and Barbar, prompt another question about the sacred and particular character of the island in Sumerian times. All Sumerian cities were built around the temple, which, in most cases, was their original purpose for coming into existence. The process of city-making is complex and various: in the case of the proto-Sumerian cities it seems likely that they began as cult centres, serving the needs of a group of villages and settlements of which the city in its beginnings formed the nucleus. The city was consecrated to one or several of the gods; it belonged to them. No city was ever built without its temple.

Except for the city at the Qala'at al-Bahrain, all the buildings so far known there are secular, consecrated to trade rather than to the honour of the gods. Yet Dilmun was a land of temples: such areas in the north of the island that have as yet been surveyed confirm the presence of many large structures and each site that has been excavated, other than the tomb-fields, has produced a crop of sacred buildings. In the region of Barbar, for example, there is little doubt that further excavations will produce more temples.

The explanation, of course, may lie in the exceptional sanctity of the entire island.[52] It was the island, perhaps, that was the veritable cult centre, consecrated forever to the high gods. The sea encompassed it rather than the walls of other, lesser centres. Within its sea-girded walls, everything would have been sacred. If the main temple was located at Barbar (and indeed if it does not still await discovery) four miles or so from the city, this would not have been a material consideration; city and temples alike would all have been contained within the island's own holy precincts. In truth Dilmun was the first, the archetypal Holy Land, the place of assembly not only of the people but of the gods.

Another site, at Umm es Sejour, a mile to the west of Diraz, has produced some unexpected finds, which may bear upon this matter of the religious character in the island. The site is a small well-temple which achieved a later celebrity when, according to legend, the Caliph Abdul Malik Ibn Marwan, incensed at the Bahrainis' reversion to their ancient gods in the early years of Islam (the famous 'Apostasy'), invaded the island and destroyed the well as a punishment for the people's heterodoxy.[53] However, long before this, there was a sacred building here and in its ruins were found the headless statues of two stone animals. They were probably the ornaments of a portal or the decoration of a shrine built in the high days of Dilmun's influence, in the third millennium before our era; carved in limestone, the animals have been decapitated by some unkown zealot who, presumably, disapproved enough of them to wish to ensure their ritual 'killing'.

The architecture of the Barbar temples reveals a high technical standard, particularly in the careful shaping of the ashlar blocks from which the structures and the great well or bath were built. The area of sacrifice contained a number of blocks which, when assembled, formed two circular structures; around the temples a wall was built which also curved gently at its corners. Parts of the ashlar walls demonstrate one interesting characteristic: an irregular shaping of the stone courses which fit into each other, a technique of strengthening stone walls more typical of Egypt in the third millennium than of Sumer. Indeed, the assurance with which stone is handled both at Qala'at al-Bahrain and at Barbar is reminiscent more of the authority with which Egyptians built than of the work of Sumerian architects.[54]

The ashlar stone work at Barbar is characteristic of the later temples; in the first structure the stones are small, packed together tightly. They suggest an unfamiliarity with the properties of stone on a large scale: indeed they have prompted one authority to speculate whether they may not represent the work of craftsmen who were only beginning to find their way in its use, in contrast with the assurance with which the later monumental courses are handled.[55]

The site at Barbar is perhaps the most important in the Arabian Gulf yet to be excavated. It was first uncovered by the Danes between 1955 and 1963.[56] After its first clearance the site was re-filled for its protection. It was then decided, in 1983, to clear it in its entirety of excavated areas and to conserve the remains as a monument, so that visitors could comprehend something of its extent and significance. This has now been achieved, under the control of the Department of Antiquities of the State of Bahrain.[57]

These apparently deliberately decapitated animals were recovered from another of the island's sacred wells, this time at Diraz.

There are many other sites of cardinal archaeological importance in Bahrain. There is, too, an increasing awareness of their significance amongst the archaeological community, alerted by the spectacular success of the Danish excavations.

In the course of 1971 the Committee for Arabian and Gulf Studies was set up in London at the initiative of a number of scholars (and one non-scholar) with special interests in the developing field of archaeological and related studies in the east Arabian states. The Committee was a modest one in its objectives and, as it turned out, in its achievements. However, it was not undistinguished in its constitution; every major institution concerned with the region was represented on it. The British Museum led it, supported by the Institute of Archaeology and the Royal Academy in whose splendid headquarters in Burlington House, Piccadilly, its meetings were convened. A trio of the most eminent archaeological knights then extant lent lustre to its assemblies. Its funds were drawn from modest subventions from public funds and some backing from British companies trading in the area who generously committed themselves to support its work. The British committee proposed that it should send a small team to Bahrain to work on three sites which had previously been identified as being likely to repay effort. These were Al-Markh, Diraz East, near the 'Well of the Bulls' dug by the Danes in the 'fifties, and a later site at Jannusan North. The British worked in Bahrain from 1973 to 1976.

Considerable interest had been kindled in 1971 in archaeological circles by the recognition of Ubaid pottery on eastern Arabian sites.[58] The Arabian sites had been expertly and professionally excavated: altogether more than forty sites have been identified. Subsequently Ubaid pottery had been found at al-Da'asa, at Ras Abaruk, Dukhan and in the region of Bir Zikrit in Qatar.[59] Thus far no such very early pottery had been found in Bahrain.

The British team selected Al-Markh as a consequence of some sherds having been found on the surface of the site and identified as Ubaid in 1971.[60] Al-Markh lies inland from the west coast, south of the village of Zallaq. It is a low sand-covered mound and north and east of it are *sabkha*, the treacherous flats where evaporation has produced a fragile crust of impacted sand. There are considerable quantities of flint and of fish and other animal bones scattered about.

The expedition found and excavated a number of what they believed to be fire pits used for cooking. They detected two phases on the site, the earlier one when fish were predominantly represented in the remains and a later one when mammal bones became significant and evidently formed an important part of the diet of the site's occupants. The animals represented included the Bahrain hare, which still lives around the site, the dugong, the sea-cow now rarely if ever seen in Gulf waters, and, most frequently, the goat. A change in the technique of fish hunting was suggested to the excavators by the fact that in the earlier levels the fish species tended to be small whilst in the later ones they were generally larger and 'included more carnivorous fish'. It was suggested that these 'may have been caught by hook and line, by harpoon or by bow and arrow'. A greater density of flints in the upper levels compared with that of the lower suggested that more flints would have been needed to butcher the larger mammals and larger fish than would have been required for the small species.[61]

A statistical analysis of the pottery sherds found at Al-Markh led to the conclusion, at first sight surprising, that only in the earlier occupations of the site had pottery been used. The sherds are painted and are dated to c. 3800 BC.[62]

It seems most likely that there was no permanent settlement at Al-Markh at this early fourth-millennium date, but rather that it was occupied seasonally by hunters or fishermen coming from some other place. At the time the sea level in the Gulf was somewhat higher than it is today. As a result Al-Markh was a small islet off the coast of the main island in the Bahrain group. It would be interesting to know more about the people who used the site then and, particularly, of how and by what means they sailed to the island, presumably from the Arabian shore, some miles away. But of this sort of information, not surprisingly, the little site at Al-Markh, sparse even by the most austere standards of desert archaeology, communicates nothing.

Diraz East, the other important site to be dug by the British expedition, is part of a substantial third-millennium settlement in the fertile northern sector of the island. It has always been fertile and has been inhabited consistently at least since the Barbar periods. An isolated Ubaid sherd was found there.

What appear to be the remains of an important third-millennium building was described by its excavators as 'a temple'; since a partly destroyed altar was found in the remains of the building, this seems reasonable enough. The building itself is notable for the rows of large columns which originally stood inside it. There was a large stone and mortar basin adjacent to the building, though this was suspected of being later in date than the building itself, perhaps of the late Babylonian period. Sherds from pottery of this time were found and in one of the rooms the burials of at least five persons, dating from late Babylonian times, were discovered. A 'snake bowl', like the ones from the Qala'at al-Bahrain, was found but it was empty. Two crude stamp seals were also found.[63]

Because of its value as an agricultural area, many of Diraz's ancient sites have been disturbed. The discovery of the temple at Diraz East is significant however, for if it is third millennium in origin, then it is quite unlike any other building of the period known from Bahraini sites. Interestingly, if only because of the frequency with which the creature is portrayed on Dilmun seals, Diraz is notorious for the number of scorpions which abound there and which, even now, make excavation difficult.[64] To this day the scorpion, so often shown circling the seals and in the designs they display, seems to guard Diraz from intruders.

A brief excavation was conducted by the Expedition at Aali East which uncovered a double-chambered tomb of the seventh century BC. Though the tomb had been conscientiously robbed in antiquity, three seals had been overlooked. A cylinder seal, dating to c.650 BC, is of neo-Babylonian format. A stamp seal with the round boss on the reverse is obviously derived from the much earlier Dilmun seals and may, the excavators suggest, have been an heirloom or a treasured possession of whoever took it with them into the tomb. A double-sided seal is of a very unusual format, but is reminiscent of some of the late third, early second-millennium seals from Failakah.[65]

The British Expedition was not in operation for very long but its achievements were not wholly insignificant. The increasing difficulty of persuading either the controllers of public funds or private industrial benefactors to support archaeological work in states which were becoming richer by the hour than any previously known to history, brought its activities to a close.

Little has yet been said about the people who lived on the island during the long centuries of its most expansive period. This is for the simple reason that little is known of them: very few remains have been found outside the principal sites, and little evidence of how the people lived. From examinations of their skeletal remains, it seems probable that they were a healthy people, somewhat taller than their present-day successors, and relatively long-lived, a quality entirely appropriate for the island of the gods, where all had once been perfection.[66] Remarkably, the Dilmunites of the third and second millennia appear to have practised dentistry of a quite sophisticated character.[67] A number of skulls have produced evidence of carious teeth extracted in life. Only the Egyptians could claim a comparable technology so early: Hesy-re, a

One of the few neo-Babylonian cylinder seals found in Bahrain. (*Department of Antiquities, Bahrain*).

third-dynasty nobleman buried at Saqqara, was, amongst other attainments, a dentist as recorded in his tomb. The early Dilmunites had a diet high in carbohydrates, notably the dates for which Dilmun was famous. All the early inhabitants, on the evidence of their skulls, were Caucasoid in racial affiliation.

Whilst it may be said that there is comparatively little known of how men lived in Bahrain, there is abundant evidence of how they were treated after death. The last of Bahrain's major archaeological phases, which at its earliest probably overlapped with the later centuries of the Sumerian period, is represented by its gigantic graveyards.

From the Ziusudra episode in the Epic of Gilgamesh, it is not unreasonable to suppose that, in addition to its sacred and mercantile characters, Dilmun was conceived as an island of the dead, and so perhaps was the prototype of that strange and evocative concept of the mortuary isle which looms, shrouded in mist and lapped by the water of death, in so many later mythologies. Whilst there is no doubt that the island's city could provide a substantial number of candidates for the tombs over the centuries, it is only very recently that anyone has attempted to compute the likely numbers buried in the island and from that to extrapolate the inhabitants of the city.[68] It is tempting to think that Dilmun may have been like Abydos in Egypt or, more recently, Kerbala in Iraq, widely recognized as a desirable place in which to be buried. However, there is no evidence of the dead being brought to Dilmun for burial and it must be assumed that most of those buried

159

there are native to the island. But the presence of similar tombs on the mainland suggests that there must have been some sort of mortuary cult in Dilmun as a whole. There is, of course, nothing to prevent the island and mainland Dilmun serving both as a place to which the dead were brought and as a flourishing mercantile kingdom with a substantial population who lived on the profits of its many-faceted trade. Indeed, it has been suggested that some of the prosperity which was so evident a feature of life in Dilmun may have been the consequence of the stream of visitors who came to the island to bring their dead to its holy shores.[69] There are plenty of parallels for such practical benefits from the exercise of religion: after all, the riches of the western Arabian cities of Makkah and Madinah derive, in part, from their role as the holy places of Islam and, in Makkah's case, as the centre of the Pilgrimage. Lourdes, Rome and a thousand shrines of Christendom have brought wealth in this life to those fortunate enough to have them within their boundaries.

It has now been calculated that there may be at least one hundred and seventy thousand tombs in the Bahraini deserts.[70] The fields of tumuli create a curious undulating effect in the desert, stretching on and on to the horizon. In this respect they are quite unique. So closely packed are they that it would now often seem to be difficult to build a new one between the ancient mounds. Many today are broken hillocks of rubble

The fields of mound burials in Bahrain are reckoned in square miles: over 170,000 are thought to exist.

and sand collapsed upon their stone-lined chambers, and are sometimes difficult to recognize. Others still rise to more dramatic heights, their contours firm but with their sepulchral chambers empty; in one group, at Aali village, some of the mounds still stand 40 feet high with a diameter of 100 feet. The tumulus fields are of enormous proportions, extending over two or more square miles; they are widely scattered over the island, even extending down to the desert lands of the south. The large preponderance of the mounds comes from the time of Dilmun's height of prosperity, from the end of the third millennium and the beginning of the second. Two principal types have been identified: the earlier without capstones, the later, with them. Some underground burials have also been found and there seems to have been a return to mound building in Hellenistic times. Various forms of structure have been identified: the earliest small and compact with corbelled roofs some three feet in height, and the later, much larger tumuli with provision for multiple burials, probably, in effect, family mausolea, or the resting place of people linked by clan ties.[71]

The doorways of the tombs, high and strongly built, tend to be turned towards the west looking towards the region where the sun dies. The dead generally lie with their heads towards the north-west; often their hands are placed in front of the face. Perhaps the occupants of the tombs were, like the Egyptians, able thus to enjoy the sunset when, gathering at the doorways of the tombs, their spirits could daily watch the sun set out upon the journey which they had already taken. The westerly orientation of the tombs suggests elements of a solar faith and the recognition of the sun's divinity, and it will be recalled that Utu, the sun god of the Sumerians, lived in Dilmun. It has also been suggested[72] that the entrances to the tombs are aligned to Venus at sunset, recalling the supposed stellar orientation of the entrance shafts of the pyramids at Giza, where, when they were built, the light of the Pole Star may have shone directly down them.

It is very curious indeed that tumulus or mound burials are found in a great arc from the Near East to Ireland, and in parts of Northern Europe the mounds heaped up over the graves of chieftains assumed a size and splendour equalled only by the *tholos* tombs of the Mycenaeans, the pyramids of the Kings of Egypt or the huge mounds of the Dilmunite rulers. The *tholos* itself may have originated in western Asia, where houses in the forms of *tholoi* are known from northern Iraq, though the evidence comes from so early a period that it must be tenuous.

The mound burials also recall the great structures of the European

Early and Middle Bronze Ages, the megaliths, the groups of standing stones which, often following the meander or the circle, are said to represent the Mother Goddess. Stonehenge is the most celebrated of them, whilst Avebury and Carnac are almost of comparable significance and power; with them earth burials are invariably associated. Even the pyramids, those most titanic of all funerary monuments, may have originated, in the opinion of some scholars, in the little mounds of sand heaped over the modest graves of pre-dynastic chieftains.[73]

It has been suggested that the worship of the Mother may have originated around the fertile perimeter of the Arabian deserts;[74] certainly Greek and Roman historians considered that the Goddess was supreme in the region in their day and equated her (or more strictly, the Romans did) with Venus. Whether her worship had persisted over so many centuries cannot be known for certain and, with the present lack of knowledge of the early history of the Arabian peninsula, such a contention remains to be proved, if it ever can be over so broad a span of time. Evidence has been found on the Saudi Arabian mainland of a substantial goddess cult, in late times, possibly centred on Thaj; it seems also likely that some of the early inhabitants of Arabia were megalith builders, though on a relatively modest if perplexing scale. In the nineteenth century Palgrave, unhappily not a wholly reliable commentator, reported seeing in northern Arabia a circular structure of trilithons, two upright stones bridged by a third, reminiscent of Stonehenge.[75] In the north-west of the peninsula, interestingly enough, around the early copper mining and smelting settlements, great assemblages of stones, some standing, some distributed on the ground, abound. They may date from the fourth millennium.[76]

The Bahrain tumuli are generally stone-lined, with well-cut blocks designed to make a secure resting place for the dead. Behind the building of such permanent burial places lies the belief in the continued survival of the individual after death, although this is not a belief typical of all early Semitic peoples, many of whom seem rather to have believed in the extinction of all personality once death had ended the earthly existence.

Until recent years only a few of the Bahrain mounds had been opened professionally, except by that long-established 'professional' group, the robbers of tombs. It would be very unlikely that many (if indeed any) of such obvious monuments, built with no attempt to conceal them, could have escaped depredation. From the pathetically fragmentary remains that have been found scattered in the tombs it is possible to reconstruct some idea of what they originally contained.

Usually the body was placed either on its side in the attitude of sleep or seated, facing the tomb's entrance. The extreme humidity of the Bahrain climate has not allowed the survival of human remains other than bones and skulls, usually fragmented and scattered – the work of the small desert creatures which live among the tombs.

There are few hints of the riches the tombs might once have contained. Certainly much pottery has been recovered, indicating a ritual of placing offerings or providing the means of sustaining the spirit after death. Copper and bronze artefacts, swords, daggers and dress ornaments have all left their traces in the tombs. A comparatively high degree of material luxury is indicated by the ivory which has sometimes been found amongst the debris of the tombs, suggesting in at least once case that the corpse was laid upon a bed decorated with ivory carvings and ornaments. One little ivory figurine, itself fragmentary, has been found: a girl, slender-waisted and wide-hipped, her latter feature recalling, though in a greatly refined degree, the steatopygous figures of the goddess from early times, which were carved with monstrously enlarged thighs and buttocks.[77] It seems likely that many such small statues were placed in the tombs: the torso of another was found by one of the early excavators in Bahrain. What their purpose was no one can agree on the basis of the fragments which have been found. They may have been representations of the dead, guardian divinities or servants.

In one Bahraini tomb some very curious ivory objects were found. They appeared to be wands or sceptres which seemed to have been broken deliberately and cast into the tomb.[78] What significance the broken wands held is unknown: perhaps their destruction marked the dead man's final break with this world. Similar ivory wands have been found in the Indus Valley.

In several of the tombs the remains of what appeared to be ivory caskets were discovered amongst other ivory fragments, including spindle whorls. So decayed, however, that it was virtually impossible to reconstruct them, or to guess what they once contained.[79]

The examination of the ivories found in the Bahraini tombs originally produced the view, which was frequently asserted, that they were of Phoenician workmanship. However, the Phoenicians flourished later than the likely median date of the Bahraini tumuli; it is likely that the ivories are simply another link with the cities of Sumer for, whilst little has remained due to the climate of southern Mesopotamia, it is known that ivory was widely used in the cities and that it was recorded as one of the important goods trans-shipped through Dilmun. It must be remembered, too, that much ivory was imported through Dilmun from the Indus Valley. Another possibly Sumerian connection has been provided by the quantity of bronze pins found in the tombs, similar to those with which the Mesopotamians fixed their characteristics 'buns', the most common coiffure favoured by them in the latter centuries of their existence.[80]

At Aali village, now the centre of a local pottery industry, is the most remarkable group of tombs in Bahrain, concentrated together within a relatively compact area. There are some twenty of them, all exceptionally large, and many of them still rise to impressive heights. It seems likely, from their size and certain other evidence described below, that these are the tombs of ancient chiefs, perhaps even of the kings of Dilmun. They conform, except in their great size, to the general pattern of the islands' graves of the early Bronze Age period: a central shaft, stone-lined, with two niches at the head of the shaft forming a T-section. These, it is assumed, were for offerings placed by the head of the corpse. A peculiar feature of these tombs is that, after the sand and rubble had been heaped up high over the burial, a high circular surrounding wall was built to enclose the tumulus. Thus the tombs would have looked like gigantic, up-ended cylinders crowned by a dome of sand – very strange monuments indeed.

Durand, in his 1878–9 expedition, was the first to excavate at

These ivory objects, including what appear to be spatulas or wands ritually broken, were found in mounds excavated by Mackay in 1926. (*Mackay, Harding, Petrie, 1929*).

Aali.[81]. He left behind some notable drawings of the village as it was then, with a far greater density of mounds than is evident today.[82]

In the 1961–2 season some striking pottery vessels were recovered from one of the Aali tumuli.[83] The tomb had been robbed at an unknown date, but a trail of potsherds, found in the tunnel cut by the robbers into the tomb chamber, enabled the archaeologists to reassemble them and so present a 'suite' consisting of two handsome goblets, elegantly proportioned and painted with a geometric decoration in black on a red slip, and three slender-walled cups. In type the goblets recall an early design found in Iran and Pakistan and can be dated approximately to the second half of the third millennium. It is known that ostrich eggs made to serve as drinking vessels were also placed in the tombs, recalling a particularly Sumerian practice; similar deposits were found in the burials of early Dynastic Ur and Kish.[84]

But one object in particular from the Aali tombs testified to links more distant still and to connections even with remote and legendary Troy. The object, slightly smaller than a man's thumb nail, is a gold quatrefoil meander, the four spiral shapes being linked by a central bar.[85] It is extremely finely made and indicates a very high degree of metal-working craftsmanship to which the princes of Dilmun had access. The shape is a familiar one, associated throughout the Near East and right across Europe with early Bronze Age burials. It is particularly identified with the practice of mound burial and examples directly analogous to the Aali fragment have been found as far west as Greece, as well as at Troy.[86] Further west still, the same meander shape, cut into massive stones, is the most frequent motif on the large barrow tombs of Ireland.[87] Two recently published examples, which appear to be identical with that from Aali, come from the disputed hoard of Aegean gold acquired by the Boston Museum, which, from the gold cylinder seal bearing the cartouches of two Egyptian kings, can be dated to the twenty-fifth century BC.[88] This corresponds well with the upper limits of the estimated age of the principal Aali tumuli.

These gold meanders seem to have been identified throughout the ancient world with royal burials. That one should have been discovered as far south as Bahrain is quite unexpected and it postulates a much closer connection with the burial practices of the great civilizations of the ancient world in the third millennium than could ever have been reasonably anticipated. It also suggests a high degree of sophistication and luxury and, sadly, confirms the view that the original contents of the tombs must have been well worth the plundering. This one tiny gold object is, in all probability, a proof of the rich and splendid treasures originally buried with the kings, as splendid perhaps as anything buried with the kings of Egypt, Anatolia or, nearer Bahrain still, in the Royal Tombs at Ur.

It has been proposed that the Aali tombs represent royal burials through successive generations, beginning around the middle of the third millennium and continuing into the early centuries of the second. In several of the tombs, the bones of rams and sheep may be the remains of sacrifices, performed at the threshold before the tomb was sealed. Some of the tombs show that they have been re-used at various periods since their construction: material of much later times has been found in one or two of them. In one tomb, opened by Prideaux during his visits to Bahrain in 1905–6 and again in 1908, two pottery jars were found in each of which was a handful of dates, recalling the significance which the date had in the economy of Dilmun.[89]

Many more of the tumuli have been destroyed over the years by villagers using the stones to build their own houses, and, in recent times, by the demands of the Aali pottery. In recent years, road building and other phases of Bahrain's modern development programmes have added to the destruction of the tombs.

Grave mounds similar to the most characteristic form in Bahrain have been found directly to the west in Saudi Arabia, at Abqaiq near Hofuf, at Dhahran, and other mainland sites.[90] Again, relatively little work has been done on these tumuli but their methods of construction and the similarity of the pottery which they have yielded suggest the same, if equally mysterious, origins as the Bahrain burials.

Work continues on the Bahraini tomb fields. Now another hazard faces large numbers of them: the causeway which will link Bahrain with the mainland of Saudi Arabia. The causeway will land on Bahraini territory near the village of Sar, where the mounds are particularly densely concentrated.[91] Yet more types of tomb, different from others on the island, have been recognized at Sar: one rises high above the plain and is ringed by smaller subsidiary burials, for all the world like the burials of retainers around the great *mastabas* of the early kings of Egypt. But this cannot be more than chance, for the date of the Bahraini tombs seems to be early in the second millennium, at least a thousand years after the practice was current in Egypt. The tomb at Sar may merely be that of some great man or a particularly revered or patriarchal figure around whom others chose to be buried, in the hope that this propinquity would bring dividends in the afterlife.

In the same part of the island a group of burials of children has been found.[92] Since the ancients were not generally particularly sentimental about children, infant mortality being a common hazard, the presence of this group of tombs apparently reserved for children is arresting.

Perhaps it is a tribute to Dilmun's reputation as a 'pure and clean place' in which disease was the exception. The apparent longevity of the Dilmunites, suggested earlier, may have been a factor in this reputation.

A new township for the modern inhabitants of Bahrain is now being built at a site south of Aali: it is to be called Medinat Hamed, named for the eldest son of the Amir, the Crown Prince of Bahrain. The construction work has required the Department of Antiquities to undertake some urgent 'rescue archaeology', to collect the evidence which is contained in the groups of mounds which must be destroyed in the name of progress.[93]

The Medinat Hamed mounds are important in that several of them seem to be unplundered and they are, it would seem, particularly early. Their principal interest however lies in the fact that they are similar in construction and layout to the tombs on Umm an-Nar in Abu Dhabi.[94] Umm an-Nar was probably the port from which raw copper was exported to Dilmun for smelting and onward shipment to Sumer. There is also another tomb which looks as though it may have Umm an-Nar connections on the Budaiya road; these connections are of great importance in attempting to assess the likely origin of the Dilmun culture and the direction from which came the civilizing influences found in the Gulf in the mid-third millennium. Pottery from the Medinat Hamed graves also appears to sustain the Umm an-Nar connection.

A further, rather earlier indication of the archaeological riches which seem still to lie everywhere in Bahrain, just below the surface, was provided in 1970 by two large mounds at Al-Hajjar.[95] These were originally penetrated by that frequent enemy, and occasional friend of archaeology, the bulldozer. Subsequent excavation, by the Bahrain Department of Antiquities, revealed a complex and extensive cemetery containing burials from c.3000 BC, the earliest period of the island's history, down to Hellenistic times.

Some of the graves were unplundered, their inhabitants still comfortably reposing in them; most of them had been efficiently pillaged. Many of the graves were rock cut, several were compartmented and some of the early ones were sealed with a type of small portcullis. Several produced features new to the repertory of Bahrain's ancient burial practices. One third-millennium tomb at Al-Hajjar revealed the burial of a dog, evidently sent to spend the afterlife with its master. There are also examples of dogs being buried in early graves in Sumer;

This mound is surrounded by subsidiary burials.

At Sar, a large and complex field of mounds south of Aali, there are many different types of mound, dating to the early second millennium.

An unusual feature of the burials of Sar is a complex of children's graves.

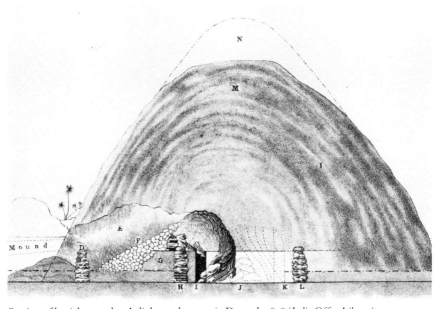

Section of burial mound at Aali drawn by captain Durand, 1878 (*India Office Library*).

(left) Mounds and excavations at Medinat Hamed, late third millennium BC.
(Right) A Jamdet Nasr seal, probably originating in Mesopotamia c. 3000 BC and no doubt a family heirloom, was found in one of the graves at Al-Hajjar.

in one particularly early burial of a boy, a dog was laid with him and thoughtfully provided with a bone to take with him to the after-life.[96]

Al-Hajjar has produced a considerable quantity of high quality artefacts from all the periods represented. It was the first site to yield a Dilmun seal in direct relationship to a burial; from its position it would appear, as might be expected, that the seal was worn around the neck.[97]

One of the graves produced a Jamdet Nasr seal which, it has been suggested, may have been ancient when it was imported into Bahrain. It had probably been re-cut and may have been a family heirloom.[98]

A considerable number of seals of all periods were found at Al-Hajjar including an unusual concentration of cylinder seals, attesting the continuation of some degree of commercial or official activity in Bahrain during the otherwise relatively obscure period in the later second millennium.

A baby buried in a round pot, its skull still clearly recognizable, recalled similar burials from the Qala'at al-Bahrain, a few miles away. One grave, from the Assyrian period in the eighth century, produced a fine painted goblet.

From all the wide range of graves extending over a time-scale of more than two thousand years, one of the most notable characteristics

(Top left) The burial site at Al-Hajjar differs from others in that the dead are interred in single graves, cut in the bedrock; most graves were covered with a capstone and the whole complex was buried under a large mound.
(Top right) A steatite 'pyxis' excavated from Al-Hajjar.
(Below) One of the tombs at Al-Hajjar included the skeleton of a dog, laid across the entrance.

of the Al-Hajjar burials was the presence of fine steatite or chlorite vessels at all periods. It does appear that vessels of this material, whether they were manufactured in Bahrain or imported from outside, were an important element in the people's economy after the third millennium

171

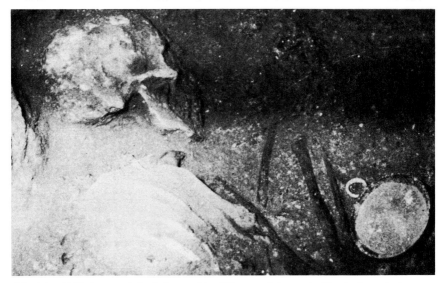

A burial at Al-Hajjar revealed a skeleton with a Dilmun seal close to it. The dead man had evidently been buried with it attached to his wrist.

when, a little surprisingly, they seem generally to be absent. The quality of manufacture and the consistency of design over so extensive a period, are remarkable phenomena.

History, in the form of written records of man's achievements and failures, began in the land of Sumer. At this time, let it be remembered, the whole of the rest of the world was still locked, for the most part, in societies which descended directly from those of Stone Age times; only in this small corner of the Near East did the light of civilization and culture begin to burn, flickering along the two great river valleys of Mesopotamia and Egypt. In the minds of the people of the elder of these great cultures, Dilmun-Bahrain occupied a special, sacred place. It may be that in Bahrain, awaiting discovery or understanding, lie more clues to the origins of our own society, certainly to very many of our most deeply-held beliefs. This small Gulf island in the dawn of history had its part to play in kindling the spark that, tended by the 'black-headed' people of Sumer, was to light the beginnings of the five-thousand-year long cycle of hope and disillusion, compassion and brutality that makes up human history, down to the present day.

But all this is only part of the story. At least as significant and certainly quite as revealing is the story of Dilmun-Bahrain as a great commercial centre, the centre, virtually, of the world's trade of its day. This is the story not of the gods of Dilmun but of the businessmen of Sumer, exploring markets overseas in search of an honest *mina*.

VII

Dilmun's Merchants, their Marks and far-ranging Trade

During the time of Sumer's greatness life went on busily in the cities, despite the sombre, occasional courts-in-death of the kings, the instability of the prevailing political system and the perennial threats of invasion and unrest. But as the Sumerians were essentially a down-to-earth people, much of their life consisted of concentrating on the simple process of making a living. The profit motive was strong in Sumer and its pursuit was more agreeable and certainly more dear to the average Urite, for example, than the pursuit of an uncertain immortality by dead courtiers or the pretensions and schemes of aggrandisement of little princes.

Most of the earliest city-states of Sumer were concentrated near the confluence of the two great rivers on which the black-headed people's civilization depended, the Tigris and the Euphrates. It was natural, especially if the legends of their origins were based upon any sort of recollected reality, that they should explore the sea routes to the south, down throughout the Gulf, the Lower Sea, and out into limitless ocean, which they believed, reasonably enough at the time, circled the world. Very soon the Sumerians became considerable though sometimes rather apprehensive seamen; they constitute, indeed, the first great maritime trading nation in the world's history. The boats which they sailed were probably not greatly different from the present day *boum* (often erroneously called a dhow) and the high-prowed *tarafa* of the Marsh Arabs.

Trade and legend are inextricably mixed in Sumer's history. Dilmun stands at the centre of both, just as the Bahrain Islands occupied a conveniently central position between Mesopotamia, the Arabian coast, Oman (the probable source of much of Sumer's copper and stone) and the markets of the Indus valley.

For many centuries Bahrain-Dilmun provided the natural entrepot and distribution centre for the trans-shipment of the raw materials vital

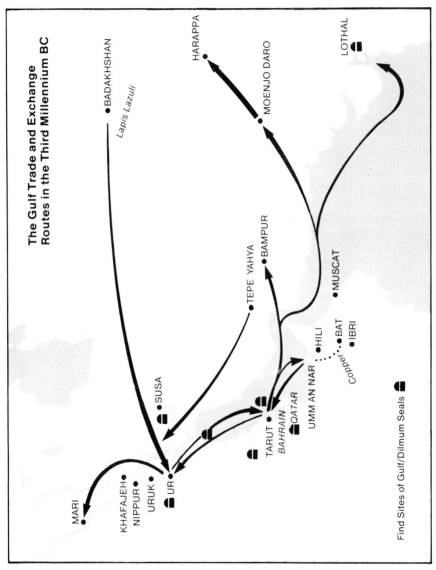

**The Gulf Trade and Exchange
Routes in the Third Millennium BC**

BADAKHSHAN

Lapis Lazuli

HARAPPA

MOENJO DARO

LOTHAL

TEPE YAHYA

BAMPUR

MUSCAT

SUSA

HILI

BAT

IBRI

Copper

UMM AN NAR

TARUT

QATAR

BAHRAIN

MARI

KHAFAJEH

NIPPUR

URUK

UR

Find Sites of Gulf/Dilmum Seals

Third-millennium trade routes with distribution of seal sites.

174

to Sumer's economy. Like the Vikings of a later age, the princes of Sumer were merchants on a lavish scale and the most substantial records of Dilmun come from the trading activities of the little states, particularly from the city of Ur. It may be appropriate here to leave the world of gods and heroes and turn to the more everyday concerns of merchants and businessmen, seeking a profit forty centuries and more ago.

Trade became possible when man had learned to exploit nature and to produce beyond his immediate needs. The surplus he thus created, he could exchange with other peoples, taking from them their surplus in turn.

Trade in artefacts, which clearly began very early, probably arose out of simple admiration, an admiration which could not be satisfied merely by clubbing the owner of the object admired. Sophisticated techniques of warehousing, distribution, banking, the exchange of value-based rates and commodities, and all the other facets of a complex economic system, were developed over these early centuries, as the result of the recognition of a need in each case and of a reasoned response to it. The dialogue, often as acrimonious as in our own day, between the needs of the state and those of the private sector of the economy, began very early on, and complaints against the level of taxation and the incursions of central government into the affairs of commerce can be heard rising clearly above the chatter of the most ancient market places.

Great cities rose and fell because of economic factors and their attendant political responses. In the documents which survive from Mesopotamia, a significant proportion are commercial records of one sort or another, bills, memoranda and even dunning letters from anxious creditors seeking the repayment of a debt.

In the trade of the ancient Near East, certainly in its earliest centuries when the great civilizations of Mesopotamia were widening the range of their influence and contacts, the Gulf, and particularly the islands and Oman, had a profoundly important part to play in the most vital trade sea route of the day, that which went south and eastward from Mesopotamia to India. At the time when the Gilgamesh legend was written down in something like the form which has reached us, a millennium or more after the actual reported voyage of Gilgamesh to Dilmun, the island is represented as a thriving and important entrepôt, with its kings recognized throughout the region as powerful merchant princes. Dilmun is no longer simply the faeryland of Sumerian legend but a place of trading ships and thronged harbours, its storehouses stacked with the wealth of the states on whose trade routes it was so strategically placed.

Trade routes were of immense antiquity and well-travelled, both those which extended over land and, later, the sea routes. Along the principal routes was strung a chain of trading posts and one of the most frequently repeated claims of a reforming monarch was that under his rule merchants could travel securely and speedily over the great distances, provisioned by caravanserai at regular stages and protected by imperial agents along the way.

Of course the mechanics of trade took many forms. In some cases, as we know from the documentary evidence, merchants would base themselves abroad, far from their home. From this distant posting they would maintain contact with their headquarters and manage the acquisition, exchange or distribution of products with the communities amongst which they had established themselves. Artefacts themselves, of course, sometimes travelled far further than even the most dauntless merchant reached. A fine vessel, a piece of jewellery or a weapon might be handed on across a widespread area and pass through the hands of many different intermediaries.

For the Sumerians trade was inextricably linked with every phase of their lives. By harnessing the waters of the two great rivers on which their prosperity and even their lives depended, they created abundance; by planning their year carefully in relation to the rivers' inundations they created leisure in which to develop crafts and technical skills of a very high order. Sumer, however, was a land barren of trees and of minerals: these resources, essential for the well-being of the land and its ambitious and intensely creative people, could only be obtained from outside their own frontiers. The abundant fertility of their crops and herds gave them scope to trade their surplus for their other needs.

From very early times the Sumerians had established a flourishing import-export economy, at first directed by the temples, later by the secular authorities and merchants operating on their own account.[1] As the cities grew they became important trading points for the caravans which came up out of the plateaux of Iran. The growth of the early cities of Iran has been the subject of intensive study. They straddled the overland routes for many of the most sought-after raw materials of the fourth and third millennia, such as chlorite (steatite) and lapis lazuli. It has indeed been postulated that these cities, some of which were considerable in scale and extensive in influence, came into being simply in response to the demands of trade and the search for raw materials.[2]

The great highway of Sumerian trade, however, ran north-south. The two rivers themselves were the most expeditious and direct means for trade to flow from the Gulf, up through Sumer proper, onwards towards the Mediterranean into what was to become Assyria, travelling north further still, into Anatolia and, to the west across the Upper Sea, possibly as far as distant Cyprus. As will be seen later, one of the most important items of trade was copper, both in the form of ingots and converted into manufactured products. The Euphrates' part in moving this trade may be commemorated by the fact that its Sumerian name was *Urudu*, 'the copper river'; the Tigris, on the other hand, a swift flowing stream, was appropriately named *Idiglat*, 'the arrow'. From the various cities on the rivers caravans busily set out, and the river routes also became the principal system for the distribution of manufactured goods and for inter-urban trade.

From the marsh lands where the Tigris and Euphrates debouch into the Gulf another route lay open to the enterprising Sumerian merchant, south to Arabia and away to the east, to the rich and powerful cities of the Indus Valley, Moenjo-Daro and Harappa. On this route, Dilmun occupied a crucial position, lying some 300 miles from the head of the Gulf, and the only safe harbourage in what were often dangerous and unpredictable seas. The probable earliest reference to Dilmun trade in the Sumerian records is of immense antiquity; far back into the third millennium Dilmun is established as an important trading post. Ur-Nanshe, king of Lagash *c.*2520 BC, records the fact that, in his reign, ships of Dilmun brought tribute to him, in what is otherwise a catalogue of the temples that he built for the honour of the gods of Sumer. The inscription is from a door socket dedicated by the king:

> Ur-Nanshe, the king of Lagash, the son of Gunidu, the son of Gurmu, built the house of Ningirsu: built the house of Nanshe: built the house of Gatumdug: built the harem: built the house of Ninmar. The ships of Dilmun brought him wood as a tribute from foreign lands. He built the Ibqal: built the Kinir: built the sceptre-house.[3]

Thus as early as the first recorded kings of Lagash, roughly at the time when the pyramids in Egypt were sparkling new, Sumer was promoting an extensive export trade to Dilmun. The king and queen of Lagash (if such titles may be used, however anachronistically) were directly involved and in exchange for Dilmun's copper and splendid dates they offered barley, cedar, oil, flour, dresses and silver

Records of the shipment of dates and onions, both specialities of Dilmun, again occur in the reign of Ur-Nanshe. The wife of Lugalanda, another ruler of Lagash, exported wheat, cedarwood, cheese and shelled barley to the island: '234 mina of copper ore; copper ore, property of Luqunntu (wife of Lugalanda) which Ur-Enki the mer-

The earliest known monumental inscription relating to trade with Dilmun is this plaque dedicated by the ruler of Lagash in 2520 BC. In it Ur-Nanshe, shown here attended by his sons, refers to bringing timber from Dilmun. (*Louvre*; after *Art in the Ancient World*, Faber).

chant has brought from the mountain of Dilmun, Lugalanda, Ensi of Lagash, has paid for in the palace.'[4] Copper from Dilmun was called, in the Sumerian language, *urudu ni-tuk-ki*. Ur-Enki, whose name is compounded with that of Enki, the benign god, is one of the earliest merchants to be known by name; it is interesting that by his time the temporal power, in the person of the sovereign's wife (or, more accurately, one of them) was engaging in trade, rather than it being the province of the temple authorities, which is generally thought to have been the case in early Dynastic times. The wives of rulers also engaged, like their husbands, in the fish trade.[4a]

The records of Lagash in Sumerian times reveal something of the mechanics of trade in the city-states, before the merchants had achieved fully independent status. The ruler evidently provided goods from some sort of central warehousing system to the merchants, enabling them to trade (in this case, with Dilmun) and to exchange Lagash merchandise for Dilmun's products.

Presumably the merchants were working on a basis of commission payments. Ur-Enki operated on quite a large scale: he is recorded as having moved something like a hundred kilograms of copper in one shipment from Dilmun. 'From the central warehouses Shubur, the Inspector, gave him a quantity of cedarwood, grain and flour for exchange in Dilmun. This was in the fifth year of the rule of Lugalanda.'[5]

Lugalanda was evidently favoured with at least two commercially-minded wives. Apart from Luqunntu we are told that 'Barrambara, wife of Lugalanda, counted out copper to the merchant Dugilam, to take to the city of Umma and exchange for silver'.[6]

Documents from the very ancient and holy city of Shurrupak, once ruled by Ziusudra, show that the dealers and sailors engaged in the trade were known as 'gal-Dilmun'.[6a] This compares with the Old Babylonian term 'Alik Tilmun' which described the guild which represented the merchants who traded with Dilmun in the early second millennium.

It may be inferred by various objects, including the distinctive 'Barbar ware' pottery found in Sumerian sites, that Dilmun had its own export industry long before then, probably originating at the time of the Sumerians' first accession to supremacy in the land, towards the later centuries of the fourth millennium. The earliest textual reference to Dilmun comes from this time and seems to refer to trade.

The Indus Valley cities spread north-west in a chain along the banks of their great river. There is little early evidence at present of developed cultures having flourished in the region, most of which is now contained within modern Pakistan, at the time of the foundation of the Sumerian cities. However, as many of the early levels of the Indus cities are hopelessly waterlogged, caution must be expressed even about this view. The sites of the Indus cities are impressive and suggest a considerable awareness of the importance of town planning; most of them are designed on a formal pattern with a preponderance of large public buildings and wide, regular streets. Indus Valley architecture tends to be monolithic, lacking in relief or features, and their cities must have been oppressive places to live in.

The people of the Indus cities had developed a pictographic script, evolved seemingly to a relatively high degree and apparently demonstrating, for example, the understanding and use of accent markings. It occurs on the pottery of the region and on their characteristic square stamp seals, of which many examples survive.[7] Despite recent attempts it remains undeciphered.

At the height of the Indus Valley civilization, around a hundred cities made up what was a fairly centrally organized state. The two cities of Harappa and Moenjo-Daro were much the largest and, it has been suggested, may have been twin capitals of a large and monolithic state. Throughout the Indus Valley there are hints of Mesopotamian, even of Sumerian, influence, but these are too slight to suggest a profound and continuing influence of what is probably the older civilization on the younger. There is, however, little doubt that the Indus Valley people, whoever they were, drew some of their initial inspiration from Mesopotamia. Beyond that fact, contact was maintained between them principally by way of trade through Bahrain-Dilmun and the Gulf.

The little of Indus art that survives suggests the presence of Sumerian influences. The so-far-unique carved stone bust of a 'priest-king' or divinity from Moenjo-Daro *could* be a provincial, orientalized Sumerian work. Pottery figurines of divinities display the pinched, almost reptilian faces of their much earlier Mesopotamian colleagues, with similar rather bizarre ideas about the headdress proper for a god.

Kidney-shaped beads found in Dilmun may have their origins in the Indus Valley and there is little doubt that the ivory which was so important a part of Dilmun's trade with the Sumerian cities came from there. A little ivory figurine, unhappily only a fragment, found in one of the tumuli in the desert near Aali is reminiscent, no more, of one of the most celebrated pieces from Moenjo-Daro, which in its elegance and mastery of form is quite uncharacteristic of the little that we know of the Indus peoples' art. This is a little bronze dancer, pert and nude, full of charm; comparable with it, if suspect in the relatively early period to which it has been ascribed, is the torso of a youth, whose impressively developed genitals and general chubbiness may lack appeal to those accustomed to judge such figures by the more slender charm of a *kouros*.

Indus Valley pottery has been found in the Arabian Gulf at Abu Dhabi, at the oasis of Buraimi and, arguably in that the Indian provenance is disputed, on the island of Umm an-Nar. However, the evidence in Bahrain itself is reasonably conclusive, and, *prima facie*, there is no reason why other points on the coast of the Gulf should not have been visited by traders journeying to or from the Indus Valley. Recently Harappan material has been identified on the Omani coast at Ras al-Hamra, not far from Muscat.[7a]

The land routes from Sumer to the Indus ran through Persia and were long and dangerous, beset with rapacious and deplorably uncommercial tribes. The sea route was to be preferred, therefore, and it was because of this that in the third and early second millennia Dilmun, the sacred island, assumed another, more mundane role as the great emporium of trade between east and west. Equally important, it was well placed between the southern, richly endowed but primitive lands and the northern states, hungry for the raw materials and for copper, stone, ivory and gold, which were needed for their rich, consumer-orientated economies.

In pre-Sargonid times trade was largely the perquisite of the temple administrations even when they were conducted in the ruler's name, a logical enough practice since, technically at least, all land and goods belonged to the god of the city and the authorities, governors and priests, merely administrated them on the god's behalf. Thus it was the practice for the temples to fit out trading expeditions, hiring sea captains and a class of merchant who specialized in the brokerage of the temple-financed trade. Apart from the merchant's payment, the profits went to the temples and they grew exceedingly rich.

Later, however, as a result of an as yet unknown change in the Sumerian social system, individual merchants appear, trading on their own behalf or as members of privately financed syndicates. It may well be that the merchants who had traded in the temples' interest grew rich and, over generations, saw the prospect of even more substantial profits as a motive still more compelling than the favour of the gods, whose payment of dividends was likely, in the Sumerian view of things, to be long deferred if, indeed, forthcoming at all. During the time when free enterprise flourished, however, the palace and sometimes certain of the temples levied a duty on imports, particularly on the all-important copper trade.

In the first year of the reign of king Ibbi-Sin of Ur (c. 2029–2006 BC) a sea captain, Ur-Gur, who commanded a large boat and thought it worth recording the fact, shipped ten talents worth of wool 'of ordinary quality' to Dilmun. There is some evidence that he was acting under the aegis of one of the temples in this transaction.[8]

Over a century later a woman, Amad-Ningal, in all probability a native of Ur, made an offering to the goddess Ningal from the proceeds of an expedition to Dilmun.[9] It is a matter of speculation whether she was making the offering, the customary tithe, on behalf of another or whether, as is equally possible, since women were at no disadvantage in Sumerian society (as witness Lugalanda's wives), she was trading in her own right.

Trade did not only flow one way, directed from Sumer to the impressionable natives of Dilmun and other distant regions, for several unmistakably Dilmunite names in texts of the time make it clear that the islanders also traded in Ur and other Sumerian cities. Thus from Larsa, at the end of the twentieth century, gifts to the temple of Ningal are recorded from one Idin-Nin-Inzak, the last part of whose name commemorates Dilmun's tutelary god.[10] Included amongst the merchandise listed in Idin-Nin-Inzak's inscription are 'fish-eyes', almost certainly the pearls of Dilmun, the trade of which was of very high antiquity. Idin-Nin-Inzak was prosperous enough for gold, a comparatively rare product in Sumer, to figure amongst his benefactions to the temple of Ningal.

Another inscription is a catalogue of the items found in the great burial tumuli of Bahrain: carnelian beads, rods of iron, copper and ivory combs, all recorded as the proceeds of an expedition to Dilmun.[11]

A Dilmunite, Iddin-ilum, appears making a tithe of silver whilst Dumu-dugga certifies the correctness of the amount.[12] The Dilmun merchants were prosperous and influential men; indeed, so considerable was their reputation that in Babylonian times *lu-tilmun-a*, the men of Dilmun, became a synonym for the profession of trader. The Sumerian term for merchant, incidentally, and itself of great antiquity, is *dam-gar*; it may be one of the supposed pre-Sumerian words taken into the language from some earlier stratum.

One of the techniques of early trading, developed to aid the interchange of goods and contacts between distant peoples, was the establishment of merchant colonies in cities linked by mutual trading interests. This obviously was desirable amongst peoples who did not possess a common language (although Akkadian was employed for this purpose by the middle of the second millennium) and whose literacy was, to say the least, limited. Thus communities grew up whose function was to broke the argosies which plied to and from the land from which the settlers came. Sometimes they lived outside the city walls; often they were independent communities, governed by their own magistrates who were responsible for the general maintenance of order and the return of taxes to the central authority. Their rights were respected, but they were aliens, forming a sort of ghetto in the midst of a foreign city or on its periphery. Seals found at Ur, obviously Indian in origin, demonstrate the existence of such communities in the Mesopotamian cities.

The Sumerians, more than their successors the Babylonians and Assyrians, seem to have been by inclination a seafaring people, but their attitude to the sea and sailing was one of extreme caution and respect; in this way they were typical of most ancient peoples. Though, in one mood they would salute the Gulf as the father of all oceans, in another they spoke of it as 'the fearful sea'. They were forced on to the sea to gain additional and, because they were far distant, more lucrative markets for their exports.

They were more confident of their merchanting ability than of their seamanship: many ex-votos survive proclaiming the gratitude of these nervous merchant venturers to the gods who have ensured their safe return from the perils of ocean. Ningal was the recipient of most of the offerings of Urite seamen; she has been well described as a sort of Sumerian 'Notre Dame de la Garde'.[13] The Mesopotamians were however far from being as alienated from the sea as some of their contemporaries. The Egyptians, the most conservative of all the ancients, regarded 'the Great Green' with positive distaste and considered the fact that Egypt was but little dependent on the sea for any of its wants as another singular mark of the favour of the gods who had, they felt, made Egypt as perfect a land as it was possible even for the gods to do. But the extent of the Dilmunite trade overland was equally formidable and is demonstrated by the appearance at the court of the King of Mari, a city on the Tigris far to the north of Sumer in northern Syria, of messengers from the island in the eighteenth century BC.[14] That its emissaries could travel these distances, apparently independently, attests to the prosperity and influence of Dilmun at that time. The king of Assyria, Shamsi-Adad I (1814–1782 BC) commanded that the Dilmunites should be given gifts of oil, sesame, boxwood and sandals. The Assyrians sent a caravan to Dilmun, which on its return was directed to deliver its goods to Hammurabi of Babylon, who reigned from 1792 –1750 BC. Before it reached the city, however, it seems to have met with difficulties on the way.[15]

Hammurabi's successor as king of Babylon was Samsu-iluna, who reigned from 1749–1684 BC. In the twenty-first year of his reign traders from Dilmun are mentioned in a text from a provincial city, Legaba.[16] This document records the delivery of a quantity of barley, perhaps the property of a Dilmunite, Samas-Nasir, resident in the Babylonian kingdom, to two others, one of whom, Inzak-gamil, has a traditional Dilmunite compound in his name.

Most ancient history is the record of the doings of kings and conquerors, figures who loom larger than life and whose shadows obscure the people whose lives went on despite them. But an engaging feature of the records of early Mesopotamia is that individuals play their part, private citizens who would be wholly recognizable today, mocking the grave significance which history gives to the events happening around them, like jesters chuckling sardonically at the feet of emperors.

The largest group of cuneiform tablets to have come down from the city mounds of Mesopotamia over these four thousand years is unquestionably that which is concerned, in general terms, with trade. Many of them are contracts between one merchant and another, with captains of ships hired for specific voyages, and bills, notes of exchange, and even agreements over the financing of trading expeditions. These last are particularly interesting in that they appear to describe the earliest examples of banking, whereby a financier would advance funds against a particular project at an agreed rate, the contract specifying in the manner of bankers ever since, that the borrowers alone would be responsible for all losses. Hammurabi tried unsuccessfully to change this and make the banker equally liable.[17] That he could not do so suggests that the legendary political power of bankers has deep historical roots. There is one particularly interesting document which appears to be a 'joint and several guarantee' by a number of partners to the banker who had advanced them a loan.

Credit makes its first helpful appearance in commercial history and is recognized as a factor in assessing how much money might reasonably be advanced to a trader. The Sumerian term *tadmiqtu* approximates to the concept of 'goodwill' as a factor in assessing the value of a business and thus in securing a loan.[18] A system of letters of credit enabled a merchant to operate at a distance far from his home-base without the need of carrying large amounts of treasure with him, with all the risks attendant upon so doing. Relationships between one merchant firm and another in a foreign market were built up and enabled members of the firm to trade together to the advantage of both. Many firms existed for long periods, often for several generations.

The idea of a currency standard first appears at the end of the third millennium, for values of goods are often expressed in terms of an equivalent in silver. Whilst the Sumerians used the silver standard they did not go to the next stage and actually produce a currency for exchange, although they did possibly exchange discs or rings of standard weight silver for services or products; coinage had to wait for its invention until the seventh-century Lydians of Asia Minor. But its absence did not prevent the Sumerians from developing a highly sophisticated system of merchant banking by using the silver standard as an agreed basis on which loans or interest might be assessed. This was largely achieved by comparisons of weights. Silver was handled in bars, with official markings and a certification of weight.

Dilmun seems to have been of sufficient importance as a trade centre around the beginning of the second millennium to have had its own measurement of weight, differing from that of the great commercial metropolis of the time, Ur. Recent research has suggested that the Dilmun weight may have been of the same value as that used in the Indus Valley cities.[19] A set of weights found in the city site of Dilmun on Bahrain is equivalent to the weights used in the Indus Valley cities and may be evidence of the presence of merchants from those cities in Dilmun.

In the time of Rim-Sin (1822–1763 BC), one of the kings of the Elamite dynasty which formed the kingdom of Isin-Larsa, there flourished in the city of Ur, for centuries one of the most important of the Sumerian trade centres, a member of the guild of Dilmun merchants whose name was Ea-Nasir. The guild, the *Alik-Tilmun* as it came to be called in the Babylonian form, consisted of those merchants who, trading on their own behalf down the Gulf, based their trans-shipment business on Dilmun's prosperous and hospitable quays. By a fortunate chance, an extensive correspondence, if it is sometimes anxious and acrimonious, between Ea-Nasir and his business associates survived in the ruins of his house in Ur, to which he had withdrawn in the hope of enjoying a prosperous retirement after his active and evidently not wholly scrupulous business career.[20] He was active in business around the turn of the nineteenth century BC.

It is, incidentally, important to recognize that this particular trade, of which we have relatively detailed knowledge, was between Dilmun and Ur. There may well have been other merchants of the status of the Urites who dealt with Dilmun but nothing is known of their organization, if any such existed. Ea-Nasir was a substantial dealer in copper, a wholesaler of copper ingots; sometimes he dealt in finished products made from the metal and, indeed, in anything else from which he could see the chance of a profit.

Amongst the mass of often tedious, but historically very important cuneiform commercial correspondence which survives inscribed on tablets of baked clay, Ea-Nasir's letters gleam mischievously, for much of what survives of his archives may be categorized as 'dunning tablets' from his creditors, often expressed in those terms of hurt surprise and reproach which would be familiar to many a debtor today. Ea-Nasir, the first part of whose name is the semitic or Babylonian form of Enki, was obviously considered a reasonably good risk at the outset, judging by the amounts which he was advanced; the records credit him with substantial borrowings in copper. Evidently at the outset of his career he was acting for the palace, buying and selling on the king's behalf. But later there appears a series of sharp and sometimes rather petulant cries of financial anguish directed to him by his backers in Ur whilst he is evidently away in Dilmun. The usual formal injunction 'speak to. . . .' precedes the text of most of the letters, indicating that in all probability neither the sender nor the recipient was literate. A letter, in fact, was known as 'a say to them' and was written and read by professional scribes who thus themselves became men of influence and power, privy as they were to all the commercial and political secrets of the time.

Nanni is particularly hurt at Ea-Nasir's casual, even discourteous

mag. N

Ea-Nasir, the Dilmun merchant who evidently spent much of his career in Bahrain, was a Urite. The ruins of his house in Ur (marked) were excavated by Sir Leonard Woolley. (From L. Woolley, *Excavations at Ur*, E. Benn)

attitude: after all, are not both of them gentlemen and surely they should behave as such?

Speak to Ea–Nasir; thus says Nanni. Now when you had come you spoke saying thus: 'I will give good ingots to Gimil-Sin' this you said to me when you had come, but you have not done it: you have

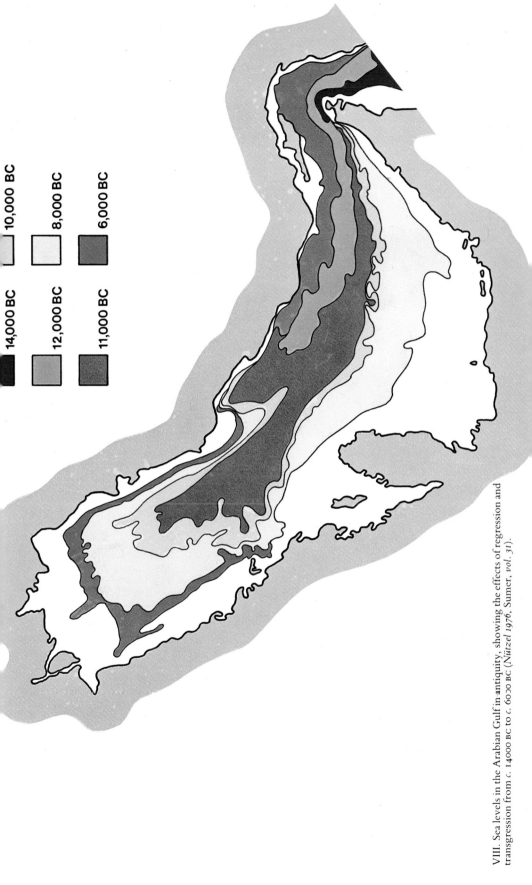

VIII. Sea levels in the Arabian Gulf in antiquity, showing the effects of regression and transgression from c. 14000 BC to c. 6000 BC (*Nützel 1976*, Sumer, *vol. 31*).

Legend:
- 14,000 BC
- 12,000 BC
- 11,000 BC
- 10,000 BC
- 8,000 BC
- 6,000 BC

IX. *Above left*. This handsome copper bull head, the most famous artefact from Bahrain, comes from Barbar, from a votive deposit in the second temple, *c.* 2000 BC.

X. *Above right*. This suite of fine painted goblets was restored from fragments recovered from one of the 'Royal Tombs' at Aali.

XI. Alexander the Great: one of a hoard of silver tetradrachms minted by one of Alexander's successors and found at Qala'at al Bahrain, the principal ancient city site on the island.

XII. This tiny gold piece, probably a dress ornament, was found in one of the 'Royal Tombs' at Aali. It is similar to other objects found in royal burials at Ur and Troy.

offered bad ingots to my messenger, saying 'If you will take it, take it, if you will not take it, go away'. Who am I that you are treating me in this manner – treat me with such contempt? and that between gentlemen such as we are! I have written to you to receive my purse but you have neglected it – who is there among the Dilmun traders who has acted against me in this way?[21]

Babylonian and Sumerian businessmen frequently demonstrate a strong sense of their own gentility and deplore the absence of it in their correspondents. They were, in fact, right to do so. The status of 'gentleman' was defined at law, certainly in Hammurabi's time. It was, for example, considerably more expensive, in terms of the compensation which had to be paid, to wound a gentleman than it was to injure a commoner or a slave.

In another letter Nanni seems to resent the fact that Ea-Nasir has removed a quantity of silver from his house and now 'you make this discussion'.[22] He is worried too that he and others have sworn as to the legality of the contract in the temple of Shamash. The Sun-God was traditionally the witness of all such oaths, thus rendering them sacred, and he had a special care of merchants. In a hymn of praise to the god it is said of him 'the merchant with his pouch, thou dost save from the flood'. Abituram follows, more concisely and with the threat that he will call in Ea-Nasir's mortgages; Abituram, wisely one feels, had actually pinned Ea-Nasir down in writing. Nigga-Nanna, a name that it would be difficult to take seriously today no matter how much one might owe him, makes the first of his several appearances.

> . . . .The silver and its profit give it to Nigga-Nanna. . . . I have made you issue a tablet. Why have you not given the copper? If you do not give it, I will bring in your pledges.[23]

Exasperation dominates the opening of the next letter, still as curt in its address to Ea-Nasir as the others have been:

> Speak to Ea-Nasir: thus says Abituram. Why have you not given the copper to Nigga-Nanna?

He ends on a kinder note, but still with a plea for his copper:

> The work you have done is good. . . . The copper . . . give it to Nigga-Nanna.[24]

The next is no doubt familiar to the modern reader, for it gives the impression of a weary banker dismissing a tiresome client:

> Speak to Ea-Nasir: thus says Imqui-Sin. May Shamash bless your life. Give good copper under seal to Nigga-Nanna. Now you have had one issue ten shekels of silver. In order that your heart shall not be troubled give good copper to him. Do you not know how tired I am? And when you arrive with Itsu-Rabi take it away and give it to Nigga-Nanna.[25]

Nanni's place in the correspondence is now taken by Appa who has the same sort of problem with Ea-Nasir and who also wants, slightly improbably, a copper kettle.

> Speak to Ea-Nasir: thus says Appa. The copper of mine, give it to Nigga-Nanna – good copper in order that my heart shall not be troubled . . . and one copper kettle which can hold 15 qa of water, and 10 minas of other copper send to me. I will pay silver for it.[26]

Ea-Nasir evidently has a partner, Ilsu-ellatsu, for one of the letters is addressed to them both. Another, a rather cagey one in which Ilsu-ellatsu seems to be worried that his partner will upset the client, is addressed by him to Ea-Nasir.

> Speak to Ea-Nasir: thus says Ilsu-ellatsu, with regard to the copper of Idin-Sin. Izija will come to you. Show him 15 ingots so that he may select 6 good ingots and give him these. Act in such a way that Idin-Sin will not become angry.[27]

It would be agreeable to think that in the end Ea-Nasir honoured all his commitments and lived happily ever after with the other financiers of Ur on the profits of the Dilmun copper trade. He appears again, this time in the garment business, a very profitable export line to Dilmun and one which it is difficult not to feel was particularly suited to the egregious Ea-Nasir.

Unhappily, all may not have gone well with Ea-Nasir in the long run. According to Woolley, who excavated his house at Ur, part of it was incorporated into the house next door at the end of the Isin-Larsa period when Ea-Nasir lived and flourished hopefully.[28] In Ea-Nasir's private records, Woolley found evidence of a diversity of interests and a variety of commercial involvement to a degree which would impress a modern entrepreneur. Land speculation, real estate, usury and second-hand clothing were all, apparently, grist to Ea-Nasir's mill.

His ambition, however, seems to have outrun his ability at least in Woolley's view, and to have forced on this agile and adventurous merchant a significant reduction in his standard of living and in the size of his house. At this distance of time, it is probably merely sentimental to hope that part of Ea-Nasir's house was incorporated into his next-door neighbour's residence because his neighbour offered him a good price for it.

It is to Woolley that we owe the location and layout of Ea-Nasir's house in Ur, at the time of Rim-Sin. Woolley was a splendid excavator and a perceptive archaeologist: he was also often idiosyncratic. When he published the results of his epoch-making researches at Ur, so much more remarkable than the findings of the burial of Tutankhamun in the same period (the 1920s), Woolley produced a clear and precisely-drawn street plan of the city as it was in Ea-Nasir's time. For some reason he chose to give the streets, or at least the principal ones, the names of the streets of Oxford where he had been an undergraduate (a contemporary of T. E. Lawrence) in the early years of the century. This produces some curious consequences: Ea-Nasir's address thus becomes 1 Old Street; after his house was combined with his neighbour's it became 7 Church Lane. It would be a courageous archaeologist today, incidentally, who would inscribe two lanes on his city plan as 'Gay Street' and 'Straight Street' respectively.[29]

It is easy to be amused by the bickerings and craftiness of these ancient businessmen whose attitudes, behaviour and even language are so totally that of their modern successors. Yet it must not be forgotten that to the immediate predecessors of Ea-Nasir and his companions, one of the supreme and most glorious achievements of the human race is due.

As far back as the middle of the fourth millennium, trade in Sumer had achieved such proportions that those engaged in it required the means to record their sales and purchases and the stocks of goods and animals which they maintained. From the system which they developed, the earliest known examples of which are baked tablets from Gilgamesh's city of Uruk and from Kish, dated roughly 3500 BC, all writing, so far as we know, descends. From its earliest form, when it was little more than the association of symbols of quantity with the representation of the object concerned, writing quickly evolved to become a sophisticated and flexible instrument for recording, not merely the number of sheep a temple possessed, but the aspirations, fears and delights of men. By the early centuries of the third millennium a formal literature already existed which culminated in the story of Gilgamesh's quest, perhaps the most moving and majestic of all the legends of antiquity; but it is wholly in character with the Sumerians that one of the earliest phonetically-written words should be *dam-gar*, a merchant.

Ea-Nasir, the Dilmun merchant, was clearly more concerned with profit than with poetry. But he has his modest place in the line which runs from the archaic scribes of Uruk and Kish, through the spiky elegance of Sumerian cuneiform and all the written languages of the world to Virgil, Dante and Shakespeare.

Agreeable though it is to associate Ea-Nasir and his colleagues with poetry, it is only part of the story; arguably it is not the most important contribution which ancient enterprises made to human progress and development. Before the creation of armies, a relatively late develop-ment in any real sense, the social and cultural character of one land was most likely to be influenced by another through trade and the contacts and exchanges which it brought about. Merchants were, of necessity, travellers, by nature observant and keen to take advantage of any opportunity which might present itself. Finding a society less de-veloped than that from which they themselves had come, they could introduce new ideas, new ways of doing things, even new beliefs and religious practices. This must have been especially true when there was something, metal perhaps or timber, that they wanted from a less sophisticated land. From those countries that had developed crafts, they brought goods which they had bartered, leaving behind the products of other lands which in turn exercised their influence and contributed to change and progress.

From the earliest times this traffic had extended far across the world. It is to the merchants, and probably in particular to the sea-faring merchants, that much of the credit must go for the bringing of the arts of civilization to backward lands and not, as so many legends would have it, to gods such as Enki or, in Egypt, to the followers of Horus, unless they too combined business with divinity.

Writing, in any fully developed sense, is one thing; the immediate, day-to-day responsibilities of running a business quite another. It is clear that few merchants were themselves literate: each firm would have had scribal staff members who were responsible for the archives and for the management of the firm's correspondence. The production of literary texts could be left to the temple scribes or to ladies of a literary turn of mind, like Sargon the Great's daughter who was a High Priestess in Uruk in the twenty-fourth century BC, and was given to occasional composition.

For the ordinary affairs of the businesses on which so much of Sumer's prosperity was founded, a technique other than the laborious, labour intensive and no doubt costly process of scribal composition was devised: the practice of marking merchandise, documents or other movable property with the impression of a design cut into the face either of a cylinder or of a stamp seal. The latter form, the stamp seal, is one of the special glories of the Gulf cities. Its use made general literacy unnecessary for, whilst it might be difficult for a hard-pressed merchant or his assistants to decipher a written text, anyone could recognize a design, their own or another's, whose repetition would make it familiar very quickly. Before describing the various caches of Dilmun seals from Bahrain and other sites in the Gulf, it may be appropriate to consider more generally the purpose of seals in antiquity for they are amongst the most enduring objects frequently to survive from these remote times. They are of special appeal to those who approach the ancient world from what is nowadays perhaps an outmoded and unfashionable humanistic standpoint, for they are highly personalized objects, most of them unique and hence attributable to one ownership.

To consider them properly we must turn aside from the Gulf for the time being, to begin the examination in much earlier times than when Dilmun and its dependencies flourished. The seals of the ancient Near East, though they are some of the smallest objects to survive from antiquity, give a profound insight into the life, manners and customs of the people of the time. However dimly, they throw light on some of the influences which fashioned the beliefs and concepts which guided the people's lives and on which the religious rituals and practices were based. But first the development of the use of seals must be set into the general context of man's evolution as a social animal, for the use of these objects marks a significant advance in the organization of his world.

The first step on his progress towards humanity was not man's invention of tools – he is not the only animal that uses them – but the evolution of speech as the means of communicating, coherently and conceptually, with the other members of his own species, and to be able to do so consistently. It is not possible to estimate at what point of hominid development speech became possible; probably it went with the assumption of an upright posture and the freeing of the hands for labour. The first words that infant man uttered are likely to have been warnings and indications of direction to the pack in hunting for food. Later, the repetition of sounds associated with objects or emotions became conventionalized and hardened into the names of things. Man has never lost his wonder at the power of language and at its mystery; that everything in the world has its name is still regarded as magical, despite the fact that it was man himself who conferred names on all the rest of creation.

Speech utterly transformed man's potential and, with the marked increase in brain capacity to which it gave rise, he began to emerge as supreme amongst all the animals; after all, as with Adam in the Garden of Eden, the animals themselves received their names from him. It was however uncountable millennia later that he took the next logical step and invented writing as the means of preserving his thoughts and expanding the use of his most valuable attribute, memory.

The lateness of man's invention of writing is the more surprising when the vastly greater antiquity of his conscious use of design is considered. In the late Old Stone Age, painting and sculpture, in both cases dependent upon most careful observation and its recording, reached an astonishing standard of technical achievement. In the darkness of European caves or around the fires of their primitive encampments, draughtsmen and painters, engravers and modellers in clay and stone produced works which, in the representation of life around them and the use of the media they employed, have never been bettered during the tens of thousands of years which separate their makers from the present day.

Art is communication; the seals of Dilmun, whose function was to communicate, are a particularly happy demonstration of that self-evident truth. But to communicate effectively art must observe certain conventions and produce symbols which evoke a response from those with whom it seeks to communicate. Very early in its history, therefore, art became stylized and form was abstracted to dimensions immediately recognizable; thereby its effectiveness as magic, and as an element in ritual inducing awe and a sense of the nearness of the divine, was profoundly deepened. Certain forms, the cross, perhaps indicating the cardinal points, the wide-curving horns of the bull, the pierced or divided circle and a bewildering repertory of stellar and solar symbols, have been sacred from the remotest times to the extent indeed that they seem to be part of man's absolute heritage, as basic to him as the patterns woven by generations of birds when they build their nests. These symbols man has always sought to identify with his environment, both to reassure himself by the sight of the familiar and to mollify the spirits and hidden forces which they came themselves to represent.

The very earliest of them are those most rewarding of study. The designs which descend from the early Anatolian sites, those which later appear in Mesopotamia and Elam and the extraordinary riches of Egyptian design are the most important elements in man's graphic heritage. Other considerations apart, they reveal what are the most potent symbols to a succession not of primitive but of highly sophisticated peoples *before* they were subject to all the influences and pressures of the world outside their own immediate environment. Such design elements are amongst the most potent products of the collective unconscious.

When man began to speculate about his relationship with the world around him and the rest of the natural order, he came to postulate the existence of a further reality which transcended that which he could see with his own eyes. At the same time, and with uncharacteristic logic, he began to hope for his own continued existence beyond death for he could not believe that all the purpose of creation was accomplished within the tiny span of a man's lifetime; indeed, in this mood, he probably discovered time itself, and the fact of death, the knowledge of the inevitability of which is another of the marks which separates him from the other animals.

Surrounded, then, by unknown powers in life as well as in death, he gave thought to deflecting malignant forces and of touching the good-will of 'the kindly ones'. He began to hang about himself charms to achieve these purposes and, in some societies, to decorate his body with magical signs and colours, both by painting himself and by tattooing.

Man has an interesting tendency to seek mechanical solutions to any problem that confronts him. In central Anatolia, at Catal Hüyük in the sixth and fifth millennia before the present era, he seems, remarkably enough, to have devised a method for the repeated impression of stylized designs by means of baked clay stamp seals, with the design scored on the flat under-surface of the seal.[30] Because the designs which they reproduced were often regarded as sacred and celebrated the gods, the seals themselves may have served as amulets and thus transmitted the benefit of their magic to the wearer. There is, further, a strongly probable link between the use of seals, writing and urbanization. As man began to live in permanent communities, the idea of individual property evolved and with it the need to protect and to identify it. To meet these needs, first the seal and then writing itself were invented, with the use of 'tokens' whose extraordinarily long history has recently been demonstrated as a stage preliminary to the development of scripts.[31]

The use of seals was to become one of the most characteristic practices of the peoples, particularly the traders, of the ancient Near East. Whether they originated in Anatolia it is not at present possible to assert positively but certainly none older are known. If they did first emerge there it seems that, although a dark night of oblivion descended on the Anatolian settlements which has only been lifted in the past generation, the practice spread from there, since some of the early forms and symbolisms seem to be preserved, travelling down into

Syria, across to Mesopotamia and Iran and southwards to the Indus Valley; in time, each region developed a form or shape of seal peculiar to it, although, as will be seen later, many of the elements of their design were common or were diffused from one culture to another. The excavator of the remarkable pre-literate, pre-urban 'cities' on the Anatolian plain proposed that the original use of the stamp seals found there was as a means of decorative tattooing on the body and, in what is surely the first glimmering of printing as a mechanical reproduction process, the imposition of designs on textiles.[32] This beginning of the practice of making seals may be dated to the seventh millennium BC.

In the Gulf, seals are the harbingers of capitalism; but they are also talismanic, powerful amulets which invoked the protection of a divinity over the goods which they marked, or even, since some have been found in positions which indicate that they were attached to their owners in their tombs, over the owner himself.

Seals fall broadly into two types, *stamp* seals of which the Gulf examples may be regarded as typical, and *cylinder* seals of which the Akkadian, Old Babylonian and Assyrian empires in Mesopotamia were notable producers. Their purpose is the same, to identify property in a largely illiterate society; not, it should be noted, in specifically pre-literate societies, for the use of seals and the practice of writing are frequently coexistent. The method employed in the actual business of sealing differs in the two types of seal: in the case of the stamp seal a single 'print' of the seal is impressed in the clay either on the object to be identified, a pottery jar, inscribed tablets or a sort of 'bulla' which might be attached to the article concerned; the cylinder seal, by contrast, is rolled out and thus gives a continuous, repeated impression of the design by which its proprietorship is to be distinguished.

Stamp seals were the earlier of the two types to be evolved; the cylinder seal is a product of the later fourth, early third millennium in Mesopotamia. One of the evidences which is frequently cited as demonstrating Mesopotamian influences in late pre-Dynastic and Archaic Egypt (c. 3200–2800 BC) is the appearance of cylinder seals which bear designs with Mesopotamian elements.[33] The adoption of cylinders in Egypt was however a temporary phenomenon, Mesopotamian influence or not; they were soon replaced by one of the most typical of Egyptian product, the scarab, which is in fact a stamp seal. However, at certain times, notably during the First Intermediate Period, immediately prior to the formation of the Middle Kingdom (c. 2000–1780 BC) Egypt developed a type of circular stamp seal very reminiscent of the Gulf forms. Whilst there is no certain evidence, it is not beyond the bounds of possibility that the early second millennium, a time of great mercantile and commercial activity in the Gulf, saw some contact between the Dilmunite culture and Egypt. It was the time of renewed Asiatic penetration of the Nile Valley. In the New Kingdom, however, and subsequently, the scarab became one of the most common of all Egyptian artefacts.

The cylinder seal was in many ways a more efficient product than the stamp seal for it allowed a larger surface to be exposed. Thus many cylinders carry textual inscriptions, an unusual phenomenon with Gulf seals; cylinders are in consequence more frequently capable of being attributed to named owners than are stamp seals.

Seals are frequently miniature works of art of great complexity and appeal. The art of the lapidary must have been highly valued in the communities of the ancient world and the stone carvers or craftsmen, as precise as the most exact jewellers, repaid whatever respect they were accorded by the high standards of their craftsmanship. No seal cutter's tools have survived but what was probably a workshop has been found in Bahrain; no doubt small drills, of copper, bronze or stone were employed in cutting the fine detail of the design once the face of the seal had been prepared by grinding and polishing the surface.

The best of the seals demonstrate one of the special glories of ancient art in the miniature dimensions employed by these archaic craftsmen: the designs can be enlarged to a monumental scale and still retain their proportions and their power. In the Gulf, seals are almost invariably made of chlorite, a relatively soft stone which is easily worked and which engraves well. Sometimes, in the manner of seals from the Indus Valley cities, they are washed with an alkaline solution which gives them a milky-white finish; equally often they are found in the uncoloured stone.

Over four hundred Gulf seals have now been recovered; the largest number comes from the island of Failakah, in the Bay of Kuwait. About seventy-five have been found in Bahrain itself. It is generally believed that the type originated in Bahrain.

There are two types of seal: the earlier with one or two parallel grooves on the domed obverse, the latter with four quarters in which are often set pierced circles. The earlier type tends to emphasise animal figures and astral and solar symbols; the later ones are notable for what appear to be ritual scenes.

The seals from Barbar are all of the second, later type as are those from Failakah. The transition from the earlier to the later form seems to have taken place during Ur III times.

The latest and most typical Gulf seals are of a highly distinctive form which seems to have evolved over a period, from the latter part of the third millennium, and subsequently into the early centuries of the second millennium. When the Kassites moved in to control the Mesopotamian plains and their dependencies in the Gulf, the stamp seal virtually disappeared to be replaced by the cylinder seal which thus finally asserted its functional superiority. The fully evolved form of the Gulf seal is a round stamp, rarely more than one inch in diameter and often smaller. Its obverse is flat and on it the design is carved: animals, cultic scenes or what often appear at first sight to be random elements which are frequently found in various combinations on different seals. The motif of the pierced circle or 'eye' found on the domed reverse very frequently appears on other Gulf products of the period and is often an element in the decoration of, for example, the steatite vessels which are found often in large quantities on sites throughout the region.

After what may have been the Anatolian precedent, the earliest-known seals, dating from the fourth millennium, have been recovered from Syrian and Iranian sites.[34] The earliest of these tend to be stamp seals, which had to be impressed firmly with the fingers into the clay that was to take their image; and often, like the seals from early Mesopotamia, they tend to portray formalized animals, perhaps with a fetishistic or totemic significance. Each level of the Sumerian cities' sites has yielded its crop of seals, the earliest showing highly stylized, abstract designs, whilst the later ages settled upon graphic designs which often appear to be narrative in their purpose. These seals show scenes which can be associated with Mesopotamian myth, such as the hero and the bull-man wrestling with animals, a design which is customarily (though probably anachronistically) ascribed to the Gilgamesh epic, or, later still, scenes of worship and ritual observance, of which the most common is the seal's owner, or perhaps his patron, being presented to one of the great divinities. Episodes from the stories of the gods are displayed, with Enki, Shamash, Nanna and Inanna being amongst those most frequently portrayed.

The Mesopotamian variety demonstrates well the dual function of the seals for, in addition to serving as amulets and thus conferring the protection of the divinity whose name they invoked over the object that they sealed, they also became the means, in predominantly non-literate societies, for property to be identified. Thus, and in time, temple administrations, the rulers of cities and later still the merchants, developed their own marks which made the identification of their property easy and certain. However, it is unlikely that the seals ever wholly lost their amuletic quality. They were also used on legal documents to attest the presence of witnesses or the consent of the parties concerned.

Although the princes of antiquity used their seals to engross treaties and official papers there seems little doubt that the majority of the seals which survive are the personal signets of merchants and businessmen. They are, it might be said, the originals of the trade mark; certainly they served the function of a personal crest and represent the beginnings of heraldry. If this be so, then the European pride in crests and the appurtenances of heraldry not only recalls some noble ancestor but also perhaps a tattooed *shaman* or a Near-Eastern businessman of four thousand years ago.

In Crete, where the extent of ancient trade is incidentally evidenced by the presence of Old Babylonian seals, the custom of seal-making was taken up keenly, and that elegant civilization predictably produced some of the most elegant examples of all. Indeed, with what appears to be the Cretan habit of over-sophistication demonstrating itself in this as in other departments of their society, the Cretan seals are really gems and are frequently classified thus.

In the Indus Valley cities a highly distinctive form of stamp seal was evolved, usually square in shape and with a remarkable massivity in the design elements which were incorporated on the face. The 'Indus Valley script' appears on many of them, often in juxtaposition with the huge, hump-backed bulls which are a significant factor in the sub-continents' agronomy even today. The reverse of the Indus Valley seal usually shows a slight elevation through which the suspension-hole has been bored. Some of the seals, incidentally, seem to portray divinities who were later assumed into the Vedic pantheon.

That trade routes had been open between the Sumerian cities and those of the Indus Valley has long been known by the discovery of Indian seals in cities such as Ur. A third, highly individual type of seal was eventually recognized, which was clearly neither wholly Indian nor wholly Mesopotamian, though the examples recovered seem to contain design elements which could be related to both societies.

This third category of seals found in Sumer, and later in Indus Valley sites, was felt to lie between the other two and so gave rise to the speculation that it might have had its origins in the Gulf. The excavations in Bahrain and Failakah have confirmed this unequivocally and it seems certain that these seals are peculiar to Dilmun, and as such they are now designated.

The distribution of the Dilmun seals follows the routes which the merchants who owned them plied between Sumer and the Indus

Valley; the excavations at Ur produced the first group, several of which are now in the British Museum. These seem to show particular Indus Valley relationships. Others have been found at Lothal, one of the sea ports on the coast of what is now Pakistan, serving the Indus cities.

The dome-shape of the reverse, in the case of the earliest forms, is frequently more of a cylindrical projection from the seal face than the fully integrated dome of the typical Dilmun seal. Some examples are simpler still and are merely round stones bisected horizontally: it is possible that it was from this form of simple 'button' seal that the dome itself later evolved. The designs, with one or two exceptions, are equally simple, in general being confined to one subject, frequently an abstract form, or an animal. Already though, two creatures which will be found throughout the lifespan of the Dilmun seals are in evidence, the scorpion and the bull.

The temple complex at Barbar has yielded its crop of seals, including those which seem to have been deliberately cast into the sacred well there. This group is fully realized in format and the designs are highly sophisticated and aesthetically pleasing; full and sensitive use is made of the circular face of the seal. The design of these seals is noticeably uncluttered when compared with some of the later ones, where the craftsmen have seemingly not been able to resist filling every available millimetre of the surface. The figures of men and animals are full of grace and vitality with that curious sense of arrested motion which is always one of the glories of ancient art.

The largest group of seals from Bahrain comes from the second city level at Qala'at al-Bahrain and thus is to be dated from the end of third millennium and the beginning of the second. The latter period was the time of the *Alik-Tilmun*; it was the apogee of Dilmun's commercial influence and importance. All obvious traces of Indian influence have now been submerged in Mesopotamian and Gulf forms, though some elements are retained from earlier times. Probably contemporary with these seals, a number of which were found among the debris of a seal-cutter's workshop, are those found in the remarkable caches amounting to nearly 500 seals discovered in the remains of an early second-millennium settlement at Failakah. Whilst these conform to the general pattern of Dilmun seal forms, for Failakah was without doubt a province of the Dilmun culture at this time, they have their own distinctive iconography and, in many ways, are the most striking and attractive of all of the seals found in the Gulf.

These later seals are remarkable for their precision, elegance, vitality and craftsmanship; the last characteristic only calling for the slight and occasional qualification that the seal cutter apparently was never able to leave well alone and displayed a tendency to over-elaboration.

They are also remarkable from one further point of view: that, at the present stage of knowledge, their iconography is largely incomprehensible. Of course, many of the elements can be identified but it is not yet possible to advance a coherent explanation of each seal's design. This, of course, presupposes that they are capable of being 'read' and are not merely amalgams of different elements (for no two seals are ever wholly alike) which served to differentiate one owner's property from another. It seems on balance, and with the precedents of both the Mesopotamian and the Indus Valley seals to go on, that they probably did convey some specific ideogrammatic significance to the people who used them.

It has already been noted that in the case of Mesopotamian seals, ritual scenes were customarily depicted, whilst the Indus valley seals frequently incorporated inscriptions, although these are also unintelligible. The Dilmun seals are different in that they often contain groupings of apparently random elements; but the repetition of certain ones, the ibex, gazelle, goat, bucranium, bird, tree, foot, scorpion and others in a variety of permutations, suggests that each element had a particular significance or could be 'read'.

The ibex is one of the most frequently depicted animals, as often found on the Gulf seals as the bull or the scorpion. Often the animal is shown in a curious juxtaposition with the other elements of the seal's design, even sometimes upside down. This may be an attempt to suggest some sort of astronomical relationship.

Many of the seals' designs seem often to be associated with the fertility of animals and men. Some of them may symbolise good and evil, the one to be identified with the owner of the seal, and the other to be propitiated and its malignancy deflected.

Attempts have been made to identify specific seals with known Sumerian myths, and to suggest that they illustrate, for example, incidents from the story of Gilgamesh or the creation myths associated with Dilmun. There is no warrant for such attributions, however, and to describe, as often has been the case, two male figures on a seal from Failakah as Gilgamesh and his friend Enkidu, whilst it is appealing, is misleading and probably quite irrelevant. Not enough is known, for example, of the understanding which the Sumerians themselves had about their own myths and the possibility must be recognized that the duality of Gilgamesh and his friend and the dualism of two figures on a seal, whilst probably representing the same principle, do not necessarily represent each other. The fact that evey figure of a hero wrestling with lions or bulls tends to be labelled with Gilgamesh's name, even in cases which clearly preceded his historical existence, has already been remarked upon and demonstrates the problem of this sort of over-simplification. However, it is only fair to add that it does not in the least matter what interpretation is put upon the seals as they are quite sufficiently potent and appealing to be admired in their own right. Indeed, they are thoroughly engaging if minor works of art, tiny documents which throw a light, however wavering, on the minds of the men who lived in this region four thousand years and more ago.

To date the seals of the Gulf, other than those from Failakah,[35] have not been published fully so that knowledge of them even in archaeology quarters, is very limited. It is to be hoped that eventually, when the corpus of Dilmun seals is published, they will be recognized as having an important part to play in the history of art. In the meantime it is possible to single out some of the seals and some of the elements which frequently appear in their design, for even what must of necessity be only a cursory examination of a few produces considerations of great interest.

The gods, or at least, superhuman beings, appear on many of the seals. They are identified with animals, with ships and with a companion figure, a mysterious part man part bull (whether he is monster or mask is not clear). Often the gods wear the typical horned crown or horned turban of Sumerian divinities.

Amongst the Bahrain seals, one of the most common designs represents the scorpion which appears by itself and in conjunction with other elements, sometimes literally represented and at others portrayed schematically. Several of the scorpion seals are closely similar to examples from Tell Brak in northern Syria but may be earlier in date. It seems possible that the scorpion motif may have originated in the Gulf, perhaps in Bahrain itself. One of the Barbar seals appears to show four scorpions circling a series of superimposed squares, which perhaps represent a sacred area or building; this design would admirably represent the successive levels of a ziggurat, seen in plan.

A design inherited from earlier times is to be recognized in a class of seals, from Failakah as well as from Bahrain, which depict whirling ibex or gazelle heads, four, five or six joined at the neck. The Gulf forms mark a return to literal representations of the symbolization of the creature's fleetness, for the shape became highly abstracted after its introduction in Samarra ware from northern Mesopotamia in the fifth–fourth millennia BC.

One class of seals, that categorized as 'erotic' in the minds of later classifiers, though perhaps less certainly in the minds of those who created them, is represented by two black seals from Barbar and the second city at Qala'at al-Bahrain. The first shows a gigantic, steato-pygous female with her massive legs spread apart being penetrated by a more modestly proportioned male. It is a remarkably athletic copulation for he grasps one of her ankles and she appears, oddly, to be standing on one leg as he enters her, a difficult enough manoeuvre one would have imagined, even for a divinity. It is possible that she is lying above him in what an older generation of anthropologists believed was the conventional position for intercourse in a matriarchal society. More surprising still is that she appears to be vomiting into a jar: even the most fervid imagination might find it difficult to know what to make of this scene. The other seal appears to depict the two same principals and shows the male, not ithyphallic this time as in the previous example, lying passively by the female's opened thighs. This scene does of course recall the healing of Enki by Ninhursag who laid him by her vulva (see Chapter V). These two seals are matched by two others from Failakah which appear to depict in one case an act of sodomy and in the other a frieze of men and monkeys (perhaps boys?) indulging in some rather curious acts. Monkeys, incidentally are known to have been imported from Melukhkha into Mesopotamia through the Gulf in early times.

Two seals stand out from the Bahrain group, both of them from Barbar, for their technique and content seem different from the others, demonstrating, as other examples from Failakah will, that despite the normally rigid conventionalism of ancient art there was still consider-able scope and opportunity for the individual artist. The first shows two confronted men, holding a shield between them, each with a spear grasped in his other hand. Above them appears an 'eye,' an extremely ancient symbol which probably signified the all-seeing divinity of the sun and of which countless examples are known from, for example, the so-called 'Eye Temple' at Tell Brak, and many other sites. The men appear to be wearing either helmets or 'top knots' with their hair shaved to the crowns of their heads.

The other seal shows a male figure standing in a rectangular surround, two sides of which each have a pot, a larger and a smaller one, fixed to them. Beyond the enclosure, on the left, a gazelle turns its head to look at the figure enclosed within it whilst on the right a scorpion is shown. It may be that the two creatures represent life and death and that the scene suggests a burial, with the pots that were customarily placed in the tomb; equally possible is that a figure in a shrine is intended.

Curiously, a painting from an Egyptian tomb, now in the Egyptian Museum in West Berlin, of the First Intermediate period (*c.* 2000 BC) appears to show much the same elements; it and the seal are probably roughly contemporary.[36] A seal from Failakah certainly depicts a

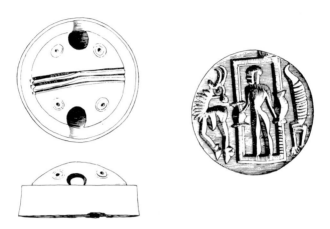

This seal, which may depict a burial, is closely paralleled by a painting on a First Intermediate period tomb from Egypt, with which it is probably roughly contemporary (*Forshistorisk Museum Moesgard*).

complicated ritual scene with two figures standing in an enclosure which bears Mesopotamian symbols of divinity.

Two appealing seals from Bahrain may be considered together; the first shows one of the most celebrated Sumerian motifs, the 'symposium' where two men sit together drinking through straws from the same pot between them. Above them is the sun. The other shows two similar figures gesticulating at each other by a palm tree, this time with the moon's crescent riding over them. It is difficult not to see two Dilmun merchants here, perhaps making their way home together after a hard day's commercial drinking. More formal representations of two figures drinking through long straws also exist on other Dilmun seals.

An important category of seals, hitherto unrecognized, has recently been identified in a perceptive study by a Bahraini scholar, Shaikha Haya Al-Khalifa.[37] The seals in question are all made from sea shells, in contrast to the chlorite or steatite examples which represent the vast preponderance of seals recorded.

The shells employed for the making of the seals are drawn from the species *Conidae*. This is a common shell in the Gulf and is distinguished by its helical form. The adaptation to a seal shape is obtained by sawing off the shell's base, the Dilmunites evidently having realized that each shell has a distinctive configuration in its interior.

So far, the shell seals have been found only in tombs.[38] In this they are different from most Gulf seals which only occasionally were buried with their owners. The shell seals have been found in most types of burial in Bahrain, particularly in those representing the Dilmunite period.

Some of the seals have designs drilled on them in a technique which has been compared with that used by seal cutters in Mesopotamia during the Jamdet Nasr period, though the Bahraini examples must be chronologically much later. Some of them seem to reproduce design elements, particularly of animals and solar and stellar symbols, which appear on the Gulf seals proper.

It is not at present clear whether the shell seals are earlier in date than the chlorite seals or whether they are contemporary. As they are only found in funerary contexts it is, of course, possible that they are simply replicas of the real thing, a relatively inexpensive way of ensuring that the dead did not go wholly seal-less to the after-life.

A notable group of seal impressions was recovered from Barbar.[39] These are flattened pellets of clay on which impressions from small seals appear to have been made, in some cases on both sides of the bullae. Their function is not known and the term *bullae* has only been applied to them as they are in appearance similar to the seal impressions customarily attached to mediaeval European official documents. They introduce a range of quite new designs, one of which appears on several of them; this seems to be a bundle of reeds, bound together at the centre and thus looking rather like the Roman *fasces*. The bundle is enclosed in a rectangle with the lower side missing. On the other side of one such impression appears a series of concentric circles, with looped, serrated edges, which bears some resemblance to a clay seal from the Indian site of Damb Sadaat.

A motif which appears on the Bahrain seals and is also to be found on those from Failakah, though apparently less frequently, is a single human foot; this may be connected with the Mesopotamian 'fringed triangle'. The frequency with which the foot appears in Gulf iconography and in other contexts in Arabia is striking to the extent indeed that it is difficult to avoid the idea that its appearance in the Barbar temple is not accidental. Perhaps it is intended to convey the idea of eternal contact with the chthonic gods, of whom Enki was certainly one and perhaps the first and greatest, by means of the one part of the human body which is generally in permanent contact with the earth, beneath whose surface the gods of the underworld dwell.

The sheer quantity of seals from Failakah is remarkable and frankly puzzling.[40] No part of the site yet suggests a settlement in any way approaching in size and importance as an urban centre the Bahrain City II site. Yet from the latter far fewer seals have been recovered than from Failakah and fewer still from the temple site at Barbar. The one site on Failakah has provided a substantial majority of all the known examples. The eastern province of Saudi Arabia has yielded five seals but, of course, no major third-millennium city site has yet been excavated there.

One explanation, though it must be regarded as wholly speculative for this concentration of seals on Failakah, would relate to the island's apparently sacred character. Perhaps it was customary to dedicate the seals to the presiding divinity, on a merchant's death, for example, or on his retirement from business. But until more of the Failakah site is excavated it is really idle thus to speculate.

The form of the Gulf seals finds its closest counterpart in the square seals of the Indus cities. A few Gulf seals indeed bear Indus characters. It would be natural to see the Gulf seals descending from contact with Indus Valley traders who, it may be presumed, would have met Dilmunite and Mesopotamian merchants in the course of business.

However, as it is doubtful whether all Indus Valley seals are as old as the earliest Gulf seals, it seems unlikely that the Indian influence could be predominant. Equally, it seems improbable that the highly developed Indus cities would have borrowed the form of their seals, with little adaptation, from the Gulf. It is more likely that both found their inspiration in some other culture, perhaps on the Persian side of the Gulf where early urban centres in Elam, Susiana and at Shar-i-Sokta and Tepe Yahya developed in a region which is contiguous both to the Gulf and to lands close to the sphere of influence of the Indus cities.

The Failakah seal designs are generally, though not always, more complex and involved than the Bahraini examples. Animal forms predominate with scenes of sacrifice being common. The principal sacrificial animal appears to be the bull, but gazelle or ibex, and scenes of the chase are frequently depicted. It will be recalled that Arrian makes the point that, in the time of Alexander, deer and wild goats were bred on Failakah for sacrifice to the island's goddess.

A variety of elements recur in the Failakah seals. A large bird, perhaps an ostrich, or, since two of them are shown on a seal surmounting a large bull of Indus type, possibly 'the bird of Melukhkha' which is thought to have been the peacock, are often included in the iconography. Whatever species it is, the bird on the seals is clearly the same as the copper bird excavated at Barbar.

A puzzling feature on many seals is a chequer design of a regular squares, sometimes nine, fifteen, sixteen, twenty, twenty-four, twenty-eight and, in one case, forty in number. These chequers are usually shown in close association with significant human – or divine – figures who may be standing on or over them as if they were an altar, holding them or presenting them. Like the Egyptian hieroglyph which has a similar form, this symbol may well represent a town or settlement and the figure with which it is associated, either the king or its tutelary divinity. Occasionally, animal heads project from the chequer design.

It is notoriously difficult to interpret the intentions of ancient craftsmen and artists in attempting to determine what real purpose was in their minds. However, there is one category of seals that is especially interesting and, by the frequency with which one particular motif is present, perhaps one of special significance to the region, though they come, in fact, from Failakah. This group of seals seems to display evidence of an extensive and highly developed bull cult.

If it were possible to speculate about the principal religious cult at Failakah, it would be reasonable to suppose this to have been concerned with bulls, as some of the most remarkable of the designs feature the bull in what are obviously ritual contexts. A figure peculiar to the Failakah seals introduces a mysterious, hieratic note; a man with hooved feet and a tail wearing what may be a bull-mask, a variation of the horned-turban of Sumerian divinities, is frequently portrayed.[41] In one seal he holds the severed head of a bull, standing on the chequer symbol as two ibexes turn their heads away; in another two masked figures support a third, less distinct, personage upon an altar. Above them, one of the great eight-petalled rosettes which frequently occur on the Failakah seals dominates the middle ground with two more beside the officiants at the sacrifice, if that is what the scene depicts. Above them, two bulls stand whilst monkeys leap on their backs.

The last of the seals featuring bulls to be described here is one which recalls, however anachronistically, the treasure of the Royal Tombs at Ur. Some of the most spectacular of the Ur finds were the great ceremonial harps and lyres which were buried with the dead princes and their courtiers. These were notable for the finely worked bull-heads which decorated the lyres' sounding boxes. On the Failakah seal a man is shown, seated and drawing his fingers across the harp's strings. But the harp itself has turned into a bull with the instrument's front strut projecting from the animal's back, an artist's extension, obviously, of the idea of the bull-headed sounding box. Gudea, the King of Lagash, incidentally, records that a lyre, which he dedicated to a temple in his city, 'bellowed like a bull' when played.

The 'harp-bull' is standing on the back of another, larger bull before whom stands a man with an axe raised over the head of what is clearly intended to be the sacrifice. A palm branch, a bird, an open square and what are probably planetary symbols complete an intricate and remarkable design.[42] Is it possible that the votive axes at Barbar commemorated the bull sacrifice, here seemingly depicted? There is evidence that animals were tethered to pierced stone blocks in the sacrificial area of the temple there.

These bull motifs on the Failakah seals do prompt speculations which, in their implications, at least, are exciting. If a cult of the bull existed in the Gulf at the end of the third millennium this itself is surprising enough: but taken with the seeming evidences of rituals and symbolism which became, in later centuries, associated with the northern Levantine coast and from there were transmitted to Crete, the prospect opened up is, in archaeological and historical terms, extraordinary. Perhaps, as so frequently has been confirmed by others about his reports, which once were regarded as wholly unreliable and then were proved to be accurate, Herodotus had sound reasons for relating the belief that the Phoenicians came originally from the Gulf; except, perhaps, that it was not the Phoenicians of whom he ought to have been speaking but their predecessors, the peoples who populated the Levantine coast at the beginning of the second millennium and who brought with them cults of the bulls which were to be transplanted so spectacularly in that other island, Crete, in the second millennium.

If it could be substantiated that the islanders of the Gulf emigrated to the Levant, perhaps around the beginning of the second quarter of the second millennium, it would explain why there seems to have been a sudden break in continuity, at least in religious practice, in Bahrain and in Failakah at that time. Though several small objects from the second millennium have been found, the ruins of the third millennium settlement at Failakah do not seem to have been succeeded by any important buildings until Hellenistic times, just as the last temple at Barbar, c. 2000 BC, seems to be followed by an abandonment of the site.

Other seals from Failakah may be mentioned briefly: a beautiful and almost Matisse-like design of two naked men apparently masked, standing in a boat; a third, smaller figure is leaping from it, his leg thrown up over the stern. One of the most handsome of all the seals and so far unparalleled is double-sided with a milled edge which, with the dignity of its design, gives it the appearance of a Renaissance medallion; on one side two men are seen in a boat, in the act of worship, one of

This seal (left), from Failakah, appears to show a sacrifice of a bull (on the back of the larger animal) which is in fact a lyre. This recalls both the bull-headed lyres from the Royal Tombs at Ur and the handsome copper bull- or ox-head from Barbar.

This design (right) of three figures in a boat is of great antiquity though rarely so beautifully produced as in this example from a Failakah Island seal.

them holding a palm branch; on the other side, a divinity is enthroned with a worshipper standing before him.

Of particular interest to the cults of Dilmun is the seal which shows a tall, etiolated, standing figure in the centre of the seal with the remainder of the surface incised with vertical registers of a cuneiform text, so far the only one to be found on any seal from Dilmun. The text is an invocation to Inzak, God of Dilmun, and recalls the Durand inscription with which it is approximately contemporary. Another seal unique in form and technique is cut in a fine green steatite. Two men stand, looking outwards from the seal, caught for ever in some ritual, perfectly symmetrical action. They are naked but for belts around their waists which are of an almost Cretan narrowness; their fingers are entwined. Both have elegantly curled wigs and beards of a form known from Sumerian precedents. On the other face of the seal a circle encloses an eight-rayed star and at the four cardinal points, an ibex stands, the creature of Enki; between each ibex is an eight-petalled rosette. The seal is banded with gold, suggesting that its owner might have been royal, and in this it has no precedent.

Egyptian influence seems curiously to be represented by a seal the reverse of which is carved in the form of a scarab, though it retains the

The boat with the animal-headed prow (top left) is found also on Mesopotamian cylinder seals and recalls some of the predynastic representations of boats from Egypt, where similar animal-headed boats are often depicted. On the right, one of the erotic seals (*Forshistorisk Museum, Moesgard*).

(Below) Banded with gold and so finely carved that it is more like a jewel than a workaday seal, this example is double-sided: on the obverse showing two heroes and on the reverse the eight petalled rosette denoting a god and the ibex, the creature of Enki.

three incised parallel lines of the typical dome seal form on the lower part of its back.[43] This is all the more surprising when it is remembered that the scaraboid seal did not become common in Egypt until the Middle Kingdom, at the end of the third millennium BC. Scarab seals are known from Ur and the Failakah example could easily be contemporary with them. At first sight, it would seem that Egyptian traders were active in Dilmun and in its Mesopotamian commercial metropolis: yet the fact that the scarab only becomes common in Egypt *after* this period is puzzling. Some apparently Middle-Kingdom scarabs have been found in Bahrain.[44]

(Left) Two warriors hold between them a buckler, surmounted by an eye(?); a duck-like bird is swimming beneath their feet. (*Forshistorisk Museum, Moesgard*).

(Right) The palm tree and the ibex, sometimes associated with the god Enki, dominate this seal (*Forshistorisk Museum, Moesgard*).

From a group of Dilmun-type seals excavated at Ur and now in the British Museum comes one which has a design strangely different from any others and which would seem more appropriate to a later age.[45] A man is portrayed bearing on his shoulders a pole from which hang two large pots; above him there are two stars or rosettes and beside him, two indeterminate creatures. This design is most evocative of the water-carrier; perhaps it is Akki, the drawer of water, commemorated in the legend of Sargon's birth and upbringing, who is here depicted.

One late Sumerian cylinder seal, dating to the very early second millennium, has been found on Bahrain; it comes from the time of the Isin-Larsa dynasty. It is thought to be comparable in date with a Dilmun seal impression found on a tablet, probably from Ur, which can be dated precisely to the tenth year of King Gugunum of Larsa, in 1923 BC. This is one of the few reasonably certain dates in the history of the region.

The study of ancient seals is profoundly revealing of the societies which made them; they also exercise a special appeal in that they are wholly personal objects and, although this cannot positively be asserted, may well represent in their design and symbolism the direct choice of the men who first owned them long ago. It may be said that some of the Dilmun seals equal the finest achievements of gem-cutters from far more celebrated cultures and that they deserve to rank high in the history of glyptic art. It would be difficult to have imagined a more unlikely prospect when excavations first began in Bahrain but, in many ways, the seals of Dilmun may prove to be among the most significant additions to the corpus of knowledge of the ancient world to have been gained in recent years.

VIII

Greater Dilmun and its Neighbours

There is a third Dilmun, to be added to the paradisial Dilmun of myth and the mercantile Dilmun of commodities and trade. Really, this third Dilmun is an extension of the Dilmun of ships and sailors, of merchants harvesting their profits from the city on the island's northern shore. This is the temporal Dilmun, the political organism whose dominion from time to time extended along the east Arabian shore as far as the Bay of Kuwait and included the islands which lie close to the point where the two great rivers of Iraq end their journey in the headwaters of the Gulf.

In the present state of knowledge and at this distance of time it is not possible to speculate meaningfully on what sort of political organization constituted the Dilmunite state in the third and early second millennia when it was at its most important. We know that Ur-Nanshe of Lagash claimed to receive tribute from Dilmun in the twenty-sixth century BC.[1] This implies that even at that time Dilmun was a state, though standing in the status of client to one of the principal Sumerian powers, if Ur-Nanshe is to be believed. Some two hundred years later Sargon would seem to have captured Dilmun and added it to his new-founded empire. Other kings after him claimed sovereignty over the Holy Land. We know the names of several of Dilmun's later kings: Uperi, who lived 'like a fish in the midst of the sea', Hundaru and Qanaia, to mention three. Throughout this long period Dilmun as a political entity seems to have extended and contracted, sometimes being confined in extent to the Bahrain islands, at others embracing the whole coast to the west and north. It is not without point, bearing in mind the extraordinarily long currency of names in Arabia, that the Hasa province of Arabia has from time to time been known as Bahrain, though this did not always imply any political control over the mainland by the islanders. In his original report to the Viceroy's Foreign Department in 1879, Durand reproduces a map from a somewhat earlier date which shows 'El-Bahrein' as embracing the Qatar peninsula as well as the whole of eastern Arabia.[2]

As far as we know Dilmun never incorporated Qatar within its boundaries. There are reports of the remains of settlements on Qatar which include Barbar material but they are scanty and do not seem to represent any major evidence of permanent or long-lasting habitation.[3]

It is the mainland which extends from due west of Bahrain up to the edge of the marshlands of southern Iraq which was often associated with the islands. From this it seems that insular Dilmun was able to sustain its territorial links with Sumer, far to the north. If the Sumerians did come to their land from the south then this identification of the mainland coastal regions with Dilmun would presumably have per-petuated the route of their migration from Dilmun. It may have been this migration indeed that they were thus disposed to commemorate by the retention of the island's name for the mainland. We know that the Sumerians, on the evidence of some of their far distant settlements in northern Syria, for example, were capable of seeding and sustaining colonies which were essentially Sumerian in character, established in an alien environment far removed from the homeland. It could be that this is at least how Dilmun began and it was sustained by its landward connection to the north with Sumer, as much as by the sea. The difference is that the Syrian settlements were heavily fortified whilst City I at Bahrain was not. In this connection it has been suggested that the Sumerians turned to the Gulf and southward in search of trade only after they were driven out of their northern outposts. The evidence, at present, is obscure.

Archaeologically speaking, the eastern seaboard of Arabia has been much less thoroughly researched than Bahrain. This has been the consequence of several random factors: the reluctance of the authorities in the past to permit surveying (a position now substantially revised), the difficulties of the terrain and, until very recent times, the general unawareness, even by scholars, of the region's historical significance. The exceptions to this generalization are Kuwait (or rather Failakah island) and parts of eastern Saudi Arabia.

It is of course on the basis of the partial excavation of the late third millennium/early second millennium settlement site, the great caches of Dilmun seals, the occasional inscription and the plentiful pottery recovered from the site, that the links between Dilmun and Failakah have been established. Parts of the Epic of Gilgamesh may be set in and around the Gulf shores and Dilmun; in that story the presence of Siduri, a goddess, is important, for she lives in an island on the edge of the ocean which is known as the Garden of the Sun. Gilgamesh visits her at the beginning of his quest. She was, in Sumerian times, the tutelary goddess of the Gulf, who resided in her garden and dispensed drinks to travellers, particularly those who were about to cross the waters of death from which, unlike Gilgamesh, they would not return. It seems most probable that Failakah was Siduri's island, as Burrows indeed proposed.[4] If this were so it would account for the sanctuary on the island and for its reputation as a place sacred to the goddess, under whatever name – a reputation so long enjoyed.

Moving down the coast, the desert coastal strip now contained within Kuwait's frontiers has not revealed any evidence of settlement, even of occasional habitation. This is a trifle surprising; it may be that the evidence is there to be recovered but has not yet been identified. It may be that what there was, perhaps sparse in any case, has been lost in the development projects, roads, the spread of oil exploitation and the building of modern towns. It is also possible that the change in shore-levels, that perennial factor in any assessment of the Gulf's earlier history, has sent what evidence there was underwater. Relatively easily accessible water resources generally decline as one moves northward along the coast towards Kuwait. However, the lack of evidence is the more surprising in that the somewhat indefinite region known as 'the Sealand', which flourished as an independent, if rather shadowy, kingdom on the northern reaches of the east Arabian shore in the later centuries of the second millennium, must have included this region in its territory.[5]

Further down the coast, in what is now the territory of the Kingdom of Saudi Arabia, the situation is markedly different. Intensive survey of the surface sites in the eastern region, as in the other parts of the Kingdom, over very recent years has revealed much already and promises more in the years to come.

The later millennia of the Stone Age are well represented in the east.[6] Unlike other parts of Arabia there appears to be no evidence of human occupation until neolithic times: what were thought to be palaeolithic (even 'Neanderthal') facies have now been shown all to come from new Stone Age times. The Palaeolithic is generally well represented in Arabia as a whole. In the Najd, the Central Region, focussed on Riyadh the capital of the Kingdom, extensive palaeolithic evidence has been recovered, yet there is so far nothing from the east.[7] The explanation can only be that in palaeolithic times the level of the Gulf was substantially higher and that the east was under water. When, in the period between 17000 BC and 9000 BC, the waters withdrew leaving the Gulf itself largely uncovered, it is probable that any humans that inhabited the region would have stayed near to the ancient course of the Euphrates which then debouched at the Straits of Hormuz. Such material evidence as they would have left behind them would therefore now lie fathoms deep beneath the Gulf's waters. Many of the neolithic tools, the blades for example, the pink tools from Khor in Qatar, the many excellently shaped arrow-heads and leaf-shaped artefacts, are distinctive and memorable suggesting that when neolithic craftsmen established themselves they were already possessed of a secure industrial tradition. But it is with the first appearance of pottery in the region that the interconnections between the mainland and the islands may properly be said to begin.

At the end of the neolithic period, about seven thousand years before the present, an entirely new factor enters the history of the Gulf. It is a factor of crucial importance and it has caused a mild recurrence of the old controversy about the origin of the Sumerians. The evidence in question was the recognition (originally by two archaeological enthusiasts from ARAMCO, the oil company whose headquarters are in the eastern region) of sherds of pottery which could be classified as belonging to the Ubaid culture of southern Iraq, the first such culture to be established in the land which was, several thousand years later, to become Sumer.[8]

The Ubaid pottery, a highly distinctive ware which, once it has been seen, is virtually impossible to mistake for any other, has a rich repertory of elegant, predominantly geometric patterns. It has now been identified on a number of sites in the northern reaches of the eastern Arabian coast, in Qatar and in Bahrain; more sites are probably now lost, submerged as a consequence of the changes which have occurred in the Gulf's sea levels since Ubaid times. Some forty Ubaid sites have been identified in eastern Arabia clustering around Ain Qannas, Dosariyah and Abu Khamis.[9]

Many of the eastern Arabian Ubaid sites are small coastal settlements, probably concerned with fishing, some of which appear to have been occupied over quite extended periods. The pottery, which incidentally is invariably discovered in association with late neolithic stone tools, is relatively late Ubaid, from the third phase of its development. One more or less complete pot from Khursaniyah shows that it was made on a slow wheel. Spectrographic analysis has produced the interesting conclusion that all of it was made near Ur.[10]

The presence of Ubaid pottery on eastern Arabian sites is probably evidence of contact, however indirectly, between the makers of the

These fine awls and borers from Ubaid sites in Eastern Arabia, may demonstrate the extreme antiquity of the pearl trade, as it is thought that they may have been used in adapting pearls to function as ornaments. (*Museum of Archaeology and Ethnography, Riyadh*, enlarged).

A reconstructed pot of Ubaid III type from eastern Arabia. (*Museum of Archaeology and Ethnography, Riyadh*).

pottery in Ur and small populations of semi-nomads who set up camp seasonally to fish; it is also a testimony to the distances over which pottery might be traded, even in this very early time. It may also be that fishermen from the early Sumerian cities came down to the Gulf in search of sea water catches. The Gulf's waters have for long been exploited; the coastal sites have yielded, from a somewhat later date than the Ubaid sites, evidence of what was most likely to have been the harvesting of the pearl beds. Most pertinent here was the discovery of tiny awls and borers associated with fragments of mother-of-pearl which suggested that even five thousand years and more ago the pearl was being adapted for ornament.[11] Spindle whorls, from the same levels, indicate that some form of fabric-making was practised.[12]

The excavation of the Ain Qannas Ubaid settlement produced much original and important evidence.[13] Not the least of it was the analysis of spring sediments which showed that during the period 5000–3000 BC the eastern Arabian climate was, from time to time, moister than today.

The houses which were inhabited at this time have left their traces. That they were made of reeds is revealed by pieces of reed-impressed plaster which were recovered from Dosariyah.[14] Similar building techniques are still used by the Marsh Arabs, living in the extreme south of Iraq, in building their splendid reed houses, the *mudhif*.

At the height of the Gulf's ancient prosperity, when Dilmun flourished and her trade was, in effect, universal since it touched most of the then known world, cities of substance and wealth were established on the Arabian mainland. Thus far, the most important settlement to be found is probably located on the small island of Tarut, close to the mainland to which it is now linked by a causeway, somewhat to the north of the Bahrain islands. Tarut, no doubt, served as the point of access to the mainland regions, with the peoples of which the Dilmunite merchants sought to trade, exchanging their goods for the produce of the region, particularly its dates.[15]. Tarut was not the only significant eastern Arabian settlement however: a substantial site has been identified near Abqaiq, by Dhahran, where there are also large tumulus fields. Mound fields in great quantity have also been located near the great Yabrin oasis in the southern part of the province. Late fourth-millennium pottery, which some observers have considered might be ancestral to Bahrain's Barbar pottery, has also been noted in this region. It is contemporary with Uruk pottery in southern Mesopotamia.[16]

It is possible to observe in eastern Arabia at this time the beginnings of two other most enduring social structures which have characterized

An extremely handsome example of Early Dynastic Sumerian-style statuary, a male figure carved in a fine white limestone *c.* 2700 BC from Tarut. (*Museum of Archaeology and Ethnography, Riyadh*).

the area ever since: the establishment of agricultural communities in the rich oases in the hinterland and, on the coast, the creation of coastal settlements. These eventually grew from fishing villages to little towns and formed the basis of the later third and second millennia trading entrepôts.

It has not been possible thoroughly to excavate the *tel* at Tarut; that it is of exceptional antiquity is, however, abundantly clear. Eventually, no doubt, excavation will begin on what could prove to be one of the most exciting of east Arabian sites.

From the environs of Tarut has come one of the most remarkable, indeed perhaps *the* most remarkable, of the antiquities of eastern Arabia, which suggests something of its importance and prosperity in Dilmunite times. This is a very fine white limestone statue, *c.* 3 feet tall, of a man in an attitude of worship.[17] He has the broad, rather podgy

face, with wide, adoring eyes with which the Sumerians were accustomed to portray themselves when engaged in prayer. He is nude,
which suggests that he may represent a priest or an official, since in early
Sumerian times there is evidence that the priests conducted their rites in
a state of ritual nudity.

The statue is exceptionally well made. If it had been found in a
Sumerian city it would have been remarkable enough and might well be
regarded as a fine piece of particularly high quality; that it was found six
hundred miles from the nearest Sumerian city is more remarkable still.
It is formidable evidence of the prosperity and importance which the
Gulf must have enjoyed at the beginning of the third millennium, to
which the Tarut statue is to be dated. It was found buried in a field by a
farmer ploughing his land. Naturally enough the villagers, for this was
in the 1950s before sophisticated notions had reached the region,
decided that this shameless object was a petrified *djinn* or evil spirit; the
statue was therefore beheaded and cut in half. It has now been reassem-
bled, almost pristine, except for some damage to the face. It is a very
remarkable work of high and quite unexpected quality.

Large quantities of worked steatite have been found on third-
millennium sites in eastern Arabia, notably at al-Rafi'ah near Tarut.[18]
There seems to have been a considerable industry in the carving of this
tractable material into bowls, vases and all manner of vessels. The style
of carving is extremely distinctive: bold, emphatic and curiously static,
often a trifle naive in concept but not in execution. The repertory of
design is remarkable: large felines, bearded men, nude and heroic, and
scenes associated with sailing, the sea and fishing. A curious survival is a
group of beard curls in chlorite, probably imitating the lapis lazuli
beards with which the statues of the gods were often adorned.

The origin of these steatite vessels, which are found throughout
third-millennium levels in the Gulf and adjacent lands, seems to lie in
south-western Persia, where evidence of steatite mining has been found
at Shar-i-Sokta, though a western Arabian source is also known. The
trade which depended upon the mining of the stone was wide ranging;
it has been extensively studied.[19] Some early vessels from Arabian sites
have a distinctly Egyptian look to them and *may* be evidence of a trade
extending far from the West. A handsome alabaster vessel of Old
Kingdom type is very like those known from Barbar, while a steatite
vessel, plain and very elegant, which was sufficiently prized to have
been repaired in antiquity, is similar to archaic period vessels from
Egypt. A macehead from the eastern region is of the bold 'Sumerian'
type which is identified in Egypt at the end of the pre-dynastic period

A large quantity of excellently carved chlorite fragments has been recovered from Eastern Arabian sites of the early third millennium. (*Museum of Archaeology and Ethnography, Riyadh*).

XIII. The rock drawings of Oman are found in many of the desert *wadis*, sometimes high up on the rock surface.

XIV. The so-called cup marks to be found in quantity on the rocks of Qatar. Their significance is still a matter of conjecture.

XV. Copper slag heaps in northern Oman are witness to the extent of the mining expeditions of the third millennium when the mines, it is believed, supplied much of Sumer's copper shipped up the Gulf via Dilmun–Bahrain.

XVI. Cairn burials are also typical of early Oman. The neatly structured piles of stone are often set along ridges or on the summit of hills.

Large archaic (Early Dynastic) pottery jars from near Abqaiq testify to connections between eastern Arabia and the Sumerian cities to the north. (*Museum of Archaeology and Ethnography, Riyadh*).

and has been seen by some commentators (though by no means all) as evidence of an invading and conquering race who inaugurated the Dynastic period.[20]

Some Dilmun seals have been found in eastern Arabia; three were picked up from the surface, lying in close proximity to each other.[21] They are of a type typical of the late third or early second millennium BC; they were found to the north of Hofuf. The extent of the Gulf's trading connections and the quality of the craftsmanship employed in the manufacture of the stone which was exported to it is demonstrated by a beautiful lapis lazuli fragment depicting a man wrapped in his cloak. It is a tiny piece but full of vitality; the Sumerians and their neighbours seem always to have worked best in a relatively small scale.

A small figure, carved in lapis lazuli, a semi-precious stone greatly valued by the people of the third-millennium cultures and found only in distant Pakistan. The figure represents a man wrapped in a cloak. (*Museum of Archaeology and Ethnography, Riyadh*; enlarged).

Throughout the eastern region there are extensive mound fields of the same types of tumulus burials familiar from Bahrain. They appear to cluster in the same periods: in the second half of the third millennium to the early centuries of the second and again in Hellenistic times.

The presence of the tombs on the mainland is a witness to the prosperity of Dilmun and the power of its appeal to the people who lived either within its boundaries or on whom it exercised a special cultic or religious attraction. It was suggested by the Danes[22] that the existence of tumulus burials of identical type on the mainland of Arabia destroyed the argument that Bahrain was a sepulchral island. They proposed, instead, that the burials in the two areas were of local, indigenous populations. Of course it could be argued that the opposite is the case: the presence of burials in mainland Dilmun as well as on the island could be taken to demonstrate the sanctity of the whole Dilmun region, not merely of its island capital. However, the evident prosperity of the region in the third and second millennia, linked with its exceptional sanctity, may well account both for a substantial population and for the importation of the cadavers of those who hoped for some great assurance of immortality by being buried in the Holy Land.

Like Bahrain, eastern Arabia seems to have enjoyed two high points of prosperity and settlement: in the third and early second millennia and again late in the first millennium BC. Nothing yet has been found of the post from which Ili-ippasra complained to his superiors in Babylon about the depradations of the Ahlamu and their seizure of the dates waiting shipment to the capital (see Chapter IV). But in later Hellenistic times the evidence is considerable, including the remains of a substantial city at Thaj.

But much remains unsure. The most abiding mystery concerns the whereabouts of the once great city of Gerrha. This is now unknown, though several locations have been suggested for it by commentators and researchers, from Durand onwards.[23]

One such putative location is at or near Uqayr. There does not appear to be any evidence to support this suggestion but two of the most engaging (if very untypical) Saudi Arabian antiquities are said to come from near there. These are a pair of tiny elephants, understood to have been purchased at Qatif in the 1930s. They are charming representations of an animal which can hardly have been very familiar to the Sumerians or the Gulf people, except through their dealings with the people of the distant Indus Valley where the elephant was indigenous. The little pair *look* Sumerian in workmanship, however, and they were evidently prized, for one is made in blue azurite, with flakes of chalcopyrite whilst its companion is made in what was originally described by the oil company geologist who examined them, as 'possibly anhydrite'. Both stones are unusual for the area. They were handed over to the Bahrain Museum some years ago: it might be appropriate to return them now to their country of presumed origin.

Near the frontier between Saudi Arabia and Qatar three Dilmun seals were found lying on the surface, some years ago. They are amongst the relative few which have been discovered in the Kingdom, and, since they tend to be associated with Dilmun's later centuries, this may be because the centre had shifted from the mainland to the island. On crossing the frontier, Qatar itself would at first sight seem unpromising archaeological territory: a small peninsula jutting out into the Gulf, which is wind- and sea-scoured, barren and inhospitable. Yet it has, in fact, much to arrest the archaeological eye and all that it has is distinctive and different from the other states in the region. Indeed it is one of the common features of the archaeology of the Gulf that each little state, superficially similar to its neighbours with which it will have certain elements in common, maintains an individuality which marks it off from the others as firmly as the often somewhat arbitrarily imposed frontiers which now divide one from another.

The neat, painstaking and, in so many ways, impressive categories into which the Qatar Stone Ages were divided by the Danes, early on in their expeditions to the Gulf, have been somewhat revised by later, French scholars.[24] The earlier divisions suggested that the first Stone-Age settlers established themselves on archaic shorelines, well into the Qatar deserts of today, and were characterized by massive, very brutish looking handaxes. They, the so-called A Group, were, it was suggested, connected with the makers of middle-Palaeolithic axes known to popular imagination as the Neanderthals. They were followed by three other principal Stone-Age industries, culminating in the so-called D Group, the makers of the fine and elegant tools of the later Neolithic. Now, the French believe, all the Qatar tools are from Neolithic times and that, in common with all the other parts of eastern Arabia (though not all the rest of the peninsula), there is no evidence of any occupation by humans before the Neolithic period.[25]

However, the fact remains that the Qatar deserts, harsh and grudging to life as they always seem to be, have yielded a fine repertory of stone tools, which remains, indeed, unrivalled in eastern Arabia. No habitation sites have been found from periods earlier than the occasional one with Ubaid material. There are many workshop sites, however, where Stone-Age craftsmen made their tools (even the finest, it seems, with speed and precision).

It was the French who first cast doubt on the previous assumption of a Palaeolithic of Mousterian date for some of the Qatar artefacts. They

Stone Age axes from Qatar.

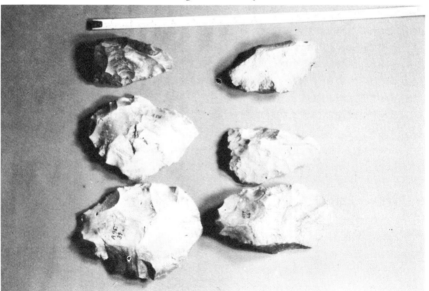

222

suggest that the sea transgressed, leaving the existing *sabkha* behind, about six thousand years before the present day. They believe they have identified Ubaid pottery, *c.*4500 BC, around the edges of what could have been permanent freshwater stands. They identify one site as a fish drying place; whilst extensive fish remains have been found, they do not include vertebrae. There is evidence of cremation on the site.

A small cairn field nearby was perhaps once an island, 12–15 feet in diameter. The Ubaid material recovered dates to Ubaid III. More interesting still is the possibility that they may have identified a Barbar structure on a small island in the Bay of Khor. Two typical Barbar pots have been recovered from the site.[26]

The products of the Neolithic inhabitants of Qatar are some of the most elegant tools produced by any Stone Age people; they are finely and beautifully made, with the best of them being fabricated by the technique of pressure-flaking. This consists of striking off tiny even flakes from the cutting edge of a tool during manufacture, thus producing a consistent edge or, if it is required, a serrated one. This technique reaches perhaps its highest manifestation in pre-dynastic Egypt, where knives in particular were expertly fashioned to produce works of art of the quality of the justly famous ceremonial knife from Gebel el-Arak, which is one of the Egyptian documents most frequently cited to demonstrate links between Egypt and Mesopotamia in the centuries immediately before the unification of Egypt into one state. The Gebel el-Arak knife displays a whole repertory of Mesopotamian motifs on its ivory hilt, which are as finely made as the blade itself. Only about two thousand years later were craftsmen in Europe producing pressure-flaked tools of comparable grace.

The flint arrowheads and leaf-shaped scrapers are unquestionably things of beauty. It is of course, an irresistible if idle speculation to wonder whether their makers themselves saw them as possessing both aesthetic and utilitarian qualities; probably they did not, though some of them are so sensitively worked, improved apparently far beyond the mere levels of their immediate usefulness, that it is impossible not to ask the question. The maker of the Gebel el-Arak knife certainly was aware of what he was doing since that knife is obviously ceremonial, made to impress rather than to cut.

Amongst the more distinctive products of the Qatar Neolithic is a find blade culture which dates from comparatively early in the sequence, from the seventh and sixth millennia.[27] Some of the Qatar neolithic products could have been used as trimming tools, such as the sickle blades which were set into hafts. There is no evidence of an early agricultural phase in Qatar (unlike its near neighbour, Bahrain) so it is likely that these tools probably served simply to assist in gathering wild grasses.

Late prehistoric man, physically and intellectually indistinguishable from ourselves, his direct descendants, comes very near us when the products of his hands are as fine and as appealing as these from Qatar. We know now, from the observation of flint knappers of the present (or near present) day, who have kept alive this oldest of man's technologies, what a marvellous technique the making of fine stone tools is. In fact, though it requires much skill, the knapping of a flint is, to a master, neither onerous nor particularly time-consuming; the finest ripple-flaked blade might be made in a morning or less, a fine arrowhead of the type found in relative profusion in Qatar, in a matter of thirty minutes or so. But one of the qualities that distinguishes the neolithic craftsman from his predecessors in the working of flint and other friable stones is that his greater industrial efficiency and his ability to select more manageable stone meant that he could produce far more cutting-edged tools per kilo of stone than was possible in earlier times. Evidently something approaching organized industrial processes was by now employed in making stone tools. Preliminary roughing out of the blanks produced from suitable 'cores' would take place at a workshop site, the blanks being taken then to a superior craftsman at a finishing site. Several such workshop sites have been identified in Qatar.

The Neolithic people, who were almost certainly migrants from outside Qatar and eastern Arabia, scattered their sites widely over the peninsula. Naturally enough though, their settlements concentrated mainly around the shoreline, for they would have been fisherfolk as well as hunter-gatherers, though their fishing would probably have been confined to trapping and spearing.

An incident in the life of a hunter which occurred on a day around 10,000 years ago is preserved dramatically in one Neolithic artefact which has survived in Qatar.[28] Urgent in pursuit of his quarry the hunter shot his arrow and, it must be presumed, missed his target. The arrow was lost, falling into a shallow pool or on to marshy ground. Over the millennia a calciferous deposit formed around the arrowhead, which is now firmly embedded in what appears to be stone. By so trivial an incident, though no doubt exasperating at the time, do the generations communicate with each other, in this case over an immensely long stretch; little could the Qatari hunter of those distant days have dreamed that his lost arrowhead would one day act as a witness to the humanity which links his day with ours.

It is possible to infer more about the way of life of the Neolithic inhabitants of Qatar, a way of life they would have shared in general with contemporaries in eastern Arabia, Bahrain, and Oman where evidence of occupation at comparable periods has also been found. It is reasonable, first of all, to assume that the population would probably have been significantly more numerous than in earlier periods, for just as Neolithic man's techniques of tool making were more skilled, so his more advanced techniques of hunting, his ability to move over a larger hunting area and to survive in conditions which in earlier times would have been insupportable, meant that a greater number could be fed regularly with a more protein-rich diet. Neolithic Qataris lived, amongst other things, on fish, gazelle and onegar and as was demonstrated perhaps by the small blades which could have been used in sickles, they harvested wild cereals and grasses. This probability in fact is made certain by the recognition of querns, used for grinding meal, though deliberate domestication of plants seems not to have been at their disposal.

The wider horizons which had opened to late Stone-Age man as a consequence of his increased skill at managing his environment and its resources, had included many new techniques which substantially improved his life. The later Qatar Neolithic sustained some elements at least of this expanded life style: a spindle whorl, an essential device in the spinning of yarn, shows that some form of cloth was produced by the people.[29] Man's insatiable need to ornament himself, in life or in death, is demonstrated by a sea-snail's shell which has been bored (itself quite a skilful procedure) so that it could be threaded and worn, perhaps as an amulet, perhaps simply as a decorative addition to what would have been, at best, a rather sparse wardrobe.[30]

This indeed is what may generally be said for the archaeological record in Qatar: despite the rich inheritances of Stone-Age artefacts which has descended from the more distant times of human experience and apart from the inferences which can be made from the evidence of neolithic times, little can be said with assurance about the people who made and used them or about their associations beyond Qatar.

The discovery of Ubaid pottery on eastern Arabian sites was first made in 1970 by a British team invited to survey the State for its planned National Museum.[31] When the British team was commissioned to go to Qatar it was, perhaps frivolously, urged upon them to find some Ubaid sites, to allow Qatar to compete, as it were, with the eastern Arabian Neolithic on equal terms. To their own, and to everyone else's surprise, find them they did.

There was no reason to expect to find any trace of the Ubaid in Qatar: such evidence as had been returned from the Arabian sites had not indicated such an extent of Ubaid influence in the Gulf coastal areas as subsequently became apparent. The presence of Ubaid pottery on the island of Bahrain, for example, had not at that time been established. If it had been it would have been reasonable to suggest that Qatar, too, might contain similar evidence. Anyway, there it was and finding it opened up an entirely new dimension in the archaeology of Qatar and of that part of the Gulf.

The pottery is invariably found in archaeological contexts with the stone tools and implements of the late Stone Age or Neolithic period. This was indeed the case in Qatar, too.

The most important 'Ubaid' site to be found in Qatar was at Al-Da'asa on the north-east coast. The site would seem to have been a small seasonal encampment, probably the lodging of a group of hunter-fisher-gatherers who returned there from time to time. The site still showed the post-holes of whatever shelter the people used; it was most likely a tent though they could conceivably have been the supports of a hut wall.

There was a peculiarly poignant find on the Al-Da'asa site which, like the embedded arrow, seems to bridge the near hundred centuries which probably separate the time of the Al-Da'asa people and the present day. Near the post-holes was found neatly stacked a group of domestic implements, a grinder, querns, a piece of coral used for scouring and the like. It was the very tidiness of the way they had been piled up together that was particularly moving, as though some neolithic tent-wife had set them carefully aside intending to return for them or to use them again. For whatever reason they lay undisturbed for nearly ten thousand years: whoever put them there so carefully never returned.[32]

Whilst the pottery found at Al-Da'asa is Ubaid in manufacture, it must not be thought that its discovery in Qatar presupposes the presence of the Ubaid people themselves. Pottery in ancient times was a greatly valued commodity and was traded over considerable distances. The value that would be attributed to a pot of the period is demonstrated by one of the larger Qatar-Ubaid sherds; this was broken in antiquity and then repaired so that it could continue to be used.

There never was, of course, any question of the Ubaid pottery found in Qatar having been made there; it is most unlikely that the region would have permitted the degree of settled occupation necessary for a pottery-producing society to flourish, with all the equipment necessary in the actual production process – kilns, paints, not to mention suitable clays.

Indeed, recent research has shown that the Qatar pottery represented by the scatter of sherds, like those found in the eastern Arabian sites, was actually manufactured in Ur and traded down to the Gulf settlements. It is interesting to speculate whether the Qatar settlements at Al-Da'asa represent the same sort of community as those identified in eastern Arabia. Presumably the sherds are part of the detritus of peoples with a very similar way of life, probably moving seasonally over a comparatively extensive territory, which might well, therefore, have included both eastern Arabia and Qatar in its range.

The later periods in Qatar, when the Gulf was the main artery of world trade and the settlements on the eastern coast of Arabia became cities of great commercial importance, are almost totally barren, with no evidence yet discovered of continuous occupation. If any should be found there it is unlikely that it will prove to be more than occasional or very minor; certain it is that no cities of the scale of those in Bahrain or eastern Arabia were ever a feature of Qatar's landscape. No doubt the environment was too harsh, the country too bleak and barren even for the hardy travellers of Sumerian, Akkadian and Babylonian times. Qatar's is a singularly scoured landscape, torn by constant winds; little vegetation grows there, the grazing is sparse and water is not readily available. There would be little incentive for settlement in times when life was harsh enough anyway.

A recent, if altogether unexpected, discovery has however, begun to qualify this view of the absence of continuous or significant settlement in Qatar. This was the uncovering by the French Expedition of a small site near Al Khor which yielded a vast quantity (estimated at some two million) murex shells.[33] The murex is the little creature on which the ancient fame and prosperity of the great city of Tyre in the Levant was based.

From this creature came the superb crimson and scarlet dyes (misnamed purple) which lent glamour and spectacular flourish to the public assemblies of the Phoenician cities and, later, of Rome. Remembering the legends of the links between the Gulf and the cities of the Levant it is remarkable to find a dye factory in so remote a place on the Qatar peninsula. From the pottery which the site has yielded it can be dated to Kassite times, late in the second millennium BC.

Most of what other antiquities there are in Qatar seem to come from much later periods, which are really beyond the scope of this present study. The Greek presence in the Gulf and eastern Arabia is witnessed by a quantity of sherds of Seleucid pottery which are of a type dating from around the second century BC.[34] The Seleucids were the rulers of much of Persia in the period following the death of Alexander the Great; they take their name from Seleucus, one of Alexander's generals, who seized the Persian throne in the anarchy which followed the world-conqueror's death. There is no evidence, so far discovered, of a settlement at Ras Uwainat Ali and it seems most likely therefore that the literally thousands of sherds of pottery of the Seleucid period found there by the Danes (who have painstakingly restored three whole vessels from the debris), are perhaps the consequence of a shipwreck or some other accidental circumstance.

A more equivocal discovery was made by the Danes by chance when a truck in which some members of their expedition were driving sank into a cavity in the sand at Ras al-Matbakh.[35] On investigating further the hole which they had opened up, they found a *pithos*, a large pot, which had been used as a coffin; the remains of the body were still contained within it. From its orientation it was clearly not Islamic for it was not directed to the west, towards the holy city of Makkah. Since the burial contained no goods nor the possessions of the dead, its dating is a matter of conjecture; however, the use of the *pithos*, which is over thirty inches tall, recalls the 'bathtub' coffins of neo-Babylonian times, examples of which were found at Qala'at al-Bahrain. Some scholars however, point to *pithos* burials in eastern Arabia which are more usually attributed to the second millennium BC rather than to the first.

In any event, it is a matter of speculation what so great a pottery vessel was doing in Qatar in the 1rst place, let alone in what circumstances it was used to enclose the body of whoever it was had the misfortune to die there. Certainly it would seem too large to have been transported by land travellers and, as in the case of the Ras Uwainat Ali sherds, there is no evidence of a settlement of either period which might have produced an artefact so majestic, in size at least. Perhaps the explanation may be that it was part of a shipborne cargo and that its occupant, too, died at sea but that the conventions demanded that he should be returned to earth, cradled in a coffin, albeit a makeshift one. The friends of the dead man may have landed at Ras al-Matbakh and buried him in this lonely place before continuing with their journey.

Two final categories of remains in Qatar must be considered, though briefly, for they too, though obscure chronologically would seem to belong to periods beyond the *terminus post quem* of this study. The first of these are the fields of cairn-burials which are found throughout the Qatar peninsula.

Cairn burial was a common form of grave construction throughout pre-Islamic Arabia: a mound of stones overlying a relatively simple interment. In Qatar the cairns are to be found at Umm al Ma, Mezruah, Ras Abaruk and Ras Uwainat Ali.[36] In no case is their chronology particularly explicit.

At Umm al Ma there were two types identified by the Danes who first investigated them. The first type is rock-cut, the grave lined with trimmed stone blocks. One such grave contained two burials, one on top of the other. The second type of graves in this group also contains worked stone blocks but is triple-chambered in plan. In such a grave a skeleton was found, lying with its legs drawn up.

At Mezruah a burial was found which seems, if only obscurely, to link customs in Qatar in pre-Islamic times with a practice known in other parts of Arabia, including Bahrain: the hamstringing of camels around the grave of a hero.[37] The grave at Mezruah consisted of an oval-shaped cairn of large flat stones; outside it were found the skeletons of camels, crouching on their hocks. In the grave a Sassanian glass, almost intact, was found suggesting that the burial might have been late pre-Islamic in date. In addition to camel sacrifices there is also evidence of horse sacrifice in pre-Islamic Qatar.

Mezruah produced the most notable of the very sparse grave goods which the cairn burials have so far yielded. The grave in question contained two burials; one at least of the occupants was, it is fair to assume, a warrior for a handsome iron sword and a group of well made iron arrowheads had been buried with him. The other skeleton bore the sinister evidence of what was evidently a warrior's last battle; embedded in the fibia, the principal bone of the forearm, was another arrowhead. It remains there to this day, the grim witness of some long-forgotten, but, for the warrior, final encounter.[38]

The last and certainly the most enigmatic of all Qatar's antiquities are to be found on the crests of two low hills in the extreme north of the peninsula, at Fuweirit and Jessessiyeh.[39] On these two little hills, both barely more than a sort of rising stone outcrop, there are countless (literally so, since nobody so far has had the determination to count them) carvings, patterns and designs pecked, cut or gouged into the rock beside some of the most desolately beautiful of Qatar's northern shores. The presence of the sea, indeed, adds to the sense of isolation of the two little hills which are backed simply by the empty desert.

It is this very isolation which contributes to the strangeness of these two sites. Rock carvings are familiar enough over the whole of Arabia to make their discovery in Qatar hardly a matter for comment or even surmise. In fact Qatar is notably bare of inscriptions and graffiti; only one other group, apart from these on the northern hills, is known outside the capital, Doha. There on what is now a military firing range, a location which discourages archaeological exploration on any but the most guarded scale, are some representations of mounted warriors, of a type common in southern Arabia, Oman and across Saudi Arabia to the north and west, pecked out on a relatively flat rock table. Except for the fact that they appear to be the only ones in Qatar, the Doha examples are quite unremarkable and are probably simply the evidence of some bored Himyarite traveller who, some two thousand years ago, found himself with time to fill in the desert outside what was to become the capital of Qatar.

But it is the carvings on the two little rocky hills to which attention must return, for they really are very curious indeed. The traveller in the Arabian deserts and the *wadis* of Oman may be forgiven if he forms the impression that, in pre-Islamic times at least, the peninsula was inhabited by a race of committed artists who, seeing a rock surface, were seized by an urge, universal and irresistible, to carve something on it. The sheer scale of Arabian rock carving, which in individual examples must amount at least to hundreds of thousands, if not to millions, suggests an earnestness and application in the decoration of rock surfaces which is perhaps surprising to those who know the desert and its people today. The tradition continues, as demonstrated in Oman where, alongside what may be third-millennium designs, the outlines of Land Rovers, rifles and other contemporary gear are delineated.

But the work of these antique desert doodlers – if doodles they are in general and not the expression of some more abiding concerns – was not the product of an idle afternoon whilst resting in the shadowed lee of some convenient rock shelter. At Jessessiyeh and Fuwerit, they assume the proportions of an industry.

By far the most frequent design to be found on the two hills is that which consists of what are most generally called 'cup-marks': small circular pits cut into the rock surface, their sides curving to a rounded depression; they are usually not more than 3 to 5 centimetres in diameter, and less in depth. In Qatar they are occasionally found singly but far more frequently are they massed together, in seemingly endless variety of formations, single lines, double and treble lines, sometimes straight and others curving, sometimes circular, sometimes a circle of cups with one in the centre, in formations of six, eight, twelve, fourteen, sixteen and onwards, with no apparent progression or sequence. They seem to be distributed at random over the surface of the little

A mounted warrior carved in the rock near Doha, Qatar.

hills; they appear to follow no evident orientation, neither solar, lunar nor stellar.

Those who have studied them have proposed, basically, two explanations for them; neither is entirely satisfactory. It has been suggested, on the analogy with similar formations in Europe, particularly in Scandinavia, that they are in some way associated with fertility, a proliferation of vulvas into which the life-giving rain pours. This may or may not be the explanation of cup forms in nothern Europe, dating from the Bronze Age; it seems unlikely in eastern Arabia if only because the cups are so small, and vulvae, other than perhaps in the most febrile imaginations, rarely come in groups.

During the lifetime of man, too, rain in the desert is a comparatively rare phenomenon, at least to the extent that it seems unlikely that so universal a practice in northern Qatar as the making of cup-marks for the purpose of catching rainfall would have prevailed so extensively. A more tenable suggestion was that the cup-mark formations were boards for playing the game called in Arabia *huwais*, but which is known throughout the world under different names and many forms. In essence the game, which is played by two people, consists in moving counters (stones, beans or any other handy alternative) round the board, the moves being determined by the throw of dice or other mechanism. The game is played amongst the Badu to this day; it has been suggested that it is African in origin and of great antiquity.

Convenient though this explanation would be, it is ultimately unsatisfactory on several grounds. The various configurations in which the cup-marks are distributed are not consistent; inconsistent too are their locations and the fact that at least one example is to be found on the side of a rock, almost in an overhang, demonstrates that it at least could not have been used to contain anything, liquid or solid.

But at the end of the day, the sheer quantity of cup-marks in countless formations destroys the argument that they were used only for *huwais*, unless the making of them had some ritual significance, as though the marking out of a roulette table or tennis court carried with it substantial indulgences, releasing its maker from so many years penance in some games-playing purgatory, for example. It seems very unlikely that the players either made a fresh board each time they wished to play – by the time they had finished making the board, night, if not their enthusiasm, would have fallen – or that there would have been so many games in progress simultaneously that several hundred (if not thousands) of boards would be necessary. It seems improbable that this very remote spot in the north of the Qatar peninsula was ever the site of so extensive and feverish a cult of *huwais*-playing as to make the saloons of Vegas or of Monte Carlo seem atrophied and empty either of activity or excitement. It simply is too far-fetched.

In such circumstances, any speculation is permissible. One pattern, which does seem often to be discernible, is the circle with one cup in the centre; when the circle consists of eight cups it is a very reasonable version of the Mesopotamian eight-petalled rosette, which in early times signified divinity, and in the view of some authorities is connected with stellar cults. The apparently random distribution of the various formations might prove to be less random than it appears if they were to be plotted on a computer; it could be that they have some astronomical or calendrical significance which could only be established by sophisticated mathematical analysis. Enough is thought to be known today about the complex astronomical knowledge and prediction available to post-Neolithic man to make the dismissal of any reasonable possibility about the extent or application of that knowledge dangerous; of course, in the case of the Qatar cup-marks, we cannot assume that they are of the period which would permit even this speculative explanation.

Another, more prosaic, explanation might be that the cup formations were associated, in some way, with the pearl trade in which

Qatar's pre-oil prosperity was grounded. The sorting of pearls of different sizes and qualities is an essential element in the trade's management and the rewards, often meagre enough, of the fishermen. The cups could have been used for this purpose, though again their quantity and the variety of their composition and disposition over the rocks makes this, too, seem unlikely.

But the cup-marks, extensive though they are, are only one form of carving on the two rocky hills, close to the sea shore. Still more enigmatic, because they are quite without precedent in Qatar or, so far as is known, anywhere else, is a series of large carvings, painstakingly cut out on the rock surface which, at first sight, appear to be representations of boats, seen in plan. Masts, cross-seats, thwarts seem all to be depicted and some of the boats appear to be trailing large anchors. However, the explanation of these carvings, of which there is a particular concentration on Jessessiyeh, as showing some sort of sailing craft is perhaps too simple: some of the drawings which initially seem to represent boats can, at a second glance, look more like fish, with long feathery tails whilst others, more remarkably still, seem to be of huge scorpions, crawling across the rock face. They are altogether strange, sinister and, seen at sunset with the dying sun glancing across them, rather disturbing.

Some of the boats, in the view of some authorities, may be pearlers. Thus far only one serious study of the rock carvings has been made.[40] The author recorded many of the carvings and, so far as the ship representations are concerned, concluded that they might be of fourteenth century AD date. Even this conclusion must be regarded as very tentative; but if this dating were to prove to be substantiated, it would still not explain why anyone should have troubled to have portrayed boats, fishes or scorpions (or perhaps something which contains the elements of all three) on such a scale, in so obscure a place.

Other carvings in the same spot add to the mystery, rather than diminish it. Circular pits cut into the rock have been compared with the fire-pits found across the Gulf and associated with Iranian fire-cults of pre-Islamic times. Others seem to be crude offering tables with long runnels extending from them, as though to allow for the running off of some liquid or other. Some of these sometimes have the look of schematic, horned beasts.

Of quite another sort, is a small, elegant and very heavily weathered carving of an ibex or other caprid. This is the most deliberately representational of all the northern group of Qatar rock carvings and would certainly not look out of place in a third-millennium, or even

Carvings on the remote hills in Qatar, at Jessessiyah and Fuwerit, which look like boats and scorpions.

A group of household implements of the Ubaid period, excavated from a living site in Qatar.

earlier, Mesopotamian context. Once again the question of what it is doing in Qatar, far from any evident signs of occupation with which it might be associated, obtrudes itself – but no answer is forthcoming. But that is the way of Qatar's archaeology as a whole; at present, it postulates more questions than it provides answers.

Further still along the coast, eastwards from the Qatar peninsula, lies the most recently invented state in the area, the United Arab Emirates, a confederation of seven little principalities paradoxically united into a highly individual and improbable republic. The seven states, Abu Dhabi, Dubai, Sharjah, Umm al-Qawain, Ras al-Khaimah, Fujairah and Ajman, represent ancient (more or less) tribal or clan territories. The first three are rich, Abu Dhabi immensely so: the latter four are not and depend on the fortunes of their richer brothers.

The interest of the various states in their archaeology has been mixed; in any case they can only be described here in a general and cursory fashion. Abu Dhabi has encouraged excavation and some rather dubious reconstructions of her important and very early monuments. Dubai has carried out spasmodic surveys, with little significant result; Ras al-Khaimah commissioned a distinguished British researcher to survey its northern regions which resulted in some of the better publications on the area.[41] Pottery has been found which links this part of the coast with the other side of the Gulf, in Iran and further to Afghanistan. Recently some evidence of copper smelting has been found there, which suggests that Ras al-Khaimah was one of the points from which copper was trans-shipped up the Gulf from its source in Oman. There has also been identified a form of tomb unlike the others for which this part of the Ras al-Khaimah coast is known. These tombs are said to be like pill-boxes in profile.[42]

However, it is Abu Dhabi which has yielded the most notable results, ones which indeed are pertinent to the early history of Dilmun-Bahrain and the Gulf generally. They have come from two principal locations: one, a small island, Umm an-Nar close to the capital of Abu Dhabi itself; the other, a site called Hili much further inland, near the great oasis of Buraimi, close to the frontier with Oman.

Umm an-Nar is another example, though a more certain one than Bahrain, of the funerary island; it was also a settlement of the living. A very distinctive type of tomb, finely built and multi-chambered, was found there, dating to very early in the third millennium. From the quality of the architecture and the grave goods recovered, particularly the pottery, it is evident that the Umm an-Nar people, though probably only a very small community, enjoyed a high and rapidly advancing level of prosperity in the early years of the third millennium. This community appears to be considerably earlier even than the first people to live in the original city at the Qala'at al-Bahrain; Umm an-Nar pottery has indeed been discovered at the bottom of the earliest harbour wall. Conceivably the Umm an-Nar people were involved in the original settlement of the site at Bahrain. Graves of Umm an-Nar type or influence may be present in Bahrain.

Umm an-Nar pottery is very distinctive. Like the later pottery from Ras al-Khaimah, it seems to have affiliations with sites across the Gulf in south-western Iran and, possibly, others in Baluchistan and Afghanistan. The importance of the Umm an-Nar community to the Gulf in the early centuries of the third millennium lies in the fact that it was probably the point from which copper, mined in what is today the Sultanate of Oman at sites to the south of Umm an-Nar, in the Buraymi and Ibri oases, was shipped via Dilmun to the cities of Sumer.[43]

One of the intriguing elements in the archaeology of the Umm an-Nar community is the evidence of their diet.[44] They were, largely, a fishing people and amongst the debris of their occupation the remains of a dugong, or sea cow have been found.[45] It was evidently butchered at Umm an-Nar to feed the settlers there. The Umm an-Nar settlement also produced evidence of the consumption of the camel, though it is not known whether this should be taken as proof of domestication; probably not, on the basis of more general evidence.[46]

At Hili an altogether different situation persisted, though it is also from an early period in the third millennium.[47] The most notable survivals are a number of remarkable carvings in relief which seem to have served as decorative elements in the architecture of some of the larger tombs. They are quite extraordinary and unlike anything else in their immediate context.[48] Whilst the decoration of rock surfaces is a practice which seems to have engaged the enthusiasm of the ancient inhabitants of much of the Arabian Peninsula (though not generally in the east except, as will shortly be seen, in Oman), to an almost obsessional degree, the Hili carvings are of quite different sort. There are several distinct scenes depicted: an erotic group of an embracing couple, a design which exactly repeats much earlier ones from Catal Hüyük in Anatolia and Ain Sakhri, a Natufian site in Palestine; two felines tearing a smaller animal; a group of travellers, looking remarkably like raffigurations of the Holy Family on the Flight into Egypt; and what may be an early representation of a camel.

The last of the territories contiguous to Dilmun-Bahrain and in many ways the most important is that which is today the Sultanate of

Oman. The second largest county in the Arabian peninsula, often spectacularly beautiful, diverse in its topography and with a rich admixture of peoples and traditions, Oman is markedly different in character from its neighbours. It is one of the few distinct *nations* in the Arab world, with a firmly defined identity of its own. This it seems always to have had; the mediaeval Arab geographers and historians tend to emphasize its essentially individual and homogeneous character.

In the ancient Sumerians' and their successors' texts Dilmun is frequently linked with two other lands, Melukhkha which is now considered to be the Indus Valley region, and Magan or, as it is sometimes transliterated, Makkan. From Magan came much of the Sumerian states' most important imported commodity, the staple of their economies, copper. Magan is today identified with Oman and parts of the northern coast now within the political boundaries of the United Arab Emirates; sometimes the term may also have embraced parts of the coast across the Straits of Hormuz.

Oman occupies much of the south-eastern quadrant of the Arabian peninsula though it is geographically, as it has always tended to have been historically, isolated from its neighbours. This isolation has contributed much to the Sultanate's particular character.

Indeed, strictly speaking, Oman is only in part a Gulf state; much of her extensive coast borders the Indian Ocean. It is this geographical factor which has most contributed to the Omani experience throughout history, a history which has been most notably a record of Oman's marriage with the sea. Oman is cut off from her northern and western neighbours by the central and southern Arabian deserts which divide the coastal strip, in which most of Oman's historic towns are concentrated, from the rest of the peninsula. This division is strengthened by the presence of the great range of mountains, the Jebel Akhdar, which runs north to south down most of the length of the country. To the west of Oman, and north of her fertile southern provinces, lies the Rub al-Khali, the Empty Quarter or, more simply, the Sands, as they are called by the local Badu. This gigantic waste, some 250,000 square miles of deep and constantly moving sands, was, in late neolithic times, a region of swamps and marshes, in particular on its northern periphery, where evidence of neolithic settlements has been found in abundance. Then, bodies of water ran down from the Rub al-Khali to the sea, making the coast of what was once called Trucial Oman, and which today is the United Arab Emirates, a string of islands of which Umm an-Nar is a survivor.

Sailing southwards from the Gulf a vessel must pass through the

The beehive tombs are finely constructed and must have been very distinctive monuments. They were apparently used as communal tombs, perhaps for the burial of a clan or other connected group.

Straits of Hormuz (to the Iranian shores of which the Empire of Oman once extended in middle Islamic times) out into the Gulf of Oman, the beginning of the Arabian Sea, and the first ocean water that the sailor meets on the route to the Indian subcontinent. The prevailing winds and currents of this region have had a considerable influence on the development of Omani history, bringing her ships eastwards to India and beyond and westwards to the east African coast.

Oman's long coastline has had a profound influence on the course of her history; her people have always been energetic and courageous seamen, from the very earliest times. Oman's ships are distinctive and her sailors were foremost amongst the seamen of Islam, their fame spreading throughout the world in the time of the Arab Empires. Omani seamen opened up the sea routes to China and the east and at the height of the Arab Caliphates her cities were reckoned amongst the most populous and splendid in Islam – which effectively meant, at that time, in the world.

Oman differs from other parts of Arabia in respect of the variety of climate and the consequently varied ecology which she enjoys. Much of the country is desert, the home of camel-rearing nomads; the mountain valleys however are in parts richly fertile and bear a variety of fruits and crops impossible to cultivate in other parts of eastern or central Arabia, whilst in the far south the green and undulating foothills of Dhofar are the home of Arabia's only cattle-breeders, archaic tribes who still speak non-Arabic languages in the security of their family groups. The south of the country catches the tail of the monsoon season, its rains bringing the prospect of intense cultivation to the land which it touches. Again, Oman is unique in this for it is the only part of the peninsula within the monsoon's reach.

The archaeology of Oman has been favoured by one special circumstance: with the exception of the equivocal activities of Dr Wendell Phillips in the early 1950s, the country's political isolation, the consequence of the somewhat peculiar and antiquated policies of the previous Sultan, very little archaeological work of any consequence had been carried out in the Sultanate before the accession of the present Sultan, Qaboos bin Said, in 1970. Many of the states of eastern Arabia, in common with those of the Near and Middle East as a whole, have been pillaged by collectors and other predators, both professional and amateur, of varying degrees of competence and probity. Oman fortunately has largely escaped this phenomenon.

It appears that even as early as the late fourth millennium and certainly by the beginning of the third Oman was in touch with other centres in the region of the Gulf. The evidence for this degree of wide-ranging contacts is the pottery found on several sites in the Sultanate which show connections with Umm an-Nar to the north, with Kulli across the Gulf in Baluchistan, with western Iran and, later, with the Barbar levels at Bahrain.[49] So far no other Gulf site has produced comparable material to show, apparently, so broadly cast a net of inter-connections which, as this pottery suggests, Oman enjoyed in such very early times. The reason for this evident concentration of foreign contact was once again trade and in particular, in Oman's case, almost certainly trade based on the ancients' search for hard stones for building and sculpture and for sources of one of the most important elements in their economies, copper.

In the early inscriptions relating to trade and the carriage of merchandise, the term 'Magan-boat' is often employed; a case in point is the myth *Enki and the World-Order* in which, it may be recalled, the god declares that he

. . . moored the Dilmun-boat to the ground, loaded the Magan-boat sky-high.[50]

This presumably is to be taken as a demonstration of the exceptional prosperity that Enki brought to both places as evidenced by the heavy loads borne by their craft; it may also refer to the type of boat which it was customary to use on the run between Magan and the markets with which it had dealings, no doubt Dilmun-Bahrain, perhaps the Indus cities, maybe Sumer itself. In the light of Oman's subsequent history of intense involvement with the sea and seamanship it is conceivable that even this early the Omanis were renowned sailors and reference to them in such a context would produce the same degree of recognition and response which might be expected from a similar reference to the better known lands of Dilmun and its sailing ships. It may be, too, that 'Magan-boat' meant something like 'China Clipper' would have done to a nineteenth-century participant in the Far-Eastern trade.

It is, of course, even possible that a particular type of boat originating in Magan is also meant. Oman has produced at least one vessel which may be peculiar to itself and which is of great antiquity: the *sewn-boat* whose planks are stitched together without the use of nails and which is used extensively in Omani waters until this day. This explanation would also require the 'Dilmun-boat', referred to in the same text, to represent a specific type; for this there is no evidence, though the representations on seals, for examples, do seem to show a variety of types of boat in use, several of which might have originated in the Gulf trade.

What particularly lured merchants and seamen to Oman in early dynastic times as well as later was the prospect of copper, present in substantial quantities and relatively easily mined. References in early texts to 'the Mountain of Copper' are thought to refer to Magan, for Oman might well be memorable to its early visitors by reason of the high mountains which are so dominating a feature of the landscape in the northern half of the country, where the copper deposits are located. This assumption is less definite now, in most scholars' views, but there is no doubt that Oman was an important source of copper in antiquity; the areas which were mined are still visible, as are the great heaps of slag remaining from the smelting operations which were evidently carried out close to the source of supply.

The fact that Oman's copper contains a relatively high concentration of arsenic trace elements, which is also found in Mesopotamian copper artefacts, is suggestive but it cannot yet be regarded as decisive proof of an Omani provenance for specific samples of Sumerian copper until analytical techniques are further refined.[51]

There are extensive workings in copper-rich areas of the Wadi Jizzi system in northern Oman which have been worked in the third millennium; the surface workings which are to be seen today date from Islamic times when Oman was once again developed as an important source. There are, in addition, extensive third-millennium workings in the Wadi Andam and Wadi Ibra. There seems little doubt that the communities which existed there came into existence as a consequence of the exploitation of copper resources. The devastation which smelting on this scale must have wrought on the forest population, particularly on the acacia trees which grew extensively on the mountain slopes of Oman, and hence the effect on Oman's ecology and perhaps on its climate, has already been noted.

Nothing very precise is known about the actual mechanism of the third-millennium copper trade in the Gulf. How the copper was mined, whether by slaves or by freemen, what was the nature of Oman's political and mercantile systems at the time, are all unknown. We do not know whether colonies of Sumerian merchants were established in Oman on the model of other outposts of their culture, or whether Oman's traders themselves travelled up the Gulf to Dilmun and Sumer. The name of only one king of Magan is known to us at present. This is Manium, whose only claim to fame is that he was defeated by Naram-Sin, the grandson and eventual heir of the great Sargon of Akkad. Manium has sometimes been confused with Menes, the putative unifier of the two Egyptian kingdoms, but Menes lived a thousand years earlier. Naram-Sin faced a general rebellion in his empire when he assumed power. Evidently control of the copper trade was worth mounting what must have been a substantial expedition, with greatly extended lines of supply, from Akkad down the Gulf to Magan. But it seems he was victorious and recorded his victory on various objects which were dedicated to his gods in gratitude.[52]

In Bahrain, on the foreshore at the Qala'at al-Bahrain city site, copper fragments and the remains of whole ingots were found, suggesting that the ore may have been exported to Bahrain and smelted into ingot-form before being sent on to Sumer. In the workshops of the little cities it would have been converted into tools and traders' vessels, weapons, statues and offerings for the gods, inlays and ornaments for furniture – a thousand different uses for a metal which helped to transform the old neolithic communities into the civilized city populations of the period. The amalgam with tin, in which copper becomes the even harder-edged bronze, it gave a name to this period of third and second millennia development, the Bronze Age, in the nomenclature of nineteenth-century archaeology.

Recent excavations have shown that, early in the third millennium, at the beginnings of the Mesopotamian cities' prosperity, Oman too was prosperous, supporting a sizeable population, some of whom lived in fortified townships of an architectural sophistication and of a character, so far as it is yet possible to judge, distinct from that of other urban centres of the third-millennium Gulf.[53] Indeed some of the earliest material in the Gulf region, other than the Ubaid (which is not present in Oman) comes from their early Omani settlements. A definite Jamdet Nasr horizon has been identified by several workers in sites such as Jebel Hafit, Ibri and Bat, amongst others.[54] This dates to c.3000 BC and is consequently earlier than any settlements known in Bahrain or eastern Arabia. One of the most remarkable phenomena in Oman, and another testament to the longevity of forms in these parts, are the observation towers which have been identified on some of these early sites.[56] They were, in all probability, observation posts protecting the little settlements against raiders; they seem generally to have contained water wells which presumably they also protected. The most notable are situated at Ibri and at Bat; there are also examples in the United Arab Emirates at Hili, where one tower was surrounded by a moat.[56] One of the towers at Hili appeared to date from around 3000 BC, much earlier than any other similar structure.[57] The towers are the direct ancestors of towers such as that which still stands in the town of Nizwa, built in the eighteenth century in the form in which it now stands and which thus has an ancestry of at least five thousand years.

An otherwise unprecedented but probably very early fragment of pottery, for so it appears, came from an unrecorded excavation of a grave in northern Oman. The sherd comes from a spouted vessel; it is of a fairly coarse red ware painted with black decoration. It is significant not only because of its notable decoration but because of the connections with other lands which that decoration recalls.

The theme of the decoration is particularly interesting for it shows a group of dancers, hand in hand in a landscape dominated by three triangles, which look suspiciously like pyramids but which, since the sherd is clearly a good deal earlier than the earliest pyramid, they certainly are not. In fact they are probably intended to represent mountains, perhaps the great central Oman chain, the Jebal Akhdar. What is notable is that the motif of the dancers appears in Elam and in Egypt, from pre-dynastic times, whilst the two elements, of dancers and mountains, are frequently combined in late pre-dynastic Egyptian pottery.

The distinctive character of Oman in antiquity is further borne out by the funerary architecture of its early inhabitants. Oman shares in the extraordinarily widespread practice of tumulus building but her tombs are different from those in, for example, Bahrain or Saudi Arabia. One group is similar to those identified at Umm an-Nar in Abu Dhabi, but the Abu Dhabi examples must really be regarded as the Omani type reaching up to the northern coastline; there can be little doubt that the form of the Umm an-Nar tombs is Omani in origin, as the same type is to be found throughout northern Oman, distributed over a widely dispersed area.

Many examples of these formidable, beehive-shaped tombs are to be found, generally built on level ground, occasionally singly but more frequently concentrated in groups; a notable concentration of beehive tombs is to be found at Bat.[58] Each tomb is probably a communal burial place, most likely for a clan or extended family group and was probably used over a quite considerable time-scale, representing the burials of several generations. They are themselves monuments of Oman's prosperity in the early third millennium for even as communal graves they must have represented a substantial expenditure of material and effort.

The tombs must have been remarkably conspicuous monuments for they were cased in fine white limestone blocks, skilfully shaped and fitted to the contours of their beehive form. So far none has been found intact and all were plundered in antiquity.

A vessel of Umm an Nar type, believed to have been found near Abqaiq. (*Museum of Archaeology and Ethnography, Riyadh*).

The second type of tombs of this period is again most distinctive: a cairn of stones, often standing up to twenty feet and more in height.[59] These are often to be found on ridges built evidently with the deliberate intention of setting them against the skyline and, perhaps, of providing their owners with an agreeable view. In this they may be reminiscent of Egyptian 'houses of millions of years'.

It may be assumed that both of these tomb types, which each represent such a substantial investment in labour and materials, were the sepulchres of the more prosperous citizens of ancient Oman. From the quantity, it may be inferred that the population of northern Oman in the third and early second millennia, was, like Bahrain in the same period and for this same reason, relatively substantial, a community certainly to be reckoned in thousands of inhabitants. The poor, it may be assumed, were not laid to rest in these handsome monuments but were buried simply in the eternally receptive desert.

But there was even earlier communal activity in Oman which has left its traces in the archaeological record. At Ras al-Hamra, not far from the capital Muscat and close to the radio, television and museum complex at Qurm, evidence of very early groups of fishermen has been found.[60] On the several promontories which mark the coastline of this

This sherd, from an unidentified site in northern Oman, shows three figures dancing, apparently in a landscape dominated by mountains.

part of Oman, burials have been found of fishermen dating back as early as the sixth millennium BC.

At this time conditions were evidently very primitive; the communities would have presented a distinctly savage appearance. Their graves, however, are well formed and the occupants were laid in them with some ritual. Ornaments and weapons have been found as well as the evidence of animal (particularly turtle) sacrifices.

The Ras al-Hamra communities flourished, if that is the right word, before the invention of pottery. Their existence, though long lasting for they continued to fish Omani waters down to the end of the fourth millennium, must have been sparse indeed. Also on the coast, to the south of Muscat, traces have been found which suggest the presence of Harappan voyagers or at least of a people who were sufficiently in touch with the Indus Valley people to have acquired their pottery.[61]

In common with what seems to have been the situation in much of the rest of the Gulf, Oman appears to have experienced a decline in activity and in the evidence of such substantial and prosperous communities after the beginning of the second millennium; the possible reasons for this phenomenon have been outlined earlier. In the case of Oman it must not be thought that so large a country, well endowed with water and fertile soil, was abandoned totally; this is most unlikely but the changed economic circumstances of the Gulf did not support large urban populations. In the case of the upper Gulf towns, whilst those in Bahrain and the mainland were probably never actually abandoned, their populations fell to a low level, to be represented

The variety of Oman's rock carvings is bewildering and appears to span the past five thousand years.

perhaps by the equivalent of squatters, with an occasional military force garrisoned there. The situation generally is obscure. In Oman it is likely that the population reverted to a closer relationship with the land, living in villages or even in mobile communities which have left few identifiable traces behind them. It is to be hoped that more intensive exploration will reveal what evidence there may be of occupation during most of the second millennium and much of the first: so far, there is little to go on.

It is significant that Alexander's advisers evidently knew nothing of Oman when he was seeking information about the peoples of Arabia as he contemplated its conquest in the last months of his life. Although he had endured the appalling rigours of the march through the Gedrosian desert on the coast opposite Oman it is evident that he knew nothing of what conditions were like on the western shore. This suggests strongly that after its earlier prosperity the downturn in the commercial and trading activity of the Gulf had resulted in the onset of barbarism in south-eastern Arabia and the towns which had grown up to serve those who sought for Oman's copper fell into decay and into the oblivion from which they are only now being recalled.

Prosperity once again returned to Oman when the extreme south of the country, the region which is now called Dhofar, came into prominence as one of the principal sources of supply of aromatics and spices, and, in particular, of frankincense.

Expeditions had been sent out from Egypt at least as early as the third millennium in search of incense. Such expeditions sailed down the Red Sea to the land of Punt, sometimes also called the Land of the God in the Egyptian inscriptions which record the journeys. The Egyptians burned large quantities of aromatics in their religious and state ceremonies. A famous relief in the funerary temple of Hasheshowi (or Hatshepsut) at Deir al-Bahari shows an expedition setting out for Punt and, later, returning with Punt's dwarfish, stout and steatopygous Queen, a visitor of State, if of improbable proportions, to the equally formidable Egyptian Queen.

Mesopotamia's comparative lack of interest in incense evidently meant that the sources of supply in south-eastern Arabia and in Oman were not exploited by the powers in Mesopotamia; there is as yet no evidence that the Egyptians ever went there themselves. It is possible that they acquired their supplies from middlemen, for the Egyptians themselves do not notably seem to have honoured the calling of merchant. However, the growth of European powers such as Greece and later Rome, appearing for the first time on any real scale in the first millennium, brought about an enormous increase in demand and, in consequence, the need to find permanent and reliable sources of supply.

The quantities of incense which Greece, Rome and the post-Alexandrian kingdoms consumed were prodigious. The altars of all the gods were perpetually wreathed with it; emperors and city corporations alike would seek to honour their chosen divinity by the consumption of yet greater amounts of costly fragrances. Thus Alexander himself, in his own lifetime renowned for his piety and the service of the gods, was never sparing in his observances. When, as a young prince, he was reproved for wasting incense by his first tutor he stored the memory in his mind and when he had conquered the world sent him a large quantity of incense, of near incalculable value, warning him not to be parsimonious in paying honour to the gods.

The cult of luxury in Rome and in the post-Alexandrian world added still further to the demand for Arabian aromatics. By their use as perfumes and unguents, the wealthier citizens, whose nostrils might be expected to be sensitive, could make living bearable in a teeming, malodorous city like Rome.

All of this meant an unparallelled prosperity for Arabia, the surest and most accessible source for the aromatics which these cults and customs demanded. Soon, kingdoms grew up in southern Arabia whose sole reason for existence was the cultivation, marketing and distribution of frankincense. Caravans, powered by the camel which now came into its own for the first time (though introduced into the desert as early as the late fourth millennium, even if probably not domesticated), began to move up and down both littorals of Arabia, along the Red Sea coasts and up the Gulf shores.[62]

At points along the route duties levied on the camel trains and the provision of food and services for the master of the caravan and his men led to the creation of permanent communities which lived almost exclusively on this trade; from these caravanserai developed the great trading cities of Arabia. Those in the West like Makkah, were later to exercise a still more stupendous role in world history when they witnessed the birth of Islam in the seventh century of the present era.

Soon the riches of Arabia entered into the mythology of Europe, never wholly to be forgotten. 'Fortunate Arabia' – *Arabia felix* – counted its wealth in the resins which were tapped from the trees, on which, it could for once be truly said, their fortunes grew. As the rumours of Arabia's limitless wealth circulated in the political centres of the world (fuelled, no doubt, by the sumptuous apparel and rich retinues of its princes and merchants who began to become familiar figures in Mediterranean cities) so European ambitions, notably those of the Roman Republic and its successor Empire, began to focus on Arabia, with the object of controlling if not subsuming the kingdoms which seemingly contained so much of the world's wealth. The parallel with circumstances today is irresistible; then as now, Arabia's wealth was based essentially on a one-product economy and one which was virtually unique in quantity and accessibility Then, as now, Arabia's resources were the envy of the world and the target of the acquisitiveness of the powers. Much of Oman's wealth in late antiquity came from the spice trade and its profits.

There is another survival from the remote past in which Oman is exceptionally rich – rock carvings. In this too her heritage is different from that of her Gulf neighbours, for in general eastern Arabia has little to show of the practice.

The distribution of rock carvings in Arabia and beyond is interesting and suggestive. Oman represents the most easterly manifestation of the phenomenon; to the west they run into the south western desert regions of Saudi Arabia and up the Red Sea coastal areas, in some cases penetrating quite far inland. They appear in great quantity in the wadi systems of the Egyptian eastern desert. In different forms, rock drawings are to be found still further to the west in the Sahara and, to the east in Iran. Some of the themes seem to be common to several of the regions, though they are separated by great distances.

Winkler, who first attempted a scientific analysis of rock carvings, using those in the Wadi Hammamat in Egypt, tried to apply a chronology to the drawings he examined.[63] In this he was followed, though cautiously, by Anati[64] who has analyzed and published many examples from the south-west Arabian repertory. They both believed they could detect various styles of drawings which, from internal evidence of the dress, weapons and manners depicted, together with the recurrence of iconographic elements familiar from other contexts, made it possible to ascribe a time-scale to them. Any such attempt at applying a chronology was necessarily broadly generalized, and depended much upon the establishment of sequences of styles for the different groups of drawings which they recognized.

Any attempt to date rock carvings absolutely is fraught with difficulty. Only the palimpsest, provided it is interpreted correctly, can allow the presumption to be made that a drawing imposed on top of another is younger than the drawing which it overlays. The patination of the rock on which the drawings lie was once thought to be a reliable indicator of age; this is no longer so for a prevailing wind constantly dusting a rock surface with sand particles can build up the most convincingly ancient-looking patination relatively quickly.

In Oman the problem is an interesting one because some of the desert people have continued the practice of engraving on rocks into very recent years.[65] Thus one case showed a replica of a drawing of an embracing couple, known from the Hili tombs of early third millennium BC; the replica appeared in Oman in a context which made it clear that it was of very recent date. Such is the persistence of certain themes in folk art the world over.

In Oman it may be possible to identify certain themes and elements from other cultures. Thus a divinity (for such the figure seems to be) is depicted seated on a throne whose form is peculiar to Sumerian art; this, if it is so, would seem to be convincing proof that the Sumerians visited Oman. A warrior with a buckler and sword is parallelled on a Bahraini seal, probably of post-Akkadian (late third millennium) date. Lines of dancing men give an almost African impression.

Great horned beasts make frequent appearances in the drawings. Some of them are of considerable size. Felines, mountain lion or leopard perhaps, both of which were native to Oman in the past, are also depicted; in one dramatic scene a huge feline is depicted in the act of devouring a little man. One handsome carving seems to show a warrior with a high-crowned helm or a feather in his hair very similar to a style known from Iran. One of the most remarkable groups yet recovered in Oman is at Colman's Rock, in the interior south of Jebel el Abri. On the rock, a large boulder in fact, are carved, expertly and in relief, four great figures, the largest of which is some seven feet tall. One of the figures, the central one of a group of three, wears a flat cap and has distinctly Caucasian features; at his side stands a huge negroid figure.[66]

This enigmatic group is quite without precedent as is the manner of their representation, fine relief carving not being among the usual techniques of rock artists, in Oman or anywhere else in Arabia, except of course in Hili. It is conceivable that the figures on Colman's Rock may bear some relationship to the Hili carvings, though it would be difficult to be more specific at this juncture.

The horse appears in a number of carvings, including spirited combat scenes where warriors brandish their little swords perpetually. These are sometimes associated with inscriptions in pre-Islamic south Arabian scripts which allows them to be dated approximately to the first century of the Christian era. As would be expected the horse is a relatively late arrival in this part of Arabia. Many are the representations of camels, from around two thousand years ago, by which time it had become a familiar part of the economy.

The siting of the carvings is often very remarkable. Naturally many are found in rock shelters, under rocky overhangs and in places generally of reasonably easy access. Some however are engraved high on the face of wadi cliffs, prompting the speculation as to how the artists worked in such difficult locations. They recall, in terms of the difficulties which they must have imposed on the artist, some of the more inaccessible places chosen by the cave artists of European Palaeolithic times ten and more thousand years before the Omani examples.

The repertory of Omani rock art is rich, varied and very extensive. Abstract designs and shapes are as popular as animals and human forms; dancers are frequently portrayed as are figures who are no doubt manifestations of man's recurring need to make his gods in his own image. The drawings are now being recorded scientifically and their eventual analysis will add much to our knowledge of the preoccupations of man in the late prehistoric and early historic periods in this part of the world. It is possible too that their detailed study will throw more light on the process of inter-connection in antiquity between Oman and other parts of the Gulf and beyond.

The archaeology of Oman is potentially very rich. The county is exceptionally ancient in its settlement and it may well hold at least one or two of the keys to the fuller understanding of the Gulf region in antiquity. Some historians of the earlier part of this century speculated that the Sumerians themselves originated in Oman: the preoccupation in their art of the people of the land of the Two Rivers with mountains suggests that their origins lay in a mountainous land and Oman seemed a fair candidate. There is not a shred of evidence yet to support the idea but enough has been said about the *possible* southern origins of the Sumerians not to dismiss absolutely any reasonable guess about their original home, always assuming that they were indeed immigrants.

However it must be said that the Sumerians seem to have known well that their copper supplies, in part at least, came from Oman. If it had also been the people's original home they surely would have remembered it? It may be that the years ahead will answer this question, as the years past have answered so many others.

IX
Gilgamesh in the Land of the Living

The Sumerians were the first people to create an heroic literature, the record of the deeds of great men, in part historical personalities and in part the figures of legend. In these stories the Mycenaean heroes of Homer and the doom-ridden protagonists of Northern myth have their forebears.

Dilmun, represented as a secure, peaceful and temperate land, figures in the first great epic poem which has survived from the earliest records of civilized urban man. In it is contained one of the great archetypes of legend found in lands all over the world, the story of the universal Deluge. It is also the story of one of the most completely realized figures of heroic myth, the generous-hearted Shepherd King of Uruk, Gilgamesh, and of his journey across the waters of death, ferried by a solitary boatman, to the 'land where the Sun rises' in search of the illusion which still obsesses man, the restoration of youth lost.[1]

Probably for as long as speech has been possible, men have invented stories in an attempt to explain the purpose of their existence, of their relationship with the natural world around them and in the hope that they might make the unseen world less fearful. Myth is of overwhelming importance in the development of man's culture. Not only does it embody many of the fundamental beliefs which man has formed about himself, but in it is often enshrined much historical reality, even if it is dimly and uncertainly recalled. The themes and subjects of myth lie at the threshold of man's discovery of art.

When myth coincides with historical experience it becomes especially powerful, for then reality mirrors the deepest longings and fears of the human psyche. Such may have happened if ever Oedipus was a limping king in Thebes or when a local catastrophe was magnified to enclose the Sumerians' fears of a recurring universal deluge. In these circumstances the event recalled in myth becomes inextricably welded into the pattern of human experience.

The oldest recorded cycle of epic myth in the world tells of the triumphs and disasters of a Sumerian king, Gilgamesh of Uruk. In his struggle against the tremendous odds which beset him, Gilgamesh is the archetypal hero, ranking with Herakles – of whom indeed he may be the inspiration – and Siegfried (that tiresome boy) but a great deal more agreeable than either. Those who have described Akhenaton,[2] the god-possessed Pharaoh of the fourteenth century – whose doubtless sublime but certainly destructive yearnings for the one god somehow (and quite unreasonably) contrast oddly with his physical appearance – as the first individual in history, overlook Gilgamesh.

Gilgamesh (his name is said to be a Babylonian corruption of the Sumerian form of the name Bilga-mes, which apparently means 'the Ancient is a Hero' or, more quaintly, 'the old man is a young man' – whatever that may mean)[3] reigned in Uruk during the twenty-seventh century BC. He is thus approximately a contemporary of Djoser, the second king of the Third Dynasty of Egypt's Old Kingdom and the inspiration of the titanic stepped pyramid at Saqqara. Little is known of the historical events of Gilgamesh's reign but it is clear that he was a sovereign well-loved by his people and remembered gratefully by them. He was the fifth king in the post-diluvian dynasty of Uruk, after the reigns of the gods. His immediate predecessors included Lugalbanda, who seems to have been an historical figure, and Dummuzi, who is described as a shepherd and is almost certainly the god later known to the peoples of the Levant as Tammuz, whose name is perpetuated in the Jewish and Arabic names of the month which commemorates him to this day. Gilgamesh speaks of Lugalbanda as his father, although his paternity is disputed. He was said to be two thirds divine for his mother was a goddess: his birth was probably the consequence of his mother's participation in one of the sacred marriage rites, the temple ceremony which year by year ensured the fecundity of the city.

Gilgamesh is one of the most popular subjects in Sumerian and Babylonian art, in which he is depicted as a young man, bearded and vigorous, enacting scenes from his epic history. Frequently he is shown in the company of gods and animals, reflecting an early belief that man stood somewhere between these two orders of creation. Almost invariably he seems to be smiling and exulting in the twin powers of his kingship and his manhood, and as a king walks as happily with beasts as with divinities. He fortified his city against invasion and gave laws to his people which anticipated the code of Hammurabi, another great Mesopotamian sovereign who was to rule in Babylon a thousand years after Gilgamesh.

The story of Gilgamesh's journey to Dilmun is recorded in the *Epic of Gilgamesh* which, in the form in which it substantially survives today, was written down during the eighteenth century before our era.[4] But this version undoubtedly drew on a much older Sumerian original, reaching us from far back into the third millennium; parts of this earlier text survive and undoubtedly the other versions call on parts of the original now lost. The most complete text is preserved in twelve tablets of baked clay, written in the wedge-shaped cuneiform script of the first Babylonian empire. The tablets were found in the ruins of the library of King Assurbanipal (668–633 BC) who, in addition to being a great conqueror, was a conscientious antiquarian, and who collected with enthusiasm and appreciation the records and legends of those who had preceded him on the thrones of Mesopotamia.

Over the past century or so various recensions of the myth have been published. A problem arises in relating them out of a scholarly context, in that the names of the principal characters are different in each version; only Gilgamesh himself seems to preserve his own consistent identity. Thus the character of the immortalized King of Shurupak, the prototype of Noah, is called Ziusudra in the Sumerian text, but Utanapishtim in the Babylonian and Assyrian.

The mysterious boatman who ferries Gilgamesh across 'the waters of death' is Sursunabi and Urshanabi respectively. In the outline which follows the names are used as they appear in the original versions though the incident quoted may only appear in the non-Sumerian recensions which survive.

The story is as follows: Gilgamesh, the young and vigorous king of one of the oldest and most important of Sumer's states, is loved by his people, but with certain distinct reservations. His nature, two-thirds divine and one-third human by his descent from the Great Goddess of Sumer and a High Priest (or from Lugalbanda, who by his kingly office would also have been a cult-priest), is tempestuous and uncontrolled. The citizens of Uruk have become increasingly unenthusiastic about his assaults on their wives and daughters and his appropriation of their sons for his campaigns. However, since the inhabitants of Uruk are a responsible people with a proper respect for both the divine parentage and earthly rank of their king, they seek the advice of the great god Enlil. They beg him to devise some distraction for Gilgamesh which will turn his energies away from their relations. The god sympathizes with their problems and creates Enkidu to be the king's companion, a wild, untamed man living in company with the animals. Enkidu may symbolize the second mainstream of the people of Mesopotamia other

than the settled city-dwellers, the semitic-speaking nomads who entered the land from earliest times, often intermarrying with the Sumerians themselves. Enkidu's destiny is to become the twin of Gilgamesh,
the king's alter ego. Not altogether surprisingly, in view of his record of
fairly indiscriminate sexuality, Gilgamesh is deeply attracted by him
and they swear eternal friendship. There are hints that their relationship
is a sexual one. In the manner of boys who ultimately become insepar-
able, this relationship only develops after they have fought a great
battle, in which Gilgamesh defeats Enkidu. 'They grappled, each other
holding fast like Bulls.'

Unhappily the seeds of the destruction of their friendship have
already begun to germinate: Enkidu has only been coaxed to the
habitations of men by the wiles of the town whore, probably a priestess
of the Mother in her character of the Goddess of Love and Lust, who
seduces him by the river bank. Hitherto he has run wild, as free and
untrammelled as the gazelles and other fauna with whom he has shared
the desert. But now, because the animals who have been his companions to this point sense the corruption of humanity on Enkidu, they
withdraw reproachfully from him, leaving him to the fortunes of gods
and men.

To some commentators, those who seek an astrological significance
in events and personalities which probably would have considerably
surprised those concerned had they known of them, Gilgamesh and
Enkidu may represent the Twins, the eponyms of the epoch of Gemini
shortly to be superseded by that of the Bull in the concept of the
Universal Zodiac which, some believe, may descend from ancient
Mesopotamia. The only problem with this interpretation is, of course,
that the Twins overthrow the Bull, as will shortly be related, and not
the other way about. Sometimes Gilgamesh and Enkidu (or rather
those two characters from an earlier time who seem to prefigure them)
appear as Bull and Ram, thus symbolizing the poetic precession of the
Equinox, a concept that, some would believe, engaged the minds of the
most ancient philosophers; these Twins even overthrow the Bull of
Heaven when it is sent precipitately to earth to destroy them. They
represent, too, that constantly returning principle of the dualism of all
the created world which so obsessed the ancients. It has been suggested
that the whole Gilgamesh cycle is in fact a solar myth with an occult,
astrological significance. There are twelve divisions in the epic – but
who knows?

Gilgamesh's love for Enkidu brings him to a sense of his responsibilities for his kingdom, and he no longer concerns himself with leaping

upon the more personable members of the Uruk community. With the blessing of Shamash, the benevolent Sun-God, the two friends set out on a quest to conquer evil manifest in the form of Huwawa, the Keeper of the Wood. Gilgamesh is anxious to create a 'name' which will endure. Enkidu is his companion and occasionally his protector. Huwawa is the prototype of the sad monster, with whom it is difficult not to feel a similar degree of sympathy as with Fafnir when he is overcome by the doltish Seigfried. Dragon or monster-slaying was a major preoccupation of the heroes of antiquity; Horus, the Archangel Michael, even Yahweh, were all given to the practice.

After many trials the pair defeat Huwawa and when he is at their mercy, Gilgamesh is inclined to be compassionate and to spare his life. Weeping, Huwawa pleads to be saved: but Enkidu, fulfilling what is evidently his destiny, is inflexible and demands his death. Huwawa is swiftly slain.

The heroes return to Uruk and are feted in a splendid and triumphant entry to the city. But they are guilty of *hubris*; Enkidu has angered the gods both by his refusal to spare Huwawa and because he joined with Gilgamesh in insulting Inanna-Ishtar, a goddess of uncertain temper at the best of times. She tries to persuade Gilgamesh to her bed but he, prompted by Enkidu, reminds her of the dismal fate of her previous lovers. The friends mock her unmercifully and with deadly accuracy. She complains to heaven of the wrong which has been done her, the more annoying as all the taunts and accusations of libidinousness and treachery which are flung at her by Gilgamesh and Enkidu when they spurn her, she knows only too well to be true. But for these faults and also because they have killed the Bull of Heaven, sent to avenge the goddess, one of the two must die. Enkidu dreams of the congress of the gods when the fearful decision is spoken by the supreme God; it is Enkidu who is stricken.

The mortal illness of Enkidu, which lasts for twelve days, is the occasion for a remarkable and moving exchange between the dying man and Shamash the Sun-God who has taken a benevolent interest in the affairs of the two companions. He alone opposed the ruling of the gods when they agreed upon Enkidu's death and now he comes to solace the last hours of one of his protégés.

Enkidu tosses miserably on his death-bed. Gilgamesh is powerless to help him. Enkidu curses his life with a bitterness made utter by his realization of the futility even of his cursing. Frenziedly he reproaches the events which drew him away from his natural existence to the haunts of men, and even inanimate objects in his delirium become the focus of his dreadful sorrow. He curses the hunter who led the people of Uruk to his steppe-lair; most bitterly he execrates the whore who was the instrument of his ensnaring. But in Heaven, Shamash hears Enkidu and speaks to comfort him. He reminds him that life with Gilgamesh has been glorious; the princes of the world have honoured him because he was Gilgamesh's companion, indeed they have kissed his feet as he was the king's beloved friend. He has lived magnificently and now he must die knowing that Gilgamesh will command the most elaborate obsequies for him.

In the words of the myth: 'when Enkidu heard the words of valiant Shamash, his vexed heart grew quiet'. Now he blesses those whom before he cursed and, although he has a dark vision of the afterworld before his eyes, he dies reconciled by the sun-god's words.

Gilgamesh mourns his dead friend with the frenzy and inconsolable grief of Achilles bewailing the death of Patroclus and, like Alexander of Macedon weeping beside Hephaestion's corpse, he clasps the body of his friend until the horrifying evidences of corruption begin to display themselves. He speaks a lament for Enkidu which anticipates that of David for Jonathan. He orders sumptuous funeral ceremonies in Uruk and then, horror-stricken, realizes that the same mortality which has claimed his friend must one day bring an end to his own life, splendid, powerful and just though he knows himself to be.

Again he sets out, this time alone, to search for the secret of eternal life, the most constant and the most fruitless of man's quests. He is still bitterly saddened by Enkidu's death and constantly speaks of his love for him, his own awareness of life's transience feeding upon his melancholy. In the words of the epic, 'the Lord towards the land of the living set his mind' across the marsh lands and southwards to the Gulf.

The rejection of Inanna-Ishtar and the subsequent death of Enkidu represent a curious episode in Gilgamesh's story because of all divinities it might have been expected that she was the one whom Gilgamesh would most honour. She was the patroness of Uruk itself, Gilgamesh's own city and his mother was probably a priestess of her cult; yet the King is clearly in opposition to her.

Some might speculate whether this episode does not record, in mythological terms, a rejection by Gilgamesh of the ultimate payment exacted for the kingship in societies which still honoured the Mother. Gilgamesh conforms admirably to the character of the Sacred King. The myth of Tammuz-Dummuzi, which still echoes in the Near East to this day, was the story of the dying king for whom the goddess mourns but always recreates that he may again be sacrificed. When male Gods began to predominate in ancient societies there was revulsion away from the archaic sacrifice of the Sacred King, consecrated to destruction for the honour of the Goddess. The transitional phase, between the sacrifice of the king and its absolute rejection, was marked by the recognition that a surrogate might die in the king's place and his royal life be thus renewed. In Greece the practice was well attested and there are hints of it amongst the ancient Jews.

In Egypt, the king underwent the ordeal of rebirth at the *heb-sed* festival when his powers were renewed. It is generally proposed that the *heb-sed* is a surrogate act for the ritual sacrifice of the king. Christianity, it has long been recognized, enshrines the age-old concept of the dying god, whose physical death is re-enacted – as similarly was the death of Osiris in Egypt through the mystery plays which were a feature of the earliest rituals – by the sacrifice of the Mass in which the central event is the ingestation of the consecrated bread, rather than the celebrant. The bread is thus a substitute for the living flesh, once consumed in a more dreadful eucharist.

It may also be that this episode in Gilgamesh's story contains some of the essential elements of the sacred marriage rite of old Sumer and that Gilgamesh was in truth intended to be the successor of Dummuzi in the love of Inanna, the city-goddess of Uruk. In later ages the rite of the sacred marriage recurs frequently and it was clearly an integral part of the Sumerian canon, surviving into times after Sumer itself had passed away and was forgotten. It has been suggested that the burial pit at Ur, in which the unbelievably rich accoutrements of a Sumerian royal interment were found, contains the principal actors in the same cere-mony. The later deification of certain Sumerian kings – in itself a wholly un-Sumerian practice – in the time of the Third Dynasty of Ur, may yet be another echo of this ancient ceremony in which the king and the god who ensures the continued fertility of crops and herds are identified together. But in Gilgamesh's case, great though his love for his people unquestionably is, he is not prepared to die at the whim of the goddess and, by his rejection of his role, marks the end of her domina-tion, Gilgamesh's denial of his sacrificial character cannot be absolute however, and therefore his surrogate, Enkidu, his twin as dear to him as any living thing, must die in his place.

North-east of Gilgamesh's city of Uruk lay the Kingdom of Shur-uppak, the modern Fara. Shuruppak was the home of Ziusudra, ('Long of Days') or as the Babylonians called him in their version of the myth which survives, Utanapishtim, a name which may mean, appropriately as it turns out, 'I have found Life'; he was also known, evocatively, as

'The Faraway'. He was said to have reigned in Shuruppak for thirty-six thousand years, a period which reflects the Sumerians' enthusiasm for the sexagesimal scale, which they invented. He was destined to become the hero of the Deluge story, like the Biblical Noah and the Greek Xisuthros, the good and wise king singled out by the gods for salvation when they determined to destroy the rest of the human race, with whom they had become disenchanted. In a long digression which must be reflected here, the Epic explains the reason for their displeasure.

The gods of Sumer were more arbitrary in their relations with mankind even than the Hebrew god Yahweh was to be, for at least in the version contained in Genesis the Deluge was occasioned by God's wrath being visited upon the sins of the created world. The gods of Sumer, and their leader Enlil in particular, could not, it seems, tolerate the noise that mankind was making and on this petulant pretext determined to destroy the race of men by flood. Man was not destined to be wholly annihilated however. Despite the stern decree of the high gods in council, Enki, the friend of man and ruler of the floodwaters, decided to intervene thus risking the wrath of Enlil. But so that he may not be accused of betraying the gods' decision he came to Ziusudra's city and, with the cunning and resource which rarely deserted the most crafty of the gods, whispered his warning to the wall of the King's reed hut. Through the wall he urged Ziusudra to build an ark, put his family and retainers on board and, with a cargo of all living creatures, to set out upon the rising waters.

The Sumerian epic contains many dramatic passages which differ from the Biblical story; the description of the mounting terror of the storm, led by the black powers of wind and thunder, is particularly striking.

> With the first glow of dawn
> A black cloud rose up from the horizon
> Inside it Adad thunders
> While Shullat and Hanish go in front
> Moving as heralds over hill and plain
> Erragal tears out the posts;
> Forth comes Ninurta and causes the dykes to follow
> The Annunaki lift up the torches
> Setting the land ablaze with their glare
> Consternation over Adad reaches to the heavens
> Who turned to blackness all that had been light
> The wide land was shattered like a pot
> For one day the south storm blew.

Gathering speed as it blew submerging the mountains
Overtaking the people like a battle
No one can see his fellow
Nor can the people be recognized from heaven
The gods were frightened by the deluge
And, shrinking back, they ascended to the heaven of Anu
The gods cowered like dogs crouched against the outer wall.[5]

Ever since the last century when the 'Deluge' tablet was first de-
ciphered, the argument has swung back and forth as to whether the
story recalls a major catastrophe actually experienced by the Sumerians
and subsequently impressed deeply on their memory, or whether it is
merely the literary expression of what must have been a constant and
deep-seated fear of a people living between two such unpredictable
streams as Tigris and Euphrates.

Woolley, who excavated so diligently and with such effect in
Sumerian cities, firmly believed in the historicity of the Biblical flood,
admittedly on slender evidence;[6] in more recent years it has been usual
to adopt the contrary view. But floods in Sumer there certainly were
and one – or all of them – may have been immortalized in the original of
the myth, told around the camp fires, perhaps even before Enki
founded his first city at Eridu.

More recent evidence has become available however, which opens
the question again. First, it now seems likely that Ziusudra/Utanapish-
tim/Noah was an historical figure and not simply the man with the
amiable manner and a taste for zoology whom the legends, both
Sumerian and Biblical, portray. At Shuruppak, Ziusudra's capital, and
at Kish, one of the most respected religious sites of ancient Sumer,
extensive flood deposits have been uncovered since Woolley's time
which are almost certainly contemporary with Ziusudra's supposed
reign and are more widespread than had been earlier believed.[7] It is clear
that the flood waters covered considerable areas of the land and could
quite easily have been mistaken for a universal deluge by the survivors,
so terrible must have been the havoc they wrought. The flood would
seem to have covered an area many square miles in extent to a
considerable depth, and the persistent legend which has survived the
millennia may thus be based upon a real and fearful experience. This
deluge at Shuruppak may have taken place towards the end of the
Jemdet Nast period, c. 3000 BC.[8]

To return to the version of the Flood which the Epic relates; like
Noah when the deluge had abated, Ziusudra releases birds as his

messengers to find dry land, but it is the raven rather than the dove which makes the landfall in the Sumerian legend. On the mountain top where his ark – a peculiar, perfectly cubical vessel – comes to rest, Ziusudra offers sacrifices to the gods who are said, rather gracelessly, to hover around the sacrifices 'like flies' hungry for the worship which has been denied them by the destruction of the creatures they created, in part for this very purpose. A slightly acid view of the behaviour of the Sumerian pantheon is not unreasonable; it is apparent from the passage quoted earlier that at one stage the whole operation was beginning to get out of hand when the gods, obviously inexperienced in directing cosmic disasters, withdrew cravenly to the higher heavens. The image of them crouching 'like dogs' against the outer wall of Anu's most distant heaven is a telling one.

Ziusudra is rewarded with immortality by the now calmer gods, a state which is to be shared by his wife, a peculiarly thoughtful touch. They are translated to 'the land of crossing', Dilmun:

Ziusudra, the King
Prostrated himself before Anu and Enlil.
Anu and Enlil cherished Ziusudra,
Like that of a god they gave him,
Breath eternal like that of a god they bring down for him
Then Ziusudra the King,
The preserver of the name of vegetation and of the seed of
  mankind
In the land of crossing, the land of Dilmun, the place where the sun
  rises they caused to dwell.[9]

In some versions of the myth, Ziusudra is said to be placed by the gods in a mysterious land 'at the mouth of the rivers'.[10] It has generally been thought that this location must be somewhere near the outflow of the Tigris and Euphrates into the Gulf through the marsh lands near the Shatt al Arab. However, an interesting light may be thrown on this typically vague piece of Sumerian geographical description by the fact that local legend in Bahrain and on the Arabian mainland maintains that the sea's fresh water springs, which feature later in Gilgamesh's story, are the 'subterranean mouths' of the two rivers. This they are not: but it is certainly possible that the legend persisting today descends from very ancient times and that it was to these springs that the Ziusudra legend refers, when it speaks of 'the mouth of the rivers' as the eternal home of the justified king of Shuruppak – and Bahrain means, in Arabic, 'the two seas'.

Gilgamesh goes out to search for Dilmun, for nowhere is it more likely that he will find the secret of eternal life than there, a land blessed of the gods, ruled by the one man who has already been transformed by them into an immortal. He travels by foot from his city, alone and meeting more adventures on the way including an encounter with a sort of celestial hostess, Siduri, who urges Gilgamesh to forget his concern for man's condition and to eat, drink and be merry.

> Gilgamesh, whither rovest thou?
> The Life thou pursuest thou shalt not find
> When the gods created mankind
> Death for mankind they set aside
> Life in their own hands retaining.
> Thus Gilgamesh let full be thy belly
> Make thou merry by day and by night,
> Of each day make thou a feast of rejoicing,
> Day and night dance thou and play!
> Let thy garments be sparkling fresh,
> Thy head be washed; bathe thou in water
> Pay heed to the little one that holds on to thy hand
> Let thy spouse delight in thy bosom!
> For this is the task of mankind.[11]

Siduri is an intriguing, enigmatic character. The Gulf in ancient times was thickly populated with goddesses; Siduri is, by any standards, one of its principal divinities. She lives on an island at the edge of the Ocean, that mysterious generalization for all unknown seas. Her land is a garden in which the Sun walks in the mornings: the trees bear jewels. Siduri has sisters, or perhaps the other goddesses are really herself under other guises. One of them, Sinara, is described as the goddess of the Gulf, given charge of it by the Lord Enki himself. Lakhamum is conflated with Serpanit of Dilmun[12] and is represented bearing the scales of a mermaid or a fish goddess. Then there are the several goddesses associated with holy Dilmun: Ninsikilla, the lady of pure decrees and spouse to Enki, and Ninhursag, the great goddess whose terrible epiphany brought death near to Enki, are but two of them.

Siduri survived her encounter with Gilgamesh to become, in Hellenistic times, the Erythraean Sibyl. She was then represented, anachronistically, as the daughter of Berossus, the Chaldaean historian whose *Babyloniaca* contained the weird story of the appearance in the Gulf in legendary times of the *apkallu*, the part-men part-fish who brought the arts of civilization to the black-headed folk of Sumer.[13]

The garden of which Siduri was the mistress is said to bear trees laden with jewels. It has been suggested that this is a reference to the frequently intense phosphorescence of the Gulf's waters, caused by the coral in the shallows. A possible candidate for Siduri's island must be Failakah, in the Bay of Kuwait; in this event Siduri is also to be indentified with Artemis, to whom Failakah, under its name of Ikaros, was consecrated.

A pretty little Greek temple on Failakah has been excavated by the Danes. This, it must be presumed, was connected with the oracle for which, in Greek times, the island seems also to have been celebrated. The oracle, however, might be less permanent in its structure, a sacred grove perhaps or some wise woman lurking in a cave.

Cornwall, who, when he prepared his thesis, did not know of the identification between Failakah and Ikaros, recorded Strabo's and Arrian's description of an oracle, said to be dedicated to Diana Tauropolis, situated on Ikaros.[14] He suggests that the oracle's name meant something like 'Diana, of the City of the Bulls': but of what city, what bulls? In fact, Cornwall is incorrect in transcribing the epithet as 'Tauropolis'; it is 'Tauropolos' which is a very different matter. In this form it could mean 'Diana, the Slayer of Bulls'.

Diana is the Roman form of Artemis whom Alexander named as the guardian goddess of Failakah and to whom its animals were sacred. The island in the Aegean after which he is said to have named the Gulf island is Ichara, not Ikaros; but it too, had a high bull cult, of the sort which increasingly, it appears, was prevalent on Failakah. Thus it would appear that Alexander, recognizing the sacred character of the Gulf island and its bull cults, which by the evidence of the seals were ceremonies of immense antiquity, brought all these elements together and identified Failakah with Ichara, because of their common preoccupation with rituals involving bulls.

It is difficult to propose what might have been the nature of the oracle on Failakah. However, it is not impossible that the ancient goddess who was identified with the island was Siduri who, according to the Epic of Gilgamesh, lived on the 'edge of the Ocean' in 'the Garden of the Sun'. Her later identification with the Erythraean Sibyl brings her into association with a very visionary and prophetic creature indeed. Perhaps this linking of the island celebrated for its bull cults, with a goddess of ancient prophecy accounts, in Alexander's time, for its reputation as the site of an oracle of Diana and the bulls.

After his encounter with Siduri, Gilgamesh continues on his way: he meets sinister scorpion men, the guardians of the Gates of Yesterday and Tomorrow (also known as the Keepers of the Place of Sunrise), and is fearful of them: they warn him that no one has accomplished the journey which he has set himself. He meets Shamash and even the god is awed by Gilgamesh's presumption:

> Shamash was distraught, as he betook himself to him;
> He says to Gilgamesh
> 'Gilgamesh, whither rovest thou?
> The life thou pursuest thou shalt not find.'
> Gilgamesh says to him, to valiant Shamash:
> 'After marching [and] roving over the steppe,
> Must I lay my head in the heart of the earth
> That I may sleep through all the years?
> Let mine eyes behold the sun that I may have my fill of the light!
> Darkness withdraws when there is enough light.
> May one who indeed is dead behold yet the radiance of the sun!'[15]

But Gilgamesh is not to be turned from his course: he crosses the marsh lands and reaches what must be the head of the Arabian Gulf. There he summons Ziusudra's boatman to take him by sea to Dilmun. This mysterious character, whose responsibility, like Charon's in Greek mythology, is to ferry the dead to paradise, is called Sursunabi in Sumerian and Urshanabi in Babylonian. He agrees to carry Gilgamesh across the waters of death which separate Dilmun from the living world. However, it is essential that Gilgamesh shall not touch the waters and Sursunabi instructs him to cut one hundred and twenty poles sixty cubits in length to punt the boat; the Sumerian cubit was 19½ inches long. This generous allocation of gigantic poles, each one just under one hundred feet long, is necessary so that Gilgamesh may let each one fall back into the sea of death; thus he will avoid touching the lethal waters.

The journey according to the epic might reasonably be expected to take a month and fifteen days; Gilgamesh and Sursunabi however, reach Dilmun in three days, a testimony to Gilgamesh's more than human qualities. In fact, three days is about the time it would have taken a ship of Sumerian times to sail from the head of the Gulf to Bahrain.

As the boat approaches Dilmun Ziusudra is watching from the shore; at once he recognizes that Gilgamesh is no man of his, for Gilgamesh is living. It is of some significance that the Epic makes this point, the recognition by Ziusudra that the figure standing in Sursunabi's boat is untouched by death and thus is not truly ready to be brought to his (and Dilmun's) shores. This suggests, however tentatively, that the place to which Ziusudra had been transported was a place to which others were to be brought; since they had to cross the waters of death to reach it, it may be presumed that they, too, were dead. This may be an echo of the belief which gave occaion to Dilmun's sepulchral reputation. The deeply evocative concept of the 'island of the dead' which so haunted the imagination of nineteenth-century romantic artists may have had its remote beginnings here. Boeklin's celebrated painting, transposed to the blood-warm waters of the Gulf, may lose something of its mournful, cypress-haunted solemnity but it gains immeasurably in its antiquity.

Ziusudra welcomes Gilgamesh, but asks for the reason of his mournful appearance; Gilgamesh at once rehearses the story of Enkidu's death and their love for one another, his fears of his own dissolution and his quest for immortality. He realizes that unless he finds the secret, one day soon he too will die and be laid in the earth forever. He pleads with Ziusudra to tell him how he may find the eternal life which he has dedicated himself to seeking, enduring all hardships and tribulations in the quest for it. Ziusudra is emphatic and discouraging:

> There is no permanence. Do we build a house to stand for ever, do we seal a contract to keep for ever, does the flood of rivers endure? It is only the nymph of the dragonfly who sheds her larva and sees the sun in his glory. From the days of old there is no permanence. The sleeping and the dead, how alike they are, they are like a painted death. What is there between the master and the servant when both have fulfilled their doom? When the Annunaki, the judges come together, and Mammetum the mother of destinies, together they decree the fates of men. Life and death they allot but the day of death they do not disclose.[16]

Yet Ziusudra is the only mortal to escape the universal fate of mankind; to explain this destiny he begins to tell the weary Gilgamesh of the story of the Flood and his part in it. What Ziusudra, presumably delighted to have a new audience for the recital of his life-story, has to tell him seems to have little relevance to Gilgamesh's problems, except perhaps to demonstrate that the king of Shuruppak was merely fulfilling the role which destiny and the gods had determined for him.

When his recital is finished Ziusudra puts Gilgamesh to another test; all he needs to do to become immortal he tells him, is to resist sleep for six days and seven nights. Gilgamesh tries his best, but wearied by his journeys, and in all probability by the story of the Deluge, he falls asleep. So tired is he that far from remaining awake for seven nights, he sleeps for all that time, outside Ziusudra's reed hut in Dilmun.

The immortal, who has watched over him with affectionate compassion, wakens him at last and Gilgamesh, endearingly and wholly in character, cries that he had only just dropped off into a light sleep. Gently Ziusudra tells him it is not so, and the realization that he cannot resist even the little death of sleep brings panic and despair to Gilgamesh. 'Already', he says 'the thief in the night has hold of my limbs, death inhabits my room: wherever my foot rests I find death'.

Ziusudra offers Gilgamesh some consolation, but it is tinged with irony, for if he cannot give him eternal life he can give him a new set of clothes which will keep their pristine quality until he returns to his own city. Sometimes even mere possessions outlive their owners.

Gilgamesh is about to leave Dilmun and return despondently home to Uruk, when Ziusudra's wife prompts her husband to reveal one mystery of the island to him. At its revelation Gilgamesh becomes wildly excited, for it seems to be the very object of his quest. Under the water, Ziusudra tells him, there grows a plant, similar to the buckthorn, which if plucked will bring the possessor the return of lost youth. At once Gilgamesh joyously prepares to set off in search of it convinced, mistakenly, that it is the secret of immortality that awaits his grasp.

At this point of the narrative, the storyteller comments specifically that it is a sweet water current that bears Gilgamesh to the sea-bed where the plant grows. He weights himself with heavy stones tied to his feet in the way which is the practice of the pearl-fishers of the Bahrain seas to this day. It seems not impossible that it might have been one of the sea's freshwater springs that carried Gilgamesh down to find the flower of restored youth.

These springs, it has already been remarked, are a peculiar feature of the seas around Bahrain, fountains of pure water which burst up surprisingly from the shallows a mile or so offshore. It is clear from the poem that Gilgamesh is in the sea, for it is stated that when he picked the flower he cut the weighted stones from his feet 'and the sea carried him and threw him on the shore'.

The actual nature of the 'plant' that Gilgamesh seeks is still unknown. One possibility is that it is the coral which is the object of his quest.[16a] Coral grows abundantly in the Gulf; its phosphorescence has already been referred to in connection with Gilgamesh's encounter with Siduri. One of the candidates for the place where Gilgamesh plunged into the sea must be Fasht Khor, off the north shore of the principal island for there is located a substantial fresh water spring which forces its way up out of the sea-bed itself.

Now Gilgamesh reveals one of the traits of his nature which may have caused him to be so loved by his people while he was king of Uruk and which ensured that the recollection of him grew over the centuries until he assumed heroic and semi-divine proportions in the memory of the generations that delighted in his story. Excitedly he shows the magic plant to Ziusudra's ferryman; he announces that he will return to Uruk with it and there give it to the old men to eat that they may become young again. Only when the old men are restored will he, the king, eat it himself.

Gilgamesh leaves the house of Ziusudra on the shores of Dilmun and begins his journey home, bearing his magic plant and accompanied by Sursunabi who has been banished from Dilmun for bringing a mortal to its shores; but he is now Gilgamesh's friend. This time, presumably because Sursunabi has had his boat taken away from him, they are on foot. But Sursunabi is something more than a simple boatman, a Sumerian Charon ferrying the dead to Dilmun. He is a member indeed of the principal family of gods for he married the daughter of the great god, Enki of the Abyss; his name, it has been suggested, means 'Servant of Enki'. Thus Enki's dominion over Dilmun is demonstrated.

After a while upon their journey, they stop by a cool and inviting pool. Gilgamesh flings off the splendid clothes given him by Ziusudra and plunges in, leaving the precious flower of youth on the bank.

Deep in the pool, a serpent lives. Disturbed by Gilgamesh splashing joyfully above it, the serpent rises to the surface and smells the sweetness of the magic plant. Quickly it rears out of the water, seizes the plant, swallows it, and at once sloughs its skin, the invariable sign of the snake's immortality in the eyes of the ancients.

Thus destiny and the gods played their final deception upon Gilgamesh. He wept by the waters, mourning now not only Enkidu and his own certain dissolution, but also the hopelessness of his quest and the wreck of his hopes to change man's destiny.

In Bahrain near the north-east end of the island is the Pool of Adari; though there is not the slightest evidence to warrant it, it is pleasant to think of it as the place where Gilgamesh, having pitted himself as the champion of mortal man against the fates, was finally conquered. Today it is a happier place, full of boys bathing, few of whom have ever thought of the king who might have bathed there before them.

The pool is a few miles to the south of the two principal Sumerian sites in Bahrain, Barbar and Qala'at al-Bahrain. Offshore, about a mile due north of Barbar lies another of the freshwater springs which bubble up from the sea-bed, called al-Sharaiba in Arabic. It is tempting to place all the main events of Gilgamesh's visit to Dilmun in this corner of the island that was, with little doubt, the heartland of the Sumerian Eden. Adari, incidentally, was probably a place of ritual sacrifice in pre-Islamic times, for in Arabic the word means 'virgin' and this suggests that an ill-fortuned girl was once marked out as an offering to the island's divinities, and cast into its depths. To this day popular belief in Bahrain insists that a serpent in Adari pool demands an annual sacrifice and that every year a swimmer will be drowned there.

But there is another possibility: in some versions of the myth Gilgamesh is said to have bathed in a well. Given the frequently recorded practice of goddesses bathing their heads in wells or fountains, this seems a reasonable possibility. There was a well, of great cultic importance, in the temple site at Barbar.

A recurring factor in mythology and ancient belief has appeared in the Epic at this point in the form of the serpent which stole Gilgamesh's hope of eternal youth. Snakes were sacred from the earliest times and the serpent was as frequently a creature of good omen as it was of evil, for it was one of the attendants of the ambiguous Great Mother, the original divine creative force recognized and worshipped by man from high paleolithic times onward. The serpent that played so deplorable a part the garden of Eden was almost certainly Sumerian or Babylonian in its mythical origins though the biblical story was probably based upon a misunderstanding of the original source. A snake cult was still maintained in Bahrain a thousand years after the time from which the earliest versions of the Epic of Gilgamesh dates and two thousand years after the events which it describes.

Gilgamesh returned to Uruk with the knowledge that man's life is destined to be brief and that there is no escaping the ultimate summons of death and the rule of the Iggigi, the dark and terrible gods who were the judges of the Underworld. However, he finds some cause for pride in his city and he points out to Sursunabi (for he has befriended the now unemployed boatman) the high ramparted walls he has built of burnt brick, dependable and strong, and the orchards and temple lands which march with the city's limits. At least his life has not been wholly wasted if he can build a strong city and bring good government to his state; is he not Gilgamesh, the King, the shepherd of his people?

> Go up and walk upon the wall of Uruk,
> Inspect the base terrace, examine the brickwork,
> Is not its brickwork of burnt brick?[17]

At length the number of Gilgamesh's days in Uruk are realized; still protesting against his fate and the fate of all men, he dies and must descend into the sombre underworld of the spirits. His people prepare a solemn funeral for him, for the panoply of death is as splendid as that which marks the progress of a living king. The young Gilgamesh, wild and insatiable, is forgotten and only the royal shephed who suffered much for his people is remembered. Gilgamesh the King who was enjoined by Enlil, the master of the gods, to deal justly before the face of the sun, is taken to his tomb lamented by all the people of the city:

> The King has laid himself down and will not rise again
> The Lord of Kullun will not rise again;
> He overcame evil, he will not come again
> Though he was strong of arm he will not rise again
> He had wisdom and a comely face, he will not come again
> He is gone into the mountain, he will not come again
> From the couch of many colours he will not come again.[18]

The foundations of the walls of Uruk, so proudly acclaimed by Gilgamesh may still be made out and they are nearly six miles in circumference.[19] The city itself has become a mound raked over earnestly by archaeologists, the splendour of its temples and towers reconstructed from fragments and impressions in the Mesopotamian soil. But Gilgamesh has achieved eternal life, at least to our day and, it is to be hoped, for as long as men are moved by heroes and the sagas of their exploits. And surely he warrants such remembrance, for he symbolizes man's protest against the little time which he is allowed to wander in the garden of this world and his eternal struggle against the harsh lottery of the gods.

Of course, it would be foolish to try to trace too literally, step by step, Gilgamesh's journey to Dilmun. The voyage described in the Epic may well *not* be capable of being placed strictly in any real location at all; for all we know today, it may be astronomical, cosmological or purely fictional.

The majesty of the myth and its expression through the medium of the Epic is, however, neither increased by being rooted in place or time nor diminished by not being so. It is part of the universal heritage and its real significance in the present context is that the culmination of Gilgamesh's journey is sought for and, in a sense, fulfilled in Dilmun's land, which in this case lies beyond the borderlands of reality. Again, it is the faery quality of Dilmun which pervades those parts of the Epic which touch it.

So many strands of myth run into this most ancient of all Paradise lands that those of Gilgamesh's story are only part of the warp and woof of the Dilmun tapestry. The gods cluster around Dilmun as once they were said to cluster, like flies, around Ziusudra's sacrifices after the Flood, and, in addition to Gilgamesh the most splendid among heroes, there is a significant company of other heroic figures whose stories, like his, find much of their expression in Dilmun and the lands of the Gulf. The heroes passing in review, are Ziusudra, Alexander, the Lord Enki, Oannes and Al-Khidr: it is the last, in particular, who now merits some special consideration.

These heroic figures are a special element in the Gulf's mythology. Thus Gilgamesh and his counterpart, Alexander, distant in time but comparable in their heroic status and enduring legend, are not alone as the most powerful figures who bridge the realms of myth and reality. Enki himself is there, the most puissant of divinities, who has his *alter ego* in Oannes, part-man, part-fish, the aquatic didact after whose time men, it was said, learnt nothing more than he had taught them.[20] Ziusudra, too, must qualify as an heroic figure, certainly as something more than mortal, but there is another still more mysterious being, who enters the story of the 'place of the two seas' and who may subsume all of these mighty entities – at least in the version of his legend with which we are dealing – in his own shadowy self.

The myth relates the activities of one of the more enigmatic characters in Near Eastern folklore, Al-Khidr, the Green One. Al-Khidr features initially in the archaeology of the Gulf by virtue of a shrine dedicated to him on Failakah island, close to the site excavated by the Danes and recognized by them as part of 'greater Dilmun'. Bibby has described both the shrine and the legends which attend it; it is obviously of considerable antiquity, demonstrated by the mound on which the present shrine stands.[21]

The shrine is particularly venerated by the Shi'ite sect of Islam, the second great stream of dogma and practice of the Faith of which the orthodox Sunni branch is the larger part, dominant on the Arabian shores of the Gulf. Kuwait is overwhelmingly Sunni in observance but respect for belief, even if it may appear to be heterodox, prevents any interference with a shrine sacred even to a small minority. Thus the shrine of Al-Khidr is inviolate, safe from the probings of archaeologists, a triumph for Faith if a loss for knowledge. There can be little doubt that the site would repay excavation, for it has obviously been a sacred place over many millennia: indeed, it is likely that its position today is a consequence of the ancient concept that certain points on the earth's surface were immemorially sacred and hence were for ever consecrated to a divinity. Thus did the ziggurat originate in Sumerian cities and no doubt, if it were possible to penetrate the lower levels of Al-Khidr's Failakah shrine, evidence would be found of its own origin; it might even reveal who, and what, Al-Khidr was.

In Islamic lore Al-Khidr is an intriguing figure; he has no precise analogy in Christian or Jewish mythology. In the Quran it is never clear exactly what Al-Khidr is, other than that he is a messenger and a servant of God (like Sursunabi who was a servant of Enki); he is, presumably, a spirit who, since he is visible to men, can assume human form. He is one of the agents of the divine power and is himself something of an elemental, with much of the apparent capriciousness and unpredictability of a primaeval divinity.

Al-Khidr is the protagonist of one of the most remarkable, complex and disturbing Surahs (chapters) of the Quran. This is Surah 18, commonly titled *The Cave*.[22]

The Cave contains many different elements: stories, precepts and injunctions, as well as the account of Moses' meeting with and attachment to Al-Khidr. Al-Khidr is never named as such in the Quranic accounts; he is called 'one of Our Servants to whom we have vouchsafed Our mercy and whom we had endowed with knowledge of Our own'. But all the commentaries agree that it is Al-Khidr's intervention in human affairs, an intervention wholly countenanced by God, that is described in the episode.

The Cave is many-levelled; the Surah begins with the sequence which gives it its name, but which is not immediately relevant to our purpose here. It relates the story of the Seven Sleepers (and their dog) who, in the Quranic version of a wide-spread myth, are boys who fall asleep for an unknown time in the depths of the cave. When this story is told the Surah goes on to warn of the catastrophes which await the nations of unbelievers and wrong-doers; then, suddenly, Moses appears and an entirely different narrative begins. It is at this point that *The Cave* begins to assume a particular significance and interest in the context of the Gulf. It must however be remembered that the account belongs essentially to the realm of legend; nothing is precise and clearly defined but all is hazy and allusive. *The Cave* has much of the quality of a dream sequence.

Moses announces to his servant that he plans to journey to 'the place where two seas meet'. It must be said that traditionally the commentaries on the Quran have always assumed the objective of Moses' journey to have been Suez where two seas, the Red Sea and the Mediterranean, may be said to meet.[23] However, modern scholarship has tended to suggest that the Quran means precisely what it says and that it is to 'the place of the two seas'; that is, to Bahrain in the Gulf, that Moses directs his wanderings.

Moses is himself attended by a servant whose name, in the commentaries on the Quran, is called Joshua son of Nun. Joshua is Jesus; Nun is the Deep, the primaeval waters. He is also sometimes identified as a fish. Thus all the elements in the story of Al-Khidr constantly run together in the most intriguing way.

Moses and his servant journey on together, and the Quran reads: 'But when they came at last to the place where the two seas met, they forgot their fish, which made its way into the water, swimming at will.' The loss of the fish, a miraculous creature, evidently, which has not been referred to before in the account, is not realized by Moses until he asks his servant for food. The servant admits the fish's loss; Moses recognizes that the event is a miraculous one and 'they return by the way they came' – presumably once more to the place where the two seas meet. Here they find the Servant of God – was he perhaps the fish, disguised? Recognizing him for what he is, Moses begs to be permitted to follow him that he may learn from his wisdom. The Servant of God warns Moses that he will find it difficult to bear with him and with the accession of knowledge which is beyond him; Moses insists, however, and they set off together.

Then follow three episodes in each of which Al-Khidr carries out an action which appears to Moses to be either malignant or inexplicable. In the first Al-Khidr bores a hole in the bottom of the boat in which they are travelling and sinks it; in the second they meet a youth on the road and at once Al-Khidr kills him; in the third they find a wall on the point of collapse and Al-Khidr restores it, but seeks no payment for doing so.

Moses has promised Al-Khidr not to question his acts, but cannot contain his bewilderment at what Al-Khidr does, so perplexing do his actions seem to be.

At each event therefore, Moses (who in this episode is presented as a rather frivolous and irresponsible chatterer) demands an explanation from Al-Khidr, only apologizing abjectly as, each time, the Servant reminds him of their bargain. Al-Khidr, when he is pressed by Moses, now warns him that they must part but first he explains each of his strange proceedings. He knew that an enemy was in pursuit of the boat in which they were travelling so to thwart him, he scuttled it. The boy he killed was the only son of his parents, true believers to whom the boy would bring much distress by reason of the sinful life which Al-Khidr knew lay in his future; he would beg his Lord to give them another, more pious son whose worth would bring them joy. The wall he rebuilt, because beneath it was buried a treasure which belonged to two orphan boys, which they would find when they grew to manhood and could protect it. All these events were directed, not by Al-Khidr's will but by the will of God.

Apart from his appearance in *The Cave* Al-Khidr is an important figure in popular Muslim and Near-Eastern myth. Sometimes he is said to be the son of Adam: sometimes his true name is given as Elijah. On occasion he is identified with St George.[24] As well as being a contemporary both of Moses and of Alexander he is said to have been living in the time of Abraham. He lives, variously, on an island or on a green carpet in the midst of the sea. In some of the legends associated with the life of Alexander he is the commander of the King's vanguard, his vizier, even his cousin, certainly his friend. They journey together to the spring of life and Al-Khidr discovers a miraculous well.[25]

Al-Khidr is said to worship God on an island. By his association with islands he is taken to be the patron of seamen and seafaring folk; indeed, on the sea he is said to be God's *Khalifa* or successor. In India he is a river-god, a spirit of wells and streams who is portrayed seated on a fish. One of his principal shrines is on an island in the Indus river. He can find water below ground and speaks the languages of all peoples. He is a particular friend of the archangel Raphael and his name is even substituted sometimes for that of the still greater Michael.

After relating the story of the three episodes involving Al-Khidr and Moses, *The Cave* abruptly changes the course of its narrative once again. Al-Khidr and Moses vanish, to be replaced by yet another powerful figure in Islamic lore, Dhul-Qarnein, the Two-Horned One.

There is general agreement among the commentators as to the identity of Dhul-Qarnein; to their collective mind he is beyond doubt Alexander, son of Philip King of Macedon and, customarily, surnamed the Great. Alexander's legend lives on fervently in the Near and Middle East, even to this day; he is moreover enshrined in the Quran as one chosen by God and particularly favoured by Him. In *The Cave* we learn that Dhul-Qarnein is given by God the rulership over many peoples. He journeys to the west where he sees the sun setting in a pool of black mud and to the east where he builds a rampart of iron and molten brass against the depredations of those two familiar figures in the mythology of London, Gog and Magog, who, perhaps rather surprisingly, make their appearance here. Then the Two-Horned One in turn disappears and the narrative of *The Cave* is concluded.

The Cave is a text of great subtlety and complexity; to unravel all of its many strands would require the invention of a Quranic scholar of deep learning and skill. However, it may be possible to detect one or two more elements which are relevant to the larger theme and which contribute to an understanding of the importance of myth in the development of the Gulf's historical character.

C. G. Jung, the most perceptive *magus* of our century who probed deeply into the nature and structure of myth, chose Al-Khidr as one of his 'Four Archetypes'.[26] For Jung, Al-Khidr stood for the figure of the Trickster, the almost elemental and catalytic force which produces effects but conceals their (and his) reality. Thus, nothing is wholly what it seems to be under Al-Khidr's dispensation and the victim of his wiles must be careful neither to seek for premature understanding of what his actions mean nor to attribute to them solutions which are rooted simply in what seems to be.

A better candidate than Al-Khidr for the Trickster would, however, surely be Enki himself, the wise divinity who, by a cunning device, saved the race of men from the Flood and the misdirected wrath of the other gods; often in his dealings with his fellow divinities Enki adopted subterfuge and displayed a predilection for obscuring the reality of his actions. Jung probably did not know of Enki's existence when he was considering the origins of myth. Then the Greek and Hebrew legends, with the addition of the occasional Egyptian example, were considered to be formative to man's developing consciousness. The immensely more ancient Akkadian and, more ancient still, Sumerian myths were then largely unknown. It is interesting to speculate what Jung might have made of them had he known of their existence, in the form in which they are understood today. Had he known Enki, the god's enigmatic and ambiguous nature could hardly have failed to intrigue him.

It is reasonable to assume that the story of Moses and Al-Khidr takes place in the Gulf waters where the two seas meet, somewhere therefore in the general locations of Bahrain, perhaps on the Arabian mainland rather than on the island. The miraculous fish and the appearance of Nun recall the fish cults which are known to have been a feature of early religious practice in Sumer as witnessed by the evidence of such cults in the earliest shrines at Eridu. Enki's priests were often represented wearing a sort of fish costume, emphasizing the god's concern with the creatures of the deep.

A popular myth of great antiquity, still current in Bahrain in this century, has a giant striding up the Gulf, its waters only up to his ankles, who reaches down into the water to take a fish for his meal. Having caught it he holds it up against the sun to grill it. Clearly the giant is another fish-connected wonder-worker, still haunting these waters. His name is Ishnaq bin Inak and it obviously recalls, over these several thousand years, Enki and his son, Enshag or Inzak.[27]

The Two-Horned One is Alexander as he is most frequently portrayed on his coinage, after his coronation as King of Egypt. He is shown, often in Herakles' lion-skins, wearing the horned headdress by which his descent from ram-headed Amon, the ruler of the Egyptian pantheon in his day, is portrayed. But horned men and horned gods are powerful symbols from long before Alexander's time, particularly in Mesopotamia and the Gulf; it should not be forgotten that Moses himself is often portrayed wearing the ram's horns, even in mediaeval iconography. Horned men abound in the seals of the Gulf, particularly those from Failakah island.

Of the real nature of both cult and myth we can only guess. Indeed all of this topic is essentially speculative but it seems not impossible that the elements of fish, horned divinity and sacred king may suggest that Al-Khidr, who is the common denominator of them all, may in reality be Enki, the benign god of Dilmun and Eridu, on the one hand; and at the other end of the chronological sequence with which we are concerned, he merged into the figure of Alexander Dhul-Qarnein, when he assumed legendary proportion and status. Many of the aspects of Alexander's legends recall those of Gilgamesh, who is thus further brought into the equation. But the appeal which Gilgamesh has exerted on the world over the forty-five centuries which divide his time from the present day is that he represents one of the most enduring archetypes of man in historical time, the hero who sets out on a quest and, despite sufferings and all the odds against him, endures. That Gilgamesh failed in *his* quest only adds another dimension to his essential humanity.

X

The Future of Dilmun

One hundred years of archaeology in Bahrain have revealed much about the material culture which flourished in the centuries during which it was the heart of the far-famed land of Dilmun.[1] The post-war period has provided at least the beginnings of an understanding of the part played by the lands of eastern Arabia and Oman in the development of a Gulf-wide culture over the past fifty or so centuries. But two fundamental questions remain as inpenetrably unanswered as ever they were.

Who were the Dilmunites and where did they come from?

We are reasonably certain that the Dilmunites were not Phoenicians; we are by no means certain now that the Phoenicians were not Dilmunites.[2] There is no evidence that the Dilmunites were Sumerians, though the destinies of the two peoples were closely linked. We do not know what was the language of Dilmun. That inscriptions in most of the historic languages associated with the region have been found either in the insular or the continental Dilmun (the islands or the mainlaind) prove only that Dilmun had contact with the peoples of many lands and that, in all probability, people to whom these languages were native resided here.

We may be reasonably sure that there would have been a significant component in the Dilmunite stock drawn from the proto-Arabians (if such a term may be permitted) who inhabited the eastern part of the Arabian peninsula in the historic period and who probably had always done so.[3] These were the relatives of the Mar-tu, the Ahlamu and eventually of the Arameans; they tended, all of them, to have connections with the western Semitic linguistic groups but whether the Dilmunites spoke a western Semitic tongue, in post-Sumerian times, must be considerably in doubt.

We do not know what a Dilmunite looked like. We do not know what his customs of dress were, other than the odd fragments of jewellery which have survived. We do have the mildly satisfying information that the reputation of Dilmun as a particularly favourable place in which to live seems to have been borne out by the fact that the Dilmunites' skeletal remains show them to have been rather taller, better built and somewhat longer living than the average of their contemporaries.[4] It is all an agreeable little mystery.

On the matter of the origins of the Dilmun civilization, it may now just be possible to discern some tentative landmarks through the haze which surrounds them, which may in time lead to their fuller recognition. Even this, however, will not necessarily tell us all that we would wish to know about the Dilmunites themselves, though it may begin to suggest at least some associations for them.

It now appears more and more likely that the essential impetus which led, in the later centuries of the third millennium, to the establishment of what was evidently a rich and sophisticated society on the principal Bahrain island, came from the south and east.[5] There are more and more hints of connections in the third millennium between the island of Bahrain and what is today the Sultanate of Oman, particularly its northern reaches and beyond Oman to the Indus Valley and its coastal regions. There is no doubt also, that, as matters stand at present, the settlements in Oman are notably earlier in date than the earliest so far known in Bahrain.

There is a curious chronological hiatus in Bahrain archaeology, which in effect seems to mean than between the late Ubaid period in the fourth millennium BC and the end of the third millennium, a gap of well over a thousand years, there was no settlement in the Bahrain islands. Since the Mesopotamians of the earlier period evidently had some contact with the eastern Arabian seaboard and since people using Ubaid pottery landed on Qatar and on the little off-shore island to Bahrain which is now the inland site of Al-Markh, this is puzzling.

Having got as far as Al-Markh, they must have been aware of the larger island only a mile or so away to the east, yet, seemingly, they did not venture there.

It is the more strange since the holy character of Dilmun-Bahrain seems to be bound up with its insular character and clearly it is strongly identified in the minds of the Sumerians with the origins of their society. It is considered the place where many of the benefits of civilization originated: this ought to refer, in terms of the Sumerians' own chronology, to some time in the middle of the fourth millennium.

The Sumerians were certainly capable of sailing the Gulf's waters this early. We can presume that they did so in pursuit of the raw materials which they so earnestly sought in lands far from their own home. The conversion of copper was very ancient; by the late fourth millennium it was a familar medium and by the early third its use was virtually industrialized. Oman represents the most convenient source of copper that the Sumerians could tap, but nonetheless it is about a thousand miles distant from the most southerly Sumerian settlement. The odds against their finding it accidentally must be formidable; the idea cannot be wholly discarded, therefore, that the Sumerians themselves *did* come up the Gulf from the south, perhaps from Oman itself or somewhere near to it and brought with them the knowledge of its resources. As was earlier proposed the affection in which they seem always to have held Dilmun-Bahrain may have originated because it sheltered them on their northward journey. In which case, why did they apparently delay establishing the temples (if they are, in any real sense, Sumerian) at Barbar until virtually the end of the Sumerian period? Or are there still earlier shrines awaiting discovery?

It would seem that the Sumerians either maintained contact with or themselves established bases on the eastern Arabian seaboard. They could hardly have failed to be aware of Bahrain's existence, yet apparently they did not use the island during the time of their own greatest prosperity and creative outpourings.

It may be that the explanation may lie in the erratic character of the Gulf itself over this period. The Gulf is significantly lower today than it was in the fourth and early third millennium; it is conceivable that any early settlements that there might have been were built of very fragile materials, such as *burasti*, and simply perished. The sites themselves would be beyond the original shorelines and may now be buried beneath wind blown sand, a substantial distance inland. But, despite the many surveys which have been undertaken of Bahrain's land surface over the past thirty years, no trace of earlier settlements has, in fact, been found.

The extensive structures at Barbar which still wait for the spade of the archaeologist (and for the even more sophisticated survey equipment which he has at his disposal today) could well reveal earlier evidence than has so far been the case. Indeed, it would be very surprising if they did not.

Whether the discovery of fourth- or early third-millennium remains on Bahrain will resolve the long disputed matter of the Sumerians' own origins is another matter altogether. Perhaps it will; certainly no one seems inclined nowadays to suggest any convincing alternative, so a southerly approach may be at least as defensible as any other and more so than most. If, in the closing pages of a book which has tried to take a broad-based but reasonably objective view of the evidence of the past of this region, it were permissible to speculate, then there is one prospect which teases the imagination, once it is planted there.

In late neolithic times, between seven and six thousand years ago, the Gulf and the eastern reaches of the Arabian peninsula presented a markedly different appearance from its present-day topography. With the level of the Gulf significantly higher, by as much as two metres, the sea reached far into parts of the coastal area and beyond, which are now well removed from it.

Al-Markh would have been only one of many such little islands, strung along the coast; Umm an-Nar, off the northern coast of the Omani peninsula, was another. The sea ran deep into the Empty Quarter, Ar-Rub al-Khali, and into the Omani desert. The little communities of hunters who lived on the edges of the lakes which were formed along the desert's perimeter and who subsisted on the larger game which the region could then support, were, by the evidence of their stone tools, talented craftsmen; we do not know what other products they produced since these would have been made from perishable materials. As the sea withdrew and the desert supervened, this people must have been driven away to find new pastures. As they were lake dwellers they were probably competent boatmen; the Gulf (which would hardly have been recognizable to them as such) would not have represented any insuperable barrier to their movement, rather, indeed, the opposite.

As the environment changed the lake dwellers may have moved eastwards and south to form the root population of Oman, whilst others may have moved northwards, working up the Arabian coast or, some of them, skirting it by sea. Eventually the most adventurous of them – and perhaps they were also amongst the earliest to undertake this putative 'trek' – reached the southern Mesopotamian marshlands and founded Eridu. They were unquestionably fisherfolk, wherever they came from, and as such they would be primary candidates to know the Gulf islands intimately; Enki, after all, was their patron. If they were the progenitors of the later Gulf populations this would explain their attachment to its habitable islands: Umm an-Nar, Bahrain, Tarut and Failakah were all important centres of the Dilmun culture or its contemporaries.

These early migrants may have been the ancestors of the Ubaid pottery makers. This is not to assert that they were responsible for the Ubaid pottery found in east Arabian sites, Qatar and Bahrain. This is later in time than the period about which we are now speculating. The earlier Ubaid pottery has however, been identified with early levels at Eridu. The first wave of migrants may have been followed by others, not all of whom perhaps went all the way to Sumer but stayed on the Arabian mainland, though, if they did, they seem to have kept some contact with their cousins to the north.

Over the centuries the south-east Arabian lake dwellers could have fanned out over a wide area.[6] There may even have been a corresponding movement towards the west which, if it is not wholly fantasy, might account for some of the similarities which seem to exist between, for example, the rock art of the early inhabitants of Oman and that of the western Arabians, who lived far away from the Gulf in the region now called the Hijaz and there energetically undertook the decoration of most available rock faces in the area, using forms and motifs strikingly similar to those in the south-east quadrant of the peninsula.[7] These western Arabians incidentally were probably the carriers of many of the Asiatic influences which appear in late pre-dynastic Egypt, in the second half of the fourth millennium. Even some of the rock art of Egypt seems to echo forms to be found in the wadis of Oman. But this is more speculative still, and, for the present, must remain so. However, it may be recalled in passing that the Egyptians seem to have sustained a memory of an island, in the midst of the sea, far away beyond the eastern horizon, 'the island on the edge of the world'.[8]

Much more will be known about Bahrain's antiquity when the as yet unexcavated areas of the principal island are opened up. The whole of the northern fertile strip of Bahrain is archaeologically viable; it is by far the richest repository known of the island's past and one of the most important areas in the region as a whole for the study and understanding of man's societal ancestry.

It may well be that one of the most tantalizing omissions from the catalogue of Bahrain antiquities, the archives of Dilmun, still survive and will one day be recovered, perhaps from the library of a Dilmunite king, the tablets room of a great temple or the filing system of a member of the Alik Tilmun; for all of these there are precedents in Mesopotamia. In very recent years the discovery of the huge *cache* of tablets at Ebla (Tell Merdikh), in northern Syria, which reveals an entire literature in a language previously unknown, demonstrates the wonders which chance or the archaeologist's skill can still recall. The archives of Dilmun must exist somewhere; it is unthinkable that what must have been a very substantial corpus in long-enduring materials can have been irrevocably lost.

The discovery of such an archive might conceivably throw light on one of the most enigmatic elements in the character of Dilmun–Bahrain in antiquity. It is early enough to comprehend the importance of the island in trade and to accept it as the centre of an important late third-millennium culture in the central Gulf whose influence spread to quite distant lands. What is more difficult to understand is why it occupied so very special a place in the Sumerian (and later) traditions, why, in particular it was celebrated as *the* holy Land.[9] Its essential holiness is possibly Dilmun's most powerful characteristic; it is the first of all sacred lands and its legend endured over long ages. Its influence was, as will have been seen, profound. It was even more important than the shrines of Greece, even of Egypt's holiest place, at Abydos where Osiris was reputed to have been buried.

Geoffrey Bibby who, perhaps more than any man living, has been responsible for recalling Dilmun to the world of today, has argued, persuasively, that the Sumerian believed that Dilmun was holy because the Dilmunites themselves insisted that it was so.

If we assume that by the time the Sumerian cities established themselves, the temple administrators flourished and the scribes of Sumer found time from their recording of the numbers of sheep the temple owned to compose the marvellous songs and stories which are the glory of Sumer, the people of the islands and the Arabians were distinct (or thought themselves to be) from their cousins in the north, their view of the holiness of their land might well be impressive to a visiting Sumerian merchant. The merchant, or the scribe, or court official or whoever, might thus take back to Sumer the story of a distant land lit by a strange and numinous light.

Well and good. But why did the Dilmunites themselves consider their land to be so uniquely, so exceptionally sacred? It cannot have been simply chauvinism ('*my* land is holier than *your* land') or merely the consequence of ample supplies of fresh water, *pace* Enki, in an otherwise desertic environment. There must be some other, more compelling explanation, but thus far it evades us.

The rich and complex designs of the seals will clearly repay further study, containing, as they must do, much information waiting to be released. It may eventually be possible to 'read' the seals; it certainly should be possible to understand the significance of some of their symbolism, particularly of the inter-relationship of the symbolic and the frequency with which some of them are employed.

Beyond Bahrain there are important issues to be resolved. The nature of the relationship between the Umm an-Nar culture of the north of Oman and the high Dilmun culture needs to be further refined. In Oman itself the extent and character of its third-millennium society needs further to be clarified; it may be that even earlier, perhaps fourth-millennium, connections will be established as a consequence of further study.

In eastern Arabia, possibly the coastal regions, and others which are now quite deep into the desert, will almost certainly produce evidence that will be at least as remarkable as that which Bahrain can provide. The nature of early third-millennium settlements, the influence, if any, which the mainlanders exercised on the people of the islands, if they were not the same, need to be analyzed still further. It may even be that some light can still be shed on the vexed, perpetually recurring question of the origins of the Sumerians.

If this book has a theme, other than the simple presentation of the evidence of a high culture which, since it is ancestral to us all, demands to be known, it is the quest. The quest for the terrestrial paradise, Gilgamesh's quest for the flower of eternal youth, the merchant's search for materials and profit, are all elements which go to make up the story of Dilmun, of Bahrain and the Arabian Gulf in centuries long past. It is fitting that it should end with a small and tentative signpost pointing directions (even if they prove to be hopelessly misguided) for those who enjoy quests for their own sake, or who engage in them for the sake of archaeology, where yet more remarkable discoveries may still await those who search for them.

FOOTNOTES

Introduction
1. Rice 1977
2. *Atlal*, the *Journal of Saudi Arabian Archaeology* and the *Journal of Oman Studies*

Chapter 1.
1. Glob, 1954d, 1968b
2. Kramer 1963
3. Rawlinson 1880, Burrows 1928
4. Wilson 1928
5. Rice 1984
6. H. Frankfort 1968, University of Chicago Press 1948
7. See Daniel, *The Arabs and Medieval Europe* Longman 1975.
8. Izzard M., *The Gulf* John Murray 1979
9. H. Frankfort, *Kingship and the Gods*
10. Kenyon K., *Digging up Jericho* Benn 1957
11. Melaart 1967
12. Ibid
13. Kramer 1961
14. Cornwall 1964a. Kramer 1963.
15. Alster 1983
16. On the Sumerian view of the date palm generally see Landsburger, *The Date Palm and its By-products according to the Coneiform Sources* Graz 1967.
17. See Kramer 1944, revised as Chiera's original.
18. Kramer 1969
19. Ferrara 1979
20. Albright, *Cuneiform Texts from Babylonian Tablets* in Cornwall 1974a.
21. Bibby 1969
22. See Ch. 3 n. 28.
23. Sanders 1972
23a ANET
24. A. de Selincourt 1954, Penguin Books Ltd.
25. A. de Selincourt, 1970, The Folio Society, London
26. Ptolomaeus, Claudins, 'Tabula Asiae Sexta' in *Arabia in Early Maps* Tibbetts, GR, Falcon-Oleander 1978
27. See Ratnagar S., 1981, for a broadly based discussion.
28. Masry 1974
29. Ibid
30. Nielsen 1959

31. Lloyd 1978
32. N Groom 1981, *Frankincense and Myrrh* Longman Group Ltd
33. Lombard, 1984
34. Herodotus, op. cit.
35. Ibid
36. Bowersock 1984
37. Ezekiel 27:3–4; 28:13 (Quoted in D. N. Talbot, *The Saturn Myth* Doubleday)
38. Potts 1984
39. Niebhur, *Travels in Arabia* Edinburgh 1792
40. Wilson, op. cit.
41. Durand 1880
42. Durand 1879
43. Rawlinson 1880
44. Smith G., *Assyrian Discoveries*, London 1874
45. Palgrave W. 1865, *Central and Eastern Arabia* Macmillan
46. Bent J T. 1890
47. Bent MVA 1900
48. Jouannin 1965
49. Prideaux 1912
50. Mackay 1929
51. Petrie W.M.F. 1939, *The Making of Egypt*
52. Petrie W.M.F. 1917, *Ancient Egypt*
53. Cornwall 1946
54. Cornwall 1943a
55. Glob 1954a, Bibby 1969
56. Bibby 1969
57. The late Sir Charles Belgrave, pers. comm. to author.

Chapter 2.
1. Mclure 1971
2. Baker B. H. 1970, *The structure patterns of the Afro/Arabian rift system in relation to plate tectonics*, Phil. Trans. Royal Soc. Series AV267
3. Al-Asfour 1978, *The Marine Terraces of the Bay of Kuwait* in Brice
4. Kassler P. in Purser 1973
5. Ibid
6. Ibid
7. De Cardi 1978
8. Andrews, Hamilton, Whybrow 1978, 'Dryopithecine from the Miocene of Saudi Arabia', *Nature* vol. 224
9. Mclure op. cit. 9a, Reported in *Atlal* vol. 4

10. Ibid
11. Ibid
12. Ibid
13. Tosi 1914
14. Mclure op. cit.
15. Kassler op. cit.
16. Ibid
17. Larsen 1983b
18. Kassler op. cit.
19. Mclure op. cit.

Chapter 3.
1. Frankfort 1948 op. cit.
2. Solecki 1972
3. Wendorf, *Prehistory of Nubia*; Wendorf and Schild, *Prehistory of the Nile Valley*
4. Strommenenga and Hirmer, *Art of Mesopotamia* Thames and Hudson 1964
5. Woolley, *Ur Excavations – The Early Periods* British Museum and the American Philosophical Society, Philadelphia 1955
6. Oates J. 1960
7. Ibid
8. Kramer 1963
9. Ibid
10. Marshack A. *The Roots of Civilization* McGraw Hill, 1972
11. See Muller-Karpe, *Handbuch der Vorgesichte Band II* CH Beck 1968
12. Schmand – Bassaret
13. Muller-Karpe op. cit.
14. Ibid
15. Kramer 1963
16. Leemans 1950
17. Leemans 1960a
18. Muhaly 1973
19. Goettler, Frith and Huston 1976; Weissgerber 1978
20. Bibby 1969
21. For example, Barton cited in Cornwall 1944
22. Oates J., Kamili, McKersell 1977
23. Burstein 1978
24. Kramer 1961
25. Ibid
26. Larsen 1975
27. Lloyd 1978
28. Witzel cited in Goetz Appendix to Cornwall 1952
29. See Popenoe 1973, *The Date Palm* Field Research Projects, Coconut Grove, Miami

30. See Adams and Nissen 1972, *The Uruk Countryside* University of Chicago Press
31. Oates J. 1960
32. Lloyd S. and Safar F. 'Eridu' *Sumer* 3 and 4 (1947/8)
33. Safar, Mustafa, Lloyd 1981
34. Baumgartel E., *Predynastic Egypt* vols. 1 and 2
35. Jacobsen T. 1970
36. Kramer 1961
37. Ibid
38. Woolley 1934
39. Whitehouse R. 1977. *The First Cities*, Phaidon
40. Woolley op. cit.
41. Iraq Museum, Baghdad
42. Brooklyn Museum, Brooklyn
43. Amiet P. 1966, *Elam* Archee Editeur, France
44. Amiet 1961
45. Kohl 1978
46. Lamberg-Karlovsky 1972
47. Vallat 1983
48. Baumgartel op. cit.
49. Petrie op. cit.

Chapter 4.
1. Tigay 1982, Sanders 1972
2. ANET, The Sumerian King-List
3. Kramer 1963
4. Nissen 1984, Englund 1983
5. Woolley op. cit.
6. Ibid
7. ANET
8. Kramer 1969 for reference to the *hieros gamos*
9. ANET
10. Bibby 1984b
11. Bibby 1958a
12. ANET
13. Iraq Museum, Bagdhad
14. ANET vol II
15. Roux 1966
16. Kramer 1963
17. Ibid
18. Leemans 1950, 1960a
19. Nielsen 1959
20. ANET vol II
21. Cornwall 1944
22. Ibid
23. Cornwall 1952
24. Zarins 1984, Buccellati 1966
25. ANET
26. Luckenbill D. D. *Ancient Records of Assyrian and Babylonian roll*, University of Chicago Press
27. Cited Luckenbill 'The Annals of Sennacherib' in Alster 1983
28. In Cornwall 1944
29. Weidner, noted in Cornwall op. cit.
30. ANET
31. ANET
32. Oppenheim 1954
33. Lombard 1984
34. De Selincourt, *The Life of Alexander the Great* Folio Society London 1970
35. Salles 1984: 1984a, 1984b
36. Bibby 1969
37. See Badian E., 'Alexander the Great and the Unity of Mankind' in Griffith, *Alexander the Great, the Main Problems* Heffer, Cambridge 1968
38. Bibby 1969

39. Reported in Gulf Mirror, Bahrain
40. Bibby op. cit.
41. Al-Ansary A. R. 1981, *Qaryat al-Fau. A portrait of pre-Islamic civilization in Saudi Arabia*, Croom Helm, London
42. Bibby op. cit.
43. Ibid

Chapter 5.
1. Kramer 1961b
2. Heidal 1963; ANET 'The Epic of Gilgamesh'; Sandars 1972
4. Kramer 1961b
5. Ibid
6. Albright, cited in Cornwall 1944
6a After Kramer 1961
7. Witzel T25 1932: in Goetz, *The Texts Ni 615 and N 641 in the Istanbul Museum*
8. Kramer 1963
9. ANET
10. In Cornwall 1944
11. Cornwall 1952
12. Kramer 1961
13. Alster 1983
14. Griffith, *The Conflict of Horus and Seth from Egyptian and Classical Sources* Liverpool 1960
15. Kramer 1984
16. Cornwall 1944
17. Burstein 1978
18. Nagel 1968
19. ANET

Chapter 6.
1. Durand 1880
2. Pers. comm, Christies (Auctioneers) to author.
3. Durand 1880
4. Rawlinson – 1880
5. Durand 1879
6. Roux 1966
7. Vallat op. cit.
8. Rawlinson op. cit.
9. Bowersock op. cit.
10. Burrows 1928
11. Kramer 1963
12. Nielsen 1959
13. Deimel in Cornwall 1944
14. Heyerdahl T. *The Tigris Expedition* George Allen and Unwin, London 1980
15. McNicholl, 1975
16. Glob 1954c
17. Bibby 1958a
18. Bibby 1984b
19. Bibby 1977–78
20. Kohl 1978, Zarins 1978
21. Potts, 1978
22. Laessoe J. 'A cuneiform inscription from the Island of Bahrain', *Kuml*
23. Mortensen 1984
24. Frohlich 1984
25. Bibby 1969
26. Krauss, Lombard, Potts, 1983
27. Luckenbill D. D. *Annals of Assyrian and Babylonian roll*, University of Chicago Press
28. Glob 1958b
29. Ibid
30. Frifelt 1975b
31. Burstein op. cit.
32. Andersen 1984, Doe 1984a, 1984b Mortensen 1984

33. Durand 1880
34. Glob 1955
35. Glob 1954d
36. Andersen 1956, Rice 1983
37. Glob 1955
38. Ibid
39. Glob 1954d
40. Mortensen 1971a
41. Kjaerum 1983
42. Mortensen 1971a
43. Frankfort 1968
44. Petrie, *Ancient Egypt* 1917; *Egypt and Mesopotamia; The Geography of the Gods* 1917; *The Making of Egypt* 1939
45. Glob 1955
46. Kjaerum op. cit.
47. Potts 1983
48. Woolley 1934
49. Kramer 1961b
50. Emery, *Archaic Egypt* Penguin
51. Emery, *Great Tombs of the First Dynasty* vol III 1958
51a Cornwall 1944
51b Ibid
52. Bibby 1984a
53. Rice 1983
55. Doe 1984b
56. Mortensen, 1956, 1971b, 1984
57. Rice 1984
58. Burkholder and Golding 1971, Masry 1974
59. De Cardi 1978
60. McNicholl op. cit.
61. Roaf 1974
62. Ibid
63. Pers. comm. from Shaikha Haya bint Ali Al-Khalifa
65. Kjaerum op. cit.
66. Frohlich 1984
67. Hojgaard 1983, 1984
68. Frohlich 1983
69. Lamberg-Karlovsky 1982, 1984
70. Frohlich 1984
71. Ibrahim 1983, Mughal 1983
72. Cornwall 1943b
73. Edwards, *The Pyramids of Egypt* Penguin Books Ltd
75. Palgrave, *Eastern and Central Arabia* MacMillan 1865
76. Zarins 1979, 'Rajajil: A Unique Arabian Site from the Fourth Millennium BC', *Atlal* vol 3.
77. Mackay 1926
78. Ibid
79. Ibid
80. Cornwall 1943b
81. Durand 1879
82. Durand 1880
83. Madsen H. J. *Kuml* 1964
84. Woolley 1934
85. Rice 1983
86. See no 88 below
87. O'Kelly M. J., *New Grange* Thames and Hudson 1982
88. Vermeule C. and E., 'An Aegean Gold Hoard and the Court of Egypt', *Illustrated London News*, 21 March 1970
89. Prideaux 1912
90. Cornwall 1940
91. Ibrahim op. cit. Mughal op. cit.
92. Ibid
93. Ibid
94. As yet unpublished

95. Rice 1972
96. Lloyd 1978, reference to Eridu burials; see also *Illustrated London News* 11 September 1948
97. Rice 1972
98. Ibid

Chapter 7.
1. Diakonoff 1974, *Structure of Society and State in early dynastic Sumer* Undena Publications
2. Lamberg-Karlovsky 1972
3. Kramer 1963
4. Cited in Leemans 1950
4a. Ibid
5. Leemans 1950
6. Cornwall 1944
6a. Deimel in Cornwall 1944
7. Fairservis 1971
7a. See ch. 8 n. 60
8. Leemans 1960a
9. Ibid
10. Ibid
11. Ibid
12. Ibid
13. Oppenheim 1954
14. In Potts 1984
15. Ibid
16. Leemans 1960a
17. Oppenheim op. cit.
18. Ibid
19. Bibby 1971b
20. Leemans 1960a
21. Ibid
22. Ibid
23. Ibid
24. Ibid
25. Ibid
26. Ibid
27. Ibid
28. Woolley, *Ur of the Chaldees* Benn, London 1955
29. Ibid
30. Melaart 1967
31. Schmandt-Basserat 1977
32. Melaart op. cit.
33. Frankfort 1968
34. Amiet 1961
35. Kjaerum 1983
36. Aegyptisches Museum, Berlin 1967 (Taf. 299)
37. Al-Khalifa H. 1984
38. Al-Khalifa H. in Ibrahim 1983
39. Mortensen 1971b
40. Kjaerum op. cit.
41. Ibid
42. Ibid
43. Ibid
44. Pers. comm. from Shaikha Haya bint Ali Al-Khalifa
45. Gadd 1932

Chapter 8.
1. Kramer 1968
2. Durand 1979

3. *Mission Archaeologique Française à Qatar*, Tome I 1980, Ministry of Information, State of Qatar
4. Burrows 1928
5. Dougherty 1932, *The Sealand of Ancient Arabia* Yale
6. Masry 1974
7. See Zarins, Ibrahim, Potts, Edens, *Atlal* vol 3: Adams et al 1977
8. Burkholder and Golding 1971
9. Masry op. cit.
10. Oates 1976
11. Masry op. cit.
12. Ibid
13. Ibid
14. Ibid
15. Bibby 1973
16. Said to be from a site near al-Uyun
17. Rashid 1972, *The Museum of Archaeology and Ethnography, Riyadh, Saudi Arabia* Catalogue, Department of Antiquities and Museums, n.d.
18. Zarins 1978
19. Kohl 1978
20. Emery W. E. 1961, *Archaic Egypt* Penguin Books Ltd
21. Golding 1974
22. Bibby 1969
23. See Bibby 1969
24. Kapel 1967
25. *Mission Archaeologique Française à Qatar*, op. cit.
26. Ibid
27. Kapel op. cit.
28. De Cardi 1978
29. Ibid quoting earlier Danish reports
30. Ibid
31. Ibid
32. Ibid
33. *Mission Archaeologique Française à Qatar*, op. cit.
34. Kuml 1964
35. Ibid
36. Ibid
37. Ibid
38. Ibid
39. Ibid
40. Kapel H.
41. De Cardi 1971, 1975b
42. De Cardi, Collier, Doe 1971
43. Weisgerber 1978, 1984
44. Tosi 1974
45. Ibid
46. *Kuml* 1962; Tosi 1974
47. Friefelt 1975a, 1978b
50. Kramer 1963
51. Peake H. 1928, 'The Copper Mountain of Magan', *Antiquity* 2, 1928.
52. Cornwall 1944
53. Friefelt 1970, 1975b
54. Friefelt 1975a
55. Friefelt 1976
56. Friefelt 1975b

57. Friefelt 1968
58. Friefelt 1975b
59. Ibid
60. Durante and Tosi, *JOS* 3 Pt. 2
61. Tosi M., 'A possible Harappan Seaport in Eastern Arabia, Ras al-Jurrayz in the Sultanate of Oman' 1st International Conference on Pakistan Archaeology, Peshawar
62. Groom N. 1981, *Frankincense and Myrrh* Longman
63. Winkler H. 1938/39
64. Anati 1968
65. Preston 1976
66. Clark 1975

Chapter 9.
1. Sandars 1972
2. Particularly Freud
3. Tigay 1982
4. Ibid
5. ANET
6. Woolley, *Ur of the Chaldees* Benn, London 1955
7. Schmidt E. F. quoted in Campbell J. *Oriental Mythology*, Penguin 1976
8. Ibid
9. ANET
10. ANET
11. ANET
12. Burrows 1928
13. Burstein 1978
14. Cornwall 1944
15. ANET
16. Sandars op. cit.
16a During-Caspers 1982
17. ANET
18. Sandars op. cit.
20. Burstein op. cit.
21. Bibby 1969
22. *The Koran* trans. N. J. Dawood, Penguin Classics 1956
23. *Shorter Encyclopaedia of Islam*, Brill, Leiden
24. Ibid
25. Ibid
26. Jung C. G. 'The Archetypes and the Collective Unconscious', *Collected Works* vol 9, Routledge and Kegan Paul, London 1959
27. Pers. comm. by Y. A. Shirawi to author

Chapter 10.
1. Rice 1983
2. Bowersock 1984
3. Zarins 1984
4. Frohlich 1984
5. Bibby 1984b
6. Mclure 1971
7. Zarins, *Atlal*, vol. 5
8. Rice 1984b
9. Bibby 1984a

Bibliography

There is now an extensive bibliography of books, articles and references to Bahrain and the Gulf States in antiquity. Certain works are essential reading: Durand and Bibby's *Looking for Dilmun* in particular. The pattern of publication throughout the States is very uneven: Bahrain and Saudi Arabia are generally well referenced; Kuwait is woefully under-published as is the United Arab Emirates. The Sultanate of Oman is relatively well served.

Two important journals concerned with archaeology have been introduced in the course of the past decade: *Atlal, the Journal of Saudi Arabian Archaeology*, published by the Department of Antiquities and Museums of the Kingdom of Saudi Arabia, and the *Journal of Oman Studies*, published by the Ministry of National Heritage of the Sultanate of Oman. Both of these journals contain, in various of the articles which they publish, a wealth of references to sites and specific aspects of their own and their neighbours' archaeology and history.

Year by year the Proceedings of the Arabian Seminar, held alternately in London, Oxford and Cambridge since 1970 contain a great deal of important material contributed by the most committed researchers in the field.

The *Proceedings of the Bahrain Historical Conference* now in preparation, will provide the most up-to-date summary of Dilmun-Bahrain references. In addition, *Dilmun: New Studies in the Archaeology and Early History of Bahrain* (ed. D. T. Potts: Dietrich Reimar Verlag, Berlin 1983) represents a collection of valuable studies.

The Department of Antiquities of the State of Bahrain is leading the way in itself publishing well-prepared reports of major excavation taking place in the State.

ADAMS, R. McC; PARR, P. J; IBRAHIM, M; AL-MUGHANNUM, A.S. 1977, 'Saudi Arabian Archaeological Reconnaissance – 1976'. Preliminary Report on the First Phase of the Comprehensive Archaeological Survey Program – Eastern Province. *Atlal* Vol. 1.

ALSTER, B. 1983. 'Dilmun, Bahrain, and the Alleged Paradise in Sumerian Myth and Literature'. In Potts, BBVO Vol. 2.

AMIET, P. 1961. *La Glyptique Mesopotamienne Archaique*. Paris, CNRS 1966. 1975. 'A cylinder seal impression found at Umm an-Nar'. *East and West* n.s. 25 (3–4). 1984. 'Suse et la Civilization de Dilmun' *PBHC* (in prep).

ANATI, E. 1968. *Rock Art in Central Arabia*. Vol. I: 'The Oval-Headed People of Arabia'; Vol II: pt 1, 'Fat-tailed Sheep in Arabia'; pt 2, 'The Realistic-dynamic Style of Rock Art in Jebel Qara'. Universitè de Louvain, Institut Orientaliste.

ANDERSEN, H. H. 1956. 'The Building by the Barbar Temple' *Kuml* 1956. 1984. 'The Barbar Temple: its stratigraphy, architecture and interpretation'. *PBHC* (in prep).

BARRELET, M. T.. 1978. *L'Archaeologie de l'Iraq du debut de l'epoque neolithique a 333 av. n. ere: perspectives et limites de l'interpretation anthropologique des Documents*. CNRS Colloque No. 580, Paris, June 13–15.

BENT, J. T. 1890. 'The Bahrein Islands in the Persian Gulf', *Proceedings of the Royal Geographical Society* 12 and Mrs Bent 1900. *Southern Arabia*, London.

BIBBY, T.G. 1954. 'Fem af Bahrains hundrede tusinde gravhoje' (Five among Bahrain's Hundred Thousand Grave-Mounds) *Kuml* 1954. 1954. 'Tyrebronden' (The Well of the Bulls) *Kuml* 1954. 1958. 'Bahrains oldtidshovedstad gennem 4000 ar' (The Hundred-meter section), *Kuml* 1957. 1958. 'The "Ancient Indian Style" Seals from Bahrain', *Antiquity* 32. 1965. 'Arabiens arkaeologi' (Arabian Gulf Archaeology), *Kuml* 1964. 1966. 'Arabiens arkaeologi' (Arabian Gulf Archaeology), *Kuml* 1965. 1967. 'Arabiens arkaeologi' (Arabian Gulf Archaeology), *Kuml* 1966. 1969. *Looking for Dilmun*, New York. 1971. *I Dilmun Tier Ravnen*, Hojbjerg. 1971. '. . .efter Dilmun norm' (according to the standard of Dilmun'), *Kuml* 1970. 1973. 'Preliminary Survey in East Arabia 1968,' Jutland Archaeological Society Publ. XII, Aarhus. 1977–8. 'Gensyn med Bahrain.' *Sfinx* 1. 1984. 'The Land of Dilmun in Italy,' *PBHC* (in prep). 1984. 'The Origins of the Dilmun Civilization', *PBHC* (in prep).

BOWERSOCK, G.W. 1984. 'Tylos and Tyre: Bahrain in the Graeco-Roman world', *PBHC* (in prep).

BRICE, W.C. ed. 1978. *The Environmental History of the Near and Middle East*, Academic Press, London, New York, San Francisco.

BRUNSWIG, R.H. Jr., PARPOLA, A. and POTTS, D. 1983. 'New Indus Type and Related Seals from the Near East', in Potts, ed., 'Dilmun', *BBVO 2*.

BUCCELLATI, G. 1966. *The Amorites of the Ur III Period*. Istituto Orientale di Napoli, Pubblicazioni del Seminario di Semitistica, Naples.

BURKHOLDER, G. and GOLDING, M. 1971. *A Surface Survey of Ubaid Sites in the Eastern Province of Saudi Arabia*, informal paper (mimeographed) delivered at the Third International Conference on Asian Archaeology, Bahrain, March 1970.

BURROWS, E. 1928. 'Bahrain, Tilmun, Paradise', *Scriptura Sacra et Monumenta Orientis Antiqui*, Pontifici Istituti Biblici, Roma.

BURSTEIN, S.M. 1978. *The 'Babyloniaca' of Berossus* Undena Publications, Malibu.

BUTZ, K. 1983 'Zwei kleine Inschriften zur Geschichte Dilmuns'. In Potts ed., *BBVO 2*. 1983. 'Dilmun in Wirtschaftstexten der Ur-III-Zeit'. In Potts ed., *BBVO2*. 1983 'Dilmun in Altbabylonischen Quellen' In Potts, ed., *Dilmun: New Studies in the Archaeology and early History of Bahrain*, BBVO 2.

CARTER, T.H. 1981. 'The Tangible Evidence for the Earliest Dilmun', *JCS* 33. 1972. 'The Johns Hopkins University Reconnaissance Expedition to the Arab-Iranian Gulf', *BASOR* 207. 1984. 'Eyestones and Pearls', *PBHC* (in prep).

CLARKE, A. 1981. *The Islands of Bahrain*, The Bahrain Archaeological and Historical Society, 1981.

CLARKE, C. 1975. 'The Rock Art of Oman', *JOS* 1.

CLEUZIOU, S. 1984. 'Dilmun and Makkah during the third millennium and the early second millennium BC: a tentative view', *PBHC* (in prep).

CLEUZIOU, S., LOMBARD, P. and SALLES, J.-F. 1979. Excavations at Umm Jidr, Bahrain, *ADPF*, Paris.

CORNWALL, P.B. 1943. *Dilmun: The History of Bahrain Island before Cyrus*, unpubl. PhD, diss., Harvard University. 1943. 'The Tumuli of Bahrein' in *Asia and the Americas*, XLIII. 1946. 'On the Location of Dilmun', *BASOR* 103. 1946. 'Ancient Arabia: Explorations in Hasa, 1940–41'. *Geographic Journal*, No. 107. p. 28 1952. 'Two Letters from Dilmun', *JCS* 6.

COSTA, P.M. 1978 'The Copper Mining Settlement of Arja: A Preliminary Survey', *JOS* 4.

DANI, A.H. 1984. 'Bahrain and the Indus Civilization', *PBHC* (in prep).

DE CARDI, B. 1967. 'The Bampur Sequences in the 3rd Millennium BC', *Antiquity*, XLI. 1969. 'A Preliminary report of Field Survey in the Northern Trucial States', *Kuml*. 1971. 'Archaeological Survey in the Northern Trucial States', *EW*. 1975a. 'Survey and Excavations in Oman', *JOS* 1. 1975b. 'Archaeological Survey in Northern Oman', *EW*. 1977. 'Surface collections from the Oman Survey, 1976', *JOS* 3, Part 1. 1978. *Qatar Archaeological Report, Excavations 1973*, OUP.

DE CARDI, B.; BELL, R.D. and STARLING, N.J. 1979. 'Excavations at Tawi Gilaim and Fawt Sa'id in the Sharqiyah, 1978', *JOS* 5.

DE CARDI, B.; COLLIER, S. and DOE, D.B. 1971. 'Archaeological survey in the northern Trucial States', *EW* n.s. 21 (3–4).

DE CARDI, B.; COLLIER, S.; DOE, D.B. 1976. *Excavations and Survey in Oman 1974–5*, *JOS* 2

DE CARDI, B.; DOE, D.B.; ROSKAMS, S.P. 1977. 'Excavation and Survey in the Sharqiyah, Oman 1976', *JOS* 3, Part 1.

DOE, D.B. 1977. 'Gazetteer of Sites in Oman, 1976', *JOS* 3. 1984a. 'The Barbar Temple site in Bahrain', *PBHC* (in prep). 1984b. 'The Masonry of the Dilmun Temple at Barbar, *PBHC* (in prep).

DURAND, Capt. E.L. 1879. 'Notes on the Islands of Bahrain and Antiquities, as submitted from the Political Resident, Persian Gulf, to the Foreign Department, Calcutta'. 1880. 'The Islands and Antiquities of Bahrain', *JRAS* (New Series), XII, (Part II) 1880.

DURANTE, S. and TOSI, M. 1977. 'The Aceramic Shell Middens of Ra's al-Hamra: a preliminary note', *JOS* 3, Part 2.

DURING-CASPERS, E.C.L. 1971a. 'New Archaeological Evidence for Maritime Trade in the Persian Gulf during the Late Protoliterate Period', *EW* 21. 1971b. 'The Bull's Head from Barbar Temple II, Bahrain: A Contact with Early Dynastic Sumer', *EW* 21. 1972–74. 'The Bahrain Tumuli', *Persica* VI. 1973a. 'Sumer and Kulli meet at Dilmun in the Arabian Gulf', *AfO* 24. 1973b. 'Dilmun and the Date Tree', *EW* 23. 1973c. 'Harappan Trade in the Arabian Gulf in the Third Millennium BC', *PSAS* 3. 1976. 'Cultural Concepts in the Arabian Gulf and the Indian Ocean: Transmissions in the Third Millennium and their Significance', *PSAS* 6. 1977. 'A Dilmun Seal Cutter's Misfortune', *Antiquity* 51. 1979a. 'Westward Contacts with Historical India: A trio of Figurines', *PSAS* 9. 1979b. 'Statuary in the Round from Dilmun', in J.E. van Louhuizen-de Leeuw, ed., *South Asian Archaeology 1975*, Brill, Leiden. 1980. *The Bahrain Tumuli: An Illustrated Catalogue of Two Important Collections*, Uitgaven van het Nederlands Historisch-Archaeologisch Instituut te Istanbul 47. 1982. 'Corals, Pearls and Prehistoric Gulf Trade', *PSAS* 1983. 1984. 'Animal Designs and Gulf Chronology', *PBHC* (in prep).

DURING-CASPERS, E.C.L. & GOVINDAKUTTY, A. 1978. 'R. Thapar's Dravidian hypothesis for the location of Meluhha, Dilmun and Makkan'. *JESHO* XXI (2).

EDENS, C. 1982. 'Towards a Definition of the Western Ar-Rub al-Khali "Neolithic"', *Atlal* 6. 'Bahrain and the Gulf: the Second Millennium Crisis', *PBHC* (in prep).

ENGLUND, R. 1983a. 'Exotic Fruits', in Potts ed., *BBVO* 2. 1983b. 'Dilmun in the Archaic Uruk Corpus', in Potts ed., *BBVO* 2.

FAIRSERVIS, W. 1971. *The Roots of Ancient India*, Allen and Unwin, London.

FALKENSTEIN, A. 1967. 'The Prehistory and Protohistory of Western Asia', in Bottero, E. et al (ed), *The Near East*, Delacorte Press, New York.

FERRARA, A.J., 1979. *Nanna-Suen's Journey to Nippur*, Biblical Institute Press, Rome.

FIELD, H. 1958. 'Stone Implements from the Rub' al-Khali, Southern Arabia', *Man*, No. 121. 1960. 'Stone Implements from the Rub' al-Khali', *Man*, No. 30. 1960. 'Carbon-14 Date for a "Neolithic" Site in the Rub' al-Khali', *Man*, No. 214.

FOSTER, B. 1977. 'Commercial activity in Sargonic Mesopotamia', *Iraq* XXXIX.

FRANKFORT, 1968. *The Birth of Civilization in the Near East*, Benn, London.

FRIFELT, K. 1968. 'Archaeological investigations in the Oman Peninsula', *Kuml*. 1970. 'Jamdat Nasr fund fra Oman', *Kuml*. 1971. 'Excavations in Abu Dhabi (Oman)', *Artibus Asiae* XXXIII (4). 1975a. 'A possible link between the Jemdet Nasr and the Umm an-Nar graves of Oman', *JOS* I. 1975b. 'On prehistoric settlement and chronology of the Oman Peninsula', *EW* n.s. 25 (3–4). 1976. 'Evidence of a third millennium BC town in Oman', *JOS* 2. 1984. 'Grave Mounds near Aali excavated by the Danish Expedition', *PBHC* (in prep).

FROHLICH, B. 1983. 'The Bahrain Burial Mounds', *Dilmun* 11. 1984. 'The Human Biological

History of the Early Bronze Age in Bahrain', *PBHC* (in prep).

GADD, C.J. 1932. 'Seals of ancient Indian style found at Ur', *Proceedings of the British Academy* XVIII.

GELB, I.J. 1970. 'Makkan and Meluhha in early Mesopotamian sources', *Revue d'Assyriologie* LXIV.

GLOB, P.V. 1954a. 'Bahrain, Oen med de Hundredtusinde gravhoje' (Bahrain – Island of the Hundred Thousand Burial-Mounds), *Kuml* 1954. 1954b. 'Bahrains oldtidshovedstad' (The Ancient Capital of Bahrain), *Kuml* 1954. 1954c. 'Flintpadser i Bahrains orken' (The Flint Sites of the Bahrain Desert), *Kuml* 1954. 1954d. 'Templer ved Barbar' (Temples at Barbar), *Kuml* 1954. 1955. 'Udgravninger pa Bahrain, Dansk Arkaeologisk Bahrain-Ekspeditions 2. udgravningskampagne' (The Danish Archaeological Bahrain-Expedition's Second Campaign), *Kuml* 1955. 1956. 'Et nybabylonisk gravfund fra Bahrains oldtidshovedstad' (A Neo-Babylonian Burial from Bahrain's Prehistoric Capital), *Kuml* 1957. 1958a. 'The Prosperity of Bahrain five thousand years ago: Solving the riddle of the 100,000 burial mounds of the island', *Illustrated London News* 232. 1958b. 'Slangeofre i Bahrains oldtidshovedstad: Dansk Arkaeologisk Bahrain-Ekspeditions 4. udgravningskampagne' (Snake Sacrifices in Bahrain's ancient capital), *Kuml* 1958. 1958c. 'Investigations in Kuwait', *Kuml*. 1959a. 'Alabasterkar fra Bahrains templer. Dansk Arkaeologisk Bahrain-Ekspeditions 5. udgravningskampagne' (Alabaster Vases from the Bahrain Temples), *Kuml* 1958. 1959c. 'Arkaeologiske undersogelser i fire arabiske stater' (Archaeological Investigations in Four Arab States), *Kuml* 1959. 1960. 'Danske arkaeologer i Den Persiske Golf' (Danish Archaeologists in the Persian Gulf), *Kuml* 1960. 1968a. *Al-Bahrain, De danske ekspeditioner til oldtidens Dilmun*, Gyldendal, Copenhagen.

GLOB, P.V., and BIBBY, T.G. 1960. 'A Forgotten Civilization of the Persian Gulf', *Scientific American* 203.

GOETTLER, G.W.; FIRTH, N. and HUSTON, C.C. 1976. 'A preliminary discussion of ancient mining in the Sultanate of Oman', *JOS* 2.

GOLDING, M. 1974. 'Evidence for pre-Seleucid occupation of eastern Arabia', *PSAS* IV.

HALLO, W.W., and BUCHANAN, B. 1965. 'A Persian Gulf seal on an old Babylonian mercantile agreement', *Assyriological Studies* 16 (Landsberger volume).

HANSMAN, J. 1973. 'A periplus of Magan and Meluhha', *Bulletin SOAS* 36(3).

HASTINGS, A.; HUMPHRIES, J.H. and MEADOW, R.H. 1975. 'Oman in the third millennium BC', *JOS* I.

HEIDEL, A. 1963. *The Gilgamesh Epic and Old Testament Parallels*, 2nd ed., University of Chicago Press.

HERRMANN, G. 1968. 'Lapis Lazuli: the early phases of its trade', *Iraq* XXX (I).

HOJGAARD, K. 1983. 'Dilmun's Ancient Teeth', *Dilmun* 11. 1984. 'Dental Anthropological Investigations on Bahrain', *PBHC* (in prep).

HOJLUND, F. 1984. 'The Chronology of City II and III at Qala'at al-Bahrain', *PBHC* (in prep).

HRUSKA, B. 1983. 'Dilmun in den Vorsargonischen Wirtschaftstexten aus Suruppak und Lagas', in Potts ed., *BBVO* 2.

HUMPHRIES, J.H. 1974. 'Some later prehistoric sites in the Sultanate of Oman', *PSAS* IV.

IBRAHIM, M. 1983. *Excavations of the Arab Expedition at Saar El-Jisr*, Ministry of Information, State of Bahrain.

JACKLI, R. 1980. *Rock Art in Oman. An Introductory Presentation*, Zug, Switzerland.

JACOBSEN, T. 1970. *Towards the Image of Tammuz*. Harvard Semitic Series, Harvard.

JOSHI, P.J. 1984. 'India and Bahrain – a survey of Cultural Interaction during the third and second millennia', *PBHC* (in prep).

JOUANNIN, M. 1905. 'Les tumuli de Bahrein', *MDP* VIII.

KAPEL, H. 1967. *The Atlas of the Stone-Age Cultures of Qatar*. Jutland Archaeological Society Publ. VI, Aarhus.

KERVRAN, M. 1984. 'Qala'at al-Bahrain. A Strategic Position from the Hellenistic period to modern times', *PBHC* (in prep).

KJAERUM, P. 1983. *Failaka/Dilmun: The Second Millennium Settlements*, Vol. 1.1.: 'The Stamp and Cylinder Seals', Jutland Archaeological Society Publications, XVII:1. 1984. 'The Dilmun seals as testimony of long distance relations', *PBHC* (in prep).

AL-KHALIFA, H. A. 1984. 'The shell seals of Bahrain', *PBHC* (in prep).

KOHL, P.L. 1978. 'The Balance of trade in southwestern Asia in the mid-third millennium BC', *Current Anthropology* 19(3). 1981. *The Bronze Age Civilization of Central Asia*, M.G. Sharpe

Inc., New York. 1984. 'The Lands of Dilmun: Changing cultural and economic relations during the third and early second millennia', *PBHC* (in prep).

KOMOROCZY, G. 1977. 'Tilmun als "Speicher des Landes" in Epos "Enki und Ninhursag"', *Lag* XXXIX, Part 1.

KRAMER, S.N. 1944. 'Dilmun, the Land of the Living', *BASOR*, December 1944. 1961. *History Begins at Sumer*. Thames and Hudson, London. 1961b. *Sumerian Mythology*, Harper Torch Book, New York. 1963. *The Sumerians*, University of Chicago Press. 1963b. 'Dilmun: Quest for Paradise', *Antiquity* XXXVII. 1969. *The Sacred Marriage Rite*, Indiana University Press, Bloomington, and London.

KRAUSS, R.; LOMBARD, P. and POTTS, D. 1983. 'The Silver Hoard from City IV, Qala'at al-Bahrain', in D. Potts ed., *BBVO* 2.

LAESSOE, J. 1958. 'en Kileskrift fra Bahrain' (A Cuneiform Inscription from the Island of Bahrain), *Kuml* 1957.

LAMBERG-KARLOVSKY, C.C. 1972. 'Trade mechanisms in Indus-Mesopotamian interrelations', *JAOS* 92(2). 1982. 'Dilmun: Gateway to Immortality', *JNES* 41. 1984. 'Death in Dilmun', *PBHC* (in prep).

LAMBERT, W.G. and MILLARD, A.R. 1969. *Atra-Hasis. The Babylonian Story of the Flood*. OUP.

LARSEN, C.E. 1975. 'The Mesopotamian delta region: a reconsideration of Lees and Falcon', *JAOS* 95(1). 1983. *Life and Land Use in the Bahrain Islands: The Geoarchaeology of an Ancient Society*, University of Chicago Press. 1983b. 'The Early Environment and Hydrology of Ancient Bahrain', in Potts, ed., 'Dilmun. . .', *BBVO* 2. 1984. 'Variations in Holocene land use patterns in the Bahrain Islands: Construction of a simple land use model', *PBHC* (in prep).

LEEMANS, W.F. 1950. *The Old Babylonian Merchant*. Brill, Leiden. 1960a. 'Foreign Trade in the Old Babylonian Period', *Studia et Documenta ad Iura Orientis Antiqui Pertinentia* VI, Brill, Leiden. 1960b. 'The trade relations of Babylonia and the question of relations with Egypt in the Old Babylonian Period', *JESHO* III. 1968. 'Old Babylonian letters and economic history: a review article with a digression on foreign trade', *JESHO* XI.

LEES, G.M., and FALCON, N.L. 1952. 'The Geographical History of the Mesopotamian Plain', *Geographical Journal*, Vol 118.

LLOYD, Seton 1978. *The Archaeology of Mesopotamia from the Old Stone Age to the Persian Conquest*, Thames and Hudson, London.

LOMBARD, P. 'Iron Age Dilmun: A reconsideration of City IV al Qala'at al-Bahrain', *PBHC* (in prep).

LOMBARD, P. and SALLES, J.-F. 1983. 'La Necropole de Janussan, Bahrain', *Maison de l'Orient Ancien*, Lyon.

MACKAY, E., HARDING, G.L., and PETRIE, F. 1929. *Bahrein and Hemamieh*, Publications of the British School of Archaeology in Egypt, Vol. 47, London.

MASRY, A.H. 1974. *Prehistory in Northeastern Arabia: the Problem of Interregional Interaction*. Field Research Projects, Coconut Grove, Miami, Florida.

MATTHIAS, Paolo. 1977–80. *Ebla*, Hodder and Stoughton, London.

MCCLURE, H.A. 1971. *The Arabian Peninsula and Prehistoric Populations*. Field Research Projects, Coconut Grove, Miami, Florida.

MCNICOLL, A. and ROAF, M. n.d. *Archaeological Investigations in Bahrain 1973–75*, unpubl. ms, Dept of Antiquities, Bahrain.

MCNICHOLL, A.W. 1975. 'Al-Markh excavations', Committee for Arabian and Gulf Studies, Vol 6, 1976, Institute of Archaeology, London.

MELLAART, J. 1967. *Catal Huyuk*, Thames and Hudson, London. 1970. *Excavations at Hacilar*, Edinburgh University Press for the British Institute of Archaeology at Ankara.

de MIROSCHEDJI, P. 1973. 'Vases et objets en steatite susiens du musee du Louvre', *Cahiers de la Delegation Archeologique Française en Iran* 3.

MITCHELL, T.C. 'The Indus and Gulf type seals from Ur', *PBHC* (in prep).

MORKHOLM, O. 1973. 'En hellenistisk montskat fra Bahrain' (A Hellenistic Coin Hoard from Bahrain), *Kuml* 1972.

MORTENSEN, P. 1956. 'Barbartemplets ovale anlaeg' (The Temple Oval at Barbar), *Kuml* 1956. 1971. 'On the Date of the Barbar Temple in Bahrain', *Artibus Asiae* 33. 1984. 'The Bahrain Temple – its chronology and foreign relations reconsided', *PBHC* (in prep).

MOSCATI, S. 1959. *The Semites in Ancient History*, University of Wales Press, Cardiff.

MUHLY, 1973. *Copper and Tin*, The Connecticut Academy of Arts and Sciences, New Haven.

MUGHAL, M.R. 1983. 'The Dilmun Burial Complex at Sar'. *The 1980–82 Excavations in Bahrain*.

Ministry of Information, Directorate of Archaeology and Museums, State of Bahrain.

MULLER, W.H. 'Tylos, Hagar, Gerrha – a triangle of Arabian oases in antiquity', *PBHC* (in prep).

NAGEL, W. 1968. *Fruhe Plastik aus Sumer und Westmakkan*, Verlag Bruno Hessling, Berlin.

NASHEF, K. 1984. 'The Deities of Dilmun', *PBHC* (in prep).

NEILSEN, V. 1959. '-vidt beromt for dens mange perler' (Famed for its many Pearls), *Kuml* 1958.

NISSEN, H.J. 1984. 'Mentions of Dilmun in the earliest Mesopotamian Texts', *PBHC* (in prep).

OATES, D. 1984. 'Dilmun and the Assyrian Empire', *PBHC* (in prep).

OATES, J. 1960. 'Ur and Eridu, the Prehistory', *Iraq*, Vol. XXII. 1976. 'Prehistory in northeastern Arabia', *Antiquity* 1. 1984. 'The Gulf in Prehistory', *PBHC* (in prep).

OATES, J., KAMILLI, D. and MCKERRELL, H. 1977. 'Seafaring Merchants of Ur?', *Antiquity* LI.

OATES, D. and J. 1976. *Rise of Civilization*, Elsevier-Phaidon, Oxford.

OPPENHEIM, A.L. 1954. 'The Seafaring Merchants of Ur'. *JAOS* 74.

PHILBY, H. 1933 'The Empty Quarter', Constable, London.

PHILLIPS, C.S. and WILKINSON, T.J. 1970. 'Recently Discovered Shell Middens near Quriyat', *JOS* 5.

PORADA, E. 1965. 'The Relative Chronology of Mesopotamia. Part II', in Ehrich, R. (ed), *Chronologies in Old World Archaeology*, University of Chicago Press. 'Remarks on Seals Found in the Gulf States', 3rd International Conference on Asian Archaeology in Bahrain, March 1970, *Artibus Asiae*, Vol. XXXIII, 4, Institute of Fine Arts, New York University.

POTTS, D. 1978. 'Towards an Integrated History of Culture Change in the Arabian Gulf Area: Notes on Dilmun, Makkan, and the Economy of Ancient Sumer', *JOS* 4. 1983. 'Dilmun: Where and When?' *Dilmun* 11. 1983b. 'Dilmun: New Studies in the Archaeology and Early History of Bahrain', *BBVO* 2. 1983c. 'Barbar Miscellanies', in D. Potts, ed., 'Dilmun. . .', *BBVO* 2. 1984. 'The Chronology of the Archaeological Assemblages from the Head of the Arabian Gulf to the Arabian Sea (8000-1750 BC)', in R. W. Ehrich, ed., *Chronologies in Old World Archaeology*, 3rd ed., University of Chicago Press. n.d. 'Proto-Elamite problems'. Paper read at the XXVth 'Rencontre Assyriologique Internationale', Berlin, 3–7 July 1978. 1984. 'Dilmun's further relations: The Syro-Anatolian evidence from the third and second millennia BC', *PBHC* (in prep).

POTTS, D., al-MUGHANNUM, A.S., FRYE, J., SANDERS, D. 1978. 'Preliminary Report on the Second Phase of the Eastern Province Survey 1397/1977'. *Atlal* Vol. 2.

POWELL, M.A. 1983. 'The Standard of Dilmun', in D. Potts, ed., 'Dilmun . . .', *BBVO* 2.

PRESTON, K. 1976. 'An Introduction to the Anthropomorphic Content of the Rock Art of Jebel Akhdar', *JOS* 2.

PRIDEAUX, Capt. 1912. 'The Sepulchral Tumuli of Bahrain', *Archaeological Survey of India*, Annual Report, 1908–1909.

PRITCHARD, J.B. 1969. (ed.) *Ancient Near Eastern Texts Relating to the Old Testament*, Princeton University Press.

PULLAR, J. and JACKLI, B. 1978. 'Some Aceramic Sites in Oman', *JOS* 4.

PURSER, B.H. 1973. *The Persian Gulf: Holocene Carbonate Sedimentation and Diagenesis in a shallow Epicontinental Sea*, Springer, New York.

RAIKES, R.L. 1967. *Water, Weather and Prehistory*, John Baker, London.

RAO, S.R. 1969. 'A Bronze Mirror Handle from the Barbar Temple, Bahrain', *Kuml* 1969. 1973. *Lothal and the Indus Civilization*, Asia Publishing House, London. 1984. 'Travel and Cultural contacts between Bahrain and India in the third and second millennia BC', *PBHC* (in prep).

RASHID, S.A. 1972. *Eine fruhdynastische Statue von der Insel Tarut im Persischen Golf*. Bayerische Akad. d. Wiss., Phil.-Hist. Kl. Abb. NF. 75

RATNAGAR, S. 1981. *Encounters, The Westerly Trade of the Harappan Civilization*, OUP, Delhi.

RAWLINSON, Maj.-Gen. Sir H. 1880. 'Notes on Capt. Durand's Report upon the Islands of Bahrain', *JRAS* XII.

READE, J.E. and BURLEIGH, R. 1978. 'The 'Ali Cemetery: Old Excavations, Ivory, and Radiocarbon Dating', *JOS* 4

READE, J.E. 1984. 'Variations in the Mesopotamian-Dilmun relationship', *PBHC* (in prep).

RICE, M. 1972. 'The Grave Complex at Al-Hajjar Bahrain', *PSAS* 2. 1983. 'The Barbar Temple Site, Bahrain', The Ministry of Information, State of Bahrain. 1984. *Dilmun Discovered* Longman, London. 1984b. 'The Island on the Edge of the World', *PBHC* (in prep).

ROAF, M. 1974. 'Excavations at Al Markh, Bahrain: a fish midden of the fourth millennium BC', *Paleorient* 2.

ROUX, G. 1966. *Ancient Iraq*, Pelican, London.

SAFAR, F., MUSTAFA, M.A., LLOYD, S. 1981. *Eridu* Ministry of Culture and Information, Baghdad, Republic of Iraq.

SALLES, J.-F. 1981. 'Le Golfe Arabe dans l'Antiquité', *Annales d'Histoire de l'Universite Saint-Joseph*, Fasc. I. 1982. 'Gulf Area During the First Millennium', *Dilmun* 10. 1983. 'Bahrain "hellenis-tique": données et problèmes', in Boucharlat and Salles, eds., *AOMIM*. 1984. 'Le Golfe entre le Proche et l'Extreme Orient à l'epoque Hellenistique', in E.C.L. During–Caspers, ed., *Beatrice De Cardi Felicitation Volume*, Academic Publishers, Leiden. 1984b. 'The Necropolis of Janussan and burial customs at the end of the first millennium BC', *PBHC* (in prep).

SANLAVILLE, P.J. 1984. 'The evolution of Bahrain shore levels through the ages', *PBHC* (in prep).

SANDARS, N.K. 1972. *The Epic of Gilgamesh: An English Version with an Introduction*, Penguin Books, London.

SCHMANDT-BESSERAT, D. 1977. *An Archaic Recording System and the Origin of Writing*, Undena Publications, Malibu.

SMITH, C.H. 1890. 'The Bahrain Islands in the Persian Gulf', Discussion: *Proceedings of the Royal Geographical Society*, Vol. XII. London.

SMITH, G.H. 1977. 'New Prehistoric Sites in Oman', *JOS* 3, Part I.

SOLECKI, R. 1972. *Sharidar*, Allen Lane, The Penguin Press, London.

SOLLBERGER, E. 1970. 'The Problem of Magan and Meluhha', *Bulletin of the Institute of Archaeology*, Nos. 8–9, 1968–69.

STRIXA, F.L. 1984. 'The Tarut statue as a peripheral contribution to the knowledge of early Mesopotamian plastic art', *PBHC* (in prep).

SUELL, D. 1982. *Ledgers and Prices – Early Mesopotamian Merchant Accounts*, Yale Babylonian Collection.

THAPAR, R. 1975. 'A Possible identification of Meluhha, Dilmun and Makkan'. *JESHO* XVIII(I).

THORVILDSEN, K. 1962. 'Burial cairns on Umm an-Nar', *Kuml*.

TIGAY, J.H. 1982. *The Evolution of the Gilgamesh Epic*, University of Philadelphia Press.

TIXIER, J. 1978. 'La mission archaeologique Française au Qatar', in *Barrelet* 1978. 1984. 'The Prehistory of the Gulf', *PBHC* (in prep).

TOSI, M. 1974. 'Some data for the study of prehistoric cultural areas on the Persian Gulf', *PSAS* IV. 1975. 'Notes on the distribution and exploitation of natural resources in ancient Oman', *JOS* I. 1976. 'The dating of the Umm an-Nar culture and a proposed sequence for Oman in the third millennium BC', *JOS* 2. 1984. 'Early maritime cultures of the Arabian Gulf and the Indian Ocean', *PBHC* (in prep).

VALLAT, F. 1983. 'Le Dieu Enzak: Une Divinité Dilmunite Venerèe à Suse'. In Potts ed., *BBVO* 2.

WEISGERBER, G. 1978. 'Evidence of Ancient Mining Sites in Oman: a Preliminary Report', *JOS* 4. 1984. 'Dilmun – a trading entrepot, evidence from historical and archaeological sources', *PBHC* (in prep).

WHEELER, Sir M. 1953. 'The Indus Civilization', in *Cambridge History of India*, Cambridge University Press. 1968. 'The Indus Civilization', Cambridge University Press.

WHITEHOUSE, R. 1977. *The First Cities*, Phaidon Press, Oxford.

WINKLER, H.A. *Rock Drawings of Southern Upper Egypt*, 2 vols. The Egyptian Exploration Society 1938 (vol. I), 1939 (Vol. II), London.

WILSON, A.T. 1928. *The Persian Gulf*, George Allen and Unwin, London.

WOOLLEY, C.L. 1934. *Ur Excavations*, Vol II: 'The Royal Cemetery', Oxford University Press. 1956. *Ur Excavations IV, The Early Periods*. British Museum and the University Museum of the University of Pennsylvania, Philadelphia and London.

ZARINS, J. 1978. 'Steatite Vessels in the Riyadh Museum', *Atlal* Vol. 2. 1984. 'Martu and the Land of Dilmnn,' *PBHC* (in prep).

ZARINS, J., WHALEN, N., IBRAHIM, M., MORAD, A., KHAN, M., 1980 'Preliminary Report on the Central and Southwestern Provinces Survey', *Atlal*, Vol 4.

Abbreviations

AfO	Archiv für Orientforschung, Berlin
AOMIM	Arabie Orientale, Mesopotamie, et Iran Meridional
Atlal	The Journal of Saudi Arabian Archaeology
BASOR	Bulletin of the American School of Oriental Research
BBVO	Berliner Beitrage zum Vorderen Orient
CNRS	Centre National des Recherches Scientifique
EW	East-West
JAOS	Journal of the American Oriental Society
JCS	Journal of Cuneiform Studies
JESHO	Journal of the Economic and Social History of the Orient
JOS	Journal of Oman Studies
JNES	Journal of Near Eastern Studies
JRAS	Journal of the Royal Arabic Society (New Series)
JRCAS	Journal of the Royal Central Asian Society
Kuml	Journal of the Jutland Archaeological Society
MDP	Memoires de la Delegation en Perse
PBHC	Proceedings of the Bahrain Historical Conference
PSAS	Proceedings of the Seminar for Arabian Studies

Acknowledgements

The author gratefully acknowledges the following: the Department of Antiquities and Museums, the State of Bahrain; the Department of Antiquities and Museums, the Kingdom of Saudi Arabia; the Department of Antiquities and Museums, the State of Kuwait; the Department of Antiquities and Museums, the United Arab Emirates; the Department of Antiquities and Museums, Sultanate of Oman; the State of Qatar. Bahrain National Museum; the Baghdad Museum; the C.N.R.S.; the Forshistorisk Museum, Moesgard; the Musée du Louvre; the Museum of Archaeology and Ethnography, Riyadh; the Royal Asiatic Society; the Trustees of the British Museum. David Williams, of Michael Rice and Company, for his drawings of seals and maps; Roger Wood for his photographs, including the author's on the back flap. The University of Chicago Press; Indiana University Press; Princeton University Press; E. Benn Ltd; E. J. Brill; Faber & Faber Ltd; Penguin Books Ltd; Thames and Hudson Ltd; the *Illustrated London News*.

Index

Aalii, tombs of 27, 119, 158, 161, 164–6, 180., *pl. X, XII*; *see also burial mounds*
Abqaiq site 215, 217
Abu Dhabi, archaeology of 17, 36–7, 39, 138, 167, 180, 235–6
Agade (Akkad) 74–5, 78; *see also* Akkadians
agriculture:
  Bahrain 16, 126, 128–9
  development of 8, 41–2, 44, 47
  of eastern Arabia 18, 107, 216, 223–4
  of Sumeria 41
Ahlamu 87–9, 221, 276
Aim Qannas site 213, 215
Akkadians 12, 16–17, 60, 194
Alexander the Great 17, 92–8, 112, 138–9, 228, 248, 263, 270, 273, 275, *pl. XI*
Anati, E. 249
Androsthenes 22
Arabian peninsula:
  archaeologists' neglect of 3–5, 27, 211
  decline of trade from 23–4
  influence of oil on 2–3, 6, 8
archaeology:
  early, of Bahrain iv–v, 3, 7, 26–9, 116–17
  revival of interest in 30–1, 156
  see also Arabian peninsula; *and under individual countries and sites*
Arrian 92–6, 204, 263
art 9, 192–3, 197–8, 253
  Indus Valley 180
  Sumerian 61–2, 75–7, 250
  see also carvings; seals; sculpture
Assurbanipal, Assyrian king 91–2, 254
Assyrians 11–12, 60, 77, 85, 89–92, 183, 194

Babylonians 11–12, 15–16, 52, 60, 77, 83, 85, 114, 183, 194
  influence on Gulf 21, 88–9
Badu 25, 33, 88, 232
Bahrain:
  and Britain 116
  centrality of 7–8
  copper-smelting 18, 52
  early sites 128–9
  as harbour 128
  links with Saudi Arabia 138
  modern development 124–6
  as necropolis 16, 28, 134, 159–60, 220, 265
  as religious centre 15, 54

as site of Dilmun 13, 14–15, 26–7, 30–1, 52, 86–7, 95, 111, 121–3, 129, 276, 280–1
  see also Barbar; burial mounds; Dilmun; Qala'at al-Bahrain; springs, underground
Barbar 15, 129–30, 132, 134, 138–55, 157, 206, 278, *pl. I, III, V*
  Temple I 140–1, 142–3, 148
  Temple II 141–4, 148–9, *pl. III, V, IX*
  Temple III 144–5, 147, 149, 206
  seals 195, 198, 200–1, 203–4
  well 141–5, 146–7, 198, 268, *pl. I, V*
Bat, Omani site 242–4
Belgrave, Sir Charles 30
Bent, Theodore and Mabel 27
Berossus 112–13, 138, 262
Bibby, Geoffrey v, 30, 96, 270, 281
Bible, influence of biblical scholarship 5, 10–11
boats 233–4
  Omani 240
  reed 127
  sailing 18, 55–6, 173
Bowersock, G. W. 22
Britain, influence on Gulf 24–5, 116
bronze working 90, 92, 136–7, 150, 163–4, 242
buildings:
  in mud brick 43, 59, 130, 144
  in stone 43, 129–30, 132, 144, 154–5, 162, 240
bull, importance of 23, 148, 150–2, 192, 198–9, 204–7, 263, *pl. IX*
burial mounds:
  Bahrain 16, 26–8, 97, 117–18, 134, 159–72, 182, *pl. II*
  eastern Arabia 218
  Omani 243–4
  see also Aali; cairn burials
Burrows, Fr E. 122–4, 212

cairn burials 228–9, 244, *pl. XVI*; *see also* burial mounds
camel:
  domestication of 20, 37, 236, 248, 251
  sacrifice 229
carvings 9, 236
  rock 36, 229–35, 246, 249–51, 280, *pl. XIII*
Catal Hüyük 9, 150, 193, 236
children, burials of 136–7, 166–7, 169, 170

294